Rules, Games, and Common-Pool Resources

Rules, Games, and Common-Pool Resources

Elinor Ostrom, Roy Gardner,
and James Walker

with
Arun Agrawal,
William Blomquist,
Edella Schlager, and
Shui Yan Tang

Ann Arbor

THE UNIVERSITY OF MICHIGAN PRESS

To our parents and families
for their love and inspiration

To our Workshop family
for their friendship and support

Copyright © by the University of Michigan 1994
All rights reserved
Published in the United States of America by
The University of Michigan Press
Manufactured in the United States of America

1997   1996   1995   1994   4   3   2   1

A CIP catalogue record for this book is available from the British Library.

Library of Congress Cataloging-in-Publication Data

Ostrom, Elinor.
    Rules, games, and common-pool resources / Elinor Ostrom, Roy Gardner, and
James Walker.
        p.   cm.
    Includes bibliographical references and index.
    ISBN 0-472-09546-3 (alk. paper). — ISBN 0-472-06546-7 (pbk. alk. paper)
    1. Public goods.   2. Natural resources—Management.   3. Game
theory.   I. Gardner, Roy, 1947–   .   II. Walker, James, 1950–   .
III. Title.
HB846.5.085   1993
333.7—dc20   93-44406
                                                                    CIP

Preface

In 1987, the three principal authors of this book received the first of two National Science Foundation grants to study an institutional theory of common-pool resource (CPR) dilemmas. This research is the foundation for this book. All of us involved in the writing of this volume are deeply appreciative of the continued support of the National Science Foundation (Grant Nos.: SES 8619498 and SES 8921884). Additional support from the Resources and Technology Division, Economic Research Service, United States Department of Agriculture (Cooperative Agreement No. 43-3AEM-1-80078), is also appreciated.

Many of the chapters in this volume draw on papers that have been previously published. Early in the process of writing, we decided against doing the book as an edited series of papers. We wanted to ensure that the book had an internal coherence that is not possible when one simply brings together previously published papers. Thus, the resemblance between the prior publications and chapters in the book has become rather faint in some instances.

Any research team that has written many previous papers accrues an enormous indebtedness to many colleagues at their home institution as well as at other universities. In Bloomington, we are particularly appreciative of the extraordinary talents of Patty Dalecki, who has somehow kept track of a very complex and evolving manuscript under the condition that changes may come from any and all directions. Her skill as a production manager, editor, and layout artist will be apparent to all who read this book. Her cheerfulness and willingness to go through revision after revision after revision is something only those of us who have worked with her can recognize. In addition, Stanra King provided many hours of very helpful editing on the penultimate version of this book.

Dean Dudley has also been a helpful partner in the experimental aspects of this project. Dean has read and commented on many of the chapters in this book, recruited subjects, run experiment "trainers," helped Walker and Ostrom cope with the complexities of recording communication, handed out fee and fine slips, and done anything and everything needed to keep an experimental research program on track. We appreciate his help very much.

We have also been blessed with colleagues at the Workshop in Political Theory and Policy Analysis who have been willing to listen to our many colloquium presentations, work over conference papers, journal articles, and various drafts of this book. Arun Agrawal, Bill Blomquist, Edella Schlager, and Yan Tang all played a special role in the development of this research that goes beyond the chapters they have written for this book. All were willing to challenge us in many long discussions and to help us create some order out of the highly complex field materials we were studying. In addition, we have received very useful comments from other workshoppers, including Elizabeth Anderson, Sue Crawford, Gina Davis, Steve Hackett, Bobbi Herzberg, Claudia Keser, Mike McGinnis, Shmuel Nitzan, Vincent Ostrom, Roger Parks, and George Varughese. We have also benefited from the comments given us by Peter Aranson, Rudolf Avenhaus, Peter Bernholz, Werner Güth, Jack Knight, Michael Maschler, Akim Okada, Charles Plott, Todd Sandler, Urs Schweitzer, Reinhard Selten, Kenneth Shepsle, and an anonymous reviewer. The opportunity to present our ideas at BoWo 1991 at Bonn University came at a particularly useful time for all three of us. Randy Calvert assigned the last draft to a seminar at the University of Rochester and gave us a very useful critique for which we are appreciative. Finally, we would like to express a special thanks to Rick Wilson and David Feeny, who spent a great deal of time pouring over the first "complete" version of this manuscript. Their thorough review and discussion were instrumental in helping us rethink the organization and synthesis of materials in the book.

Grateful acknowledgment is made to the following publishers and journals for permission to reprint previously published materials:

Sage Publications, Inc. for material in chapter 1 which is adapted from "The Nature of Common-Pool Resource Problems," *Rationality and Society* 2, no. 3 (July, 1990): 335–58. © 1990 by Sage Publications, Inc. Reprinted by permission of Sage Publications, Inc.

Kluwer Academic Publishers for material in chapter 4 which is adapted from "Rules and Games," *Public Choice* 70, no. 2 (May, 1991): 121–49.

Academic Publishers for material in chapter 5 which is adapted from "Rent Dissipation in a Limited-Access Common-Pool Resource: Experimental Evidence," *Journal of Environmental Economics and Management* 19 (1990): 203–11. © 1990 by Academic Press.

Economic Journal for material in chapter 6 which is adapted from "Probabilistic Destruction of Common-Pool Resources: Experimental Evidence," *Economic Journal* 102, no. 414 (Sept., 1992): 1149–61.

American Political Science Association for material in chapter 8 which is adapted from "Covenants with and without a Sword: Self-Governance is Possible," *American Political Science Review* 86, no. 2 (June, 1992): 404–17.

Contents

Part 3. Field Studies

Tables

Figures

Part 1
Theoretical Background

CHAPTER 1

Rules, Games, and Common-Pool
Resource Problems

In June 1991, the Ocean Hound sank in thick fog just off the Dover coast, taking all five members of her crew with her. This was not the first time during 1991 that a fishing ship from Brixham Harbor in England sank. During the first six months of 1991, more than thirty fishers were lost. Fishing is always a dangerous occupation, but something different was happening. About the same number of fishers died during the entire years of 1990 and 1989 as died during the first six months of 1991. No single cause appears to underlie the doubling of the death rate during 1991. "But on the docks of Brixham and other ports along the rugged coast of southwest England, there is talk that growing competition in the fishing grounds and hard economic times at home may be forcing some fishers to take more chances with weather and their boats" (*New York Times*, 13 September 1991).

The Brixham fleet numbered about ninety boats in 1991, almost twice what it was in 1981. Monthly payments on boats rose from $3,116 (on a $200,000 debt) in 1987 to $4,250 in 1991. Fuel cost $3,672 per week in 1991 compared with $3,128 just one year prior. Paul Jarrett, who runs the Royal National Mission to Deep Sea Fishermen—the Salvation Army of the sea— indicated that he had been in this work "for 25 years and this is the worst period yet" (ibid.). Jarrett said that pressure to pay mortgages and bills has led fishers to put in more time and take more risks.

In California during the summer of 1991, another instance of excessive investment in the exploitation of a resource occurred. The generators built by Pacific Gas and Electric to tap the geothermal resources at The Geysers, located 150 kilometers north of San Francisco, to produce two thousand megawatts of power, were actually yielding only fifteen hundred megawatts. Even worse, the pressure in the wells was dropping fast. It appears the underlying problem is simple. "The earth beneath those northern California mountains is running dry. As a result, the outlook for The Geysers is grim: By the mid or late 1990s, power output may slip to half its 1987 level. A $3.5

billion investment is in danger of turning into a white elephant" (*Science*, 12 July 1991, 134).

Common-Pool Resource Problems

The basic problem illustrated by each of these stories is overdevelopment of a resource. Just as the fishing fleet of Brixham had jumped from forty-five boats to ninety boats within the course of a decade, the amount of capital investment in generating capacity at The Geysers doubled between 1981 and 1991, accelerated by economic incentives offered by the U.S. government. In 1981, there were 14 generating units with a total output of 942 megawatts. By 1991, generating capacity had jumped to 2,043 megawatts, involving the investments of five utilities and six developers (or developer-utility combines). "Put simply, there are too many straws in the teapot," was the graphic comment of Thomas Box of Calpine Corporation of Santa Rosa, one of the firms involved.

The incentives toward excessive resource exploitation, illustrated by Brixham Harbor and The Geysers, are not isolated or unique events. The temptation to overextract fish, steam, or other resource units from a resource system shared with others occurs in many guises in diverse resource systems throughout time and space. As we define the term, these resource systems are all common-pool resources (CPRs), where excluding potential appropriators or limiting appropriation rights of existing users is nontrivial (but not necessarily impossible) and the yield of the resource system is subtractable. It is not always the case, however, that individuals jointly using CPRs behave so as to produce the tragic results of Brixham Harbor or The Geysers. As documented in chapters 10–13 and in many recent books (Berkes 1989; Blaikie and Brookfield 1987; Blomquist 1992; Bromley 1992; McCay and Acheson 1987; E. Ostrom 1990; V. Ostrom, Feeny, and Picht 1993; Pinkerton 1989; Sengupta 1991), individuals in many CPR situations avoid tragic outcomes.

In chapter 13, for example, William Blomquist describes how water producers pumping groundwater from a series of groundwater basins underlying southern California sought to change their incentives and capacities to engage in a pumping race that threatened their basins. At one time, they also had "too many straws in the teapot." At a later juncture, however, in all but one groundwater basin, the pumpers had used institutional arrangements such as an equity court system and the establishment of special districts to regulate their use of the basins. Basins that had been threatened with destruction were in such good shape during the recent drought in southern California that water producers were able to draw on supplies in reserve to cope with six years of below-normal rainfall.

In *Governing the Commons*, a book based on the initial stages of the research program that is more fully elaborated in this study, E. Ostrom (1990) described a series of long-enduring CPRs and the institutions—rules-in-use—that enabled individuals to utilize these resources over long periods of time. *Governing the Commons* challenged the indiscriminate use of three metaphors commonly applied to CPR situations to predict suboptimal use and/or destruction of the resource: (1) G. Hardin's tragedy of the commons (1968), (2) Olson's logic of collective action (1965), and (3) the Prisoner's Dilemma game. The arguments laid out in Hardin's and Olson's work can be quite insightful for understanding the basic issues faced in many, but not all, CPR situations. The simple structure of the Prisoner's Dilemma game is a useful device for demonstrating the conflict between individual rationality and group rationality. When individuals withdraw scarce resource units from the same CPR, when they cannot communicate and establish agreed-upon rules and strategies, and when no other authority has established and enforced effective rules, predictions of suboptimal use of the resource are likely to be correct. Users will overappropriate, individuals will defect on one another, and potential collective benefits will not be achieved. Too many straws will be in the teapot.

In *Governing the Commons*, however, it was shown that in many instances individuals jointly using a CPR communicate with one another and establish agreed-upon rules and strategies that improve their joint outcomes. By devising their own rules-in-use, individuals using such CPRs have overcome the "tragedy of the commons." Further, where the institutions they devise have been sustained over long periods of time, it is possible to describe a series of design principles that characterize the robust institutions and to identify the variables most likely to be associated with successful institutional change.

The current study follows the research leading up to *Governing the Commons* as part of a continuing effort to understand how individuals behave in CPR situations like Brixham Harbor, The Geysers, and the groundwater basins of southern California. Our approach has been to address CPR issues using the theory of *N*-person, finitely repeated games. Our mode of analysis has been to embed the resulting games in a broader institutional framework. Our approach to testing and evaluating these models is through the use of both experimental and field data. By testing formal models in the controlled environment of an experimental laboratory, we are able to examine more closely the conditions under which the theoretical results predicted by noncooperative game theory are supported, and where the theory fails. By analyzing empirical studies from four field settings—fisheries, irrigation systems, forests, and groundwater basins—we are able to begin to assess the generality of the findings from controlled experiments. Some of our empirical findings are consistent with currently accepted theory, while others are anomalous. In fact, our findings are sufficiently puzzling that we are faced with the need to begin the process of formulating a better positive explanation for individual behavior in CPR situations than currently exists in accepted theories.

But we are getting ahead of ourselves. Before turning to a discussion of the theoretical foundation for analysis, and a discussion of results from experimental and field studies, we need to lay out our definitions of key terms and the central questions that we address in this volume.

Conceptual Foundations and Key Terms

Common-Pool Resources and Other Types of Goods

This study focuses on a particular class of goods or events in the world that share two important attributes. These two attributes are (1) the difficulty of excluding individuals from benefiting from a good and (2) the subtractability of the benefits consumed by one individual from those available to others. Let us discuss each attribute.

Exclusion

The goods and events in the world that individuals value differ in terms of how easy or costly it is to exclude or limit potential beneficiaries (users) from consuming them once they are provided by nature or through the activities of other individuals. Fencing and packaging are the ultimate physical means of excluding potential beneficiaries from a good. To be effective, however, fencing and packaging efforts must be backed by a set of property rights that are feasible to defend (in an economic and legal sense) in the legal system available to individuals within a country. It follows that the legal and economic feasibility of excluding or limiting use by potential beneficiaries is derived both from the physical attributes of the goods and from the institutions used in a particular jurisdiction.

Subtractability

The goods and events that individuals value also differ in terms of the degree of subtractability of one person's use from that available to be used by others. If one fisherman lands a ton of fish, those fish are not available for other fishermen. On the other hand, one person's use of a weather forecast does not reduce the availability of the information in that forecast for others to use.

Four Types of Goods

Arraying these attributes of exclusion and subtractability provides a very general classification of four types of goods as shown in figure 1.1. The four kinds of goods so identified—private, public, and toll goods and common-

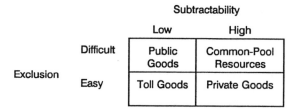

Fig. 1.1. **A general classification of goods**

pool resources—are broad categories that contain considerable variation within them (V. Ostrom and Ostrom 1977). They are similar to four large "continents" in the world of goods. Each of these four types of goods differs from the other three, notwithstanding the substantial variety present within each broad type.

Private goods, which are characterized by the relative ease of exclusion in an economic and legal sense and by subtractability, are the commodities best analyzed using neoclassical economic theory of markets. Public goods are the opposite of private goods in regard to both attributes. Toll goods (sometimes referred to as club goods) share with private goods the relative ease of exclusion and with public goods the relative lack of subtractability. Common-pool resources share with private goods the subtractability of resource units and with public goods the difficulties of exclusion.

Common-Pool Resources

This book focuses on common-pool resources. This focus is not because we consider the other types of goods to be uninteresting. Rather, as the reader will soon see, understanding human behavior related to CPRs is itself a substantial challenge. Given the wide diversity of CPRs that exist in field settings, the task of understanding behavior related to this class of goods is both difficult and of considerable policy import. We focus on CPR settings where the individuals involved make repeated, rather than single, decisions. While interesting CPR problems exist that involve single decisions, most of the important questions related to the use of CPRs involve situations where a set of individuals use the same resource over and over again.[1]

Excluding or limiting potential beneficiaries from using a CPR is a nontrivial problem due to many causes. In some cases, it is the sheer size or, more generally, the physical attributes of the CPR. For example, the total cost of fencing an inshore fishery, let alone an entire ocean, is prohibitive. In other

---

1. This discussion relies significantly on Gardner, Ostrom, and Walker 1990.

cases, the additional benefits from exclusion, or placing restrictions on use, are calculated to be less than the additional costs from instituting a mechanism to control use. In still other cases, basic constitutional, legal, or institutional considerations prevent exclusion or limiting use. A constitution, for example, might explicitly provide unlimited access to the fisheries within a jurisdiction to all citizens of that jurisdiction. Again, traditional considerations or norms, issues of fairness, ethics, and so on may preclude serious consideration of excluding some beneficiaries. The difficulty of exclusion leads to CPRs being used by multiple individuals, with severe restrictions on the ability to effectively limit use. Since these users could be fishers, farmers, herders, mainframe computer users, or groundwater producers, to name only a few types, we will use one term—*appropriator*—to refer to all individuals who withdraw or appropriate resource units from any kind of CPR.[2]

A CPR "facility" creates the conditions for the existence of a stock of resource units. This stock makes available a flow of resource units over time that are appropriable and subtractable in use. Examples of CPR facilities and their resource units include (1) a groundwater basin and acre-feet of water, (2) a fishing grounds and tons of fish, (3) an oil field and barrels of oil pumped, (4) computer facilities and processing time, and (5) parking garages and parking spaces. It is the resource units from a CPR that are subtractable. The fish being harvested are a flow, appropriated from a stock of fish.

The distinction between the resource stock and the flow of resource units is especially useful in connection with *renewable* resources, where one can define a regeneration rate. As long as the number of resource units appropriated from a CPR does not exceed the regeneration rate, the resource stock will not be exhausted. When a resource has no natural regeneration (an *exhaustible* resource), then any appropriation rate will eventually lead to exhaustion. Although our primary focus in this book is on renewable resources, many of the general issues we treat apply to the problems of regulating the use of nonrenewable resources such as oil pools.

Classifying CPR Situations: Appropriation and Provision

While all CPR situations share much in common, the analytical problems that appropriators face in one CPR may vary markedly from those faced by appropriators using other resources. The task of developing a set of rules that assigns fishers to a set of fishing spots with differential returns is different

---

2. We follow Plott and Meyer 1975 in calling the process of withdrawing units "appropriation" and thus the term *appropriator* for all those who withdraw units including groundwater pumpers, irrigators, fishers, hunters, herders, computer users, and so on.

from designing a set of rules to induce labor contributions by fishers to maintain aquatic breeding grounds.

Below, we lay out a typology that is useful for classifying the assortment of problems faced by appropriators in CPRs. CPR problems can be usefully clustered into two broad types: *appropriation* and *provision*. In appropriation problems, the production relationship between yield from the CPR and the level of inputs required to produce that yield is assumed to be given. The problems to be solved relate to excluding potential beneficiaries and allocating the subtractable flow. This is accomplished by various means, including agreement on the level of appropriation, the method for appropriation, and the allocation of output. Provision problems, on the other hand, are related to creating a resource, maintaining or improving the production capabilities of the resource, or avoiding the destruction of the resource.[3] In other words, in appropriation problems, the *flow* aspect of the CPR is what is problematic. In provision problems, the *resource facility or resource stock* of the CPR is problematic. Clearly, within each of these two broad classes of problems, there exist a set of complex subproblems.

Any discussion of the types of problems faced in the allocation of resources (and the solutions to those problems) forces one to consider some criteria to evaluate resource allocations. In this book, we will use the concepts of economic efficiency (often referred to as optimal or the optimal solution) and Pareto optimality as such benchmarks. In its simplest terms, economic efficiency implies the maximization of discounted net present value. Pareto optimality implies an allocation of resources where no individual can be made better off without making some other individual (individuals) worse off. These conceptual notions have difficulties. In the field, they may be very difficult (if not impossible) to measure or observe. Heterogeneous individuals may have different discount rates. What is the "proper" discount rate for "society"? Further, these notions do not address important issues of fairness that groups of individuals inevitably confront. But, even with these shortcomings, they provide a useful benchmark for theoretical modeling and conceptualization in empirical settings. We will develop these concepts further as we use them throughout this book.

Appropriation Problems

Appropriation problems can be conceptualized as either one-shot static situations or as iterated, time-independent situations. In its most fundamental form, the solution to the problem of the *efficient level* of appropriation deals simply with equating the marginal costs of appropriation with the marginal

---

3. We use the term *provision* in the same sense as V. Ostrom, Tiebout, and Warren 1961 and Advisory Commission on Intergovernmental Relations 1987, 1988.

returns from appropriation. However, solving appropriation problems may go beyond the fundamental problem of achieving the efficient level of appropriation. Specifically, efficient appropriation may also require solutions to the optimal timing and location of appropriation, and/or an understanding of how alternative appropriation technologies may impact each other. As elaborated below, we use the terms *appropriation externalities*, *assignment problems*, and *technological externalities* to differentiate these problems.

Appropriation Externalities
To understand the problem of appropriating the efficient level of resource units from the CPR, one must understand the externality generated whenever resource users appropriate from a CPR. The appropriation externality reflects the production relationship by which one user's increased appropriation reduces the yield obtained by other users for any given level of appropriation activity. That is, increased appropriation by a user reduces the average return others receive from their costly investments in appropriation. For example, as one fisher increases his or her appropriation activity, the yield other fishers receive from their fishing activities is reduced; increased water withdrawal by one pumper reduces the water other pumpers obtain from a given level of investment in pumping inputs. In the case of production externalities, the average return for any given investment in appropriation activities is decreased *to all users*. If this externality is not suitably accounted for, the externality leads to a suboptimal allocation of inputs in the appropriation process.

The simplest model leading to suboptimal appropriation assumes identical appropriators who have unrestricted access to the CPR, resource units distributed homogeneously across space, and a single technology available to all appropriators. The classic example of an appropriation externality is described in H. Gordon 1954 for a group of homogeneous fishers. Here, Gordon argues that fishers will increase their fishing activities until the average return from fishing equals the additional (marginal) cost of inputs used in fishing. Since average return is greater than the marginal return, this will imply a level of fishing activity where the marginal return from fishing is less than the marginal cost. From neoclassical theory of markets, however, the marginal cost of an input used in the appropriation process serves as a measure of the value that others place on that input. If inputs are used in the appropriation process at a level such that the marginal return is less than the marginal cost, this implies that a reallocation of this input to some alternative use would enhance efficiency.

The reason appropriators might employ inputs at this level is that it is only inefficient from the point of view of the group. As a single user appropriates from the resource, that user reduces the average return to all appropriators, thereby creating an externality. However, individually rational appropriators who consider only their own returns ignore the impact of their own increased appropriation on overall returns from appropriation. By ignoring the negative impact of an individual's appropriation on *others'* returns, the appropriator creates a negative externality. The presence of the externality leads to overinvestment of resources into the appropriation process. Net yield to appropriators from the resource is driven below optimal levels.[4]

Assignment Problems

Changing the assumption of homogeneity in the spatial distribution of resource units within a CPR creates an assignment problem. CPRs with a heterogeneous distribution of resource units are characterized by a patchy environment in which patches may differ dramatically in yield. Many fishing grounds, for example, are characterized by "hot spots" where fishing is very good and "cold spots" where it is not. Similarly, farmers who take water from a location on an irrigation canal near the head of the system obtain more water for their effort than farmers who take water from a "tail-end" position. In such cases, it is not only important to determine who can benefit from the CPR but also how to make assignments to beneficiaries in better or worse locations.

Assignment problems lead to an inefficient use of the CPR if appropriate solutions cannot be obtained. In many CPR situations, frequent conflict occurs over access to the good patches. In some instances, however, a wide diversity of local rules are used to give a clear order (based on time, location, type of appropriator, and other attributes) to how appropriation activities are to be organized. In such cases, assignment problems are solved and conflict is eliminated or reduced. Note that these rules may go unrecognized since they are frequently embedded in what outsiders think of as quaint customs. Messerschmidt describes one irrigation system where the potential conflict between head-end and tail-end irrigators was solved by reversing the order by which fields were irrigated for the two major crops grown during the year:

> To make distribution equitable for all farmers over the course of the year, the barley crop was watered from the top of the north fields downward; that is, the fields closest to the head received first water. For buckwheat, the watering order was reversed so that the farther fields were watered first. This traditional rule was remembered in a Thakali rhyme: *kar vaalaa, nhaa mhalaa*, meaning "barley from the top, buckwheat from the bottom." (1986, 463)

---

4. See H. Gordon 1954 for one of the earliest expositions of this dilemma and Johnson and Libecap 1982 for a more recent discussion.

A rhyme such as this is one means that nonliterate peoples pass their rules on from one generation to another. The rules are never written down. Outsiders may have no idea—unless they ask quite specific questions—about the ordering principles that the appropriators use to organize withdrawal activities.

Technological Externalities

Changing the assumption regarding the presence of a homogeneous technology creates a technological externality when the use of one technology increases the costs (or productivity) for the users of other technologies. For fishing trawlers to operate efficiently, they need to travel over a large domain. Fixed nets operating in the same territory increase the operating costs for both trawlers and fixed net users. Similarly, if one group of fishers uses dynamite in its fishing efforts, the costs for other fishers rise as a result of this production technology. Many fishing communities have established extensive rules allocating fishing space to alternative technologies at different seasons to reduce these external costs. A well-documented case of allocation rules designed to cope with technological externalities is the fishing village of Fermeuse, Newfoundland, described in chapter 11. There the cod fishers have divided their inshore fishery into distinct fishing areas. Each area is assigned to fishers who use a particular fishing technology.

The linkages among appropriation problems are illustrated in figure 1.2. Suboptimal allocation is the underlying behavioral problem. The specific form of suboptimal allocation varies within CPRs depending on such variables as spatial heterogeneity and technological heterogeneity.

Provision Problems

An analysis of provision problems begins by considering the optimal size and productive nature of the resource facility in relation to the cost of providing that facility and the set of beneficiaries to be included. Provision problems focus on the behavioral incentives for appropriators to (*a*) alter appropriation activities within an existing CPR that alters the productive capacity of the resource, *demand*-side provision, or (*b*) contribute resources for the provision or maintenance of a CPR, *supply*-side provision. Depending on the specific characteristics of the situation, provision problems may be represented as one-shot games, time-independent repeated games, or time-dependent repeated games. For most CPR problems, the most natural representation is a time-dependent repeated game. One-shot games or time-independent repeated games are adequate representations when the natural replacement rate is at least as great as current and foreseeable withdrawal rates so that the CPR is able to maintain itself. In many CPRs, this condition is frequently not met, and one is forced to deal with the time-dependent features of the situation. In

APPROPRIATION PROBLEMS

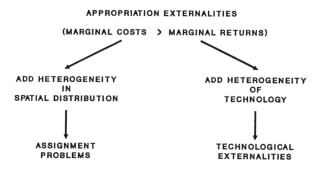

Fig. 1.2. A framework for appropriation problems

time-dependent situations, appropriators face an environment in which the strategies they have undertaken in time periods $t - 1$, $t - 2$, . . . affect the strategies available to them in time periods t, $t + 1$, $t + 2$, ... Time-dependent provision problems can be arrayed as in figure 1.3.

Demand Side

The source of demand-side provision problems is the way in which appropriation impacts on the productive capacity of the resource. For example, increased fishing beyond some critical level will reduce fish stock to the extent that the productivity capacity of the fishery is reduced. Solutions to demand-side provision problems involve the maximization of the discounted present value of net returns. In the extremes, when the discount rate used is sufficiently large, the extinction of biological species can result as a consequence of an appropriation rate higher than the minimal safe yield (see Clark 1976; Smith 1968).[5] Fieldwork by Blomquist (see chap. 13) describes the problems faced by a group of water producers utilizing groundwater basins located adjacent to the Pacific Ocean. When water withdrawn exceeded the average safe yield of the basin, salt water intruded, destroying the capacity of the basin to hold potable water. Since surface reservoirs are extraordinarily expensive, the provision problem facing the producers was to reduce withdrawal rates sufficiently to preserve the basin.

---

5. The demand-side provision problem is conceptually akin to the choice problem investigated in earlier experimental research such as Brechner 1976, Cass and Edney 1978, Jorgenson and Papciak 1980, Messick and McClelland 1983, and Messick et al. 1983. In these experiments, subjects face a general problem of appropriating resources from a common pool whose regenerative powers depend on the stock of existing resources.

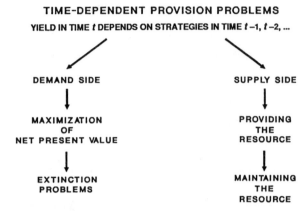

TIME-DEPENDENT PROVISION PROBLEMS

YIELD IN TIME *t* DEPENDS ON STRATEGIES IN TIME *t* −1, *t* −2, …

DEMAND SIDE   SUPPLY SIDE

MAXIMIZATION
OF
NET PRESENT VALUE

PROVIDING
THE
RESOURCE

EXTINCTION
PROBLEMS

MAINTAINING
THE
RESOURCE

Fig. 1.3. · A framework for provision problems

Supply Side

The source of supply-side provision problems lies in the individual incentives to free ride on the provision activities of others. Conceptually, the supply-side CPR situation parallels the theoretical and empirical literature focusing on public-goods provision. Similar to pure public good provision, maintenance or provision of a CPR facility may suffer from free riding because it is difficult to monitor or prevent access. A classic supply-side provision problem is that of the maintenance required to keep an irrigation system operating effectively (see Coward 1980a; Chambers 1977; and Easter and Welsch 1986, for analyses of this problem). E. Martin and Yoder (1983a) provide an in-depth description of the extensive efforts that local farmers have undertaken in the mountainous areas of Nepal to build and maintain their own irrigation canals, as well as the rules they use to ensure the continued maintenance of these systems. De los Reyes (1980a, 1980b) provides similarly detailed accounts of how forty-seven different communal irrigation systems in the Philippines have kept locally constructed irrigation canals in good working order.

The Relationships between Appropriation and Provision Problems

In natural settings, individuals most frequently face combined (nested) appropriation and provision problems. Any humanly constructed CPR, such as an irrigation system, must be provided before anyone can appropriate from it. Even those CPRs provided by nature, such as groundwater basins or fisheries, may involve extensive demand-side provision activities to provide for economically beneficial appropriation or avoid their destruction through overuse.

Further, supply-side provision activities related to maintenance of the resource affect the resource flow available for appropriation. Thus, the nature of the appropriation problem is affected by how well the provision problem is solved.

Analytically, however, it is useful to separate these classes of problems to clarify what is involved in reducing the severity of each type of problem. In many instances, appropriation problems are an easier class to analyze. Also, there are many problems that appropriators face in CPRs that are strictly appropriation problems. Consequently, in our theoretical and experimental chapters we will address these problems independently so as to gain better understanding of the types of actions associated with variously structured appropriation and provision problems. When problems have complex relationships, it is difficult to understand them without first focusing on their subparts. We do recognize, however, that provision and appropriation problems are linked together in natural settings, and this linkage is addressed in the chapters reporting on research conducted in field settings and again in the concluding chapter.

CPR Situations and CPR Dilemmas

Individuals jointly providing and/or appropriating from CPRs are thought by many analysts to face a universally tragic situation in which their individual rationality leads to an outcome that is *not* rational from the perspective of the group. When this actually occurs, we call the behavioral result a *CPR dilemma*. Contrary to the conventional wisdom, many CPR situations are not CPR dilemmas. In some CPRs, the quantity demanded of the resource unit is not sufficiently large to induce appropriators to pursue individual strategies that produce suboptimal outcomes. Such situations are not problematic, even though they might become so if the demand for the resource unit were to increase or appropriation costs were to decrease. In other CPRs, the quantity of resource units demanded is sufficiently large that appropriators are motivated to pursue individual strategies that would produce suboptimal outcomes if they had not already adopted their own rules to cope with these problems.

Conditions Leading to a CPR Dilemma

Because all situations where multiple individuals use CPRs are not dilemmas, we need to distinguish between those CPRs that are dilemmas and those that are not. To do so, we introduce two conditions that may or may not apply in any particular CPR situations. These are: (1) suboptimal outcomes and (2) institutionally feasible alternatives.

Condition 1: *Suboptimal Outcomes*
The strategies of the appropriators—given a particular configuration of the physical system, technology, rules, market conditions, and attributes of the appropriators—lead to suboptimal outcomes from the perspective of the appropriators.

Condition 2: *Institutionally Feasible Alternatives*
Given existing institutional arrangements, there exists at least one set of coordinated strategies that are more efficient than current decisions and are institutionally feasible. That is, (1) a set of strategies exists in which total discounted benefits exceed total discounted costs including production, investment, governance, and transaction costs and (2) given existing rules for institutional change, there exists a necessary consensus for such a change. A sufficient (but not necessary) condition for such a set of feasible alternatives would be the existence of a Pareto optimal set of coordinated strategies that are *individually* advantageous to all appropriators or potential appropriators. Institutionally feasible alternatives include changes in the operational rules affecting the rights and duties of appropriators and nonappropriators accomplished by procedures authorized in the basic constitution of a political regime.

Both Conditions 1 and 2 are needed to distinguish a CPR *dilemma* from a CPR *situation*. If suboptimal outcomes are not produced by the current combination of the physical system, technology, rules, market conditions, and attributes of the appropriators, there is nothing problematic in the CPR situation. If no alternative set of institutionally feasible strategies (given discounted benefits and costs) could produce a better outcome for appropriators individually or for the group of current and potential appropriators, there is no dilemma. When a CPR dilemma does exist, a resolution of the dilemma requires a change in appropriation and/or provision activities. One type of solution is for resource users to evolve a set of *coordinated strategies* related to appropriation and/or provision.

Coordinated Strategies to Resolve CPR Dilemmas

A coordinated strategy is defined as a feasible strategy adopted by appropriators regarding (*a*) how much, when, where, and with what technology to withdraw resource units and/or (*b*) how much and/or when to invest in supply or maintenance inputs to the CPR facility or stock. Two types of coordinated strategies occur in field settings.

The first type of coordinated strategy is the result of learning or evolutionary processes by which appropriators eventually reach and maintain a set of individual strategies that increase joint (and individual) payoffs relative to problematic outcomes. In other words, the structure of the situation remains the same, but the appropriators adopt strategies that reduce the suboptimality of outcomes. An example of this type of coordinated strategy is when individuals can communicate with one another and agree that each will follow a particular strategy so long as others also follow that strategy. If the strategy agreed upon obtains the best possible joint outcome, the appropriators have coordinated their actions so as to reach the optimal outcome. Given the difficulty of calculating optimal solutions to complex problems, however, individuals adopting coordinated strategies within a given structure frequently approximate rather than achieve full optimality.

The second type of coordinated strategy involves changing the rules-in-use affecting the structure of the situation. Individual incentives in the re-formed structure lead to better outcomes than before. This kind of coordinated strategy can be conceptualized as a shift in the level of action by appropriators to change the rules of the CPR game. An example of this kind of strategy is when appropriators not only agree on the particular actions they will adopt if others adopt them but also agree upon rules for monitoring and sanctioning one another. The importance of the latter is that if someone breaks the agreement, there is a line of defense (sanctioning the offender) before the entire agreement disintegrates. Rules that authorize self-monitoring and self-sanctioning actions are added by the appropriators themselves to whatever rules existed prior to the adoption of these new rules.

In some, but not all, field settings, appropriators use both types of coordinated strategies to extricate themselves from CPR dilemmas. The use of either type of coordinated strategy is not, however, normally predicted as the outcome of a finitely repeated, CPR dilemma game (see chap. 3). Viewing the game as finitely repeated, the standard game theory prediction is that individuals will repeat the equilibrium of the one-shot game. Viewing the game as infinitely repeated, the standard game theory prediction is embodied in the Folk Theorem (see chap. 3). This basic result shows that sufficiently patient appropriators may adopt strategies that improve joint outcomes, but they may also continue to use strategies that do not improve joint outcomes.[6] Most game theorists do not consider the second type of coordinated strategy at all. The rules of the game are considered to be fixed.[7]

Any theory predicting that appropriators will not adopt coordinated

---

6. The term *Folk Theorem* is used because its implication—cooperation is one equilibrium among many in an infinitely repeated game—was commonly understood by most game theorists a generation ago and not attributed to any one of them.

7. See the important work of Randall Calvert 1993, who also explores how the rules of the game change over time. Calvert views these rules as increasingly structured equilibria that involve communication and differentiation.

strategies supports the view of appropriators as pawns in a tragedy of their own making that they cannot resolve. The policy advice most often based on this view is to call upon the government to impose new rules and regulations from outside the situation. These rule changes are supposed to restructure the entire situation for the better. But agents of the central government may lack both the incentives and the information necessary to devise optimal rules. Moreover, how such rules will be understood and agreed upon by those affected, how such rules will be monitored, and how such rules will be enforced are rarely addressed. A goal of this book is to address precisely these concerns.

Consistent policy prescriptions cannot be based solely on the Folk Theorem. It is a gigantic leap of faith to deduce that, simply because a mathematical solution exists to an infinitely repeated CPR dilemma, appropriators will automatically find such a solution and follow it. Even if participants understand the reasoning behind the theorem, they will inevitably face a plethora of solutions from which to choose. No formula works by itself. Finding one of the better solutions in the sea of possible solutions depends on the acquisition of considerable experience, time and effort devoted to coordination, and common understanding of the task. Making such a choice is a difficult coordination problem, as difficult in principle as the coordination problem in the one-shot CPR. The challenge for theory is to predict when appropriators' outcomes will approximate those given by good Folk Theorem outcomes, and when not. A further challenge is to describe precisely appropriators' behavior when they adopt coordinated strategies of either kind, and see to what extent their strategies approximate Folk Theorem strategies. A goal of this book is to understand these challenging problems.

No existing theory provides a consistent explanation for how and why many appropriators extricate themselves from CPR dilemmas, why this is not universally the case, or why many laws imposed by national governments on local CPRs produce the unintended consequences that they do. Consequently, policies are adopted based on an inadequate theoretical foundation. Government policymakers working without a coherent and effective theory of CPRs may easily be misled and misguided. It should come as no surprise that such policies may do more harm than good.[8]

Policy analysis needs to be based on theory that is supported by empirical evidence. Even though existing theory may lead to inadequate predictions about the ways that appropriators extricate themselves from CPR dilemmas in some settings, it is still better than no theory. It remains extremely useful as a

---

8. Matthews 1988 and Matthews and Phyne 1988 document how fisheries in Newfoundland that had been organized to cope with many problems were destroyed by actions taken by the Canadian national government. See also Barrett 1991, who describes a similar situation in Bermuda.

benchmark for exploration. Consequently, the task we set for ourselves is not so much one of rejecting theory as one of amending theory. The amendments we exploit, such as coordinated strategies of the second kind, are useful only insofar as they improve our explanatory power in the areas troublesome for existing theory and do not adversely affect our explanatory power in other areas.

The theoretical issues that we address in this book will strike many readers as relatively technical, if not arcane. We owe it to our readers to be up front about this. We have been working on these issues as a team for seven years, and the questions are tough. There is no easy road, there is no shortcut, to the right answers. We have made every effort to reach the widest possible audience, but we have not watered down our presentation to make it easy, if that would compromise clarity and precision. The CPR dilemmas confronting the world today are sufficiently urgent to demand better explanation and improved policy options. Otherwise, we face increasingly irrelevant theoretical predictions, and increasingly dire resource outcomes. The best way to achieve a firmer theoretical foundation for policy analysis of CPRs is to dig into the subject, even if it gets technical, and this is what we will do. For those unfamiliar with this terrain, but willing to make the investment in understanding the issues, we assure you that your investment will be rewarded.

The Central Questions to Be Addressed

Given the gap between received theory and empirical results, we intend to address the following three central questions.

1. In finitely repeated CPR dilemmas, to what degree are the predictions about behavior and outcomes derived from noncooperative game theory supported by empirical evidence?
2. In CPR dilemmas where behavior and outcomes are substantially different from that predicted, are there behavioral regularities that can be drawn upon in the development of improved theories?
3. What types of institutional and physical variables affect the likelihood of successful resolution of CPR dilemmas?

The first question is difficult to address in field settings. Observers rarely know enough about the structure of the field situations to make point predictions about expected behavior or what behavior would lead to optimal outcomes. Without specific predictions, one cannot measure the degree of deviation of actual outcomes from predicted or optimal outcomes. In the first part of the book, we provide the analytical tools that we use in making predictions and in understanding these core problems. These include the general framework within which we are working (the Institutional Analysis and Development, or IAD framework) and some basic game theory applied to CPRs. Once we have done this, we rely primarily on evidence from the experimental laboratory to assess the degree to which predictions about behavior and outcomes are confirmed by empirical evidence. In some experimental settings, empirical results are relatively close to those predicted. In others, the empirical results are substantially different from those predicted. Thus, the second question becomes relevant.

We address the second and third questions using both experimental and field research. The behavioral regularities that we observe in experimental and field settings—where individuals achieve joint outcomes substantially more beneficial than predicted—are both complex and subtle. Answering the second question is one of the most challenging and important tasks that we undertake in this volume. Relating that answer to factors in the physical and institutional worlds is our effort to tie our theoretical endeavors to the development of an improved set of policy tools.

The Plan for This Book

We have identified a series of resource utilization problems that may occur whenever more than one individual appropriates from a common-pool resource. We examine these problems from three perspectives: theoretical, laboratory experiments, and field settings, in that order.

The first part of the book lays out the theory. In chapter 2, we present the IAD framework that we use as an organizing tool in all of our work. In chapters 3 and 4, we use noncooperative game theory as a formal language for applying the IAD framework to CPR problems. In chapter 3, we illustrate the application of game models by presenting a simple analysis of appropriation externalities, of assignment problems, and of provision problems related to monitoring. In chapter 4, we tackle the difficult relationship between changing rules and their effect on the structure and outcomes of a game. These results have implications for the further study of rule provision.

In the second part of the book, we present the findings from a series of empirical studies conducted in an experimental laboratory. Our experimental work focuses on appropriation externalities in the context of time-independent and time-dependent settings. We also focus on the provision of rules. While there is considerable overlap between the questions addressed in the field and in the laboratory, we are able to address some questions more precisely in the laboratory than can ever be done in richer, but more complex, field settings.

In the third part of this volume, four colleagues who have worked with us during the years in which we have developed the theoretical and experimental studies of CPRs present findings from a series of closely related field studies. Four sectors are represented. In chapter 10, Shui Yan Tang provides an overview of the effects of providing irrigation through farmer-owned versus government-owned systems. In chapter 11, Edella Schlager provides an overview of the type of institutional arrangements that fishers using inshore fishing grounds around the world have developed. In chapter 12, Arun Agrawal focuses on the types of enforcement and sanctioning mechanisms that are associated with successful self-organized village institutions that govern and manage local forests in India. In chapter 13, William Blomquist describes the evolution and comparative performance of institutions for governing and managing groundwater basins in southern California.

We have learned much from our research leading to this book. Noncooperative game theory is an extraordinarily useful tool for developing precise theoretical predictions across similar settings that vary in subtle but important ways, reflecting different underlying physical laws or institutional rules. The predictions are supported, at least at an aggregate level, in many of these settings. We have, however, encountered anomalies in our research, anomalies supported by other empirical research. At the end, we are confronted with the need to rethink our original theory. We argue that the next step is an amended theory that remains within the IAD framework and is anchored in noncooperative game theory.

CHAPTER 2

Institutional Analysis and Common-Pool Resources

The substantive concerns of this book involve understanding how rules affect the behavior and outcomes achieved by individuals using common-pool resources (CPRs). To address these concerns effectively requires us to raise fundamental questions about how to explain observed behavior in laboratory and field settings. The three basic questions that we identified in chapter 1 are *theoretical* questions. They have to do with how we think about CPRs. Policies are fashioned from the way that public officials, citizens, and scholars think about problems. We hope that our readers recognize how important the ideas used in policy analysis are. Unless empirically well-grounded theories are developed to enhance the prediction and understanding of behavior, the likelihood of changing rules so as to improve outcomes is slim.

Models, Theories, and Frameworks

Empirically well-grounded theories, however, do not just appear out of thin air. Nor is all theoretical work accomplished at the same conceptual level. Theoretical work related to the study of rules proceeds on at least three different levels: formal models, theories, and frameworks. These levels are all important in the long-term development of empirically grounded theory.

The Formal Model Level

Formal models make explicit assumptions about the elements and structure of a particular situation and use the logical tools of a theory to derive predictions about the likely outcomes of a particular set of parameters. Chapters 3–6 of this book are examples of work at this conceptual level. In chapter 3, we initially develop the simplest possible two-person models of four types of CPR games—appropriation, assignment, provision, and monitoring. In chapter 4, we focus on how various types of rule configurations affect the structure (and thus the predicted outcomes) of the assignment game that we initially present in chapter 3. In chapter 5, we expand the two-person appropriation game into an N-person game that can be tested in an experimental laboratory. Chapter 6 extends the analysis to a time-dependent situation.

Models are always models of something else. Our formal models are models of CPR situations that draw on a more general theory—noncooperative game theory—in providing the logical tools and techniques for building specific models. Game theory is at a more general conceptual level than the models that apply game theory to particular problems.[1] Further, one can generate many game-theoretical models of similar situations. For example, the model of a two-person appropriation game using complete information, presented in chapter 3, could be contrasted with a two-person appropriation game using incomplete information. This would be a different model with the potential for a different predicted equilibrium. Without going outside the confines of game theory, alternative models of the same situation can be developed so that the precise implications of using one or another assumption can be explored. Game theory, then, is the metalanguage for game-theoretical models.

The Theory Level

At this conceptual level, theorists are concerned with puzzles that apply to general classes of models rather than specific models. A theory provides a metatheoretical language for formulating, postulating, predicting, evaluating, and changing various models of that theory. A recent concern among game theorists is the number of game-theoretic models that discover multiple, rather than single, equilibria. Theories of equilibrium selection (Harsanyi and Selten 1988) and equilibrium refinements (van Damme 1987) focus on games that have more than one equilibrium and address how the theorist should proceed. Applications of game theory draw on the developments made at the theory level.

In addition to noncooperative game theory, there are many other theories of human behavior upon which scholars interested in CPRs and in institutions can draw. Theories of bounded rationality are quite relevant—as we discuss later—for the analysis of more complex situations that exist in CPR settings. Cooperative game theory is relevant when the players may freely communicate and commit to binding agreements enforced by a third party, such as some forms of bargaining. Where individuals making economic decisions do not encounter strategic interaction, the microeconomic theory of perfect competition is appropriate. To think about, develop, and evaluate diverse theories, one needs a general framework. Before microeconomic theory was fully

---

1. Duncan Snidal 1985 stresses the important difference between game theory and game models.

developed, the general theoretical framework of classical economics provided the paradigmatic foundations for theoretical work in economics. A framework provides a metatheoretical language for thinking about diverse theories and their potential usefulness in addressing important questions of relevance to the analyst.

The Framework Level

At the conceptual level of a framework, theorists identify the broad working parts and their posited relationships that are used in an entire approach to a set of questions. Frameworks help to organize diagnostic and prescriptive inquiry. The framework we use is called the Institutional Analysis and Development (IAD) framework, which has been the object of considerable thought and reflection by many colleagues over the years.[2] We use the IAD framework as a general organizing tool that helps us develop a long-term research program not only for research on CPRs but also on other problems where individuals find themselves in repetitive situations affected by a combination of factors derived from a physical world, a cultural world, and a set of rules.

Historical Roots of IAD

The IAD framework has its roots in classic political economy (specifically the work of Hobbes, Montesquieu, Hume, Smith, Hamilton, Madison, and Tocqueville); neoclassical microeconomic theory, institutional economics (the work of Commons 1957 and Coase 1937); public choice theory (Buchanan and Tullock 1962; Downs 1957; Olson 1965; Riker 1962); transaction-cost economics (North 1990; Williamson 1975, 1985); and noncooperative game theory (Harsanyi and Selten 1988; Luce and Raiffa 1957; Shubik 1982). The working parts of the IAD framework, which we discuss below, do not always overtly show in an institutional analysis. That is the case with all frameworks. Since a framework orients the analyst to ask particular questions, it is the questions that are generated by using the framework that appear in most analyses rather than the intellectual scaffolding used by the analyst to diagnose, explain, and prescribe.

The IAD framework has influenced the analysis of a myriad of issues during recent decades. It has been applied to the study of metropolitan organization (Advisory Commission on Intergovernmental Relations 1987, 1988, 1992; V. Ostrom, Tiebout, and Warren 1961; V. Ostrom, Bish, and E. Ostrom 1988); the theory of public goods (V. Ostrom and Ostrom 1977); the suste-

---

2. See Kiser and Ostrom 1982; Oakerson 1992; E. Ostrom 1986a, 1986b, 1991; V. Ostrom, Feeny, and Picht 1993; Schaaf 1989; Tang 1992; and Wynne 1989.

nance of rural infrastructures in developing countries (E. Ostrom, Schroeder, and Wynne 1993); privatization in developed and developing countries (Oakerson et al. 1990); to the study of macropolitical systems (Kaminski 1992; V. Ostrom 1987, 1991; Sawyer 1992; Yang 1987) and to a considerable amount of work on CPR problems (Oakerson 1992; E. Ostrom 1990, 1992; Thomson, Feeny, and Oakerson 1992). Work has been carried on related to patterns of order, not only in the United States but in Bangladesh, Botswana, Cameroon, Ghana, India, Indonesia, Ivory Coast, Liberia, Mali, Madagascar, Nepal, the Netherlands, Nigeria, Norway, Poland, the Sudan, the former Soviet Union, and the former Yugoslavia.

The IAD framework does not limit an analyst to the use of one theory. Depending upon the context of the decision environment, an analyst may in fact use the framework as a foundation for investigating the predictive power of complementary or competing theories and models. The initial research approach we develop in this volume combines the IAD framework with the formal theory of noncooperative games and full rationality. For some field and experimental CPRs, noncooperative game theory is particularly useful, and empirical evidence (at least at the aggregate level) is consistent with predictions. For the experimental settings that we describe in chapters 5 and 6, the suboptimal outcomes associated with the game equilibria of limited-access CPR games are broadly supported by the data. This suggests that in field settings where individuals with short time horizons cannot communicate, do not trust each other, or do not have access to reliable external enforcers, outcomes are likely to be broadly consistent with noncooperative game theory.

In other experimental and field CPR situations described in this volume, the data are not consistent with predictions derived from noncooperative game theory under standard assumptions. In some instances, the changes needed to improve game-theoretical tools for the analysis of CPR problems are relatively minor. As we note in chapter 4, for example, game theory does not distinguish between the types of constraints that affect the structure of a game: the constraints of the physical and biological world and the constraints imposed by the rules that individuals evolve or design to limit what can be done in a particular setting. Since all the rules of the game are considered to be immutable from within the game, the possibility that individuals can themselves change the rules of the game (in a time-out or a different arena) cannot easily be addressed without making the distinctions we introduce in chapter 4.

Closely related to the lack of attention to the distinction between physical and biological constraints and the humanly designed rules of the game is how rules get enforced. An underlying assumption of modern game theory is that the rules of the game are unambiguously enforced by some agency external to the game. How and why agents are motivated to enforce rules fully and fairly cannot, therefore, be addressed, as the enforcers are "outside" the game. To understand many CPR environments, however, it is necessary to bring the enforcers inside the game. Further, in many CPR field settings, the enforcers are not even different actors but rather the same individuals who appropriate from a resource. In chapter 3, we construct an irrigation game where we allow appropriators in the first position to decide between following or breaking the rules of the game and the appropriators in a second position to decide between monitoring or not monitoring the behavior of the first. To do this we must use a contrivance that a "legal" move within the formal game is to break the rules of the game we are modeling. Without this contrivance, the issue of rule breaking and rule enforcing cannot be addressed by a noncooperative, game-theoretic model. With this contrivance, we are able to show that self-monitoring can lower rule-breaking behavior but never eliminate it. In recent papers, Weissing and Ostrom (1991, 1993) have shown that external agents cannot fully eliminate rule-breaking behavior either.

We find modern game theory to be a powerful and useful tool for under-standing behavior and outcomes within CPR situations, particularly when brought within the umbrella of the IAD framework with the consequent attention paid to rules. However, as we continue to conduct empirical work on CPR situations in field and experimental settings, we have encountered ever greater problems in explaining empirical results with only modest changes in the theoretical tools we use. In chapter 9, we identify experimental findings that cannot be explained relying on small modifications of received theory. These anomalies are closely related to those found in other environments that have led many scholars to challenge theories based on assumptions of com-plete rationality and unlimited computational capability. Thus, having reached the limits where modern game theory with fully rational players provides consistent theoretical guidance, we apply a theory of bounded rationality to explain the degree of cooperation reached among individuals who are given a chance to devise their own rules.

In all of our work, we have relied on the IAD framework as the general scaffolding that supports our inquiries, helps us identify relevant variables to explore, and provides a broader language that any specific theoretical lan-guage we, or other social scientists, might want to use. Consequently, we will provide a brief overview of the IAD framework in this chapter so that we share our general paradigm with others before turning to some of the theoret-ical tools we use to explore versions of that paradigm.

The Institutional Analysis and Development Framework

Markets, hierarchies, and collective-action situations are sometimes presented as fundamentally different "pure types" of situations. Not only are these situations perceived to be different but each is presumed to require its own language and explanatory theory. Scholars who attempt to explain behavior within markets may rely exclusively on neoclassical microeconomic theory. Scholars who attempt to explain behavior within hierarchies may rely exclusively on political and sociological theory. Scholars who attempt to explain behavior in a collective-action environment may rely exclusively on noncooperative game theory. Such a view precludes the development and use of a more general explanatory framework that, together with its constituent theories, could help analysts make institutional comparisons and evaluations.

Given the multiple levels of analysis involved in institutional analysis, there are several ways that one can approach a question. One of the first steps that can be taken in an institutional analysis using the IAD approach is the identification of a conceptual unit—called an *action arena*—that is subsequently the focus of analysis, prediction, and explanation of behavior and outcomes within fixed constraints.[3] Action arenas include an *action situation* component and an *actor* component (see fig. 2.1). Action situations refer to the social space where individuals interact, exchange goods and services, engage in appropriation and provision activities, solve problems, or fight (among the many things that individuals do in action situations). In field settings, it is hard to tell where one situation ends and another begins. Life continues in almost a seamless web as fishers move from home to a harbor to a nearby fishing grounds and then to a market where the day's haul is sold.

The observer who wants to analyze the recurrent structure of situations must, however, find ways of separating one situation from another for the purpose of analysis. Further, individuals who participate in many situations must also know the difference among them. The actions that can be taken on the fishing grounds are *not* the same as those that can be taken in the fish market. An individual who repeatedly is mixed up about what situation he or she is in is not considered to be competent.

What is distinctive about the IAD framework, as contrasted to many frameworks that are closely tied to a single social science discipline, is that all situations are viewed as being composed of the *same set of elements*.[4] Markets, CPRs, hierarchies, and legislatures are all viewed as being constituted

---

3. An important aspect of the IAD framework is, however, that the analysis of changes in these same parameters is an important part of a full institutional analysis. Thus, for many purposes, we assume a given physical and institutional world and ask what difference these fixed constraints make in outcomes. But, as we discuss later in this chapter and again in chapter 4, many institutional analyses focus precisely on the effects of changing the constraints known as rules. Consequently, one can start an institutional analysis by first looking at the factors that affect action arenas rather than with the arenas themselves.

4. One of the reasons that game theory is particularly compatible with the IAD framework is that it also views all action situations, now conceptualized as games, as constituted of similar working parts.

AN ACTION ARENA IS COMPOSED OF

•   An Action Situation involving

> Participants in
> Positions who must decide among diverse
> Actions in light of the
> Information they possess about how actions are
> Linked to potential
> Outcomes and the
> Costs and Benefits assigned to actions and outcomes

•   Actors, the participants in Action Situations who have

> Preferences,
> Information-processing capabilities,
> Selection criteria, and
> Resources.

Fig. 2.1. Components of action arenas

by a similar set of elemental parts. A minimal action situation is characterized using seven clusters of variables: (1) participants, (2) positions, (3) actions, (4) potential outcomes, (5) a function that maps actions into realized outcomes, (6) information, and (7) the costs and benefits assigned to actions and outcomes. Since many of these elements are themselves relatively complex, the variety of action situations that can be constructed from these elements is immense. Thus at the same time that the framework stresses a universality of working parts, it also enables theorists to analyze unique combinations of these universal working parts. Further, each of these parts are constituted by combinations of physical, cultural, and rule-ordered attributes, as we discuss later in this chapter.

The Action Situation

We will now discuss the elements of an action situation and then turn to how actors are conceptualized in this framework.

Participants

The first element of an action situation includes the actors who have become participants in a situation. This is also the element that links actors, given the way they are conceptualized, to an action situation. In the minimal action situation, there is only a single participant. The theories that are relevant to such a situation include all of the various approaches to decision science, including linear programming and statistical decision theory. At least two participants (but only one position) are necessary for an analyst to use game theory. There is a fundamental difference between two-player games and games involving more than two players. The theory of perfect competition (and some voting theories) are limiting cases when the number of players becomes so large that the actions of one player are negligible to others.

Positions

Positions are simply place holders to associate participants with an authorized set of actions (linked to outcomes) in a process. Examples of positions include first movers, bosses, employees, monitors, voters, elected representatives, judges, appropriators, and citizens. In some situations, every participant holds the same position. In others, every participant holds a different position. In most situations, the number of positions is less than the number of participants. The capabilities and limitations of being in a particular position depend on the way the other elements are defined.

Once the other elements of an action situation are specified, for example, a first mover may be a very powerful or a very weak position. That depends upon the options left to others once the person authorized to move first makes a decision. Similarly, being told that a participant is a "boss" does not tell us the full story about the relative status and power of that individual. To get a complete picture, one needs to know more about the actions the individual can take and the outcomes that can be affected. Whether an actor is a "boss" in a civil service system where decisions about hiring and firing are made by others or is the owner of a private business with considerable discretion to hire and fire employees without much need to confer with others affects what it means to be a boss. Even the type of information available to a participant may be tied to the position that actor currently holds. What is essential is that in the IAD framework, analysis is undertaken about the actions that individuals who hold particular positions are likely to take, rather than focusing on individual personalities independent of the structure of the situation in which they are acting. Thus, once all the other components are settled, the full meaning of a position is articulated.

Actions

The third element is the set of actions that participants in particular positions can take at different stages of a process (or, nodes in a decision tree). Examples of actions include decisions to fish or not to fish during a defined time period; to go to one fishing spot or another; and to fight or not with another fisher about fishing in a particular location. These are the actions we examine in the assignment game in chapter 4. In many action situations, the array of actions that are available is immense and may exceed the capacity of current theoretical tools to analyze. Most analyses attempt to identify only those actions that are the most important in a situation, in the sense that choices made about them make an essential difference in the outcomes achieved.

Potential Outcomes

The fourth element is the outcomes that participants can potentially affect through their actions. Examples of potential outcomes include the quantity of fish caught in a fishing spot, the extent of damage imposed by one participant on another, the physical condition of an irrigation system, or destruction of the regenerative capacity of a CPR. In other words, these are the potential outcomes of individuals interacting with one another in a regularized setting.

Transformation Functions

The fifth element of an action situation is the set of functions that map participants (and/or random actions) at decision nodes into intermediate or final outcomes. In some action situations in economics, these functions are called production functions. They link various combinations of inputs into some type of product. In a voting situation, the transformation function takes the symbolic actions of individuals and produces a collective decision. Transformation functions can be determinate or stochastic in nature. The degree of certainty regarding the transformation function can vary with the situation. In most quid pro quo situations within a defined market, for example, participants know the exact conditions for an exchange to be completed. But in some situations, neither participants nor observers fully understand the complex transformations involved. This is the case, for example, in regard to many fishing grounds where fishery biologists do not yet understand the combination of factors that affect the relationship between fishing effort in one year and availability of fish in the next year.

Information

Closely allied to the type of transformation function is the sixth element—the set of information available to a participant in a position at a stage in a process. When the transformation function is simple and determinant complete information about actions, outcomes, and their linkages may be generated. Many situations generate only incomplete information because of the physical relationships involved or because the rules preclude making all information available.

Payoffs

The seventh element is the set of payoffs that assign benefits and costs to actions and outcomes. Examples include the price of rice offered to the irrigator for crops brought to market, the costs of traveling to a fishing spot, the fines attached to illegal actions, or taxes paid on various activities. Thus, payoffs differ from outcomes as they are the method of assigning positive and negative weights to the outcomes and the actions leading to outcomes. During the monsoon season in an Asian country, particular actions taken in irrigating fields are transformed in a relatively predictable manner into a quantity of rice produced. Thus, the outcomes achieved are consistent from one year to the next. The payoffs achieved, however, may differ radically from one year to the next depending on the costs of inputs (such as labor and fertilizer) and the price that a farmer can command when selling rice. In some formal models, outcomes are not overtly separated from payoffs, but they are implicitly assumed. To understand many situations, however, keeping outcomes and the payoffs assigned to combinations of actions and outcomes is quite essential.

A specification of these seven elements—plus a set of assumptions about the attributes of an actor—is made whenever a theorist undertakes an analysis of a CPR setting, one-shot or repeated. In chapter 3, we provide several examples of how these elements are used to construct different types of CPR games. We consider these to be a minimal set of necessary elements for the construction of theories and models of settings where outcomes depend on the acts of individuals. This is a minimal set in that it is not possible to predict behavior in an interdependent situation without such a specification.

A standard mathematical structure for representing an action situation is a game (Selten 1975; Shubik 1982). The decision environment faced by participants in a well-designed laboratory experiment also represents an action situation. The concept of an action situation is, however, broader than any particular theoretical instance. Any action situation, be it a CPR, a committee, a market, or a hierarchy, can be constructed from these seven elements.[5]

---

5. The simplest possible representation of a committee, for example, can be constructed using the following assumptions:
   1. One position exists; that of member.
   2. Three participants are members.
   3. The set of outcomes that can be affected by the member contains two elements, one of which is designated as the status quo.
   4. A member is assigned an action set containing two elements: (a) vote for the status quo and (b) vote for the alternative outcome.
   5. If two members vote for the alternative outcome, it is obtained; otherwise, the status quo outcome is obtained.
   6. Complete information is available about elements (1) through (5).
For this simplest possible representation of a committee, and using a well-defined model of the

A change in any of these elements produces a different action situation and may lead to very different outcomes. More complex models of CPRs, committees, markets, or other interdependent situations are constructed by adding to the complexity of the elements.[6]

Actors

To predict how actors will behave, the analyst must make assumptions about four clusters of variables: (1) the preference evaluations that actors assign to potential actions and outcomes; (2) the way actors acquire, process, retain, and use knowledge contingencies and information; (3) the selection criteria actors use for deciding upon a particular course of action; and (4) the resources that an actor brings to a situation. The actor in a situation can be thought of as a single individual or as a group functioning as a corporate actor.

Individual Preferences

In most theories of rational behavior, individuals are presumed able to construct a complete preference ordering over outcomes to which payoffs are assigned. Preference theory is itself a vast subject. Many different theories exist about how actors acquire preferences, what they do when outcomes imply extreme trade-offs among valued objects, and how preferences are assigned when outcomes are unknown. Utility theory is a richly developed body of theory for how individuals assign a valuation—utility—to the outcomes and costs of actions.

Individual Information-Processing Capabilities

To explain how individuals make decisions, the theorist specifies the level of information actors possess and process. A frequent assumption made in theo-

---

rational actor, we know whether an equilibrium outcome exists. Unless two of the members prefer the alternative outcome to the status quo and both vote, the status quo is the equilibrium outcome. If two members do prefer and vote for the alternative outcome, it is the equilibrium outcome. The prediction of outcomes is more problematic as soon as a third outcome is added. Only when the valuation patterns of participants meet restricted conditions can an equilibrium outcome be predicted for such a simple committee situation with three members and three potential outcomes using majority rule (Arrow 1966; Plott 1967).

6. A more complex committee situation is created, for example, if a second position, that of a convener, is added to the situation, and the action set of the convener includes actions not available to the other members (e.g., Haney, Herzberg, and Wilson 1992; Eavey and Miller 1982; Isaac and Plott 1978). See also Gardner 1983 for an analysis of purges and recruitment to committees.

ries of full rationality is that individuals have *complete* information. Specifying that participants have complete information means that they know

1. the actions that each participant can take at every stage of a decision process and those acts that are governed by a random operator;
2. the intermediate and/or final outcomes that can be reached as a result of the moves of various participants combined with chance moves where relevant; and
3. the preference ranking placed by each participant on all outcomes.

If a participant knows all of the above, the participant knows the full decision or game tree in extensive form. *Perfect information* requires all aspects of complete information, and in addition, that all actions taken by participants are known to all others.[7] Chess is an example of a game with perfect information if one assumes that chess players are fully capable of remembering all past moves and calculating forward into the indefinite future at any particular stage in the game. Rational players process all available information infallibly. Such players can place past information into long-term storage without loss or bias, and they can bring adequate information into short-term storage to make a correct analysis.

The models of chapters 3–6 assume complete information and infallible processing. In chapters 3 and 4, where there are only two players and each player has only two actions, these assumptions are reasonable, and enable us to make precise predictions. In chapters 5 and 6, where we model eight-player versions of the appropriation game in a finitely repeated setting, the game is more complex but still tractable to analyze. The complexity of the game grows with the number of players, the number of feasible actions, and the number of repetitions (see chap. 3). All this makes the assumption that individuals are perfect and infinite information processors heroic in more complex situations.

Bounded rationality is a much weaker assumption about players' information-processing capabilities. In many situations, the amount of information generated is larger than what individuals can amass and record. They may not utilize all of the information available to them, and they may make errors in processing the information they do use. Boundedly rational individuals possess various heuristics or shortcuts to cope with informationally complex problems they face.

---

7. Technically, this means that all information sets are singletons and that participants know exactly where they are in a game tree.

Individual Selection Criteria

Theories differ in regard to the criteria they posit actors to follow in making decisions. In many theories that assume complete information and infallible processing, actors maximize expected utility, compute best responses, or obey the minimax criterion. Sometimes these criteria all lead to the same prediction. Usually, however, the predicted outcome is criterion dependent. Under bounded rationality, the information needed for many of the rigorous selection criteria is not assumed to be present. Selection criteria are then built into the heuristics that individuals are posited to use. Sometimes these involve selecting the first alternative that exceeds a minimal threshold. Other heuristics involve more complex processes, but not the necessity of undertaking a full analysis and choosing the maximal set from it.[8]

Individual Resources

Many theoretical analyses assume that all actors possess sufficient resources to take any of the actions available to them. But in situations where some actions involve high costs, the monetary and time constraints facing individual actors are important constraints. Budgetary constraints may eliminate all but a very narrow band from the feasible set of some actors.

Given that most of the actions that we analyze are feasible to the CPR appropriators, these constraints are not as important in our analysis as they are in many other settings. It does turn out, however, that the amount of the endowment given to subjects in a laboratory setting has a major and unexpected effect on behavior (see chap. 5).

Explaining Behavior in Situations

In order to derive inferences about the likely behavior of each actor in a situation (and, thus, about the pattern of joint results that may be produced), one must make assumptions about the preferences, information-processing skills, selection criteria, and resources of the actors who are participants. The actor is, thus, the animating force that allows the analyst to generate predictions about likely outcomes given the structure of the situation (Popper 1967).

Classical game theory (e.g., Von Neumann and Morgenstern [1944] 1964, chap. 2) assumes that players are fully rational. This has come to mean that players assign complete preferences over outcomes, have unlimited com-

---

8. Tversky and Kahneman 1990 provide a concise overview of research on bounded rationality.

putational powers, conduct complete analyses, and possess the resources necessary for any feasible action. This assumption is intended to apply to both cooperative and noncooperative games. In part because of the extremity of this assumption, powerful mathematical results can be deduced. For many field settings, these theories are highly successful explanatory and diagnostic tools. Even if individuals do not initially behave as predicted, their behavior tends to converge toward predicted behavior over time. For those settings, using these assumptions about individual choice is a useful way of doing institutional analysis. However, empirical results do not always accord with mathematical deductions from these assumptions even after adaptation, learning, or evolution has taken place.

Thus, the theorist has to choose which tools to use to analyze diverse arenas. Within the IAD framework, all of these tools are seen as valuable and having a place in the tool kit of an institutional analyst. The challenge, as we see it, is learning how best to use the full array of tools to undertake theoretical analyses of a wide diversity of situations.

When a theorist analyzes an action arena, specific assumptions are made regarding the structure of the situation and the actors. The task of the theorist is viewed as one of predicting the type of behavior and results, given these assumptions. Questions concerning the presence or absence of retentive, attractive, and/or stable equilibria and evaluations of the efficiency and equity of these results are pursued. The general question being investigated is, given the analytical structure assumed, how does this situation work to produce outcomes?

Evaluating Outcomes

After predicting and explaining outcomes, policy analysts evaluate the outcomes achieved using a diversity of evaluative criteria. The key question addressed in an evaluative effort is: How do predicted outcomes conform to evaluative criteria? As we mention in chapter 1, we rely to a large extent on evaluation criteria related to the concepts of efficiency and Pareto optimality. When individuals craft their own rules, they are apt to rely on additional criteria. Conceptions of fairness are extremely important in deciding upon what type of rules will even be considered as appropriate in a particular community. Whether it is possible for individuals to learn from their mistakes and improve on the outcomes they achieve over time is another important evaluative criterion. Whether rules can be transmitted from one generation to the next without the introduction of substantial error is still another criterion. Thus, there are more criteria to evaluate outcomes than we can rigorously address in this volume.

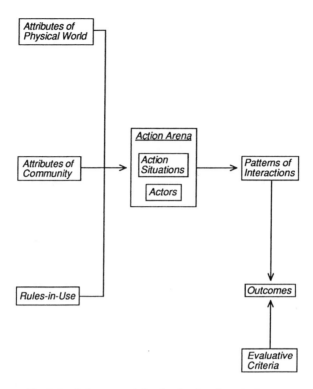

Fig. 2.2. A framework for institutional analysis

Factors Affecting Action Arenas

Underlying the way analysts think about action arenas are explicit or implicit assumptions about the *rules* individuals use to order their relationships, about attributes of *a physical world*, and about the *nature of the community* within which the arena occurs (see fig. 2.2). While many analyses are undertaken without an overt attempt to address how these deeper factors affect the situation of interest, theorists interested in institutional questions have to dig deeper to understand how rules combine with a physical and cultural world to generate particular types of situations. Implicit or explicit assumptions about rules, physical variables, and the nature of a community all influence the way the seven elements of an action situation are conceptualized. Thus, an institutional analysis might begin with an analysis of these factors first and proceed to identify some of the typical action situations that result from particular combinations of these factors. Below, we lay the foundation for clarifying the meaning and attributes of rules, physical conditions, and community. We focus primarily on how rules affect the structure of action situations, since it is rules that are usually the object of efforts to change this structure.

The Meaning of Rules

Rules, as we use the term, are prescriptions that define what actions (or outcomes) are *required, prohibited*, or *permitted*, and the sanctions authorized if the rules are not followed (S. Crawford and Ostrom 1993). All rules are the result of implicit or explicit efforts to achieve order and predictability among humans by creating classes of persons (positions) who are then required, permitted, or forbidden to take classes of actions in relation to required, permitted, or forbidden states of the world (E. Ostrom 1986a).

Rules are contextual, prescriptive, and followable (Shimanoff 1980). They are contextual in the sense that they apply to a general set of action arenas but do not apply everywhere. The rules of chess apply *only* to situations in which participants wish to play chess, and they apply to every such situation. The game of chess provides the context for the application of its rules. Rules are prescriptive in the sense that "those who are knowledgeable of a rule also know that they can be held accountable if they break it" (Shimanoff 1980, 41). Rules provide information about the actions an actor "must" perform (obligation), "must not" perform (prohibition), or "may" perform (permission) if the actor is to avoid the possibility of sanctions being imposed. Rules are followable in the sense that it is possible for actors to perform obligatory, prohibited, or permitted actions as well as it is possible for them *not* to perform these actions. In other words, it is physically possible for actors to follow or not to follow a rule. This distinguishes actions that are explained by reference to rules or norms from behavior that is explained by the physical characteristics of the situation.

Understanding the relationship between rules and games often requires one to investigate the origin of such rules. In totalitarian governance systems, a central government attempts to impose rules on most action situations occurring within its domain. It attempts to be the source of all rules and their enforcement and invests heavily in police and organized terror mechanisms in this effort. Given the extreme sanctions that can be imposed, individuals interacting with strangers try to stay within the "letter of the law" as prescribed. Behind the scenes, however, many activities are organized using rules other than those prescribed by a central regime (Kaminski 1992). Government officials try to extort bribes from citizens (or businesses), who may try to evade government regulations by keeping some things hidden and paying off officials. Special accommodations are made in secret that are exactly counter to the letter of the law. Thus, in a totalitarian regime where individuals have had an opportunity to begin to make accommodations with one another, there are many sources of the rules used in daily life. Some of these rules are exactly counter to the prescriptions laid down by the formal government.

In open and democratic governance systems, there are also many sources for the rules that individuals use in everyday life. It is not considered illegal or improper for individuals to organize themselves and craft their own rules, and enforce these rules so long as the activities involved are lawful. Much of the character of law presumes autonomy on the part of diverse, self-organizing patterns of relationships—voluntary associations, families, corporations, municipalities, provinces, and so on. Within private firms and voluntary associations, individuals are authorized to adopt their own specific rules so long as these are within the broad set of potentially lawful rules that are theoretically consistent with the larger constitutional system. Thus, many collective-choice arenas can be used to affect the structure of any particular operational action situation.

When individuals participate in the crafting of multiple layers of rules, some of that crafting will occur using pen and paper. Much will occur, however, as problem-solving individuals interact trying to figure out how to do a better job in the future than they have done in the past. Colleagues in a work team are crafting their own rules when they say to one another something like: "How about if you do A in the future, and I will do B, and before we ever make a decision about X again, we both discuss it and reach a joint decision?" In a democratic society, problem-solving individuals do this all the time. Individuals also participate in less fluid decision-making arrangements, including elections to select legislators. Elected representatives may then engage in open, good-faith attempts to solve a wide diversity of problems brought to them by their constituents. It is also possible in a governance system where individuals are elected, for patterns to emerge that are not strictly problem solving. Incentives exist to create mechanisms whereby one set of individuals dominates over others.

Thus, in undertaking an institutional analysis relevant to a field setting, one needs first to understand the working rules that individuals use. Working rules are the rules used by participants in ongoing action arenas. They are the set of rules to which participants would refer if asked to explain and justify their actions to fellow participants.[9] Rules-in-use may be remembered by participants in local sayings like the Thakali rhyme mentioned in chapter 1. While following a rule may become a "social habit," it is possible to raise to

---

9. It is not always the case, however, that participants will explain their actions to outsiders the same way they will explain them to fellow participants. Consequently, learning about the working rules used in a particular CPR may be very difficult.

conscious awareness the rules used to order relationships. Individuals can consciously decide to adopt a different rule and change their behavior to conform to such a decision. Over time, behavior in conformance with a new rule may itself become habitual (see Shimanoff 1980; Toulmin 1974; Harrè 1974). The capacity of humans to use complex cognitive systems to order their own behavior at a relatively subconscious level makes it difficult for empirical researchers to ascertain what the working rules are for an ongoing action arena.

Rule following or conforming actions are not as predictable as biological or physical behavior explained by physical laws. Rules are formulated in human language. As such, rules share the problems of lack of clarity, misunderstanding, and change that typifies any language-based phenomenon. Words are "symbols that name, and thus, stand for classes of things and relationships" (V. Ostrom 1980, 312). Words are always simplifications of the phenomenon to which they refer (V. Ostrom 1994).

The stability of rule-ordered actions is dependent upon the shared meaning assigned to words used to formulate a set of rules and how they will be enforced. If no shared meaning exists when a rule is formulated, confusion will exist about what actions are required, permitted, or forbidden. Regularities in actions cannot result if those who must repeatedly interpret the meaning of a rule within action situations arrive at multiple interpretations. Because "rules are not self-formulating, self-determining, or self-enforcing" (V. Ostrom 1980, 312), it is human agents who formulate them, who apply them in particular situations, and who attempt to enforce performance consistent with them. Even if shared meaning exists at the time of the acceptance of a rule, transformations in technology, in shared norms, and in circumstances more generally change the events to which rules apply. "Applying language to changing configurations of development increases the ambiguities and threatens the shared criteria of choice with an erosion of their appropriate meaning" (V. Ostrom 1980, 312; see also V. Ostrom 1994, chaps. 1 and 6 for an in-depth development of this thesis).

A myriad of specific rules are used in structuring complex action arenas. Classification of these rules in a theoretically useful typology is a necessary step in developing a cumulative body of knowledge about the effects of rules. Anyone attempting to define a useful typology of rules must be concerned that the classification is more than a method for imposing superficial order onto an extremely large set of seemingly disparate rules. Asking how rules affect the structures of action situations is the method developed as part of the IAD framework to cluster rules. This is seen as a first step in a theory about how rules relate to the structure of action situations, thereby affecting the way individuals behave and achieve outcomes. A similar method can be used in identifying those aspects of the physical and cultural world that affect behavior and outcomes.

Types of Rules and Rule Configurations

From sets of physically possible actions, outcomes, payoffs, decision functions, information, positions, and participants, rules alter the feasible sets of the values of these variables. The action situation is the intersection of these feasible sets. In regard to driving a car, for example, it is physically possible for a 13 year old to drive a car at 120 miles per hour on a freeway. If one were to model the action situation of a freeway in a state with well-enforced traffic laws, one would posit the position of licensed drivers filled by individuals 16 and over traveling an average of 60 to 65 miles per hour (depending on the enforcement patterns of the state). The values of the variables in the action situation are constrained by the type of physical world involved and then, further affected by the rules-in-use. Most formal analysis of a game focuses primarily on the structure of an action situation: this is the surface structure of our formal representations. The rules are part of the underlying structure that shapes the representations we use. But, how do we overtly examine this part of the underlying structure? What rules should be examined when we conduct analysis at a deeper level?

We identify seven broad types of rules that operate configurally to affect the structure of an action situation. In the list of rules we present here, we emphasize the working part of an action situation (game) that a particular kind of rule directly affects.[10]

1. Position rules specify a set of *positions* and how many participants are to hold each position.
   EXAMPLE: Farmers who constitute an irrigation association designate positions such as member, water distributor, guard, member of a tribunal (to adjudicate disputes over water allocation), and other officers of the association.
2. Boundary rules specify how *participants* enter or leave these positions.

---

10. In this effort, we concentrate primarily on the direct effects of rules (or the physical and cultural factors affecting an action situation). Since all of these factors operate configurally, the final constellation of elements in an action situation depends on more than just one rule per element. The information available to an individual at a node, for example, is directly affected by information rules but also affected by the sequence of activities that are part of an authority rule. One cannot know the action that someone else takes if they must take their action simultaneously with one's own.

EXAMPLE: An irrigation association has rules that specify how a farmer becomes a member of the association and the qualifications that individuals must have to be considered eligible to hold a position as an officer of the association.

3. Authority rules specify which *set of actions* is assigned to which position at each node of a decision tree.

   EXAMPLE: If a farmer challenges the actions taken by another farmer or the water distributor, the rules of an irrigation association specify what a water distributor or guard may do next.

4. Aggregation rules specify the *transformation function* to be used at a particular node, to map actions into intermediate or final outcomes.

   EXAMPLE: When a decision is made at a meeting of an irrigation association about changing association rules, the votes of each member present and voting are weighted (frequently each vote is given equal weight, but it may be weighted by the amount of land owned or other factors) and added. When 50 percent plus one of those voting (presuming a quorum) vote to alter legislation, the rules are altered. If less than 50 percent plus one vote for the change, the rules remain unchanged.

5. Scope rules specify the *set of outcomes* that may be affected, including whether outcomes are intermediate or final.

   EXAMPLE: Rules that specify that the water stored behind a reservoir may not be released for irrigation if the level falls below the level required for navigation or for generating power.

6. Information rules specify the *information* available to each position at a decision node.

   EXAMPLE: Rules that specify that the financial records of an irrigation association must be available to the members at the time of the annual meeting.

7. Payoff rules specify how *benefits and costs* are required, permitted, or forbidden in relation to players, based on the full set of actions taken and outcomes reached.

   EXAMPLE: Rules that specify whether a farmer may sell any of the water received from an irrigation system, what crops may be grown, how guards are to be paid, and what labor obligations may be involved to keep the system maintained.

The wide diversity of rules that are found in everyday life could be classified in many ways. The IAD method has several advantages. First, rules are tied directly to the variables of an analytical entity familiar to all game theorists. Second, one has a heuristic for identifying the rules affecting the structure of that situation. Finally, one has a conceptual tool for inquiry about how rules affect a given situation. For each variable identified in the action situation, the theorist interested in rules needs to ask what rules affect the variable as specified. For example, in regard to the number of participants, the analyst asks: Why are there N participants? How did they enter? Under what conditions can they leave? Are some participants forced into entry because of their residence or occupation?

In regard to the actions that can be taken, the analyst asks: Why these actions rather than others? Are all participants in positions assigned the same action set? Or, is some convener, or other position, assigned an action set containing options not available to other participants? Are sets of actions time or path dependent?

In regard to the outcomes that can be affected, the analyst asks: Why these outcomes rather than others? Are the participants all principals who can affect any state variable they are defined to own? Or, are the participants fiduciaries who are authorized to affect particular state variables within specified ranges but not beyond? Similar questions can be asked about each variable overtly placed in a model of an action situation.

Answers to these sets of questions are formalized as a set of relations that, combined with the structure of a physical world and the type of community involved, produces the particular values of the variables of the situation. As we show in chapter 4, a particular model of a situation could be produced by different underlying factors. Given the frequency of situations with the structure of a Prisoner's Dilemma, for example, it is obvious that the structure of this action situation results from many different combinations of rules, physical variables, and attributes of a community. This many-one relationship is not problematic when one focuses exclusively on predicting behavior within the one situation. The flip side of this relationship, which is a one-many relationship, is extremely problematic if one were to want to change the situation. From the action situation alone, one cannot infer the underlying factors.

Besides providing a general heuristic for identifying the relevant rules that affect the structure of a situation, a second advantage of examining the rules that directly affect the seven components of an action situation is that doing so leads to a relatively natural classification system for sets of rules. Classifying rules by what they initially affect enables us to identify rules that all directly affect the same working part of the situation. Specific rules used in everyday life are named in a nontheoretical manner—frequently referring to the number of the rule in some written rule book or piece of legislation. Theorists studying rules tend to name the rule they are examining for some feature related to the particular type of situation in which the rule occurs. In the interests of systematic cumulation, rules structurally the same but called by different names need to be classified the same.

Attributes of a Physical World

The variables of an action situation are also affected by attributes of the relevant physical world. The physical possibility of actions, the producibility of outcomes, the linkages of actions to outcomes, and the knowledge of actors all depend on the physical world and its transformations. The same rule configuration may yield entirely different types of action situations depending upon the types of events in the physical world being acted upon by participants. The difference between goods that are subtractive in nature, such as CPRs and private goods, as contrasted to those that are not subtractive, such as public goods and toll goods, strongly affects how rules affect outcomes. Allocation rules that are essential to achieve better outcomes related to CPRs make no difference in situations where goods are not subtractive. As we discuss in chapter 14, whether a CPR has storage facilities and whether the resource units are mobile also makes a substantial difference in the kinds of rules that one can utilize.

The physical attributes of the relevant world are explicitly examined when the analyst self-consciously asks a series of questions about how the world being acted upon in a situation affects the outcome, action sets, action-outcome linkages, and information sets in that situation. The relative importance of the rule configuration and the physical world in structuring an action situation varies dramatically across different types of action situations. The rule configuration almost totally constitutes some games, like chess, where physical attributes are relatively unimportant. There is little about the size of a chessboard or the shape of the pieces that contributes to the structure of a chess game. On the other hand, imagine, for a moment, switching the balls used in American and European football. The strategies available to players in these two games, and many other sports, are strongly affected by the physical attributes of the balls used, the size of the field, and the type of equipment.

The relative importance of working rules to physical attributes also varies dramatically within action situations considered to be part of the public sector. A legislature is closer in many respects to chess than to football. Rules define and constrain voting behavior inside a legislature more than the physical world. Voting can be accomplished by raising hands, by paper ballots, by calling for the ayes and nays, by passing before an official counter, or by installing computer terminals for each legislator on which votes are registered. In regard to organizing communication within a legislature, however, attributes of the world strongly affect the available options. The physical limit that only one person can be heard and understood at a time in any one forum strongly affects the capacity of legislators to communicate effectively with one another (see V. Ostrom 1987).

Attributes of a Community

A third set of variables that affect the structure of an action arena relates to the community in which an action situation is located. The attributes of a community that are important in affecting the structure of an action arena include generally accepted norms of behavior, the level of common understanding about action arenas, the extent to which the preferences are homogeneous, and distribution of resources among members. The term *culture* is frequently applied to this bundle of attributes.

If children are taught to extend trust to others so long as the others behave in a trusting manner, adults acquire norms of behavior that enable them to accomplish far more in life in their interactions with other trusting individuals than those who are taught to distrust others in their interactions with other nontrusting individuals.[11] This is especially true in relatively homogeneous communities where individuals repeatedly interact with one another along many different dimensions (Taylor 1987). These norms of behavior become a form of social capital that can be drawn on repeatedly as the foundation for cooperative solutions to CPR dilemmas.

Linking Action Arenas

While the concept of a "single" arena may include large numbers of participants and complex chains of action, most of social reality is composed of multiple arenas linked sequentially or simultaneously. Farmers who jointly use an irrigation system, for example, must organize a variety of provision activities primarily related to maintenance. If breaks in the sides of canals are not fixed and the canals themselves not cleaned, the amount of water that actually gets to each farmer's gate declines substantially over time. Organizing the provision side of an irrigation CPR may involve deciding upon how many days a year should be devoted to routine maintenance, how work will be allocated to individual farmers, how emergency repairs should be handled, who is responsible for repairing broken embankments caused by grazing animals, and how new control gates and regulatory devices are to be installed and paid for. Appropriation activities are closely linked to these provision activities. How much water is available for distribution is dependent upon

---

11. It is important to note that the results achieved by individuals who adopted a norm of trusting others depend on the norms adopted by others with whom they come in contact regularly. If the population of "others" contains many who are nontrusting, then those who are trusting may be worse off for following their learned norm.

whether a system is kept in good repair. The level of conflict over water distribution is apt to be higher on a poorly maintained system than on a better-maintained system. In many places in this volume, we will focus on one arena rather than the linked arenas for analytical clarity.

Multiple Levels of Analysis

Action arenas are also linked across several levels of analysis. All rules are nested in another set of rules that, if enforced, defines how the first set of rules can be changed. The nesting of rules within rules at several levels is similar to the nesting of computer languages at several levels. What can be done at a higher level will depend on the capabilities and limits of the rules (or the software) at that level and at a deeper level. Changes in the rules used to order action at one level occur within a currently "fixed" set of rules at a deeper level. Changes in deeper-level rules usually are more difficult and more costly to accomplish, thus increasing the stability of mutual expectations among individuals interacting according to a set of rules.

It is useful to distinguish three levels of rules that cumulatively affect the actions taken and outcomes obtained in any setting (Kiser and Ostrom 1982) (see fig. 2.3).

1. *Operational rules* directly affect day-to-day decisions made by the participants in any setting.
2. *Collective-choice rules* affect operational activities and results through their effects in determining who is eligible and the specific rules to be used in changing operational rules.
3. *Constitutional-choice rules* affect operational activities and their effects in determining who is eligible and the rules to be used in crafting the set of collective-choice rules that in turn affect the set of operational rules.

At each level of analysis there may be one or more arenas in which the types of decisions made at that level will occur. The elements of an action situation and of an actor are used to construct these arenas at all three levels. As we discuss above, the concept of an "arena" does not imply a formal setting, but can include such formal settings as legislatures, governmental bureaucracies, and courts. Policy-making regarding the rules that will be used to regulate operational-level action situations is usually carried out in one or more collective-choice arenas as well as being enforced at an operational level. Dilemmas are not limited to an operational level of analysis. They frequently occur at the collective-choice and constitutional levels of analysis.

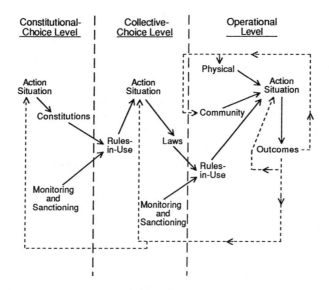

Fig. 2.3.   Linking levels of analysis

Multiple Levels of Analysis and Solving
Higher-Order Dilemmas

In chapter 1, we discussed two types of coordinated strategies that enable appropriators to extricate themselves from CPR dilemmas. One type of coordinated strategy exists within a set of preexisting rules. The second type of coordinated strategy is an effort to change the rules themselves by moving to a collective-choice or constitutional-choice arena. The possibility of switching to collective-choice or constitutional-choice arenas is frequently ignored in current analyses.

This lack of attention to the possibility of changing the rules of a game results from two different views. The first is a methodological position that eliminates analysis of structural change while examining the effects of one structure on outcomes. In other words, the givens that one uses to specify a problem for analysis are not to be changed in the process of analysis. It is easy to overcome this limit by overtly taking a long-term perspective. It is with a long-term perspective that the given constraints of a particular physical facility are changed into variables that can be changed and thus analyzed. A similar approach can be taken with rules.

The second reason that the possibility of individuals changing their own rules has been ignored is the assumption that a set of rules is itself a public good. Once developed, the rules are available to all individuals, whether or not they contribute to the effort to design the new rules.[12] Thus, changing rules is a higher-order, supply-side provision problem (Feeny 1988, 1993). Agreement on better rules affects all individuals in the group whether they participate in the reform effort or not. The temptation to free ride in the effort to craft new rules may be offset by the strong interest that most appropriators have in ensuring that their own interests are taken into account in any set of new rules. Further, the group might be "privileged" in the sense that one or a very small group of individuals might expect such a high return from provision that they pay the full cost themselves (Olson 1965).

The higher the order of a CPR dilemma, the more difficult it is to solve. An even higher-order dilemma than a rule change is the dilemma involving monitoring and sanctioning to enforce a set of rules. Even the best rules are never self-enforcing. It is usually the case that once most appropriators follow these rules, there are strong temptations for some appropriators to break them. If most farmers take a legal amount of water from an irrigation system so the system operates predictably, each farmer will be tempted from time to time to take more than a legal amount of water because his or her crops may be in severe need of more water. Once some farmers take more than their allotment of water, other farmers will be tempted to do the same, and the agreed-upon set of rules can crumble rapidly. Monitoring each other's activities and imposing sanctions on one another are costly activities. Unless the rewards received by the individual who monitors and sanctions someone else are high enough, each potential monitor faces a situation where not monitoring and not sanctioning may be the individually preferred strategy even though everyone would be better off if that strategy were not chosen. Thus, designing monitoring and sanctioning arrangements that sustain themselves over time is another delicate, difficult, higher-order, supply-side provision task involved in transforming a CPR dilemma.

In many theories of collective action, rules are enforced by outsiders. It is important to inquire into how rules are enforced and how much sanctioning deviant behavior costs. Appropriators may punish one another in several different ways.[13] In relatively small groups that interact with one another on a wide diversity of fronts, appropriators may impose social sanctions and openly criticize the offender. Further, they may refuse to participate in other types of economic exchanges with an offender. If most members of a community refused to cooperate with an offender, for example, the costs to an

---

12. It is, of course, possible for a group to change their rules and produce a worse outcome. Whether rule changes improve or worsen the outcomes of a situation, the important characteristic of the provision of rules is that everyone using a CPR is affected whether or not they spent time and effort in devising a new rule system.

13. See Jankowski 1991 for a discussion of the costs of using different types of punishment mechanisms and how these costs may vary with the size of a group.

offender may be rather substantial, while the costs to other members of the community may be relatively modest. Actions that involve physical coercion or the impoundment of property represent a somewhat higher level of cost for the person who undertakes sanctioning. When several individuals jointly undertake the sanctioning, however, individual costs are reduced and costs imposed on the offender can be very high.

A third type of punishment involves a form of retaliation whereby individuals stop abiding by the rules they have established for some time so as to "teach" the offenders the costs of breaking agreements. This is the type of punishment posited as the means of solving an infinitely repeated social dilemma game. The term used to describe this type of punishment is *trigger strategy*. What is meant by this term is that appropriators would stand ready to retaliate with strategies leading to suboptimal outcomes at any point that someone consciously or by error adopted such an action themselves (see chap. 3). Punishment by withholding cooperation can be very costly for all involved since those who take action also reap lower payoffs.

Conclusions

Substantial theoretical issues are involved in undertaking institutional analyses of any complex and important set of problems, such as those related to the study of common-pool resources. Without recognizing that theoretical languages are nested from the most specific to the most general, scholars conducting work at one conceptual level may not recognize the array of alternative conceptualizations that are potentially possible and useful for analysis at a particular level. Because one model provides insight into a particular problem does not preclude the possibility of alternative models that usefully illuminate the problem as well, in some cases leading to complementary insights. Having alternative models enables one to carefully specify variable contingencies pertaining to empirical work. Alternative models generate competing hypotheses that can then be tested. Similarly, alternative theories may be needed to address different types of situations that look initially as if they are the same. Because one theory is more useful for some situations than another does not negate the potential usefulness of both theoretical explanations. Similarly, there are many frameworks that can potentially be used in the social sciences, but given the organizing character of a framework it is more difficult for scholars to work across different frameworks.

In this book, we rely on the IAD framework as our general organizing mode that can be used to orient oneself to a large variety of problems. We started with one theory—noncooperative game theory—as our primary tool to construct models of diverse CPR situations. We have found this theory to be an extremely useful and powerful tool throughout our research effort. We have, however, found empirical evidence that we cannot explain with the initial theoretical tool that we adopted. Thus, we have added a complementary tool—the theory of bounded rationality—to the set of theories we use for explaining behavior related to CPRs. We do not address the question of alternative frameworks within this volume as we have not yet encountered problems where the IAD framework is not a useful tool for addressing policy problems. However, we do not presume that the IAD framework is the only framework available to social scientists interested in understanding questions of social order.

CHAPTER 3

Games Appropriators Play

Even in the simplest CPR environments, the number of variables that simultaneously affect individual behavior is quite large. In addition, these variables
are often related in a complex way. Informal reasoning may lead to broad
insights in such situations, but it may also lead to conclusions that are not
logically valid. Precise logical conclusions and sound predictions, both quantitative and qualitative, depend on the exact configuration of key variables in a
formal model. In this chapter, we develop a series of closely related formal
models using game theory and apply those models to the various types of CPR
problems.

The Use of Formal Models

A formal game is one method of analyzing an action situation. The seven
components of an action situation are the basic elements of every game: (1) a
set of players, (2) a set of positions, (3) sets of actions assigned to positions at
choice nodes including chance moves, (4) a decision function that maps
choices into intermediate or final outcomes, (5) a set of outcomes, (6) the kind
of information available at a node, and (7) payoffs based on benefits and costs
of actions and outcomes. Our discussion begins with simple 2-person games
to highlight the ways in which alternative CPR games may have very different
strategic consequences.

   Figure 3.1 presents the simplest possible game situation. All the following elements are contained in the figure. There are two players, called player 1
and player 2; this is the set of players (1). Using the language of game theory,
there is a single position that is held by both players. Each player makes a
single decision simultaneously and independently of the other player. Thus,
the set of positions (2) has only one position. Each player can take one of two
possible actions, called strategy 1 and strategy 2. In terms of the matrix in
figure 3.1, player 1 chooses over the two rows of the matrix, while player 2
chooses over the two columns of the matrix. The set of actions (3) possible for
each player is therefore (strategy 1, strategy 2). The outcome function is

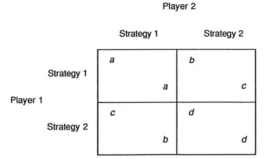

Fig. 3.1.   Game with two players, two strategies

portrayed by the matrix structure itself. If player 1 chooses strategy 1 and player 2 chooses strategy 1, then the outcome is the cell of the matrix corresponding to the first row and column, that is, the cell in the upper left-hand corner. The four cells of the matrix represent the entire outcome function (4). The outcomes themselves are the contents of the four cells of the matrix. Each cell has a different outcome. Each outcome consists of a pair of numbers, one in the upper left-hand corner of a cell (this corresponds to player 1), and one in the lower right-hand corner (this corresponds to player 2). For example, if both players choose strategy 1, then the outcome is the pair of numbers a for player 1 and a for player 2. If, on the other hand, player 1 chooses strategy 1 and player 2 chooses strategy 2, then the outcome is b for player 1 and c for player 2. The set of outcomes (5) is the set of four possible outcomes in the four cells of the matrix. The information available to each player is all that portrayed in figure 3.1. The matrix, together with its labeling, constitutes the information set (6). The letters a, b, c, and d in the matrix stand for various amounts of cash or other valued objects to be received by players when the game is over.[1] These cash payoffs define the payoff function (7).

The decision task facing each of the players in the game of figure 3.1 is which strategy to choose, strategy 1 or strategy 2. This is a complicated decision to make. It depends not only on the payoff parameters a, b, c, d, but also on the choice of the other player. To appreciate the complexity, we consider in some detail the case where the payoff parameters satisfy the following inequalities: $b < d$, $c > a$. Player 1 must consider all possible actions by player 2. Suppose that player 1 first considers the consequences for himself or herself if player 2 chooses strategy 1, so that column 1 is the only

---

1. The assumption just made is very strong. A more general assumption is that payoffs to players are a function of outcomes, called the utility function. Our assumption makes cash a metric for utility. In terms of Von Neumann–Morgenstern utility theory (and many others), our assumption further implies risk neutrality on the part of the players.

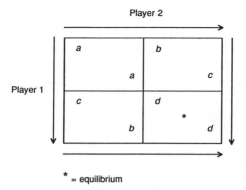

Player 2

Player 1

* = equilibrium

Fig. 3.2. Prisoner's Dilemma, (*a* < *c*, *b* < *d*)

column relevant to player 1's choice. Since $c > a$, player 1 makes more money by choosing strategy 2 instead of strategy 1. We denote this conclusion by an arrow pointing from top to bottom along the left side of the matrix in figure 3.2. If player 2 were to choose strategy 1, then player 1's *best* response would be to choose strategy 2. Next, suppose that player 1 considers the consequences for himself or herself if player 2 chooses strategy 2. Since $d > b$, player 1 would make more money by choosing strategy 2 instead of strategy 1. We denote this conclusion by an arrow pointing from top to bottom on the right side of the matrix in figure 3.2. Now both arrows point down, which means that in the case we are considering, player 1 would make the same choice regardless of what player 2 might choose: player 1 chooses strategy 2. In this special case, player 1's choice is not so hard after all.

We can now perform the same reasoning for player 2. Suppose player 2 first considers the consequences for himself or herself if player 1 were to choose strategy 1, so that the first row of the matrix is the only row relevant to player 2's choice. Since $c > a$, player 2 would make more money by choosing strategy 2 instead of strategy 1. We denote this conclusion by the arrow on the top of the matrix pointing from left to right. Suppose player 2 next considers the consequences for himself or herself if player 1 were to choose strategy 2. Since $d > b$, player 2 makes more money by choosing strategy 2 instead of strategy 1. This is represented by the arrow on the bottom of the matrix pointing from left to right. Both arrows for player 2 point in the same direction. Thus, player 2's choice is also clear: choose strategy 2 regardless of what player 1 chooses.

We are now ready to propose a solution for the game in figure 3.2. There is only one outcome toward which the arrows for both players point to simultaneously. This is the outcome where each player chooses strategy 2. At this outcome, each player receives the payoff d. This outcome has the very special property that each player has maximized his or her payoff, given what the other player does. Any pair of strategies with the property that each player maximizes his or her payoff given what the other player does is called a *Nash equilibrium*. Being a Nash equilibrium is a necessary condition for a pair of strategies to be a solution to a game.[2]

To identify which pairs of strategies are Nash equilibria and which are not, one needs to identify those pairs where arrows point in from both the player 1 and the player 2 directions. The game of figure 3.2 is rather special in that it has only one Nash equilibrium. Although every finite game must have at least one Nash equilibrium, oftentimes there are more. To see this, consider figure 3.3, which is much more general than figure 3.2. It describes the four basic inequalities on the payoff parameters, depending on whether a is less than or greater than c, and on whether d is less than or greater than b. The case we have just considered is shown in the upper left-hand corner, figure 3.3a. Its mirror image, again with a single equilibrium, is shown in the lower right-hand corner, figure 3.3d. The cases shown in figure 3.3b and 3.3c have multiple equilibria.[3] We will explain the relevance of these four cases to CPRs shortly.

Our goal is to explain behavior in many types of CPR action situations. Game theory explains such behavior in terms of maximizing behavior at Nash equilibrium.[4] Since Nash equilibrium involves maximization, it embodies the basic individual rationality assumptions of neoclassical economics. Besides the appeal to neoclassical economic principles, there are two other arguments for Nash equilibrium. One argument is based on rational expectations. If every player expects a particular equilibrium to be played, then maximizing behavior will indeed lead to that equilibrium, and the expectations are fulfilled (McGinnis and Williams 1989, 1991; Williams and McGinnis 1988). Another argument is metatheoretical. Suppose that a theory of games predicts that equilibria are *not* played. Pick a prediction by this theory and assume every player is playing according to this theory. Then, at least one of the players is not maximizing his or her payoff. Such a player has an incentive to disobey the theory. This defeats the theory.

There is a certain vocabulary associated with strategies, which (like any technical language) must be acquired to use the analytical tools. This

---

2. Sufficient conditions are much more difficult to explain. These are called refinements of Nash equilibria, and equilibrium selection principles. We will encounter some of these sufficient conditions later in the book.

3. There is a third equilibrium as well, which cannot be detected by the method of arrows. We will identify it later in the chapter.

4. We are referring exclusively to noncooperative game theory. Cooperative game theory, while also predicated on maximizing behavior, has an entirely different set of solution concepts.

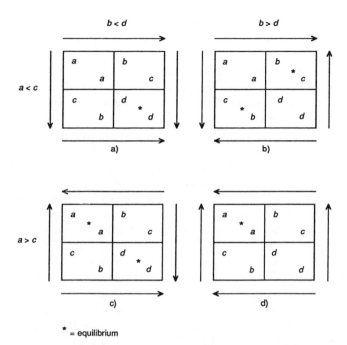

* = equilibrium

Fig. 3.3. Arrow diagrams, general payoff possibilities

vocabulary is represented by the adjective pairs pure/mixed and symmetric/ asymmetric. A *pure strategy* is a strategy that does not involve chance. A *pure strategy equilibrium* is an equilibrium with each player playing a pure strategy. The equilibrium of the game in figure 3.2 is a pure strategy equilibrium. A special case of a pure strategy is a *dominant* strategy. A player with a dominant strategy has an incentive to play that strategy regardless of what the other player does. In the game of figure 3.2, strategy 2 is a dominant strategy for each player.

A *mixed strategy* is a strategy that involves chance. Mixed strategies require that players select their actions according to a probability distribution that determines expected payoffs. A *mixed strategy equilibrium* is an equilibrium where each player plays a mixed strategy. We will give examples of mixed strategy equilibria in the assignment game and monitoring game below. A *symmetric equilibrium* is one in which every player chooses the same strategy. The equilibrium in the game of figure 3.2 is symmetric. An *asymmetric equilibrium* is one in which at least two players choose different strategies. We will give examples of asymmetric equilibria in the assignment game and monitoring game below.

Many games have proper names. For example, the game in figure 3.2 is called the Prisoner's Dilemma when one has the additional condition on payoff parameters that $a > d$. The Prisoner's Dilemma is perhaps the most famous of all games with two players, each having two strategies. This game, as we have seen, has a unique Nash equilibrium. The dilemma consists in the fact that the payoffs at the equilibrium outcome are not very desirable. Since $a > d$, the outcome associated with each player choosing strategy 2 is strictly inferior to the outcome associated with each player choosing strategy 1. Such a situation is termed Pareto inferior since there is an outcome where both players would be better off. The Pareto criterion is an example of group rationality. Invisible Hand doctrines allege that there is no conflict between individual and group rationality. The Prisoner's Dilemma was invented as a counterexample to such doctrines.

CPR problems have many times been equated with the Prisoner's Dilemma, but this is misleading. As can be seen from figure 3.3, the pattern of arrows associated with the Prisoner's Dilemma is rather special. There is no compelling theoretical reason for any particular game to be a Prisoner's Dilemma. Empirically, many subproblems within the context of a CPR dilemma can be represented as having this incentive structure (see Dasgupta and Heal 1979; Dawes 1973; and R. Hardin 1982). On the other hand, not all of the suboptimal outcomes produced in CPR dilemmas are the result of a set of incentives with the same structure as Prisoner's Dilemma. Maintaining the assumption that $a > d$, the two games called Chicken and Assurance also arise in many CPR problems (Taylor 1987). If the payoff parameters satisfy the inequalities $c > a$ and $b > d$, the game that results is Chicken (see fig. 3.3b). Alternatively, if the payoff parameters satisfy $a > c$ and $d > b$, the resulting game is Assurance (see fig. 3.3c). Chicken has a payoff structure and set of strategies such that individual players no longer have a dominant strategy. Chicken has multiple equilibria. We show in the next section that some assignment problems lead to Chicken. Assurance can represent many CPR situations where one person's contribution is not sufficient to gain a collective benefit but both person's contributions will produce a joint benefit. Thus, both players would prefer to contribute to the provision of a collective benefit if and only if the other player also contributes. We show in the next section that some provision games lead to Assurance. Like Chicken, Assurance has multiple equilibria.

CPR Games with Two Players and Two Strategies

This subsection analyzes four games. The games illustrate game-theoretic techniques in the following CPR dilemmas: (1) appropriation externality, (2) assignment, (3) resource provision, and (4) monitoring. In each case, we demonstrate that a change in the structure of the game can lead to equilibria that are distinct in their prediction of strategic behavior. These games illustrate the importance of carefully documenting the decision situation one might observe in field settings or in making policy decisions based on general models.

Appropriation Externality

As discussed in chapter 1, one fundamental prediction for CPR dilemmas is that players will ignore the impact of their input decisions on that of others' yield from the CPR. This appropriation externality leads to overappropriation from the CPR. One can model a simplified version of this problem as a game with two players, each with two strategies. Both players act as appropriators from a CPR. Each player has one unit of a productive input, which could represent his or her labor, capital, or both, in units called tokens. A player can invest a token in a safe outside opportunity, and receive a payoff w, regardless of what the other player does. For example, this could represent working as a wage earner outside the game. A player can also invest his or her token in the CPR, where things get more complicated. Let x_i be the number of tokens invested in the CPR by player i. Then $x_i = 0$ denotes taking the outside opportunity, while $x_i = 1$ denotes investing in the CPR. Output from the CPR is a function of total investment by the players, $F(\Sigma x_i)$. A player's share of CPR is proportional to his or her input into the CPR. Thus, player i's share of CPR output is 0 when he or she does not invest in the CPR, and $(x_i/\Sigma x_i)F(\Sigma x_i)$ when he or she does. This leads to the game depicted in figure 3.4a.

We now turn to solving the game. The solution will depend, as we have already seen, on the relationship between w, $F(1)$, and $F(2)/2$. If the CPR is subject to strictly diminishing returns to scale, then $F(2)/2 < F(1)$, which we will assume for the time being. If the CPR has any economic value whatsoever, then $F(1) > w$. It pays to invest the first token into the CPR rather than elsewhere in the economy. With diminishing returns to scale and economic viability, we have the arrow pattern in figure 3.4a, and see that $x_i = 0$ cannot be part of a Nash equilibrium for either player. What happens at this point depends on the relationship between a half share in the CPR, $F(2)/2$, and the outside opportunity, w. Suppose that returns on the CPR are quite sharply diminishing, so that even though $F(1) > w$, $w > F(2)/2$. Then we have the arrow pattern in figure 3.4b, with two equilibria, each of the form: one player invests in the CPR, the other stays out, and the player investing in the CPR earns more than the player staying out. The game that results in this case is a particular parameterization of Chicken.

The other possibility is that the CPR does not get crowded quite so fast, and $F(2)/2 > w$. The arrow diagram is now seen in figure 3.4c. There is a

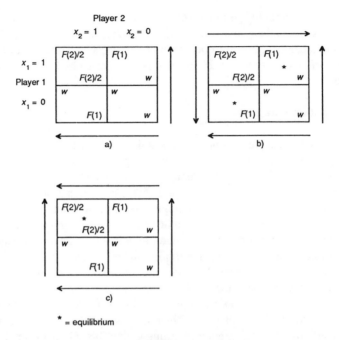

* = equilibrium

Fig. 3.4. Appropriation externality

unique Nash equilibrium, with both players investing in the CPR. The situation is reminiscent of the Prisoner's Dilemma, since each player has a dominant strategy, but it may not be tragic at all. The existence or extent of tragedy, if any, is going to depend on the specific shape of F and the value of w. For instance, if F is a convex, increasing function, such as $(\Sigma x_i)^2$, and $w < 1$, then the outcome with both players investing in the CPR is the best of all possible worlds. On the other hand, if F is strictly concave, then the outcome with both players on the CPR may be socially inefficient. Take F to be the square root function, and set $w = .7$. Then one has the specific payoffs (referring back to fig. 3.2) of $a = .707$, $b = 1$, $c = d = .7$. When both players invest in the CPR, total group payoff is 1.414, substantially less than the group payoff of 1.7 when just one player invests in the CPR. This is indeed a CPR dilemma. At the same time, it takes rather special conditions on outside opportunities (w) and on CPR production (F) to get a Prisoner's Dilemma.

An Assignment Problem

When players face a variety of "appropriation spots" that are differentiated in productive yield, they confront an assignment problem. The simplest example

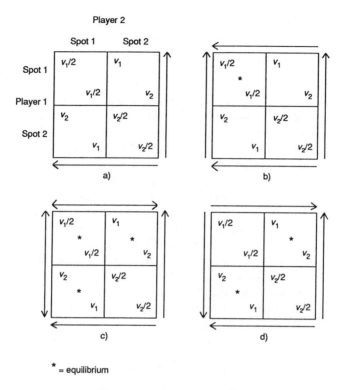

* = equilibrium

Fig. 3.5. Assignment games

of an assignment problem is the following game. The CPR, say a fishing grounds, consists of two spots of known value v_i. The value of fishing at spot 1 is greater than the value of fishing at spot 2; $v_1 > v_2$. There are two users. Each user may use the same spot, in which case they split its value. The resulting 2-player noncooperative game is portrayed in figure 3.5a, together with arrows showing that both players fishing the bad spot 2 is not an equilibrium.

There are two major cases and one borderline case to consider. One major case is $v_1 > 2(v_2)$, in which case the good spot is very much better than the bad spot. In this case, player 1 has an arrow pointing up toward spot 1 on the left side of the matrix, and player 2 an arrow pointing left toward spot 1 on the top of the matrix in the arrow diagram of figure 3.5b. Since spot 1 is always better than spot 2, each player also has an arrow pointing away from (spot 2, spot 2) on the right side and on the bottom. With this arrow configuration, each user has a dominant strategy, to use spot 1. Thus a unique equilibrium point exists, with both users on the best spot. This outcome is always problematic. Since both fishers are on the same fishing spot, the total payoff to the players is v_1. However, there are enough fishers available to achieve the total payoff $v_1 + v_2$. The game outcome fails to be optimal for the entire group.

The borderline case is $v_1 = 2(v_2)$. Each CPR user still has a dominant strategy to use spot 1. Therefore, both players on spot 1 continues to be an equilibrium. Now, however, we have two-headed arrows for the first time. Player 1 is indifferent as to which spot he or she fishes if player 2 is on the good spot. This is reflected by the two-headed arrow on the left side of figure 3.5c. The same is true for player 2. There are now three pure strategy equilibria, two of which actually avoid the CPR dilemma. (Remember, if two arrows point in toward an outcome, that outcome is an equilibrium.)

The other major case is $v_1 < 2(v_2)$. The arrow diagram is shown in figure 3.5d. This is another example of Chicken. Neither player has a dominant strategy. In this case, there are two pure strategy equilibria. Either of these, with one player on each spot, maximize group payoff. However, one should not be overly sanguine about the likelihood of a group payoff maximizing outcome from this assignment problem. There is only one position in this game, fisher. A game with a single position is called *symmetric*. Every symmetric game has a symmetric equilibrium. Since the situation in this assignment game is inherently symmetric, the players may not be willing to accept unequal payoffs via an asymmetric equilibrium. The asymmetries that institutions like private property or conventions often provide to players are precisely what are absent here.

The symmetric equilibrium of the assignment game involves chance. Every symmetric equilibrium has the property that the players get the same payoff and use the same strategy. We will now go about computing this symmetric, mixed-strategy equilibrium of the game. The best way to follow the necessary computation is by an example. Suppose $v_1 = 8$, $v_2 = 6$. Neither player is certain what the other will do, but knows there is a positive probability that the other will wind up on a given spot. Suppose these probabilities are the same for each fisher, and denote them P, the probability of going to spot 1, and $1 - P$, the probability of going to spot 2. At a mixed-strategy equilibrium, a player is indifferent between going to one spot or going to the other. To see this, first compute the expected value of going to spot 1. With probability P, someone is already there and the payoff is 4; with probability $1 - P$, no one is there and the payoff is 8. Adding up, the expected value of going to spot 1 is $4P + 8(1 - P) = 8 - 4P$. Now perform the same calculation for spot 2. With probability P, no one is there (they went to spot 1 instead) and the payoff is 6; with probability $1 - P$, someone is there and the payoff is 3. Adding up, the expected value of going to spot 2 is $6P + 3(1 - P) = 3 + 3P$. At equilibrium, the expected value of going to spot 1 equals the expected value of going to spot 2, that is, $8 - 4P = 3P + 3$. The required probability of going to spot 1, $P = 5/7$; the probability of going to spot 2, $1 - P = 2/7$. The expected value of either spot is $8 - 4(5/7) = 3 + 3(5/7) = 36/7$. Note that even though the players are now paid the same, 36/7, the payoff they receive is lower than that of the *worst* spot, 6. This is a more subtle CPR dilemma than the Prisoner's Dilemma, but no less problematic.

Resource Provision

Many users of a CPR are faced with the problem of providing the resource (e.g., digging irrigation ditches) or maintaining the resource (repairing the irrigation ditches). Such a decision problem can be modeled as the provision of a pure public good. In this example, we demonstrate how such a problem can turn out to be either Prisoner's Dilemma or Assurance, depending on the details of the provision technology.

There are two players. Each player has an endowment of one unit of input (measured in tokens) to contribute to the provision, if he or she desires. A token has an outside value of w if it is not contributed to provide for the resource. For each token contributed to provision, each player receives v. Let x_i be the number of tokens contributed to provision of the CPR by player i. Then $x_i = 0$ denotes taking the outside opportunity, while $x_i = 1$ denotes contributing to provision of the CPR. Payoff from providing the CPR is proportional to total contribution by the players, Σx_i. A player's payoff from provision of the CPR is $v(\Sigma x_i)$, regardless of whether that player contributed or not. Two possible games that result are shown in figure 3.6.

First, suppose $2v > w > v$. Then one has a Prisoner's Dilemma. Each player has a dominant strategy not to contribute, but both would be better off if both contributed. This is shown in figure 3.6a. Next, suppose $2v > v > w$. Now the incentives to contribute are so strong that each player has a dominant strategy to contribute, and the CPR functions in an optimal fashion at equilibrium. This is shown in figure 3.6b.

Now suppose the game is changed in the following way. If only one token is contributed toward provision, there are insufficient funds for provision and the value of the contributed token is 0. This might be the case in physical environments in which the good being provided is discrete (for example, an incomplete bridge has no value). Now, the single contributing player receives a payoff of 0 since he or she has foregone his or her outside opportunity. If both tokens are contributed, the resource is provided at a value of $2v$ as before. This change in the provision technology leads to the game of figure 3.7a. The arrows attached show that there is always one equilibrium involving no contribution by either player, regardless of the value of v or w. If

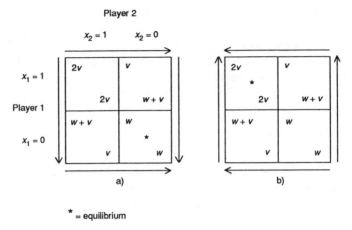

Fig. 3.6. **Provision games, intermediate value**

you know the other player is not going to contribute, you should not contribute either.

Besides the equilibrium where no one contributes, there may be another pure strategy equilibrium. Assume first that $2v > w$. In this case, there is an incentive to contribute if the other player is contributing. Thus, there is an equilibrium where both contribute, as well as an equilibrium where neither contributes. This is an example of Assurance (fig. 3.7b). The equilibrium with both players contributing is strictly better for them than the equilibrium where neither is contributing. The other major case is $2v < w$. Now it is a dominant strategy not to contribute, hence a unique equilibrium (fig. 3.7c). Note that this case is not a Prisoner's Dilemma: providing the resource is of such a low value that the best thing the players can do is not provide it.

Monitoring

In each of the examples given so far, there was a single position: appropriator in the appropriation externality game, fisher in the assignment game, and contributor in the resource provision game. We now relax this restriction, and study a game in which there are two distinct positions. The positions are motivated by the physical reality of irrigation systems, where players at the head of the system have access to the water flow before players at the tail. Players at the tail, however, have an opportunity to monitor what players at the head do. Player 1 is the player at the head of the system. His or her strategies are to take his or her fair share of the water, or to take more than his or her share. Player 2 is the player at the tail of the system. His or her strategies are to monitor, or not to monitor, what player 1 does. Payoffs are

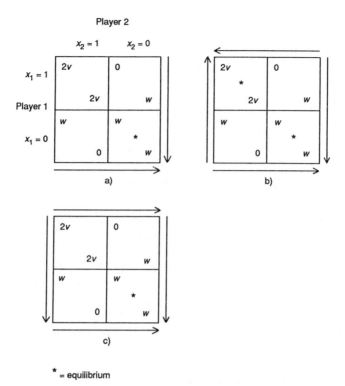

* = equilibrium

Fig. 3.7. Provision games, no intermediate value

calibrated to a (0,0) benchmark where player 1 takes his or her share and player 2 does not monitor. Indeed, the maximum possible total payoff to the players in this game is 0.

If player 1 takes more than his or her share, he or she gets a positive benefit B from the extra water. If at the same time, player 2 is not monitoring, then the water taken is gone from the flow, and player 2 loses the benefit of that water, a payoff to him or her of $-B$. In addition, it costs player 2 an amount C to go to the expense of monitoring. If player 1 is only taking his or her share, the outcome to the two players is 0 for player 1 and $-C$ for player 2. Finally, suppose player 1 takes more than his or her share and player 2 is monitoring. In this event, there is an imperfect detection technology available to player 2: sometimes he or she detects the excess taking by player 1 and sometimes he or she does not. With probability P, player 2 detects player 1 taking more than his or her share when he or she monitors; with probability $1 - P$, player 2 does not detect player 1 taking more than his or her share when he or she monitors. In case of detection, player 2 gets all of the water back

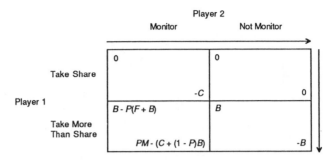

Fig. 3.8. Monitoring

plus a bonus M for successfully monitoring; player 1, besides giving back the water, pays a fine F for getting caught. With probability $1 - P$, no detection takes place, even though player 2 is monitoring. In this event, player 2 pays the cost of monitoring and nothing else happens. We now compute the expected payoffs for this outcome. For player 1, with probability P there is detection, paying $(-F)$; with probability $1 - P$, there is no detection, paying (B). The expectation thus is $P(-F) + (1 - P)(B) = B - P(F + B)$ for player 1. For player 2, with probability P there is detection, paying $(M - C)$; with probability $1 - P$, there is no detection, paying $(-B - C)$. The expectation thus is $P(M - C) + (1 - P)(-B - C) = PM - (C + (1 - P)B)$. These are the payoffs for the monitoring game in figure 3.8.

The monitoring game is the most complicated game we have considered so far.[5] It has four different complete arrow diagrams, depending on the payoff parameters. It is always the case that an arrow points toward "Not Monitor" for player 2 when player 1 takes his or her share. This shows that the strategy pair (player 1 takes share, player 2 monitors) can never be an equilibrium. Again, there is always an arrow pointing toward "Take More Than Share" for player 1 when player 2 does not monitor. This shows that the strategy pair (player 1 takes share, player 2 does not monitor) is never an equilibrium. All this is shown in figure 3.8. There are four cases to study, since the arrow on the left can point either up or down, and the arrow on the bottom can point either left or right. Figure 3.9 depicts these four cases in turn.

Case 1: Consider figure 3.9a. The arrow on the left points down, and the arrow on the bottom points to the left. The parameter conditions for this case are $B > P(F + B)$ (the arrow on the left points down) and $P(M + B) > C$ (the arrow on the bottom points to the left). The equilibrium is for

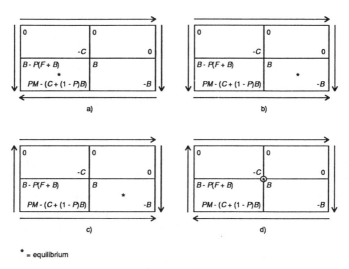

* = equilibrium

Fig. 3.9.   The four cases of monitoring

player 1 to take more than his or her share and for player 2 to monitor. This is a pure strategy, asymmetric equilibrium. Even though player 1 knows his or her behavior is going to be monitored, he or she still goes ahead and takes more than his or her share.

Case 2: Consider figure 3.9b. The arrow on the left points down, and the arrow on the bottom points to the right. The parameter conditions for this case are $B > P(F + B)$ (the arrow points down) and $P(M + B) < C$ (the arrow points to the right). The equilibrium is for player 1 to take more than his or her share and for player 2 not to monitor. This is a pure strategy, asymmetric equilibrium. The strategic possibility of monitoring has no effect on the temptation to take more than one's share in this parameter configuration. Two changes that could ultimately drive an irrigation system from case 1 to case 2 would be an increase in the cost of monitoring C or a decrease in the probability of detection P.

Case 3: Consider figure 3.9c. The arrow on the left points up, and the arrow on the bottom points to the right. The parameter conditions for this case are $B < P(F + B)$ (the arrow points up) and $P(M + B) < C$ (the arrow points to the right). The equilibrium is for player 1 to take more than his or her share and for player 2 not to monitor. This is a pure strategy, asymmetric equilibrium. Indeed, it is the same outcome as in case 2: only the arrow diagram is different.

Case 4: Consider figure 3.9d. The arrow on the left points up, the arrow on the bottom points to the left. The parameter conditions for this to happen are $B < P(F + B)$ (the arrow points up) and $P(M + B) > C$ (the arrow points to the left). There is no pure strategy equilibrium: an arrow points away from every outcome. There is, however, a mixed strategy equilibrium. To compute this equilibrium will require two steps.

First, in equilibrium, the probability of player 2's monitoring must be just high enough that player 1 is indifferent between taking his or her share and taking more than his or her share. Let m denote the probability of monitoring. If player 1 takes exactly his or her share, his or her payoff is 0. If player 1 takes more than his or her share, then with probability m he or she gets monitored and his or her payoff is $B - P(F + B)$; with probability $1 - m$, he or she does not get monitored and his or her payoff is B. The expected value of taking more than his or her share is thus $m(B - P(F + B)) + (1 - m)B$. This expected value must be equal to 0, the value of taking his or her share: $m(B - P(F + B)) + (1 - m)B = 0$. The solution to this equation is the equilibrium probability of monitoring, m^*, by player 2. This is player 2's equilibrium mixed strategy. Solving for m^*, we have $m^* = B/(P(B + F))$. Second, the probability of player 1 taking more than his or her share must be just high enough so that player 2 is indifferent between monitoring and not monitoring. Let t denote the probability that player 1 takes his or her share. If player 2 does not monitor, then with probability t player 1 takes his or her share and player 2 gets the payoff 0; with probability $1 - t$, player 2 takes more than his or her share and player 2 gets $-B$. Thus, if player 2 does not monitor, he can expect the payoff $t(0) + (1 - t)(-B) = (1 - t)(-B)$. If player 2 does monitor, then with probability t player 1 takes his or her share and player 2 gets the payoff $-C$; with probability $1 - t$, player 1 takes more than his or her share and player 2 gets the payoff $PM - (C + (1 - P)B)$. Thus, if player 2 does monitor, he or she can expect the payoff $t(-C) + (1 - t)(PM - (C + (1 - P)B)$. Setting player 2's payoff from monitoring equal to his or her payoff from not monitoring yields:

$$t(-C) + (1 - t)(PM - (C + (1 - P)B) = (1 - t)(-B).$$

Solving, one has $1 - t^* = C/P(M + B)$, where t^* is the equilibrium value of the probability with which player 1 takes exactly his or her share, and $1 - t^*$ is the probability player 1 takes more than his or her share. An asymmetric, mixed strategy equilibrium is (m^*, t^*). Case 4 is the first example we have seen of a game with only a mixed strategy equilibrium.

To summarize the results of the above four cases, we have shown that there is always some tendency to take more water than one's share at equilib-

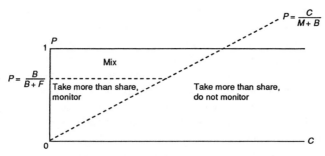

Fig. 3.10. **Regime diagram, monitoring**

rium. In three cases, player 1 always takes more than his or her share. In the fourth case, player 1 takes more than his or her share with a positive probability. Thus, player 1's inherent physical advantage by being at the head of the irrigation system shows up as an equilibrium strategic advantage as well.

A useful graphic for summarizing game equilibrium analysis is a regime diagram. Such a diagram shows how the equilibrium of a game depends on the underlying payoff parameter values, which, in turn, are related to underlying physical and rule-governed relationships. Figure 3.10 is a regime diagram corresponding to the preceding discussion of the monitoring game. The axes of the diagram are C on the abscissa and P on the ordinate. There are two major boundaries in the diagram. The boundary $P = B/(B + F)$ separates the cases where the arrow on the left of figure 3.9 points up from those where it points down; the boundary $P = C/(M + B)$, the cases where the arrow on the bottom of figure 3.9 points to the left from those where it points to the right. The four different cases lead to three observationally distinct equilibrium behaviors, so the regime diagram has three different regions. Take the region denoted "Take More Than Share, Monitor" on the left side of the regime diagram. In this region, $P < B/(B + F)$ and $P < C/(M + B)$. A quick check will show that these two inequalities are equivalent to those that define case 1. Cases 2 and 3, which are observationally equivalent at equilibrium, are represented by the region called "Take More Than Share, Do Not Monitor." The final region, called "Mix," corresponds to case 4. A regime diagram such as this one shows how equilibrium behavior depends on physical and payoff characteristics (here, the parameters P, F, B, M, and C). It also aids one in predicting what will happen to the way a game is played if there is a large change in these parameters. A large change will move the game equilibrium out of one regime and into another.[6]

---

6. Our use of the term *regime* in this context is similar to its use in the international relations literature. See Keohane 1980, 1984, 1986 and Oye 1986.

In some instances, the consequences of a change in a variable seem fairly clear. Obvious primary effects are often, however, confounded with secondary effects that can easily be overlooked when relying solely on verbal reasoning. To take a specific example, consider a change in the cost of monitoring, C. Routine economic intuition suggests that, as the cost of monitoring rises, less monitoring would be supplied. We shall now show, however, that there are several possible responses, not just one, to an increase in C. The precise game equilibrium response depends on which regime the system is in and how large the increase in C is.

In the regime diagram, an increase in C means a move to the right. If the system is in the regime "Mix" and the increase in C is small, the system stays in the regime "Mix." Anywhere in this regime, the probability of monitoring is the same. This might easily be thought to be counterintuitive; however, the reasoning leading up to the formula for $m^* = B/(P(B + F))$ shows that C plays no role in the regime "Mix." On the other hand, if the increase in C is large, then the system leaves the regime "Mix" and enters the regime "Take More Than Share, Do Not Monitor." Monitoring drops to 0. Next, suppose that the system is in the regime "Take More Than Share, Monitor." If the increase in C is small, the system stays in the regime and monitoring does not increase. If the increase in C is large, the system enters the regime "Take More Than Share, Do Not Monitor," and monitoring drops to 0. Finally, suppose that the system is in the regime "Take More Than Share, Do Not Monitor." Monitoring is at its minimum level in this regime, and no matter how large an increase in C, monitoring cannot decrease. Even though this model is very simple, the above analysis of the equilibrium behavior response to an increase in C shows how complex and nuanced the response really is—in contrast to intuition.[7]

Even in those cases where the qualitative effects of a change in a variable are unambiguous, more specific information about the strength of this effect is often desirable. Consider a community of irrigators who are faced with the problem of how to reduce stealing. An increase in the detection efficiency of monitoring farmers, a more severe punishment imposed on cheaters, and the employment of an external guard all appear to be appropriate means to reduce the incentive to steal water. Which device, however, is the most effective? This question cannot be addressed without a formal analysis that compares the costs and benefits of accomplishing objectives in a complex system of related variables.[8]

---

7. To be fair to intuition, we should point out that this pattern of game equilibrium responses depends in large part on modeling monitoring as a binary choice variable.

8. This question is addressed in Weissing and Ostrom 1991.

Repeated CPR Games

All the games presented in the previous section had the feature that they were played exactly once. This is a fairly restrictive assumption. Although some games played on CPRs are played once and only once, more often the game will be played repeatedly. For instance, the appropriation externality might be repeated whenever appropriators return to the CPR. The assignment problem might arise every time fishers go out to fish. The resource provision problem might arise every time the CPR requires maintenance. The monitoring problem might arise every time there is a crop to water. Thus, a theory of strategic behavior on CPRs must also consider games played more than once. We will consider some of the elements of such a theory here.[9]

A *repeated game* consists of a game played more than once. The game that is played each repetition, here denoted by G, is called the constituent, or one-shot, game. For example, suppose that two players are going to play the Prisoner's Dilemma (recall fig. 3.2) twice. Then the Prisoner's Dilemma would be G, and the entire game would be G-G (play G, play G again). Repeating a game retains all the complexities inherent in the constituent game, as well as creating new ones.

One major source of added complexity is the proliferation of strategies. A strategy is a complete plan of the play of a game. In the Prisoner's Dilemma, each player has 2 strategies to choose from. However, when the Prisoner's Dilemma is played twice, each player has 32 strategies to choose from. Take player 1, who has to form a complete plan for playing the Prisoner's Dilemma twice. This player has to decide what to do the first time the game is played, and also to decide what to do the second time the game is played. A plan for play the second time must take into account the four different contingent outcomes that may precede the second play. Let s denote strategy 1; t, strategy 2. Also, let (s,t) represent (player 1 played s, player 2 played t). Here is one possible plan for player 1:

Strategy I
First Round: play s
Second Round: play s if the first round outcome was (s,s)
                play s if the first round outcome was (s,t)
                play s if the first round outcome was (t,s)
                play s if the first round outcome was (t,t).

---

9. Our discussion barely scratches the surface of this vast subject. The interested reader should consult J. Friedman 1990 for an in-depth treatment.

Thus, a complete plan must take into account the real life complication that "things do not always go according to plan."[10] Even though strategy I prescribes that player 1 play s in the first round, it must still specify what happens if player 1's plan in the first round goes awry. This is why strategy I takes into account the first round outcomes (t,s) and (t,t). Strategy I is the one and only strategy for the Prisoner's Dilemma played twice, which prescribes that player 1 play s under all circumstances. In all contingencies, it prescribes the play of s. Now at each place where "play s" occurs, one could substitute "play t." Since there are five such places, there are $2^5 = 32$ different possible strategies for the twice repeated game. This is what is meant by strategy proliferation. The proliferation only gets worse as the number of repetitions increases.[11]

Strategy I provides a format for programming unconditional strategies. Repetition creates the possibility of strategies that are conditional as well. The following very famous strategy for the Prisoner's Dilemma is called tit-for-tat, and is conditional:

Strategy II
First Round: play s
Second Round: play s if the first round outcome was (s,s)
                  play t if the first round outcome was (s,t)
                  play s if the first round outcome was (t,s)
                  play t if the first round outcome was (t,t).

Strategy II starts out with player 1 playing s. If player 2 also plays s in the first round, then in the second round player 2 continues playing s. However, if player 2 plays t in the first round, then player 1 plays t in the second round. This is a very different strategy from the unconditional strategy that always plays s. This is a tit-for-tat strategy. Tit-for-tat is an example of a *trigger strategy*. In a trigger strategy, a player is committed to playing one way in the one-shot game (say, s) unless the other player plays something other than s. The latter action by the other player triggers player 1 to play t instead of s. Here is another example of a trigger strategy, only now for a repeated game of Assurance (fig. 3.3c):

Strategy III
First Round: play s

10. When things do not go according to plan, then the game is in disequilibrium if it was in equilibrium up to that point.
11. The strategy proliferation is truly explosive. For instance, if Prisoner's Dilemma is played three times, each player has 2^{21v} pure strategies.

Second Round: play *s* if the first round outcome was (*s,s*)
play *t* if the first round outcome was (*s,t*)
play *t* if the first round outcome was (*t,s*)
play *t* if the first round outcome was (*t,t*).

Recall that Assurance has two pure strategy equilibria, with the equilibrium at (*s,s*) paying better than the equilibrium at (*t,t*). The trigger strategy III is committed to playing the good equilibrium *s*, unless something happens and the good equilibrium is not played in the previous round. Then strategy III switches to the bad equilibrium. Trigger strategies like II and III play an important role in sustaining cooperation in repeated games. This is the content of the Folk Theorem discussed in chapter 1. See J. Friedman 1990 for details.

The concept of Nash equilibrium—that each player maximizes his or her payoff given what the other does—remains the same despite the increased complexity of players' strategies. Now, however, the technique of arrow diagrams becomes difficult to employ. Even the simplest game, with two players and two strategies, played twice, would lead to a 32 × 32 matrix to label with arrows! For this reason, we will not take a brute force approach to finding equilibria. Instead, we will discuss some useful recipes for constructing repeated game equilibria based on the equilibria of the one-shot game.

Suppose that the one-shot *G* has a single equilibrium, (*t,t*), such as is the case with the Prisoner's Dilemma. Construct the unconditional strategy (like strategy I) that always plays *t*; call this strategy "Unconditional *t*." Then the pair of strategies (unconditional *t*, unconditional *t*) is an equilibrium for repeated *G*. To see this, consider any strategy for repeated *G* other than unconditional *t*. Then one of two things can happen. One, this other strategy is observationally equivalent to unconditional *t*, in which case it pays the same as unconditional *t*. Two, it is observationally different, in which case it pays less than unconditional *t* at some point in the game. In no case does the other strategy do better than unconditional *t*, so unconditional *t* is payoff maximizing. Here is an example of a strategy that is observationally equivalent to unconditional *t*, when played against unconditional *t*:

Strategy IV
First Round: play *t*
Second Round: play *s* if the first round outcome was (*s,s*)
play *s* if the first round outcome was (*s,t*)
play *s* if the first round outcome was (*t,s*)
play *t* if the first round outcome was (*t,t*).

Strategy IV plans to play t in round 2 as long as (t,t) is played in round 1. But since both unconditional t and strategy IV play t in round 1, (t,t) will be played that round and in the next round. This is observational equivalence.

We can extend the above recipe for repeated game equilibria to repetitions of one-shot games that have multiple equilibria, such as Assurance and Chicken. Suppose that both (s,s) and (t,t) are equilibria of G. Then, just as above (unconditional s, unconditional s) and (unconditional t, unconditional t) are equilibria. There are also equilibria that rotate among the one-shot equilibria. Consider the following strategy:

Strategy V
First Round: play t
Second Round: play s if the first round outcome was (s,s)
                 play s if the first round outcome was (s,t)
                 play s if the first round outcome was (t,s)
                 play s if the first round outcome was (t,t).

Strategy V programs the rotation, play equilibrium (s,s) in round 1, and equilibrium (t,t) in round 2, in all contingencies. A similar rotation over the strategies (s,t) and (t,s) of Chicken can overcome the asymmetry problem we noted earlier with the asymmetric equilibria of the assignment problem. The strategy pair (strategy V, strategy V) is also an equilibrium for repeated G. So is the pair of trigger strategies (strategy III, strategy III). Just as strategies proliferate in a repeated game, so also do equilibria proliferate.[12]

There are other ways to construct repeated-game equilibria, in addition to building them up with one-shot game equilibria. However, such constructions are inherently problematic, for they program choices that, under some contingencies, are not payoff maximizing. The basic sufficient condition for a solution to a repeated game is that repeated game equilibria always be constructed on the basis of one-shot game equilibria. This sufficient condition is known as *subgame perfection*.[13] A way to guarantee that an equilibrium for a finitely repeated game is subgame perfect is to solve the game from the last round to the first, so-called backward induction. Backward induction is tantamount to using dynamic programming to perform the maximization by each

---

12. Equilibrium proliferation occurs even when the one-shot game has a unique equilibrium. This is due to observational equivalence. There are seven strategies observationally equivalent to Unconditional t. Since any pair of strategies observationally equivalent to Unconditional t constitutes an equilibrium, there are $8 \times 8 = 64$ equilibria for Prisoner's Dilemma played twice. All these equilibria have the same outcome: (t,t) the first round, (t,t) the second round. These equilibria only differ along unreached parts of the game tree, differences that should not be observed in equilibrium.

13. A classic discussion can be found in Selten 1971.

player. We will use subgame perfection extensively in the next chapter, as well as in our design and analysis of laboratory experiments.

Conclusions

The particular decision situations we have modeled as games are of considerable relevance for policy analysis. The levels of appropriation that occur on many CPR-based production systems throughout the world threaten their productivity and sustainability. The same is true of the maintenance of such systems. Even the simplest games, those with two players, played once or twice, allow us to address policy questions of importance to the organization of more general and more complex systems. The fundamental ideas that apply to games with two players apply more generally to games with many players, repeated many times. Bigger games are essential for modeling more complex CPR systems. We use such games throughout the rest of the book.

We have given four examples of strategic interactions that occur in CPRs the world over, and shown how game theory can be used to model and analyze such interactions. Game theory is predicated on the notion of strategic equilibrium. Since this is a theory of play by rational beings, one should not be overly surprised to encounter data from human play that is not entirely consistent with it. Although the ability of game theory to explain the data we present in this book is good, it is far from perfect. Arguments exist as possible explanations for this lack of perfect fit. Among these are bounded rationality on the part of the players, payoffs not captured by the game model, or complicated attitudes toward risk. We will encounter some of these phenomena in the empirical part of the book. Still, despite all these potential complications, game equilibrium is a good first step in organizing behavior data from a CPR, even if further steps are necessary later.

CHAPTER 4

Rules and Games

In this chapter, we further investigate the formal connection and difference between rules and games. Games are usually described by mathematical objects, like the matrices of the last chapter. Rules are often described by modal logic. Thus, there is a major categorical difference between the type of formal languages we use to describe rules and games.[1]

The term *rules of the game* as used in classical game theory includes both physical and deontological statements. *Physical statements* tell what is physically necessary, possible, or impossible to do. *Deontological statements* tell what is obligatory, permitted, or forbidden to do.[2] When one is primarily interested in predicting the outcomes of a given game, the difference between the type of regularities that constitute the game is not of major import. When one is also interested in understanding how to change the outcomes of a game, however, knowing the difference between physical and deontological regularities is essential.

The physical regularities referred to by physical statements and the deontic regularities referred to by deontic statements are subject to different forms of change. Human intervention cannot change fundamental physical regularities, such as the laws of physics and biology. People can use knowledge about fundamental physical and biological regularities, however, to develop new technologies that reduce the cost of many actions. While water will not flow upstream in a natural watercourse, water can be lifted over physical barriers at costs that technological improvements may reduce. Change is wrought by using the knowledge of physical laws to find more efficient uses of energy or new combinations of raw materials rather than by changing physical laws themselves. Deontic regularities ("Keep your promises," "Don't commit murder") exist primarily within a human domain. These regularities involve

---

1. This chapter relies extensively on Gardner and Ostrom 1991.

2. See G. H. von Wright 1963, 1971 for a discussion of deontological (also called "deontic") statements. See also Hirshleifer 1985, who argues that the "protocols" for games are substantively different from the physical characteristics that produce many of the payoffs in a game. Hirshleifer's concept of a protocol is very close to our concept of deontic statement.

what people perceive to be the right or wrong actions to take or states of the world individuals choose to change in particular situations. As such, deontic regularities are context-specific constraints that human beings create and change.[3]

Game theory solves a game as given. Stepping back, one can examine how physical and deontic statements affect game structure.[4] One can then align the solution of a game (the predicted outcomes) within these physical and deontic statements. Schematically, we think about the relationship between rules and games as shown in figure 4.1.

When physical or deontic statements are changed, the resulting games may produce incentives leading to the same, improved, or worse outcomes for the participants.[5] Of special interest to policy analysts are rule changes that lead to improved outcomes. A game is *reformed* when a rule change increases the total payoff to the players. This is of course the criterion of classical utilitarianism, as first introduced by Bentham.[6] The role of the policy analyst as a social reformer, which we now take for granted, was something of a novelty in Bentham's day. It is no coincidence that Bentham coined words such as *deontological* and *maximization*. He was first and foremost a reformer, and the creator of an entire vocabulary of social reform still used today.

Most games have multiple equilibria. This makes comparing the outcomes of games difficult. Whenever possible, we will use the condition of subgame perfection (see chap. 3) to reduce the number of predicted equilibria.[7] If there still remain multiple equilibria from which to choose after refinement by subgame perfection, we use *equilibrium point selection theory* to select a final equilibrium for study (Harsanyi and Selten 1988). By comparing game equilibrium outcomes, we can judge the rule configurations leading to them.

How Rules Affect the Structure of a Game

Because past emphasis in game theory has been on solving games, little systematic effort has been devoted to developing a common, theoretical lan-

---

3. Deontic regularities may evolve without conscious awareness, especially in informal situations, such as children's play on a playground (see Piaget [1932] 1969).

4. In this chapter, we do not examine deontic statements that are norms derived from a shared community that lack sanctions attached to nonconformance. See S. Crawford and Ostrom 1993.

5. See, however, Plott and Meyer 1975 for an interesting paper describing the effect of several rule changes on the structure of a game. Shepsle and Weingast 1981a, 1981b also explore similar questions.

6. We are well aware of the controversial nature of this criterion. For an extended critique, see Rawls 1971.

7. This is often remarkably effective. For instance, of the 64 equilibria of the Prisoner's Dilemma played twice, only 1 is subgame perfect.

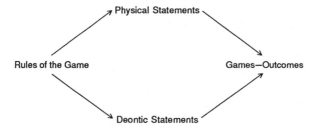

Fig. 4.1. Relationships between rules and games

guage of rules. To study institutions using game theory, we need to develop this language. As discussed in chapter 2, rules are conceptualized as prescriptions—dos and don'ts—used to provide part of the structure of an action situation. Prescriptions refer to which actions (or states of the world) are permitted, obligatory, or forbidden. Rule changes may result from self-conscious choice or may evolve over time as people develop shared understandings of what actions or outcomes may, must, or must not be done in particular situations (Commons 1957; von Hayek 1973; V. Ostrom 1980).

The basic elements of a game, as described in chapter 3, are (1) a set of players, (2) a set of positions, (3) sets of actions assigned to positions, (4) a decision function that maps choices into intermediate or final outcomes, (5) a set of outcomes, (6) the information set for each player, and (7) payoffs based on benefits and costs of actions and outcomes. Binding rules directly and indirectly affect the structure of a game by changing these key elements. A rule that forbids a player to produce a particular outcome will restrict the set of actions available to that player. A rule that creates or destroys strategies will have an effect on the entire game matrix and its entries. As discussed in chapter 2, there are seven classes of rules, depending upon which element of a game the rule directly affects. Rules that affect the set of actions available to a player, for example, are classified as authority rules. Rules that directly affect the benefits and costs assigned to actions and outcomes are payoff rules, and so on.

By simply inspecting a game matrix, it is not possible to infer which rule configuration is responsible for constituting that matrix. An outcome may be present or absent, a payoff may be positive or negative, as a result of several rules working together rather than a single rule working alone. We call this the *configural nature of rules:* frequently they operate in such a way that a change in one rule affects the working of others.[8] Because of the configural nature of rules, one needs to examine a full rule configuration rather than a single rule. To do this, it is necessary to specify a default condition in the event that no

8. See E. Ostrom 1986a, 1986b for further discussion.

rule in that class is present.[9] There is a default condition for each class. We specify the seven default conditions for the models in this chapter as follows:

Default Position Condition:	There exists one position.
Default Boundary Condition:	Each player occupies one and only one position.
Default Authority Condition:	Each player can take any physically possible action.
Default Aggregation Condition:	Players act independently. Physical relationships present in a domain determine the aggregation of individual moves into outcomes.[10]
Default Scope Condition:	Each player can affect any state of affairs physically possible.
Default Information Condition:	Each player can know what the consequences of his or her and others' actions are.
Default Payoff Condition:	Any player can retain any outcome that the player can physically obtain and defend.

If all of the rules are set at their default position, the resulting configuration embodies a Hobbesian state of nature. The only factors affecting the structure of a game in a state of nature are those related to the physical domain in which the game is played. As more and more rules are changed from a default condition, the options available to players are less and less controlled by the physical domain and more and more controlled by prescriptions.

Some Empirical Examples of Changes in Authority Rules

To provide a simple illustration of the relationship between rules and games, we start with the assignment game presented in chapter 3. We extend this elementary game to deal with various rule configurations that are stylized versions of real configurations encountered in field settings. Much of the

---

9. The concept of a default condition emerged from a long series of discussions among William Blomquist, James Wunsch, and Elinor Ostrom as we attempted to develop a systematic method for describing naturally occurring rule systems. The common law of contracts, as well as the Uniform Commercial Code, provides a set of default provisions for courts to follow when specific contested contracts remain silent.

10. If a rule configuration contains only a default authority condition, the default aggregation condition *must* be present.

world's fishing occurs in contested waters. Conflicts arise between nations when international conventions, such as the 200-mile limit, collide (Canada vs. France, United Kingdom vs. Iceland, United Kingdom vs. Belgium). Even more frequently, conflicts arise in those coastal or inland waters where neither property rights nor user rights are clearly defined (see Clugston 1984; Pollack 1983). Before modeling any games, we present some empirical examples of fishery assignment problems where different rules are in use.

An Assignment Problem without Effective Rules

On 23 December 1970, 50 trawlers were fishing inshore off the northwest coast of West Malaysia and were challenged by 10 inshore boats from neighboring villages. The trawlers caught one of the boats and burned it. They

> slashed two captured crewmen with knives, and left them to sink or swim (they survived). On December 26, aggravated by this and by threat of further trawler-licensing and further illegal fishing, over 50 inshore boats from the Perak ports chased trawlers and caught a Kampong Mee boat. The crew of five promptly got off into the water. Two could not swim. One was caught and slashed deeply on the arms with a large cleaver, but managed to escape and cling to a net-float. One was forced into the water and never seen again. The trawler was burned; the hulk, burned to the waterline. (E. Anderson and Anderson 1977, 272)

Both the trawlers and the inshore fishermen preferred to fish in the rich waters within three miles of the shore. While national legislation was on the books to exclude trawlers from this zone, trawlers ignored this legislation. No *effective* rules limited the actions of either the trawlers or the inshore boats. In other words, most of the rules were effectively at a default level. Between October 1970 and October 1971, over forty boats were sunk and at least nine fishers were killed. To quell this fishing war, the Malaysian government finally sent in over one thousand soldiers and jailed more than twenty men without trial. A "peace commission," formed by the national government, brought about a truce of sorts (E. Anderson and Anderson 1977, 274). The conflict continued to simmer, however, for at least five additional years.

Examples of violence erupting over contested fishing waters are not limited to remote locations in West Malaysia. Fights among fishers have erupted on the Great Lakes, in the English Channel and North Sea, and elsewhere. External authorities may try to impose order or pass legislation that allocates such contested waters. Unless the fishers themselves accept legislation as effective rules, however, they continue to play the fishing game as if the legislation did not exist. The possibility of violence is ever present.[11]

In contrast to the many locations where no effective rules limit who can fish in which locations, fishers living in some regions have devised relatively stable rule systems that have reduced the level of violence substantially and have produced various kinds of equilibria. A classic rule of allocation used throughout the ages to settle disputes over who can use particular locations for particular purposes is "first in time, first in right."[12] This rule is used among inshore fishers along the shores of such diverse countries as Canada, India, and Brazil (Forman 1970; Raychaudhuri 1980).

The Use of First in Time, First in Right Rules

Along the West Bengali coast, fishers use a series of flat, swampy islands for four to five months each year during the season when large shoals of fish can be expected to appear. Fishers who settle temporarily on the Island of Jambud-wip set large nets on wooden posts in semipermanent locations for the duration of the fishing season. The value of the catch depends on the skill of the fishing team in finding a good location and in setting the net properly. Further, the direction of the shoals of fish can change, necessitating a change in the location of the nets if a fishing team is to make a good harvest. The basic rule used on this island is that the first team to set a net in a particular fishing spot has a right to continue to use that location throughout the season.

> If a fishing unit changes its phar (wooden posts, etc., with which the nets are set) and sets up a new one in another place, no other fishing unit has the right to set its net in that deserted phar . . . throughout the season without prior permission. The owner may, however, set his net again in that deserted phar if the shoal of fish takes that direction. . . . Thus, the fisherfolk have developed a conventional moral code of non-encroach-ment among themselves for their livelihood. This may be termed as their tenure system valid for one fishing season only. (Raychaudhuri 1980, 168)

---

11. In many cases, those directly involved recognize that violence is too costly and develop their own rule systems that are mutually agreed upon, to allocate rights and duties. For descriptions of situations where participants have crafted their own rules, see T. Anderson and Hill 1975; Libecap 1978; E. Ostrom 1990, 1992; Umbeck 1977, 1981.

12. See the very interesting issue of the *Washington University Law Quarterly* (Fall 1986) devoted to a symposium on "Time, Property Rights, and the Common Law." In particular, Richard A. Epstein 1986 discusses the effects of rules of first possession in relationship to a variety of different kinds of situations. See also the perceptive papers by Barzel 1968, 1974 and Haddock 1986.

The Use of Prior Announcement Rules

The impoverished fisherfolk who live along the shores of Bahia in the north-eastern part of Brazil have devised a more extended set of rules that effectively assign "sea tenure" rights to the captains of canoes working in the mangrove swamps along the shore. The forms of sea tenure used in Bahia have evolved from the practices of the fisherfolk themselves, are unacknowledged by governmental authorities, and are contrary to national legislation stipulating that territorial waters are public property. Around the port of Valença, the local fishers have identified, mapped, and named 258 fishing spots, so that fishing in one spot does not interfere with fishing in the other spots. Some spots are owned permanently by the captain of a boat. The fishers have agreed that the captains from a particular village can use other spots sequentially over time. When a captain wishes to fish in a spot, he records his plans in a public forum—the local bar—and marks the location where he intends to fish.[13]

> All that is required is for another fisherman to be present as a witness. To ensure the claim, the captain must follow his proclamation by going to the chosen spot the day before fishing to leave a canoe anchored with paddles sticking up in the air. This forewarns competitors that the casting space has been taken. Fishing captains go to considerable lengths to support each other in this routine, which is part of the sea-tenure politics that shore up the entire fishing system. (Cordell and McKean 1992, 193)

The Use of Prearranged Rotation Rules

In some regions of the world, overt rotation systems have been developed to assign fishing spots on an equitable basis to all eligible fishers. A lottery-rotation system, developed by the inshore fishers living in Alanya, Turkey, is among the most intriguing. Prior to their invention of this set of rules, they had suffered considerable conflict over access to the better fishing spots in the local fishery (Berkes 1992, 170). The fishers of Alanya mapped and named all the spots where setting a net in one spot did not block the flow of fish to an adjacent spot. In September of each year, the licensed fishermen in the village draw lots to gain assignment to a specific fishing location for the first day of

---

13. See further discussion of these rules in chapter 11. While the difference between a simple "first in time, first in right" rule and a "prior announcement rule" appears to be relatively slight, it makes a considerable difference to the game outcomes, as we show below. In any situation where getting to the location involves high costs, the capacity to register in a central location an intent to use significantly reduces transportation costs and the potential for violence stemming from these costs. Land registry offices in conjunction with homesteading are examples of highly formalized mechanisms related to "prior announcement rule."

the season. "During the period September to May, each participating fisherman moves each day to the next location to the east. This gives each fisherman an equal opportunity at the best sites" (Berkes 1992, 170; see chap. 6 for
more details about these rules). This system is relatively easy to monitor and
enforce, and it has been maintained for over 15 years, primarily through the
verbal and physical actions of the fishers themselves. "Violations are dealt
with by the fishing community at large, in the coffeehouse" (Berkes 1992,
170). Other lottery systems, such as the one that cod fishers in Fermeuse,
Newfoundland, use, assign a location to a fisher for an entire season. In
Fermeuse, an elected committee of local fishers runs an annual lottery to
assign trap locations, or "berths," to fishers from the local village for use
during the summer season (K. Martin 1979, 282). During the rest of the year,
traps are not an effective technique for capturing cod, and Fermeuse fishers
have divided their local fishery into distinct zones assigned to boats using a
particular technology.

Fishing Rules and Fishing Games

An Overview

The preceding descriptions provide a brief overview of the wide diversity of
rules used in practice to assign locations of diverse value to fishers.[14] The lack
of an accepted rule that makes a clear assignment of authority regarding who
can use a particular location under specified circumstances—as in the first
example from West Malaysia—is likely to lead to conflict and violence. Many
specific kinds of authority rules that make clear assignments are possible.
Each kind of rule combined with the physical and biological domains in which
people use them may (or may not) change the structure of a game sufficiently
to produce different equilibria and potentially different welfare distributions.
    To illustrate how rules combined with physical domains affect the struc-
ture of games and resulting equilibria, we analyze four stylized rule configura-

---

14. The four authority rules just described are neither logically nor empirically exhaustive
of the authority rules that fishers use. These four authority rules are classic examples of well-
known kinds of authority rules found in practice. In this initial, formal effort to model both the
rules and the resultant games and outcomes, we wanted to (1) keep the rule configurations as
simple as possible, (2) use rules that are frequently used in other environments, and (3) illustrate
the choice of rules with real examples. An extension of the work presented here would be to
model the choice of institutional games. Shepsle and Weingast envision the choice among
institutional games as involving analysis where "it is necessary to model the equilibrium outcomes of these games under different assumptions. The choice among games is then seen as the
choice among equilibria" (1981a, 48; see also Shepsle and Weingast 1981b, 516). The choice of
games, however, always will be made from a subset of all possible games, rather than from the
full set. While the set of rules structuring games may be finite, the set of possible games that can
be constructed from these rules approaches infinity (see Chomsky 1980, 220).

tions, chosen for their simplicity. All rules, except authority rules and position rules, are set at the default condition. This means the rules allow fishers to act independently, to affect any outcome they can physically affect, and to retain the fish that they capture without external rewards or costs being imposed on them. By setting the remaining rules at the default level, one can focus on the effect of changes in the authority of fishers to use a fishing location in which to fish when there are no boundary or payoff rules to interact with a specific authority rule.[15]

As we discuss in chapters 1 and 3, an assignment problem occurs when there is competition among users of a CPR for limited use of diverse space or periods of time. The problem is not that the resource is being overexploited or that it is on the verge of destruction. Rather, the problem is that some fishing spots are better than others, with conflict erupting over who can fish where. Assignment problems arise in many situations involving major inter- and intranational conflict and warfare. The assignment problems studied here are all generalizations of the basic assignment problem studied in the last chapter.

The assignment fishing game results from particular combinations of physical parameters and rule configurations. The physical parameters include the number of fishers, the number of distinct spots, and the cost of travel between spots. These parameters are held constant while we change rules in order to assess the effect of rules on games. There are four rule configurations, differing only in their authority and position rules (see table 4.1). In the table, a 1 in a column denotes presence of a rule, while a 0 denotes absence. Rule configuration C1 has two positions, player 1 (the stronger position) and player 2 (the weaker position). The player in the stronger position is more likely to win a fight over a fishing spot than the weaker. C1 describes a Hobbesian fishing world. Rule configuration C2 has the authority rule first in time, first in right. The two positions are player 1 (the player more likely to get the first claim) and player 2 (the player less likely to get the first claim). C2 rules out fighting. Rule configuration C3 has the authority rule first to announce, first in right. The two positions are player 1 (first to announce) and player 2 (hears the announcement). Rule configuration C4 contains a prearranged rotation over spots and a single position, fisher.

The Formal Game

There are two fishers, denoted 1 and 2, and two fishing spots, denoted 1 and 2. Each fishing spot i has a value in terms of fish caught of v_i, with spot 1 being better than spot 2,

---

15. In other words, the analysis presented here is an initial analysis of how rules affect a game structure. The number of feasible rule configurations is extraordinarily large. A complete analysis of the effect of all possible combinations of rules on this game would involve immense time and effort.

TABLE 4.1.   Rule Configurations

	C1	C2	C3	C4
Authority Rules				
Default authority condition	1	0	0	0
First in time, first in right	0	1	0	0
First to announce, first in right	0	0	1	0
Prearranged rotation	0	0	0	1
Position Rules				
Position 1 is stronger	1	0	0	0
Position 1 is more likely to arrive first	0	1	0	0
Position 1 announces	0	0	1	0
Announcement rotates	0	0	0	1
Default boundary condition	1	1	1	1
Default aggregation condition	1	1	1	1
Default scope condition	1	1	1	1
Default information condition	1	1	1	1
Default payoff condition	1	1	1	1

$$v_1 > v_2. \tag{4.1}$$

These values are the same for both fishers. Travel from one fishing spot to another costs a fisher c, with c smaller than the value of the poorer spot,

$$v_2 > c. \tag{4.2}$$

Finally, each fisher can inflict damage in the amount d on the other. Depending on the game, damage can vary from mild (cutting off of a fishing trap) to serious (harm inflicted on persons and boats). The vector of physical parameters (v_1, v_2, c, d) applies across all rule configurations. Variation in all these parameters leads to different physical domains.

In addition to the four physical parameters, there is an important behavioral parameter. Since one fishing spot is better than the other, fights may occur when both fishers occupy the same spot and the authority rule does not resolve the situation. Suppose there is a fight between fishers 1 and 2 over a fishing spot. Then with probability P, fisher 1 wins the fight; with probability $1 - P$, fisher 2 wins the fight. Since fisher 1 is stronger than fisher 2, one has:

$$P > 0.5. \tag{4.3}$$

The only rule configuration where fighting occurs is C1; this is the game where the behavior parameter P affects the physical domain.

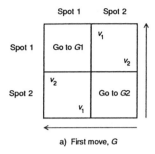

a) First move, *G*

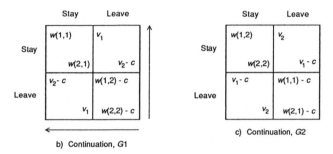

b) Continuation, *G1*

c) Continuation, *G2*

Fig. 4.2. Game according to rule configuration C1

Rule Configuration C1

We now analyze the game that follows from rule configuration C1. The game begins with each fisher choosing to go to a fishing spot. Each chooses simultaneously and independently of the other. In the event that each fisher goes to a different spot, the game is over, with each fisher receiving the value of that spot. In the event that each fisher goes to the same spot, the game continues. This is shown in figure 4.2a. The outcome according to (spot 1, spot 1), called "Go to *G1*" means that the game will continue at this point with the playing of game *G1*; similarly, if the choices (spot 2, spot 2) are made, the game will continue at this point with the playing of game *G2*.

The continuation games *G1* and *G2* may involve fighting. In these games, each fisher has the choice between staying on the spot and moving to another spot. Four things can happen once the fishers find themselves on the same spot. One of them can leave for the other spot, in which case he gets the value of the other spot minus travel cost c, while the other stays (two cases, depending on who leaves and who stays). Both can stay on the spot, in which case a fight immediately ensues. In the event of a fight: with probability P, fisher 1 wins the fight and the value of the spot and incurs no damage; with probability $1 - P$, fisher 1 loses the fight on the spot, incurring damage (the payoff $-d$), and losing the opportunity to fish altogether. Denote by $w(1,i)$ the value to fisher 1 of an immediate fight on spot i. From what has just been said, one has

$$w(1,i) = Pv_i + (1 - P)(-d).$$

Similarly, denote by $w(2,i)$ the value to fisher 2 of an immediate fight for the same spot i. Reversing the probabilities, one has

$$w(2,i) = (1 - P)v_i + P(-d).$$

From the assumption $P > 0.5$, it follows that $w(1,i) > w(2,i)$ for any spot i. Finally, both fishers can leave the spot they went to for the other spot. In this event, they again find themselves on the same spot and a fight immediately ensues on the new spot. Denoting the new spot by j, then their payoffs are $w(1,j) - c$ and $w(2,j) - c$, respectively. These are just the payoffs for fighting on spot j, after deducting travel costs of reaching the spot. Figures 4.2b and 4.2c present the continuation game $G1$, which occur when each fisher has gone to spot 1, and $G2$, where each fisher has gone to spot 2.

To analyze the play of the game governed by rule configuration C1, we begin by studying the continuation games $G1$ and $G2$. This allows us to fill in the payoff implication of "Go to $G1$" and "Go to $G2$" and so solve the game of interest G. This process of solving a complicated game by starting at the end of the game is called *backward induction*. Backward induction makes possible the construction of subgame perfect equilibria, with the continuation games being examples of subgames.

To begin the backward induction, consider the subgame $G2$. We only seek enough information about $G2$ to be able to establish arrows in the arrow diagram for figure 4.2a. Consider player 1 in subgame $G2$. His or her payoff could be $w(1,2)$, $v_1 - c$, v_2, $w(1,1) - c$, or perhaps some probability mixture of these. Notice, when player 2 is at spot 2, player 1's payoff of going directly to spot 1 instead of spot 2, v_1, is greater than any of these possibilities. Thus, we can attach the arrow for player 1 pointing away from spot 2 in the game G. This is shown in figure 4.2a. The same consideration applies to player 2 in $G2$, some of whose payoffs are even lower than player 1's, and none of whose payoffs are higher than player 1's. Regardless of what happens in the subgame $G2$, neither player will choose to go to spot 2 in the first place at equilibrium. This is shown by the arrows attached to game G in figure 4.2a.

The analysis of the subgame $G1$ is rather more complex, and requires examining a number of cases. This stands to reason. It makes little sense to be fighting over a bad spot, if there is a good spot available that you could be fighting over instead. This consideration, reflected in the inequalities $v_1 > w(2,2) - c$ and $v_1 > w(1,2) - c$, gives the arrows to $G1$ pointing away from (leave, leave). There are three possible arrow diagrams for $G1$. The first arrow diagram leads to the possible cases (C1-1, C1-2, C1-3). The second diagram for $G1$ leads to case C1-4, and the third diagram to case C1-5. For each of these cases, we will work our way back directly to the overall game G and solve it as well.

The first possible arrow diagram for $G1$ (fig. 4.3a) has the arrow at the top pointing to the left for player 2, and the arrow at the left side points to the top for player 1. Each player prefers to leave spot 2, where he or she is alone, and go to spot 1 and fight. This domain is described by the inequalities

$$w(1,1) > v_2 - c$$

$$w(2,1) > v_2 - c. \tag{4.4}$$

This is shown in the arrow diagram of 4.3a. Each player has a dominant strategy in the subgame $G1$, to stay. This means the outcome of $G1$, if it is reached, is $(w(1,1), w(2,1))$—each stays and fights for spot 1. We can now fill in the matrix game of G for rule configuration C1-1 (fig. 4.3b), C1-2 (fig. 4.3c), and C1-3 (fig. 4.3d). Remember, all these arrow diagrams are predicated on the action in $G1$ as described in figure 4.3a and inequalities (4.4).

Case C1-1. Consider first the arrow diagram of G given in figure 4.3b. In this diagram, the arrow at the top points to the left for player 2 and the arrow on the left points to the top for player 1. The equilibrium of G in this case is (spot 1, spot 1). Both fishers go to spot 1, then stay and fight. The inequalities here are

$$w(1,1) > v_2$$

$$w(2,1) > v_2. \tag{4.5}$$

This could happen, for instance, when the strengths are fairly even (P near 0.5) and spot 1 is much better than spot 2 ($v_1 >> v_2$).

Case C1-2. Consider the arrow diagram of G given in figure 4.3c. In this diagram, the arrow at the top points to the right for player 2 and the arrow on the left points to the top for player 1. The equilibrium of G in this case is (spot 1, spot 2). The stronger fisher goes to the better spot. The inequalities here are

$$w(1,1) > v_2$$

$$w(2,1) < v_2. \tag{4.6}$$

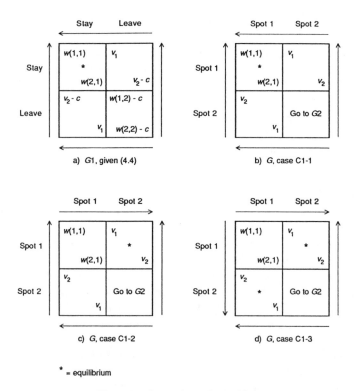

* = equilibrium

Fig. 4.3.   Cases C1-1, C1-2, C1-3

This could happen for instance when the strengths are very uneven (P near 1).

    Case C1-3. Consider the arrow diagram of G given in figure 4.3d. In this diagram, the arrow at the top points to the right for player 2 and the arrow on the left points to the bottom for player 1. The corresponding inequalities are

$$w(1,1) < v_2$$

$$w(2,1) < v_2. \qquad (4.7)$$

This could be the case for strengths fairly even (P near 0.5) and spots nearly equal in value. Game G is now an instance of Chicken and has multiple equilibria. As we have seen in the Provision Game, every game of Chicken has three equilibria. For one of these equilibria (spot 1, spot 2), the maxim "Might makes right" applies. The stronger player gets the better spot. The

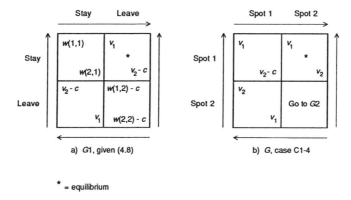

a) *G*1, given (4.8)   b) *G*, case C1-4

* = equilibrium

Fig. 4.4. Case C1-4

other pure-strategy equilibrium (spot 2, spot 1), is somewhat paradoxical, in that the maxim "Weak makes right" applies instead. Finally, since the game is asymmetric, the case for the mixed-strategy equilibrium (that it makes payoffs more equal) is also less compelling than it would be if *G* were symmetric. We will therefore select the equilibrium (spot 1, spot 2) as the outcome of *G*.[16]

We now enter the second possible arrow diagram for game *G*1, shown in figure 4.4a. This continuation game has but a single corresponding *G*.

> *Case C1-4.* In game *G*1, the arrow at the top points to the right for player 2, and the arrow at the left side points to the top for player 1. Player 2 prefers to leave spot 1 rather than fight for it, while player 1 prefers to fight rather than leave. This case is described by the following inequalities:

$$w(1,1) > v_2 - c$$

$$w(2,1) < v_2 - c. \qquad (4.8)$$

See the arrow diagram of figure 4.4a. The equilibrium of subgame *G*1 is for player 1 to stay and for player 2 to leave. This is intuitively reasonable, since player 1's strength advantage over player 2 must be considerable in order for the difference between player 1's expected value of a fight for spot 1 and player 2's expected value of a fight there ($w(1,1) - w(2,1)$) to be pronounced.

---

16. The case for this selection can be made in purely game-theoretic terms. The equilibrium selection theory of Harsanyi and Selten 1988 endorses the play of (stay, leave) for the game *G*1 in this case.

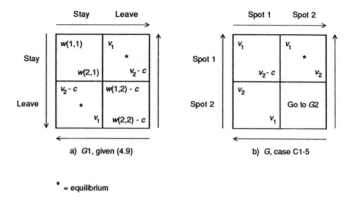

Fig. 4.5.   Case C1-5

We can now fill in the outcome of Go to $G1$ in the game G. The result is depicted in figure 4.4b. Once again, player 1 has a dominant strategy, to go to spot 1. Player 2 does best to go to spot 2. The equilibrium is for the stronger player to go to the better spot. The same reason that drives the result on the subgame (the stronger player stays on the better spot) drives the result that only the stronger player goes to that spot in the first place.

We now enter the third and final possible arrow diagram for game $G1$, shown in figure 4.5a. This continuation game again has but a single corresponding G.

> *Case C1-5.* The final case to consider is when the arrow at the top of $G1$ points to the right for player 2, and the arrow at the left side of $G2$ points to the bottom for player 1 (see fig. 4.5a). The inequalities that give rise to this pattern of arrows are

$$w(1,1) < v_2 - c$$

$$w(2,1) < v_2 - c. \tag{4.9}$$

Given these particular payoff conditions, the game that results is Chicken. As we discussed earlier, this game has three equilibria. The pure-strategy equilibrium (stay, leave) corresponds to the maxim "Might makes right." As above, the stronger player gets the better spot. The other pure-strategy equilibrium (leave, stay) corresponds to the paradoxical maxim "Weak makes right." As before, the mixed-strategy equilibrium is not compelling. Thus, using the same reasoning as earlier, the equilibrium (stay, leave) is selected as the outcome of Go to $G1$.

TABLE 4.2. Group Outcomes and Payoffs, by Rule Configuration

Domain	Group Outcome	Group Payoff
C1–1	Fishers fight	$v_1 - d$
C1–2 through C1–5	Stronger fisher gets better spot	$v_1 + v_2$
C2–1	Fishers go to better spot	$v_1 + v_2 - c$
C2–2 and C2–3	Faster fisher gets better spot	$v_1 + v_2$
C3 and C4	Fisher to announce announces better spot	$v_1 + v_2$

Returning to the initial game G, one has the matrix of figure 4.5b. Player 1 has a dominant strategy, to go to spot 1. Player 2, in light of this, goes to spot 2. On this domain, "Might makes right" rules again.

Table 4.2 summarizes the above analysis of the fishing assignment game with fighting. On physical domain C1–1, both fishers go to the better spot and fight; on domains C1–2 through C1–5, the stronger fisher goes to the better spot. The domain that is especially problematic and in need of reform is C1–1, where fighting occurs. This motivates our next game.

Rule Configuration C2

We now turn to rule configuration C2. In this rule configuration, the first fisher to arrive at a fishing spot is permitted to fish at that spot exclusively for the day. The other fisher is not authorized to fish there and would leave any previously occupied fishing spot for the other one. As in C1, each fisher decides simultaneously which spot to fish. In the event that both fishers decide on the same spot, a random mechanism determines which of them is first. There are two positions, player 1 and player 2. Player 1 is called first with probability P; player 2, with probability $1 - P$. Chance favors player 1, in that $P > 0.5$. The expected payoff to player 1 from choosing spot 1 is calculated as follows. With probability P, player 1 is called first and gets payoff v_1; with probability $1 - P$, player 1 is called second and moves to spot 2 with payoff $v_2 - c$. The expectation for player 1 is $Pv_1 + (1 - P)(v_2 - c)$. Call this expectation $w(1,1)$; this is what player 1 expects from going to spot 1 if player 2 also goes there. The expected payoff to player 2 from choosing spot 1 is calculated as follows. With probability $1 - P$, player 2 is ruled first and gets v_1: with probability P, $(v_2 - c)$. Call this expectation for player 2, $w(2,1)$. Similar calculations apply to the choice of spot 2. We have purposely used the same notation for probability and payoffs as in C1—only the interpretations here are different. The game G to which this leads is shown in figure 4.6a.

The first thing to notice about this game is that $v_1 > Pv_1 + (1 - P)(v_2 - c) = w(1,1)$. Likewise, $v_1 > w(2,1)$. Having the better spot to yourself is better than facing the chance of having to leave that spot for a worse one. This determines the two arrows in figure 4.6a, the one at the bottom pointing to the

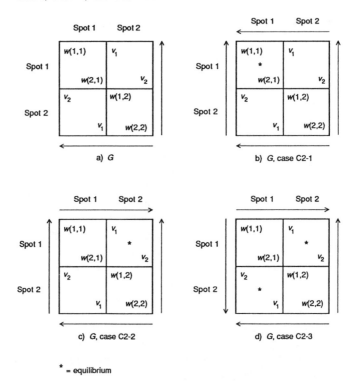

* = equilibrium

Fig. 4.6.   Game according to rule configuration C2

left for player 2 and the one on the right pointing to the top for player 1. We see that (spot 2, spot 2) is not an equilibrium.

There are still three cases to consider, depending on the physical parameters (v_1, v_2, c). These are shown in figures 4.6b–d.

Case C2-1. In this case (see fig. 4.6b), the arrow at the top of the matrix points to the left for player 2 and the arrow at the left of the matrix points to the top for player 1. The inequalities for this case are

$$w(1,1) > v_2$$

$$w(2,1) > v_2. \tag{4.10}$$

This could be the case, for instance, if P is near 0.5 and spot 1 is much more valuable than spot 2. The equilibrium is for both players to go to spot 1 and let chance decide which of them is first (and stays) and which is second (and leaves).

Case C2-2. In this case (see fig. 4.6c), the arrow at the top of the matrix points to the right for player 2 and the arrow at the left of the matrix points to the top for player 1. The inequalities for this case are

$$w(1,1) > v_2$$

$$w(2,1) < v_2. \tag{4.11}$$

This could happen, for instance, if P is near 1 and c is large. The equilibrium is for player 1 to go to spot 1 and for player 2 to go to spot 2. The chance that player 1 is first is sufficiently high for player 1 to always get spot 1.

Case C2-3. In this case (see fig. 4.6d), the arrow at the top of the matrix points to the right for player 2 and the arrow at the left of the matrix points down for player 1. The inequalities for this case are

$$w(1,1) < v_2$$

$$w(2,1) < v_2. \tag{4.12}$$

This could happen, for instance, if P is near 0.5 and the spots are nearly equal in value. The game in this case is a form of Chicken. By the same reasoning as used in previous forms of asymmetric Chicken, the equilibrium selected is for player 1 to go to spot 1 and player 2 to go to spot 2. The player who is more likely to be first on the better spot goes to the better spot.

To summarize the results of rule configuration C2, using a first in time, first in right rule does eliminate fighting. In two out of three physical domains, it even leads to a maximal group payoff, $v_1 + v_2$. However, in the domain where one spot is clearly best (Case C2-1), the social payoff is $w(1,1) + w(2,1) = v_1 + v_2 - c$, which is not optimal. This rule configuration can still be reformed (see table 4.2).

Rule Configuration C3

We now turn to rule configuration C3. There are two positions, player 1 (who announces a spot) and player 2 (who hears the announcement). As in C2, the first fisher to arrive at a fishing spot is permitted to fish at that spot for the day. The other fisher, if any, automatically leaves that spot for the other spot. Unlike C2, the player announcing always gets to the spot first. Moreover, announcing a spot commits a player to going to that spot. The strategies available to the two players are different in this game. For player 1, the two strategies are (announce spot 1, announce spot 2). A complete plan for player 2 includes what he or she will do in any contingency. Here are the four possible strategies of player 2:

Go to spot 1 if player 1 announces spot 1   (Follow)
Go to spot 2 if player 1 announces spot 2

Call this strategy "Follow." It is the plan which guarantees that player 2 will follow whatever player 1 announces.

Go to spot 1 if player 1 announces spot 1   (Spot 1)
Go to spot 1 if player 1 announces spot 2

Call this strategy "Spot 1." It is the plan which guarantees that player 2 will go to spot 1 regardless of what player 1 announces.

Go to spot 2 if player 1 announces spot 1   (Spot 2)
Go to spot 2 if player 2 announces spot 2

Call this strategy "Spot 2." It is the plan which guarantees that player 2 will go to spot 2 regardless of what player 2 announces.

Go to spot 2 if player 1 announces spot 1   (Avoid)
Go to spot 1 if player 1 announces spot 2

Call this strategy "Avoid." It is the plan which guarantees that player 2 will avoid going to whatever spot player 1 announces. One now has the matrix of figure 4.7.

This is the first nonsquare matrix we have encountered. The asymmetry in strategies available accounts for the rectangularity. Notice first of all that player 1 has a dominant strategy, to announce spot 1. All arrows point up for this player. There are two pure-strategy equilibria: (announce spot 1, spot 2) and (announce spot 1, avoid). These equilibria are observationally equivalent: the outcome is the same in both. The player who gets to announce calls for the best spot. Notice also that this outcome maximizes group payoff for all possible (v_1, v_2, c). At last, we have found a rule configuration that solves the CPR problem on all physical domains.

Rule Configuration C4
Once having solved the CPR problem played a single time, the problem of how to solve the CPR problem in a repeated setting arises. Rule configuration C4 applies C3 to a repeated assignment problem. For simplicity, we consider the fishing game played twice. In C4, the right to announce rotates between the two players. The first time the fishing game is played, player 1 gets to announce; the second time, player 2. An equilibrium sequence is for player 1 to announce spot 1 the first period, and for player 2 to announce spot 1 the

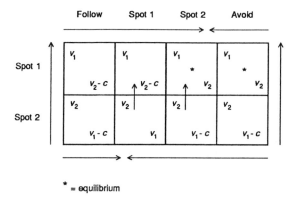

* = equilibrium

Fig. 4.7. Game according to rule configuration C3

second period.[17] Each player averages the payoff $(v_1 + v_2)/2$ over the play of the repeated game. The solution to the one-shot CPR problem can in this way be sustained over time.

Outcome Comparison

It is time to compare the outcomes of the four rule configurations we have just studied. Table 4.2 shows the group outcome and behavior of the various domains. Notice that the worst group payoff occurs in the domain C1-1, where fights always occur and are costly. This domain has two sources of inefficiency, fighting plus no fishing of the worse spot. The next worst outcome is the domain C2-1, where both spots are fished but there is excess travel. The only rule configuration among these that maximizes group payoff in all physical domains is C3, and in the repeated game case, C4.

The technique of rules and games that we have just used has uncovered several possibilities of reform. We can now be somewhat more precise about the comparisons involved in reform. Let $f(C)$ be the outcome of the game played according to rule configuration C. Let C' be another rule configuration. We say rule configurations C and C' are *outcome-equivalent* if $f(C) = f(C')$ for all possible physical domains. In such cases, one can say that the rule difference between the configurations C and C' is inessential, because it makes no difference to the outcome of rational play. For instance, the solution of tic-tac-toe is a draw, regardless of whether the player marking x or the player marking o moves first. Again, it makes no difference to the rational outcome of a secret ballot whether votes are cast on paper ballots or electron-

---

17. In particular, this is the outcome of any subgame perfect equilibrium.

ically. In the fishing assignment game, consider the following variant of C3, called C3'. In C3', player 1, instead of announcing a spot, simply goes to the spot. Player 1 arrives at the spot and player 2 sees him or her arrive at the spot. Otherwise, the rules of C3 and C3' are the same. The matrix game of C3' is the same as that of C3, so that C3 and C3' are outcome equivalent. However, none of the rule configurations C1, C2, or C3 is outcome equivalent.

Let the outcome $f(C)$ be expressed as a vector of players' payoffs. Then a rule configuration C' *reforms* a rule configuration C if $f(C') \geq f(C)$ for all players and $f(C') > f(C)$ for some player. This is the Pareto reform criterion. A reform in the Pareto sense is a reform in the utilitarian sense, but not necessarily the converse. Both criteria agree that C3 reforms C2, and that C2 reforms C1.

The phenomenon just noted, where it was possible to order all rule configurations, does not always occur. For instance, C' might be better than C for one set of physical characteristics, while C was better than C' for another. Imagine a rule configuration that used "first in time, first in right" on some physical domains, but fought it out on others. This rule configuration would not be everywhere better, worse, or the same as either C1 or C2. This observation motivates the following concept. If one is fairly certain of constancy in the physical environment, so that only a limited physical domain is likely to be relevant, then one can condition these notions on that domain. The corresponding notions are conditional equivalence and conditional reform.

Once a reform has been identified, there is still a problem to be solved. Whether the players themselves will undertake a reform depends on the costs of transforming the rules as well as more general costs of collective action (E. Ostrom 1990). If the costs of transforming the rules alone exceed the benefits of making the rule change, then players will continue to follow rules leading to suboptimal outcomes.

Conclusions

This chapter has introduced the technique of rules and games, and the notion of the configural nature of rules. These ideas have been illustrated by a rather more complicated version of the assignment problem of the last chapter. We have shown the following: (1) a simple rule change can lead to major changes in outcomes; (2) in some physical domains, a rule change may not lead to any change in outcomes; and (3) rule changes can be judged by changes in outcomes. Despite the complexity of the analysis, the particular games we have examined still make many concessions to reality—only two fishers, only two spots, and no threat of overfishing or extinction. Our main goal has been to show the reader that the technique of rules and games works and puts policy analysis on a sound logical footing. The structure of these games serves as a first approximation to the strategic and deontic considerations related to CPRs such as forests, groundwater basins, in-shore fisheries, and irrigation systems that we study later in this book. When CPR rules are effectively matched to the particular physical domain, participants in such reformed games face games with better equilibria.

Part 2
Experimental Studies

In chapter 1, we identified three core questions addressed in this volume.

1. In finitely repeated CPR dilemmas, to what degree are the predictions about behavior and outcomes derived from noncooperative game theory supported by empirical evidence?
2. In CPR dilemmas where behavior and outcomes are substantially different from that predicted, are there behavioral regularities that can be drawn upon in the development of improved theories?
3. What types of institutional and physical variables affect the likelihood of successful resolution of CPR dilemmas?

The conceptual and formal languages needed to address these questions have been presented in chapters 2–4. We now have theoretical tools to address these questions. In this section, we examine the empirical results from a large series of empirical studies conducted in the context of an experimental laboratory. While all three questions will be discussed in this section on experimental studies, we will focus on the first question.

Laboratory experiments are particularly well adapted to address this question because one can carefully create conditions in a laboratory that closely match the conditions specified in a theoretical model. In a laboratory setting, the analyst creates, and thus controls, the components of an action situation. Thus, in parameterizing CPR situations in the lab, we control (1) the number of participants, (2) the positions they may hold, (3) the specific actions they can take, (4) the outcomes they can affect, (5) how actions are linked to outcomes, (6) the information they obtain, and (7) the potential payoffs.

To take full advantage of the control made available in a laboratory setting, we need to posit a tight theoretical model of the situation and ensure that there is a one-to-one correspondence between the working parts of the model and the conditions created in the lab. A key step in accomplishing this link between a theoretical model and the conditions in the laboratory is inducing value. By inducing value, we mean that the laboratory situation must lead laboratory subjects to perceive and act on payoffs that have the same mathematical properties as the payoffs in the linked mathematical model.

In our experiments, value over alternative outcomes is induced using a cash reward structure. As discussed by Smith (1982), the following conditions constitute a set of sufficient conditions for inducing value:

1. **Nonsatiation**: Subjects' utility must be monotone-increasing in payoffs. This guarantees that given alternatives that are identical except in payoff space, a subject will always choose the alternative with the greater reward.
2. **Saliency**: In order for rewards to be motivationally relevant, or *salient*, the level of rewards must be directly tied to participants' decisions.
3. **Dominance**: An important element of the economic environment is the subjects' utility functions, which contain many arguments in addition to the rewards associated with payoffs. To successfully induce value, the cash reward structure must dominate the subjective benefits and costs of an action derived from these other utility function arguments.
4. **Privacy**: Subjects may not be autonomous own-reward maximizers. To the extent allowed by the underlying theoretical model under investigation, subjects' payoffs should be made privately.

While a laboratory situation designed to induce the incentives prescribed by an abstract theoretical model will closely match the abstract model, it cannot be expected to closely parallel far more complex naturally occurring settings to which the theoretical model may also be applied. Nevertheless, to the extent that a logically consistent model is put forward as a useful explanation of naturally occurring phenomena, laboratory experimental methods offer the comparative advantages of control and measurement. Experiments can be tailor-made for investigating a particular model, thus controlling for those particular attributes of the environment required by the model. Experiments can also induce and measure values, costs, and information flows that may be impossible to measure in naturally occurring settings. For example, as discussed in chapter 1, the measurement of criteria such as efficiency or Pareto-improving outcomes can be quite problematic in the field. In the laboratory, these concepts have clear meanings. Efficiency is measured as the percentage of maximum possible earnings (surplus) attainable from a set of possible decisions. In our experiments, this cash surplus is defined to be the gains possible from optimal investment in the laboratory CPR.

Experimental techniques enable us to examine behavior in a manner that would be infeasible if one relied entirely on field data. Over the past 25 years, the experimental methodology has become an integral part of model testing and analysis of alternative institutional designs in both economics and political science. We share Alvin Roth's (1991) enthusiasm for undertaking experimental work to test the foundations of game theory, as well as for delving deeper into findings obtained in the field. Roth particularly stresses the importance of field and experimental studies when economics, or related social sciences, are to be used as the foundation for recommending social policies:

> In summary, I think the next step in the development of game theory as an integral part of economics, and a step we must take if game theory is to continue to thrive, is to bring to the fore the empirical questions associated with strategic environments. Accomplishing this will require some changes in the kinds of theory and empirical work we do, in order to regularly confront theory with evidence, and to use theory as a guide to what kinds of evidence we should collect.
>
> I anticipate that experimental economics will play a growing role in this effort. There are many questions for which laboratory experimentation will be the most direct way to test theory, and to explore the effects of variables that are difficult to measure or control in any other way. This is not to say, of course, that experimentation in economics will come to play exactly the role it plays in any other sciences, or that there will not be many questions that are best addressed by field research, including new kinds of field research, which will pay particular attention to the details of economic environments, including both formal and informal "rules of the game," and cultural and psychological constraints on individuals' actions. (Roth 1991, 112–13)

We emphasize that laboratory investigations complement other modes of analysis. The strength of control in experimental analyses is a weakness from the standpoint of the richness that one gains from studying field data. It is for this reason that we have pursued research that combines both types of analysis, in conjunction with testing and the further development of a theoretical foundation for our work. From the perspective of field studies, our experimental designs are most closely related to decision situations in which detailed and accurate information is available on the productive nature of the resource. Further, the relationship between inputs and output is deterministic. We have, thus, chosen one of the simpler physical environments to study in the experimental lab.

In chapter 5, we lay the groundwork for our experimental study. Focusing on appropriation behavior, we examine individual and group decisions in a baseline situation with minimal institutional constraints. Our baseline decision situation is designed to examine appropriation behavior in a static situation, void of the complexities that arise when appropriation behavior is linked to the future productivity of the resource or its possible destruction. This austere and relatively simple decision environment enables us to examine the predictive success of noncooperative game theory as a benchmark for behavior. In appendix 5.1 we also summarize the major findings from closely parallel studies of the provision side of the problem.

In chapter 6, we extend the appropriation environment to capture the effects of time dependency in the resource. Specifically, maintaining our minimal institutional configuration, our experimental design allows for probabilistic destruction of the laboratory CPR dependent upon the level of appropriation. Here, we investigate subject behavior in situations where the probability of destruction increases with the level of appropriation. In our first time-dependent design, any level of resource exploitation leads to some probability of resource destruction. In many CPR situations, however, there is a natural regenerative process that enables some appropriation without damage to the CPR. We capture this decision environment by parameterizing a "safe zone" for appropriation. Inside the safe zone, the probability of destruction is zero. Outside the safe zone, the destruction probability increases linearly. In the baseline conditions examined in chapter 5, we observe behavior that leads to significant inefficiencies in net yield from the CPR. In the decision environment of chapter 6, the CPR is destroyed in every case and, in most cases, rather quickly. Thus, in CPR situations where there are *minimal institutions*, we find that the game-theoretic predictions regarding overall efficiency (derived from a CPR game situation that is finitely repeated) to be well supported by empirical evidence.

The evidence to be presented from the field in chapters 10–14 suggests that in richer institutional settings, the noncooperative inefficient outcome is not inevitable. In environments with a richer set of institutional arrangements for fostering cooperation and/or allowing sanctioning for noncooperative type behavior, subjects may adopt behavioral strategies consistent with higher levels of efficiency. In chapters 7 and 8, we take a "more controlled" look at such institutions in the experimental laboratory. Chapter 7 explores the effects of face-to-face communication on appropriation behavior. Once communication is introduced, we find behavior and outcomes that are substantially different from those predicted for finitely repeated, noncooperative CPR games. In chapter 8, we examine the behavioral properties of sanctioning as an independent mechanism and in conjunction with communication and the capacity to design and agree upon an endogenous sanctioning mechanism.

In chapter 9, we return to our core questions in light of the evidence presented in this entire section. We conclude that in institutionally sparse environments, the predicted outcomes and experimental outcomes match rather closely at an aggregate level. In institutionally richer environments, we do find behavioral regularities that help to explain why outcomes do not conform to predictions. We also find institutional and physical variables that affect outcomes in a systematic manner. Subjects who use the opportunity to communicate to agree to a joint investment strategy, who are able to communicate on a repeated basis, or can back their agreements with an endogenously adopted sanctioning mechanism, are able to achieve significantly higher levels of net yield from the CPR.

CHAPTER 5

CPR Baseline Appropriation Experiments

As discussed in chapter 1, the problems that appropriators face can be usefully clustered into two broad types: *appropriation* and *provision*. In appropriation problems, the production relationship between yield and level of inputs is assumed to be given and the problem to be solved is how to allocate that yield in an efficient and equitable manner. Provision problems, on the other hand, are related to creating a resource, maintaining or improving the production capabilities of the resource, or avoiding the destruction of the resource. In other words, in appropriation problems, we focus attention on the *flow* aspect of the CPR. In provision problems, we concentrate on the *facility* aspect of the CPR.

Both appropriation and provision problems are found in most CPR settings. In fact, in most field settings, these problems are nested in complex interrelationships that are clearly interdependent. A laboratory setting, however, allows the analytical separation of such interdependencies. To date, our experimental work has focused principally on (1) issues related to appropriation in a static environment or (2) appropriation and its relation to demand-side provision, the impact of appropriation in a dynamic sense on resource yield and on probabilistic destruction of the CPR. We have analyzed these issues in decision settings with very basic rule configurations and in settings in which rules were altered to examine how institutional changes affect appropriation decisions. Although the experimental research conducted for this book does not explicitly examine the supply-side provision or maintenance problems faced by CPR users, there is substantial experimental research closely related to this issue. We include a brief summary of this research as appendix 5.1 to this chapter.

CPR Appropriation

We now turn to our most basic appropriation setting. The first question that we need to pursue in the laboratory setting is whether subjects' decisions in a stark CPR dilemma situation are similar to those predicted by noncooperative game theory. In other words, would subjects presented with a CPR dilemma, similar to the appropriation game of chapter 3, appropriate from the laboratory CPR as predicted by the Nash equilibrium? This is our baseline game. These experiments represent a baseline in the sense that we examine behavior in a situation with minimal institutional constraints. The purpose of such experiments is twofold: (1) it allows for a close examination of individual and group behavior under conditions designed to parallel those of noncooperative complete information game theory and (2) it provides a benchmark for comparison to behavior under alternative physical and institutional configurations. Our baseline situation is designed to analyze appropriation behavior in a time-independent (stationary) condition.[1] Thus, this situation allows us to investigate appropriation behavior separate from provision behavior. The baseline situation clearly avoids the "real world" phenomena that the productive capacity and possible destruction of CPRs is dependent upon the level of appropriation from the CPR or that in some CPRs institutions have evolved in an attempt to diminish the effects of resource degradation. In the three chapters following this "baseline" chapter, we examine laboratory situations that allow for the probabilistic destruction of the CPR and institutions designed to allow communication and/or sanctioning.

Appropriation Behavior in the Laboratory

Subjects and the Experimental Setting

The experiments used subjects drawn from the undergraduate population at Indiana University. Students were volunteers recruited primarily from principles of economics classes. Prior to recruitment, potential volunteers were given a brief explanation in which they were told only that they would be making decisions in an "economic choice situation" and that the money they earned would be dependent upon their own investment decisions and those of the others in their experimental group. All experiments were conducted on the NovaNET computer system at Indiana University. The computer facilitates the accounting procedures involved in the experiment, enhances across experimental/subject control, and allows for minimal experimenter involvement.

At the beginning of each experimental session, subjects were told that (1) they would make a series of investment decisions, (2) all individual investment decisions were anonymous to the group, and (3) they would be paid their individual earnings (privately and in cash) at the end of the experiment. Subjects then proceeded at their own pace through a set of instructions that described the decisions.[2]

Subjects were instructed that in each decision round they would be

---

1. This chapter relies extensively on J. Walker, Gardner, and Ostrom 1990.
2. A complete set of instructions is available from the authors upon request.

Tokens Invested by Group	Units of Commodity Produced	Total Group Return	Average Return per Token	Additional Return per Token
20	360	$ 3.60	$ 0.18	$ 0.18
40	520	$ 5.20	$ 0.13	$ 0.08
60	480	$ 4.80	$ 0.08	$ -0.02
80	240	$ 2.40	$ 0.03	$ -0.12
100	-200	$ -2.00	$ -0.02	$ -0.22
120	-840	$ -8.40	$ -0.07	$ -0.32
140	-1680	$ -16.80	$ -0.12	$ -0.42
160	-2720	$ -27.20	$ -0.17	$ -0.52
180	-3960	$ -39.60	$ -0.22	$ -0.62
200	-5400	$ -54.00	$ -0.27	$ -0.72

Note: The table displays information on investments in Market 2 at various levels of group investment. Your return from Market 2 depends on what percentage of the total group investment is made by you.

Market 1 returns you one unit of commodity 1 for each token you invest in Market 1. Each unit of commodity 1 pays you $ 0.05.

Fig. 5.1. Table presented to subjects showing units produced and cash return from investments in Market 2 (commodity 2 value per unit = $ 0.01)

endowed with a given number of tokens that they could invest in two markets. Market 1 was described as an investment opportunity in which each token yielded a fixed (constant) rate of output and each unit of output yielded a fixed (constant) return. Market 2 (the CPR) was described as a market that yielded a rate of output per token dependent upon the total number of tokens invested by the entire group. The rate of output at each level of group investment was described in functional form as well as tabular form. Subjects were informed that they would receive a level of output from Market 2 that was equivalent to the percentage of total group tokens they invested. Further, subjects knew that each unit of output from Market 2 yielded a fixed (constant) rate of return. Figure 5.1 displays the actual information subjects saw as summary information in the experiment. Subjects knew with certainty the total number of decision makers in the group, total group tokens, and that endowments were identical. They knew that the experiment would not last more than two hours. They did not know the exact number of investment decision rounds. All subjects were *experienced*, that is, had participated in at least one experiment using this form of decision situation.[3]

---

3. Subjects were randomly recruited from initial runs to ensure that no group was brought back in tact. The number of rounds in the initial experiments varied from 10 to 20.

In the baseline experiments, eight subjects participated in a series of at least 20 decision rounds. After each round, subjects were shown a display that recorded: (1) their profits in each market for that round, (2) total group investment in Market 2, and (3) a tally of their cumulative profits for the experiment. During the experiment, subjects could request, through the computer, this information for all previous rounds. Players received no information regarding other subjects' *individual* investment decisions or concerning the number of iterations.

Note that this laboratory decision situation parallels that of an action situation described in chapter 2. A careful experimental investigation requires that each of the seven components of an action situation be clearly defined. Thus, the baseline action situation we have created in the lab has the following components of an action situation: (1) eight participants; (2) all participants hold the same position; (3) participants must make a token allocation for an experimentally controlled number of decision rounds; (4) output is in terms of units of production for Markets 1 and 2; (5) a deterministic function maps aggregate investments in Markets 1 and 2 into the number of units produced in Markets 1 and 2; (6) participants know the number of other players, their own endowment, their own past actions, the aggregate past actions of others, the payoff per unit for output produced in both markets, the allocation rule for sharing Market 2 output, the finite nature of the game's repetitions; and (7) participants know the mapping from investment decisions into net payoffs.

We interpret our baseline laboratory CPR situation in the following manner. It is limited access in the sense that an upper limit of eight players invests a maximum number of tokens in the CPR (Market 2). While this decision situation has a limited number of players, players in combination have sufficient freedom to choose investment levels that lead to extremely suboptimal yields. In fact, we examine the behavioral consequences of varying the endowments available to appropriators (the number of tokens) from 10 to 25 tokens per person per round. Although eight may be a small number of players, our baseline design approximates some of the characteristics of larger groups or conflict-ridden small groups because it does not allow explicit communication. In this baseline experiment, it is difficult for individuals to signal one another about their intentions. Information about the actions by one player is swamped by the actions of others, since players only receive information on aggregate group investment decisions and outcomes.

Further, our laboratory CPR brings together, for a relatively short period of time, players who have no relevant prior history that might implicitly enable them to coordinate behavior. The participants know the experiment will last no more than two hours and that all decisions remain anonymous to other participants.[4] Thus, while the participants do not know the specific number of rounds, they know the experiment has a relatively short finite horizon. The experimental situation has been consciously neutralized in the sense that players are not explicitly given clues to (1) what we expect of them or (2) naturally occurring parallel decision environments (e.g., we don't call them fishers or Market 2 a fishery). Finally, we emphasize again, that our baseline situation separates appropriation activity from provision. The resource is provided by the experimenters. Endowments, the production functions, the payoff functions, and the number of decision rounds are not dependent upon decisions made in any round.

Theoretical Predictions about Individual Behavior in the Baseline Experiment

Assume a fixed number n of appropriators with access to the CPR. Each appropriator i has an endowment of resources e that can be invested in the CPR or invested in a safe, outside activity. The marginal payoff of the outside activity is normalized equal to w, measured in cents. The payoff to an individual appropriator from investing in the CPR depends on aggregate group investment in the CPR, and on the appropriator investment as a percentage of the aggregate. Let x_i denote appropriator i's investment in the CPR, where $0 \leq x_i \leq e$. The group return to investment in the CPR is given by the production function $F(\Sigma x_i)$, where F is a concave function, with $F(0) = 0$, $F'(0) > w$, and $F'(ne) < 0$. Initially, investment in the CPR pays better than the opportunity cost of the foregone safe investment $[F'(0) > w]$, but if the appropriators invest a sufficiently large number of resources ($\hat{q}$) in the CPR, the outcome is counterproductive $[F'(\hat{q}) < 0]$. The yield from the CPR reaches a *maximum net level* when individuals invest some, but not all, of their endowments in the CPR.[5]

So far all CPR games we have considered had two players. This restriction was solely for purposes of exposition. Most real-world CPR problems involve many more participants. We let the parameter n represent the number of players in a CPR experimental game. For all the experiments reported in this book, n is set equal to eight. Even though many CPR problems involve more than eight participants, with eight participants one encounters most of

---

4. Contrast this finite game design with one illustrated by Palfrey and Rosenthal 1992, where a random stopping rule was used to create the theoretical equivalence of a discounted infinitely repeated game.

5. Investment in the CPR beyond the maximum net level is termed *rent dissipation* in the literature of resource economics. This is conceptually akin to, but not to be confused with, the term *rent seeking*, which plays an important role in political economy and public choice. For the latter, see Tullock 1967 and Krueger 1974.

the strategic complexity inherent with larger groups. Moreover, there is sound theoretical reason to believe that eight is a large enough number to surmount small-group effects.[6]

We now introduce some notation that will prove useful. Let $x = (x_1, \ldots, x_n)$ be a vector of individual appropriators' investments in the CPR. The amount that individual i does not appropriate to the CPR, $e - x_i$, is automatically invested in the safe outside alternative. The vector notation x reminds us of the fact that the payoff to a participant depends in general on what all the participants do. The payoff to an appropriator, $u_i(x)$, is given by:

$$u_i(x) = we \qquad\qquad\qquad\qquad\qquad \text{if } x_i = 0$$

$$w(e - x_i) + (x_i/\Sigma x_i)F(\Sigma x_i) \qquad\qquad \text{if } x_i > 0. \qquad (5.1)$$

What equation (5.1) says is really quite straightforward. If players put all their endowment into the safe alternative, they get the sure value (endowment)(value per unit of endowment) $= (e)(w)$. If players put some of their endowment into the safe alternative and some into the CPR, they get a return of $w(e - x_i)$ on that part of the endowment invested in the safe alternative. In addition, they get a return from the CPR, which equals their proportional investment in the CPR, $(x_i/\Sigma x_i)$, times total CPR output $F(\Sigma x_i)$, measured in cents.

More players in a game means more complexity. However, the basic concepts of payoff maximization and Nash equilibrium remain the same. In particular, at a Nash equilibrium, each player maximizes payoff given the strategies chosen by the other players. Let x_i be player i's strategy and $u_i(x)$ be player i's payoff function, in a general formulation of which (5.1) is a particular instance. Player i seeks to maximize her payoff by her choice of x_i, which itself is a constrained variable. When the payoff function is differentiable, as is (5.1), this maximization can be performed using calculus techniques. Consider the calculus problem:

maximize $u_i(x)$
$\qquad x_i$

subject to $0 \leq x_i \leq e$.

---

6. In an influential paper, Selten (1971) argues that five is the crucial number of players. In an oligopoly game similar to ours, he shows that with fewer than five players, the most likely equilibrium (without institutional innovation) involves considerable amounts of cooperation, while with more than five players, an effect reminiscent of a CPR problem is present at equilibrium.

Suppose that x_i^* solves the constrained maximization problem, and that $u_i(x_1, \ldots x_i^*, \ldots x_n)$ is the maximal value. This gives one equation in n unknowns. Now solve the calculus problem for each player i. Then one has n equations in n unknowns. Any solution to this system of equations is a Nash equilibrium. In other words, a Nash equilibrium requires that all n players have solved their individual maximization problems simultaneously. That is, suppose that for each player i, x_i^* is the solution to the individual maximization problem. Then at a Nash equilibrium, the problem that player i faces (if every other player is maximizing—is playing the optimal x_i^*) is

maximize $u_i(x_1^*, \ldots x_i, \ldots x_n^*)$
$\quad x_i$

subject to $0 \le x_i \le e$

is solved by x_i^*. Since there is a first-order condition for each player, solving for a Nash equilibrium in general requires that one solve n simultaneous equations in n unknowns. Computationally, solving this system can be quite challenging, which is one reason why games with many players are harder to analyze.

However, if the game is symmetric, there is a shortcut to the solution. Our baseline game is symmetric. Each player has the same endowment, the same set of pure strategies (and hence mixed strategies), and the same payoff function in cents. Under these conditions, the game is symmetric. Every symmetric game has a symmetric equilibrium. When a symmetric game has a unique symmetric equilibrium, Harsanyi-Selten selection theory selects that equilibrium.[7] To find this equilibrium, it suffices to solve a single player's maximization problem, together with the restriction that each x_i^* will be equal at equilibrium.

We illustrate this technique with the payoff function (5.1). Given our assumptions on the CPR production technology, it is easy to see that neither $x_i = 0$ nor $x_i = e$ solve player i's maximization problem. Therefore, there must exist an interior solution, where the first-order condition is satisfied. Differentiating (5.1), one has:

$$-w + (x_i/\Sigma x_i)F'(\Sigma x_i) + F(\Sigma x_i)((\Sigma x_i - x_i)/(\Sigma x_i)^2) = 0. \tag{5.2}$$

---

7. As Claudia Keser pointed out, the baseline game also has asymmetric equilibria where one player invests 7 tokens, six players invest 8 tokens, and one player invests 9 tokens. The group investment is 64 tokens, the same as the symmetric equilibrium.

Symmetry implies that at equilibrium, each player makes the same investment decision as does player i. Invoking symmetry, one has $\Sigma x_i = nx_i^*$. Substitution into equation (5.2) yields

$$-w + (1/n)F'(nx_i^*) + F(nx_i^*)((n-1)/x_i^*n^2) = 0.$$

As we show below, aggregate investment in the CPR at the symmetric Nash equilibrium is greater than optimal investment, and group return is less than optimal return, but not all yield from the CPR is wasted.[8]

There are several standard interpretations of this symmetric Nash equilibrium. First, it is the only solution to the maximization problem facing a rational player. Second, if a player does not obey (5.2), their payoff will be suboptimal. Third, once a player reaches this equilibrium, they have no incentive to change their behavior. Fourth, if one believes that strategic behavior is adaptive over long periods of time, then evolutionary forces (mimicking natural selection) will converge to an equilibrium satisfying (5.2).[9] A final interpretation is as the predicted outcome from a limited access CPR (see, for example, Clark 1980; Cornes and Sandler 1986; Hartwick 1982; and Negri 1989).[10] This is the interpretation most relevant for policy purposes.

We now compare the equilibrium to the optimal solution to the CPR problem. Summing across individual payoffs $u_i(x)$ for all appropriators i, one has the group payoff function $u(x)$,

$$u(x) = nwe - w\Sigma x_i + F(\Sigma x_i) \tag{5.3}$$

which is to be maximized subject to the constraint $0 \leq \Sigma x_i \leq ne$. Given the above productivity conditions on F, the group maximization problem has a unique solution characterized by the condition:

$$-w + F'(\Sigma x_i) = 0. \tag{5.4}$$

According to (5.4), the marginal return from a CPR should equal the opportunity cost of the outside alternative for the last unit invested in the CPR. The

---

8. See J. Walker, Gardner, and Ostrom 1991 for details of this derivation.

9. In the terminology of evolutionary game theory, this equilibrium is an evolutionarily stable strategy. See Hofbauer and Sigmund 1988 for a mathematical survey of this fascinating subject.

10. Consistent Conjectural Variations Equilibria may provide a useful method for a detailed analysis of individual subject behavior in these experiments. In the limited access version of the noncooperative CPR decision problem, full dissipation is predicted by nonzero consistent conjectures. See Mason, Sandler, and Cornes 1988 for a discussion of consistent conjectures equilibria for the CPR experiment. See J. Walker, Gardner, and Ostrom 1991 for a discussion of several alternative theories that could be used to provide a solution to the constituent game.

group payoff from using the marginal revenue equals marginal cost rule (5.4) represents the maximal yield that can be extracted from the resource in a single period. Since equations (5.4) and (5.2) have different solutions, we have shown that the equilibrium is not an optimum.[11]

Neither the Nash equilibrium investment nor the optimum group investment depend on the endowment parameter e, as long as e is sufficiently large. For the Nash equilibrium this seems especially counterintuitive, since large values of e represent high potential pressure on the CPR. Strategically, one of the most problematic aspects of a CPR dilemma is overappropriation fueled by high endowments. Big mistakes are more likely and more devastating with high endowments. The Nash equilibrium concept fails to capture this, once the corner constraint that investment not exceed endowment is no longer binding.[12]

Denote the baseline game by X and let X be played a finite number of times. Game-theoretical models do not always yield unique answers to how individuals will (or ought to) behave in repeated, social dilemma situations. Such games can have multiple equilibria, even if the one-shot game has a unique equilibrium. The number of equilibria grows with the number of repetitions. When there are finitely many repetitions, no equilibrium can sustain an optimal solution, although it may be possible to come close (Benoit and Krishna 1985). When there are infinitely many repetitions, some equilibria can sustain an optimal solution (J. Friedman 1990). In all cases, the worst possible one-shot equilibrium, repeated as often as possible, remains an equilibrium outcome. The players thus face a plethora of equilibria. Without a mechanism for selection among these equilibria, the players can easily be overwhelmed by complexity and confusion.

A commonly used equilibrium selection criterion is to require that a strategy specify equilibrium play on subgames, the requirement of subgame perfection. If the baseline game has a unique symmetric equilibrium, then the finitely repeated game has a unique symmetric subgame perfect equilibrium (Selten 1971). Thus, equation (5.2) characterizes a finite sequence of equilibrium outcomes. We get symmetry among players within a decision period, as well as symmetry between decision periods.

This prediction, like all predictions made in this chapter, is based on the assumptions of a finite game and of complete information. Our experimental procedures assure that subjects know the game is finite.[13] Although we do not

---

11. Given the extent of market failure present in CPR dilemmas, this conclusion should come as no surprise to economists.

12. Interestingly enough, this criticism does not apply with the same force to cooperative versions of the baseline game.

13. During recruitment, subjects are told they will participate in a one-to-two-hour decision-making experiment. Although the exact endpoint is not revealed, it is explicitly bounded

have complete control over our subjects' understanding of their decision task, the information we make available fulfills the requirements for complete information. We try to ensure complete information on the part of our subjects by reporting results from experiments using only subjects experienced in the baseline game. Given our instruction and question-and-answer phases, we are confident that subjects actually understand the laboratory situations they face. In the unfortunate event that they do not, then there is a bewildering multiplicity of game equilibria from which to select, one of which remains the subgame perfect equilibrium (Kreps et al. 1982).

Experimental Design

In our experimental investigation, we have operationalized this CPR situation with eight appropriators ($n = 8$) and quadratic production functions $F(\Sigma x_i)$, where:

$$F(\Sigma x_i) = a\Sigma x_i - b(\Sigma x_i)^2$$

with $F'(0) = a > w$ and $F'(ne) = a - 2bne < 0$. (5.5)

For this quadratic specification, one has from (5.4) that the group optimal investment satisfies $\Sigma x_i = (a - w)/2b$. The CPR yields 0 percent on net when investment is twice as large as optimal, $\Sigma x_i = (a - w)/b$. Finally, from (5.2), the symmetric Nash equilibrium group investment is given by:

$$\Sigma x_i = (n/(n + 1))(a - w)/b.$$ (5.6)

This level of investment is between maximal net yield and zero net yield, approaching the latter as n gets large. One additional constraint that arises in a laboratory setting is that the x_i be integer valued. This is accomplished by choosing the parameters a, b, n, and w in such a way that the predictions associated with Σx_i are all integer valued.

In particular, we focus on experiments utilizing the parameters shown in table 5.1. These parameters lead to the predictions portrayed in figure 5.2. A group investment of 36 tokens yields the optimal level of investment. This symmetric game has a unique symmetric equilibrium with each subject investing 8 tokens in Market 2.

---

above. Further, all subjects are experienced and have thus experienced the boundedness of an experiment that lasted between 10 and 30 rounds. In more recent experiments (Hackett, Schlager, and Walker 1993), the end point is public information. The behavior in these experiments closely parallels the behavior in experiments reported in this chapter.

TABLE 5.1. **Parameters for a Given Decision Round, Experimental Design Baseline**

	Type of Experiment	
	Low Endowment	High Endowment
Number of subjects	8	8
Individual token endowment	10	25
Production function[a]	$23(\Sigma x_i) - .25(\Sigma x_i)^2$	$23(\Sigma x_i) - .25(\Sigma x_i)^2$
Market 2 return/unit of output	$.01	$.01
Market 1 return/unit of output	$.05	$.05
Earnings/subject at group maximum[b]	$.91	$.83
Earnings/subject at Nash equilibrium	$.66	$.70
Earnings/subject at zero rent	$.50	$.63

[a]The production function shows the number of units of output produced in Market 2 for each level of tokens invested in Market 2. Σx_i equals the total number of tokens invested by the group in Market 2.

[b]Amounts shown are potential cash payoffs. In the high-endowment design, subjects were paid in cash one-half of their computer earnings.

Much of our discussion of experimental results will focus on what we term *maximum net yield* from the CPR. This measure captures the degree of optimal yield earned from the CPR. Specifically, net yield is the return from Market 2 minus the opportunity costs of tokens invested in Market 2, divided by the return from Market 2 at the investment level where marginal revenue equals marginal cost minus the opportunity costs of tokens invested in Market 2.[14] In our decision situation, opportunity costs equal the potential return that could have been earned by investing the tokens in Market 1. Note that for a given level of investment in the CPR, net yield is invariant with respect to the level of subjects' endowments.[15] Recall that even though the range for subject investment decisions is increased with an increase in subjects' endowments, the equilibrium and optimal levels of investment are not altered. At the Nash equilibrium, subjects earn approximately 39 percent of maximum net yield from the CPR.

Experimental Results

The baseline results from six experiments (three with 10-token endowments [experiments 1–3] and three with 25-token endowments [experiments 4–6])

---

14. In economics, this is the classical concept of rent.

15. An alternative measurement of performance would be to calculate overall experimental efficiency (actual earnings as a percentage of maximum possible earnings for the group). In our specific decision situation, this measurement has the undesirable property that it depends on subjects' token endowments. Our use of net yield, by avoiding endowment effects, gives a more accurate measure of the effect of behavior on CPR performance, our primary interest.

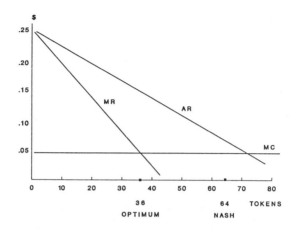

Fig. 5.2. Theoretical predictions (MR = marginal revenue, AR = average revenue, MC = marginal cost)

are summarized in table 5.2 and figure 5.3.[16] Appendix 5.3 contains round-by-round Market 2 investment decisions for all six baseline experiments. Table 5.2 displays information regarding net yield actually earned by subject groups. The most striking observation comes from increasing token endowments from 10 to 25. Aggregating across all experimental decision rounds, the average level of yields accrued in the low-endowment (10-token) design equalled 37 percent. In contrast, the average level for the high-endowment (25-token) design equalled −3 percent. From table 5.2, we see that it is in the early experimental rounds that the high-endowment treatment has its primary impact. In early rounds, a significant number of subjects make high investments in Market 2 leading to net payoffs that are as low as 382 percent below optimum. As the experiment progresses, the degree of suboptimality approaches that found in the low-endowment condition. The average tendencies for the first 20 decision rounds of the six experiments are presented in figure 5.4.

Several characteristics of the individual experiments are important. Investments in Market 2 are characterized by a "pulsing" pattern in which investments are increased leading to a reduction in yield, at which time

---

16. For clarity, the experiments in chapters 5–8 are numbered consecutively. Appendix 5.2 displays the book number for each experiment and the corresponding actual experiment number from our set of over one hundred experiments conducted in this research program.

TABLE 5.2. Average Net Yield as a Percentage of Maximum in Baseline Designs

Experimental Design	Round					
	1–5	6–10	11–15	16–20	21–25	26+
10-token (experiments 1–3)	52	35	34	36	37	30
25-token (experiments 4–6)	−43	−12	10	32	—	—

investors tend to reduce their investments in Market 2 and yields increase. This pattern tends to recur across decision rounds within an experiment. We did not find, however, symmetry across experiments in the amplitude or timing of peaks. For the high-endowment experiments, the low points in the pulsing pattern were at yields far below 0. Over the course of the experiments, there was some tendency for the variance in yields to decrease. We saw no clear signs that the experiments were stabilizing. Further, we observed no experiments in which the pattern of *individual* investments in Market 2 stabilized at the one-shot Nash equilibrium.[17] This failure of individual data to conform to the Nash equilibrium is a behavioral result that we will see throughout the next four chapters.[18]

To what extent does our data conform to the individual predictions for the equilibrium for this situation? We investigate two broad research questions and several more specific questions.

> Question 1—To what extent do round-by-round observations meet the criteria of 64 tokens allocated to Market 2?
> Question 2—What is the frequency of rounds in which individual investments of 8 were made?

Below, we present frequency counts across experiments that describe the extent to which individual decisions match those predicted by equation (5.2), namely invest 8 tokens in the CPR. We break down these two broad questions into components. The numbers in parentheses following each component question are the percentage of observations consistent with each question in 10-token (respectively, 25-token) experiments.

> Question 1—To what extent do round-by-round observations meet the criteria of 64 tokens allocated to Market 2?

17. Since the unique subgame perfect equilibrium is a sequence of one-shot equilibria, this implies that behavior did not stabilize at the subgame perfect equilibrium either.

18. We have observed disequilibrium at the individual level in every one of the more than one hundred experiments reported in this book.

Average Net Yield as a Percentage of Maximum

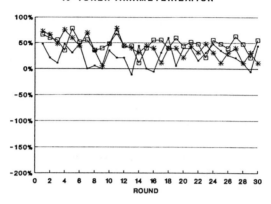

10-TOKEN PARAMETERIZATION

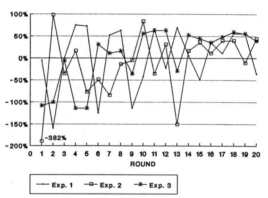

25-TOKEN PARAMETERIZATION

Exp. 1   Exp. 2   Exp. 3

Fig. 5.3. Individual baseline experiments

(a) the number of rounds in which 64 tokens were allocated in Market 2 (11 percent, 5 percent).

(b) if 64 tokens were contributed to Market 2, the number of rounds in which all subjects invested 8 (0 percent, 0 percent).

Question 2—What is the frequency of rounds in which investments of 8 were made?

(a) rounds in which all investments were 8 (0 percent, 0 percent).

(b) rounds in which all but 1 investment was 8 (0 percent, 0 percent).

Average Net Yield as a Percentage of Maximum
Means of Individual Experiments

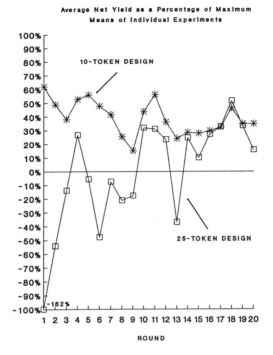

Fig. 5.4. The effect of increasing investment endowment

(c) rounds in which all but 2 investments were 8 (0 percent, 0 percent).

(d) rounds in which all but 3 investments were 8 (0 percent, 0 percent).

(e) rounds in which all but 4 investments were 8 (1 percent, 0 percent).

(f) rounds in which all but 5 investments were 8 (6 percent, 2 percent).

(g) rounds in which all but 6 investments were 8 (23 percent, 7 percent).

(h) rounds in which all but 7 investments were 8 (37 percent, 37 percent).

(i) rounds in which no investments of 8 were made (32 percent, 48 percent).

In summary, the data provide very little support for the research hypothesis that our investment environment will stabilize at the one-shot Nash equilibrium. Out of 90 investment rounds in the 10-token design, we find only 10 in which aggregate investment in Market 2 equals 64. In none of those 10 cases did we find a pattern of 8 tokens invested by each subject. Further, in all 90 investment rounds we find 4 or fewer of the 8 subjects investing the Nash equilibrium prediction of 8 tokens. In the 25-token design, we find even less support for the Nash prediction at the individual level. Of 60 investment rounds, we find only 3 in which Market 2 investment equals 64. In none of these 3 cases did all 8 investors invest 8 tokens. Further, aggregating across all 60 rounds, we find 5 or fewer individuals investing the Nash prediction of 8 tokens.

Turning to tables 5.3 and 5.4, we focus on individual strategies across rounds. Of the 24 subjects in the three 10-token experiments (table 5.3), no subject always played the strategy of investing 8 tokens in Market 2. Further, we found no subject consistently playing within one token of the Nash prediction (playing 9, 8, or 7). What happens if we analyze only the last 5 rounds of these 30-round experiments? In these final rounds, we find three subjects consistently playing within the one-token band around the Nash prediction. We also find 19 of 24 playing in the broader range of 6 to 10 tokens invested in Market 2. However, consistent with our previous designs, we find a strong pattern of players investing all 10 tokens in Market 2. In fact, in the final 5 rounds, 6 of the 24 players always invest 10 tokens. Table 5.4 provides similar information on individual behavior for our 25-token design. Similar to the 10-token design, we find very little support for the Nash prediction at the individual level. Further, our 25-token design clearly removes the allocation constraint we found in our 10-token design. No player always invested 25 tokens.

Conclusions

We can now address the first basic question posed in chapter 1: in finitely repeated CPR dilemmas, to what degree are the predictions about behavior and outcomes derived from noncooperative game theory for finitely repeated,

TABLE 5.3. Investment Patterns of Individuals, 10-Token Design

	Number of Individuals Always Investing						
	10	7–9	5–6	3–4	0–2	6–10	0–5
All rounds	3	0	0	0	0	9	0
Rounds 1–5	4	1	0	0	0	13	1
Rounds 26–30	6	3	1	0	0	19	1

TABLE 5.4. **Investment Patterns of Individuals, 25-Token Design**

	Number of Individuals Always Investing									
	25	7–9	5–6	3–4	0–2	21–25	16–20	11–15	6–10	0–5
All rounds	0	0	0	0	0	0	0	0	1	0
Rounds 1–5	0	1	0	0	0	0	0	0	1	1
Rounds 26–30	0	1	0	0	1	0	0	4	3	6

complete information games supported by empirical evidence? Using experimental methods to control for subject incentives and to induce a set of institutional arrangements that capture the strategic essence of the appropriation dilemma, the results from this chapter strongly support the hypothesis of suboptimal appropriation. At the aggregate level, results initially appear to approximate a Nash equilibrium in a limited access CPR. But, instead of a pattern that settles down at the predicted equilibrium, we observe a general pattern across experiments where net yield decays toward 0 then rebounds as subjects reduce the level of investment in the common-pool resource. Investigating across two parameterizations, we find that at the aggregate level, our results lend strong support to the aggregate Nash equilibrium prediction for the low-endowment setting. In the high-endowment setting, however, aggregate behavior is far from Nash in early rounds but begins to approach Nash in later rounds. At the individual decision level, however, we do not find behavior consistent with the Nash prediction.

Several factors may contribute to the disequilibrium results we observe in these experiments. First and foremost is the computational complexity of the task. The payoff functions are nonlinear and nondifferentiable, making them difficult for our subjects to process. Indeed, in postexperiment questionnaires we administered, we found that many subjects were using the rule of thumb "Invest more in Market 2 whenever the rate of return is above $.05 per token." Then, when the rate of return fell below $.05, they reduced investments in Market 2, giving rise to the pulsing cycle in returns we observe across numerous experiments. A related factor is the focal point effect of investing 10 tokens in Market 2 (for our 10-token design), which is indeed the modal strategic response. Here, the rule of thumb seems to be "Invest *all* tokens in Market 2 whenever the rate of return there is above $.05 per token in previous decision rounds." This behavior is clearly inconsistent with full information, best-response behavior in these experiments. Finally, the fact that equilibrium is never reached at the individual level means that each player is continually having to revise his or her response to the current "anticipated" situation. This strategic turbulence on top of an already complex task increases the chances that a player may not attempt a best-response approach to the task but rather invoke simple rules of thumb of the type reported above. In current work, Dudley (1993) has formally investigated the extent to which subjects appear to follow a reaction function consistent with Nash-type behavior.

The consistency with which we find deviations from Nash equilibrium is an important unanswered question posed by these results. It is a complex issue for experimental research in general. We know that for many institutional settings the Nash prediction can be quite robust. For example, in some of the public-goods provision situations discussed in the appendix to this chapter, there is considerable support for findings consistent with Nash. (Also see Cox, Smith, and Walker 1988 for the case of single-unit, sealed-bid auctions.) Even in this research, however, institutional changes, such as a change to multiple-unit auctions, can lead to subject behavior that is no longer consistent with a Nash model based on expected utility maximization (see Cox, Smith, and Walker 1984). Again, in duopoly experiments, Nash predictions for one-shot games are often borne out (Keser 1992 and the literature cited therein), although again predictive power seems to diminish with the number of players.

In the next four chapters, we extend the physical and institutional setting for our baseline game. In the next chapter, we explore the possibility of destruction of the CPR—a major concern in many naturally occurring CPR environments. One might hope that players would take the threat of the destruction of their resource seriously and would act accordingly—by reducing their investment pressure on it. In chapters 7–9, we explore the effect of communication and sanctioning institutions on these environments, while retaining noncooperative strategic interactions. We are interested in the possibility that, even without the ability to implement binding contracts, having a richer institutional environment leads to improved CPR performance.

APPENDIX 5.1. CPR PROVISION PROBLEMS

As discussed in chapter 1, provision and maintenance problems are linked conceptually to the general problem of public-goods provision. In situations where there must be an initial provision of the CPR, in the maintenance of a resource, or in altering appropriation behavior to affect the productive nature of a resource, users provide a public good (positive externality) to other appropriators.

To conduct an extensive examination of the experimental literature related to public-goods provision, however, is beyond the scope of this book. Even a cursory look forces one to realize this literature is broad and, as one might expect, the particular institutional design of a given experimental study is extremely important in understanding observed behavior. That is, the experimental literature points directly to the importance one must place on the institutional environment in which subjects carry out their decisions. In this brief summary, we summarize a few examples that illustrate the importance of institutions, while giving an overview of the type of behavior observed in public-goods provision experiments.

One useful method for organizing public-goods experiments is to partition experiments along two treatment variables: (1) situations in which the Nash equilibrium yields no provision of the public good and those in which the Nash equilibrium (equilibria) imply some positive (but possibly suboptimal) level and (2) simple voluntary provision versus contribution mechanisms based on more complex contribution facilitating mechanisms.

Zero Provision Environments and a Simple Contribution Mechanism

Consider the public-goods environment investigated by Marwell and Ames (1979, 1980, 1981) and by Isaac, Walker, and their colleagues (Isaac, Walker, and Thomas 1984; Isaac and Walker 1988a, 1988b, 1991). In this research, subjects are placed in an iterated game in which they must independently make an allocation of resources (tokens) between two types of goods. The first good (the private good) yields a fixed and known return per token to the subject making the allocation. The second good (the group good) yields a fixed and known return per token to the subject making the allocation, and to all other members of the group. This latter characteristic makes the group good a public good. Individual j receives value from the group good regardless of his or her decision to allocate tokens to the group good. We will refer to this simple decision situation as the voluntary contribution mechanism (VCM).

Isaac and Walker (1988b) investigate the simple case where the payoff function for the group good is continuous and the marginal value of a token placed in the group good is constant. For example, for one parameterization with group size equal to four, each subject receives a return of $.01 for each token allocated to the private account. The group account pays, however, $.003 per token to each member of the group for each token allocated by any member into the group account. The social dilemma is clear. In a one-shot game, the dominant strategy is for each subject to place all tokens into the private account (no provision of the public good). In a finitely repeated game, this is the unique complete information Nash equilibrium. The *group optimum* occurs, however, if each subject places all tokens into the group account.

Isaac and Walker examine behavior in a finitely repeated game where the end point is explicitly stated. A principal focus of their research is examining the impact of varying group size given the standard conjecture that larger groups have a more difficult task in providing public goods. A natural question is: Why should free riding increase in severity as the group size is increased? A logical response is that as the size of the group increases, the marginal return to each individual of another unit of the group good declines (due to crowding). Alternatively, public goods provided in large group settings may be characterized naturally by "small" marginal returns. These are both explanations that depend on a smaller marginal benefit from the public good with increases in group size. Is there, however, a "pure numbers" effect that influences the efficiency of public-goods provision? Defining the marginal return from the group good relative to the private good as the marginal per capita return (MPCR), Isaac and Walker investigate this question for MPCR values of $.003/$.01 $=$ .30 and $.0075/$.01 $=$ .75.

In a framework where the marginal payoff from the group good is constant (the aggregate payoff from the group good increases linearly), Isaac and Walker examine a pure numbers effect by varying the group payoff function so that the MPCR remains constant as N increases from 4 to 10. Alternatively, their design allows for the examination of group size effects based on crowding or an inherently small MPCR by allowing the MPCR to vary with group size. The findings can be summarized along three lines.

1. They observed greater provision of the group (public) good than predicted by the complete information noncooperative Nash model. Under some parametric conditions, provision reached over 50 percent of optimum, while in others, the rate of provision was less than 10 percent.
2. Provision declined with iteration of the game, but did not reach the predicted equilibrium.
3. A higher MPCR led systematically to less free riding and thus greater efficiency in the provision of the public good. No statistical support was found for a pure numbers effect. In fact, to the extent that there was any qualitative difference in the data, it was in the direction of the groups of size 10 providing larger levels of the public good than the groups of size 4. These results can be interpreted, however, as support for a crowding effect; larger groups exhibited more free riding if increases in group size generated a smaller MPCR.

The robustness of the Isaac and Walker results have been examined in depth in their work with Arlington Williams. Isaac, Walker, and Williams (1993) develop an alternative experimental methodology to circumvent the physical laboratory and budget constraints that make large group experiments generally infeasible. They use this methodology to examine the VCM environment with group sizes ranging in size from $N = 4$ to $N = 100$. The experiments presented employ two important procedural modifications relative to the research by Isaac and Walker: (1) decision-making rounds last several days rather than a few minutes and (2) rewards are based on extra-credit points rather than cash. These new experiments reported by Isaac, Walker, and Williams (and substantiated with further experimentation using cash rewards) led to several interesting findings. The results of initial extra-credit, multiple-session baseline experiments with groups of size 4 and 10 were consistent with the (cash, single-session) experimental results reported by Isaac and Walker. But Isaac, Walker, and Williams's experiments with groups of size 40 and 100 (using either extra-credit or cash rewards) led to several surprising results.

First, the impact from variations in the magnitude of the marginal per capita return from the public good (MPCR) appeared to vanish over the range (0.30, 0.75). Second, with an MPCR of .30, groups of size 40 and 100 provided the public good at higher levels of efficiency than groups of size 4 and 10. Third, with an MPCR of .75, there was no significant difference in efficiency due to group size. Further, experiments with $N = 40$ and a very low MPCR of .03 yielded the low efficiency levels previously observed with small groups and an MPCR of .30. The existence of an MPCR effect was thus reconfirmed for large groups. This research reveals that behavior in the VCM decision environment is influenced by a subtle interaction between group size and the value of the group good rather than simply the sheer magnitude of either. Experiments using both additional payoff information, more experienced subjects, and as many as 60 decision rounds provided further evidence that the public-good provision levels reported by Isaac and Walker and Isaac, Walker, and Williams could not be explained by simple conjectures of learning or insufficient iterations of the game.

Discrete Public Goods and VCM

The work described above sets the stage for an investigation of behavior in alternative experimental environments in which free riding is not a simple strategy of zero contributions to the public good. One direct way of changing the decision environment is to investigate the provision of public goods that are discrete (provision point or step function public goods; see chap. 3, fig. 3.5). Such experimental situations have naturally occurring counterparts in action situations in which a minimum level of provision support is necessary for productive services (a bridge for example).

For illustrative purposes, consider the design described above with an MPCR = .30 and $N = 4$. Isaac, Schmidtz, and Walker (1989) examined this environment, but with the following change. If allocations to the group account did not meet a specified minimum threshold, there was no provision of the public good and all allocations were lost (had a zero value). Isaac, Schmidtz, and Walker examined several designs in which they varied the minimum threshold. This type of decision situation created the "assurance problem" discussed in chapter 3. Zero contributions to the group good is no longer a dominant strategy nor the unique Nash strategy. Players have an incentive to contribute to the public good if they have some expectation (an assurance) that others will contribute. On the other hand, if others will provide the public good, the individual has an incentive to free ride on their contributions.

In a decision situation that combined the VCM mechanism with a provision point structure, Isaac, Schmidtz, and Walker found (1) in designs with provision points that require relatively low levels of contributions, numerous experimental groups were able, in early decision rounds, to overcome the assurance problem and provide the public good; (2) in experiments with higher provision points and in later decision rounds of most experiments, free-riding behavior tended to increase with resulting low levels of efficiency. These results are similar to results from a closely related provision point environment discussed by van de Kragt, Orbell, and Dawes 1983. In this study (where subjects made a binary decision to contribute or not to contribute to a group good), groups met the provision point in less than 35 percent of the decision trials.

**Discrete Public Goods and Alternative
Contribution Mechanisms**

In anticipation that the specific rules of the contribution mechanism might significantly affect decision behavior, several studies have examined the provision point decision environment using an alternative contribution mechanism. For example, Dawes, Orbell, and van de Kragt 1984, Isaac, Schmidtz, and Walker 1989, and Bagnoli and McKee 1991 investigate several versions of what is commonly referred to as the "payback" mechanism. (See Palfrey and Rosenthal 1984 for a discussion of the strategic equilibria in provision point games with and without the payback mechanism.)

Specifically, contributions are made toward the provision of the public good. If the contributions do not meet the specified minimum, all contributions are returned to players making the contributions. As one might expect, this simple change can significantly affect decision incentives and observed behavior. Certainly the risks involved in making contributions are reduced. On the other hand, there is still an incentive to free ride if others will provide the public good.

The three studies cited above examine the payback mechanism in provision point environments that differ in several respects. However, even with the specific differences, the variation in findings is quite interesting. In one-shot decisions (with no value for contributions above the provision point and binary decisions to contribute or not to contribute), Dawes, Orbell, and van de Kragt (1984) found no significant effects on levels of contributions when comparing provision point experiments with and without the payback mechanism. On the other hand (in a decision environment in which contributions above the provision point have a positive value and subjects make nonbinary choices), Isaac, Schmidtz, and Walker found using the payback mechanism substantially increased efficiency in environments with higher provision points and to a lesser extent in the low provision point environment. They still observed significant problems in low and medium provision point environments (especially later decision periods) due to what they refer to as "cheap" riding. Significant numbers of subjects attempted to provide a smaller share of the public good than their counterparts, in some cases leading to a failure to meet the provision point. Finally (in a decision environment in which contributions above the provision point have no value and subjects make nonbinary decisions), Bagnoli and McKee (1991) found very strong results regarding the cooperative facilitating features of the payback institution. In their experiments, the public good was provided in 85 of 98 possible cases. Further, there was very little loss in efficiency due to overinvestments.[19]

Appendix 5.2.
Experimental Numbers

Experiment Number in Book	Actual Experiment Number
1	31
2	36
3	38
4	35
5	39
6	40

(*continued*)

---

19. For the reader interested in more detail, a sampling of other studies related to public goods provision includes Andreoni 1988; Brookshire, Coursey, and Redington 1989; Dorsey 1992; Isaac, McCue, and Plott 1985; Kim and Walker 1984; J. Miller and Andreoni 1991; Palfrey and Rosenthal 1992; and Sell and Wilson 1991; Ledyard 1993.

Experiment Number in Book	Actual Experiment Number
7	42
8	46
9	47
10	54
11	55
12	63
13	64
14	66
15	67
16	73
17	74
18	76
19	103
20	104
21	107
22	18
23	20
24	24
25	25
26	58
27	115
28	118
29	119
30	121
31	123
32	10
33	11
34	17
35	26
36	27
37	28
38	52
39	53
40	56
41	77
42	78
43	79
44	83
45	84
46	92
47	93
48	94
49	134
50	137

(*continued*)

Experiment Number in Book	Actual Experiment Number
51	138
52	57
53	80
54	85
55	86
56	95
57	96

APPENDIX 5.3. Market 2 Group Investment Decisions

	10-Token Parameterization			25-Token Parameterization		
Round	1	2	3	4	5	6
1	62	57	55	73	115	88
2	68	59	57	94	42	87
3	70	60	62	72	78	73
4	62	65	54	54	69	74
5	66	53	59	55	84	74
6	62	61	63	90	80	66
7	72	60	56	61	85	70
8	71	65	65	58	92	69
9	72	64	71	74	73	78
10	65	62	62	79	51	60
11	68	56	53	57	78	58
12	68	63	63	76	66	58
13	74	63	64	56	93	77
14	63	70	66	71	69	61
15	72	64	63	80	65	63
16	73	60	64	65	70	65
17	66	60	70	70	64	62
18	59	64	64	60	64	59
19	71	59	64	60	74	60
20	64	63	68	78	63	64
21	64	61	63			
22	69	62	66			
23	66	68	62			
24	62	60	66			
25	65	62	70			
26	67	64	66			
27	68	58	64			
28	70	62	70			
29	73	68	66			
30	63	60	70			

CHAPTER 6

Probabilistic Destruction of the CPR

Although the dissipation of net yield in a CPR is a serious economic problem, even more urgent is the problem of the destruction of the resource. As discussed in chapter 1, many CPRs are fragile, and human exploitation can lead to destruction. The fishery resources we describe in chapter 11, the forest resources in chapter 12, and the groundwater basins in chapter 13, are all CPRs that are potentially subject to destruction through overappropriation. A more subtle example is the geothermal CPR discussed in chapter 1. The Geysers in northern California have been exploited since 1960. Although grave uncertainties surround the underground structure of this resource, it is known to be fed by groundwater. Due to expansion of electrical generating capacity, the safe yield of steam has been exceeded. The Geysers are rapidly drying up, and are almost certain to be destroyed by the end of the century (Kerr 1991). Similar considerations apply to global commons, such as the buildup of carbon dioxide in the earth's atmosphere. Trace levels of this gas do not affect life on earth. Current models of the atmosphere leave a wide zone of uncertainty as to what happens when carbon dioxide builds up in the atmosphere (Reilly et al. 1987). At some level, as on the planet Venus, the carbon dioxide concentration destroys the biosphere.[1]

A range of *safe yields* underlies each of these classes of CPRs. A natural regeneration process is present that implies a range of exploitation in which the probability of destruction is 0. When the safe yield is surpassed, the resource faces probabilistic destruction. Indeed, at high enough levels of economic activity, the resource is destroyed with certainty. The key question is the tradeoff between jeopardizing the life of the resource and earning income from it. It is the behavioral response of highly motivated decision makers to this dilemma that we focus on in this chapter. The experimental research discussed in chapter 5 concentrated on the investigation of stationary (time-independent) appropriation problems in limited access CPR environments. This chapter extends our earlier work by introducing a significant

---

1. This chapter relies extensively on J. Walker and Gardner 1992.

nonstationarity, the possibility of resource destruction, into the decision framework. Our previous results demonstrated the significance of the appropriation problem in the context of a repeated choice noncooperative decision environment. Here we investigate the behavioral question of whether the possibility of destruction will significantly alter appropriation behavior in the resulting game. Our experimental design focuses on two treatments, depending upon whether the safe zone (the range of appropriation where the probability of destruction is 0) consists of a single point or an interval. Our primary results are that (1) if the safe zone is the single point of no appropriation, the resource is rapidly destroyed in accordance with subgame perfect equilibrium; (2) if the safe zone is an interval, then group behavior in some instances tends to focus on the best available equilibrium, but in general this equilibrium cannot be sustained and the resource is destroyed. These results show how valuable agreement among appropriators of a CPR can be, not only in maximizing net yield but also in saving the CPR from destruction.

This chapter is organized as follows. The next section describes the model of the one-period CPR and the repeated game when probabilistic destruction is a treatment variable. The next two sections describe our experimental design and report our experimental results. The final section offers a conclusion and open questions for further research.

Model of a Destructible CPR

The CPR Constituent Game

The constituent CPR games from which we have drawn our designs is that of the baseline experiments presented in chapter 5. There are a fixed number n of appropriators with access to the CPR. Each appropriator i has an endowment of resources e that can be invested in the CPR or invested in a safe, outside activity. The payoff to an individual appropriator from investing in the CPR depends on aggregate group investment in the CPR, and on the appropriator investment as a percentage of the aggregate. The marginal payoff of the outside activity is w. Let x_i denote appropriator i's investment in the CPR, where $0 \leq x_i \leq e$. The group return to investment in the CPR is given by the production function $F(\Sigma x_i)$, where F is a concave function, with $F(0) = 0$, $F'(0) > w$, and $F'(ne) < 0$.

Finite Deterministic Repetition of the Constituent Game

Consider a game X that will be played more than once. We refer to the game X as the constituent game. Now consider the constituent game X played a finite number of times T. Let t index the number of periods left before play ends, $t = 1, \ldots, T$. Let $x_t = (x_{1t}, \ldots, x_{nt})$ be a vector of individual decisions at time t. Each player is assumed to choose a level of appropriation in time t that depends on the return at time t and possible returns from the CPR in future periods. Thus, an optimal return function can be defined recursively for player i, f_{it}, as:

$$f_{it}(x_t) = \max_{x_{it}} u_{it}(x_t) + f_{i,t-1}(x_{t-1}) \tag{6.1}$$

where u_{it} is the contemporaneous return function for player i at time t as in (6.1), $f_{i,t-1}$ is the optimal return function for the next period, and $f_{i0} = 0$. The solution to (6.1) for all players i and all times t is a subgame perfect equilibrium of X finitely repeated. If X has a unique symmetric equilibrium, then finitely repeated X has a unique symmetric subgame perfect equilibrium (Selten 1971). Thus (6.1) has a solution given by the solution of (5.2) in each period t.

Probabilistic Repetition of the Constituent Game

Our model of probabilistic destruction of the CPR is a one-period hazard rate depending upon the current period's decisions. That is, appropriation in the current period directly affects only the likelihood of destruction in the next period. Formally, the decision environment is a finitely repeated game, where $p_t(x_t)$ represents the probability of continuing the game past period t. The probability of continuing, $p_t(x_t)$, is endogenously determined by appropriation decisions in time t. Define LUB as the lowest upper bound on exploitation with probability 1 destruction and GLB as the greatest lower bound with probability 0 destruction. We specify the *continuation* probability as follows:

$$p_t(x_t) = \begin{cases} 0 & \text{if } \Sigma x_{it} \geq \text{LUB} \\ p(\Sigma x_{it}) & \text{if GLB} < \Sigma x_{it} < \text{LUB} \\ 1 & \text{if } \Sigma x_{it} \leq \text{GLB.} \end{cases} \tag{6.2}$$

In the event $p_t(x_t) = 0$, the resource has been destroyed and play ends. The probability of destruction depends on aggregate exploitation through Σx_{it}, with $p_t(x_t)$ a nonnegative decreasing function of its argument. One has $0 \leq$

GLB < LUB. GLB represents the limit on safe exploitation and the interval [0,GLB] the safe zone.[2]

In the presence of probabilistic continuation, the optimal return function is amended to:

$$f_{it}(x_t) = \max_{x_{it}} u_{it}(x_t) + p_t(x_t)f_{i,t-1}(x_{t-1}). \tag{6.3}$$

Thus, each player's choice of a level of appropriation in time t affects the return at time t and probabilistically affects the possibility of earning ret·ᴜs from the CPR in future periods. Since utility is linear, specification (6.3) implies risk neutrality on the part of all players. As before, a solution to the recursive equation (6.3) is a subgame perfect equilibrium. It is important to note that even if the constituent game has a unique Nash equilibrium, (6.3) may have multiple solutions.

The Experimental Design

All subjects in these destruction experiments had participated previously in an experiment using the constituent game environment with no destruction (the baseline game of chap. 5). Subjects were recruited randomly from this pool of experienced subjects. We operationalized this CPR environment with eight appropriators (n = 8) and the same parameters as the 25-token baseline design of chapter 5.

Destruction Design I

In Design I destruction experiments, the decision of the constituent game is amended in the following manner:[3]

> The subjects were notified that the experiment would continue up to 20 rounds. After each decision round a random drawing would occur that would determine if the experiment continued. For every token invested in Market 2 by any participant, the probability of ending the experiment increased by 0.5 percent. For example: if the group invested 50 tokens

---

2. Specification (6.2) is restrictive. It would be more general to make the probability of destruction depend on the entire history of the game. However, we view the ensuing complication, although interesting, as not a best starting point for our exploration.

3. The experimenter reviewed the announcement with the subjects and answered questions. Note that in the destruction experiments, subjects were told explicitly that the experiments would last up to 20 periods. This information in the destruction experiments makes the optimization task tractable.

total in Market 2, the probability of ending the experiment was 25 percent. The drawing at the end of each round worked as follows: a single card was drawn randomly from a deck of 100 cards numbered from 1 to 100. If the number on the card was equal to or below the probability of ending the experiment for that round (as determined by the group investment in that round) the experiment ended. Otherwise, the experiment continued to the next round.

Thus, the parameterization was GLB = 0, LUB = 200, and the probability of continuation (6.4) was

$$p_t(x_t) = 1 - (\Sigma x_{it}/200). \tag{6.4}$$

The safe zone consisted of a single point, zero exploitation. The optimal solution can be found by solving (6.3) with a single player in control of all resources. Similarly, the subgame perfect equilibrium can be found by solving (6.3) and exploiting symmetry.

We turn first to the maximization problem. Since achieving a maximum requires coordination among players, assume the existence of a rational agent who invests the entire group's tokens each period. Denote by Σx_{it} the amount of the group's tokens invested in the resource, when there are t periods remaining: $0 \le \Sigma x_{it} \le 200$ in our design. We solve the optimization problem of 6.3 using a dynamic programming argument assuming risk neutrality. This requires solving the optimal value function, $f_t(\Sigma x_{it})$ for each time remaining t, $t = 1, 2, \ldots , 20$ in our design.

Recall the payoff and endowment parameters for the experimental setting: (1) eight subjects, (2) endowments of 25 tokens per subject for a total endowment of 200 tokens, (3) a Market 1 return of $.05 per token, and (4) a Market 2 (the CPR) production function of $23\Sigma x_{it} - .25(\Sigma x_{it})^2$, where each unit appropriated is valued at $.01. We begin the solution with the last period remaining. From equation 6.3, $f_1(\Sigma x_{i1})$ is measured in cents and given by:

$$f_1(\Sigma x_{i1}) = \max_{\Sigma x_{i1}} 5(200 - \Sigma x_{i1}) + 23\Sigma x_{i1} - .25(\Sigma x_{i1})^2 \tag{6.5}$$

where the first term on the right represents the payoff from the risk-free Market 1 and the remaining terms represent the return from the destructible resource. A routine calculation shows that the maximum is achieved at $\Sigma x_{i1} = 36$ (this is just the optimal solution from the stationary case). Substituting in (6.5), one has: $f_1(\Sigma x_{i1}) = 1,324$ cents. Now suppose that the decision maker has two periods to go; we seek $f_2(\Sigma x_{i2})$. Here, the destructibility aspect emerges for the first time. The probability that the resource survives with two periods to go, $p_2(\Sigma x_{i2})$, is given by:

$$p_2(\Sigma x_{i2}) = (200 - \Sigma x_{i2})/200 \tag{6.6}$$

If $\Sigma x_{i2} = 0$, and no tokens are invested in the resource, it will not be destroyed; for $\Sigma x_{i2} > 0$, there is an increasing probability of destruction. Now the two-period optimal return function is:

$$f_2(\Sigma x_{i2}) = \max_{\Sigma x_{i2}} 5(200 - \Sigma x_{i2}) + 23\Sigma x_{i2} - .25(\Sigma x_{i2})^2$$

$$+ p_2(\Sigma x_{i2})f_1(\Sigma x_{i1}) \tag{6.7}$$

where $f_1(\Sigma x_{i1}) = 1,324$.

The reasoning behind (6.7) is that if the resource is destroyed in the next-to-last period, then there is 0 payoff in the last period; otherwise, the resource is exploited optimally with one period to go. The optimal solution to (6.7) is $\Sigma x_{i2} = 23$ and $f_2(\Sigma x_{i2}) = 2,454$ cents. Notice that we observe a significant reduction in investment in the risky resource, from 36 to 23. Even though the decision maker is risk neutral, the value to be gained from not destroying the resource weighs in heavily against exploiting it in the current period. As we shall now see, this consideration becomes even stronger with three or more periods to go.

For the three-periods-to-go-problem, one solves:

$$f_3(\Sigma x_{i3}) = \max_{\Sigma x_{i3}} 5(200 - \Sigma x_{i3}) + 23\Sigma x_{i3} - .25(\Sigma x_{i3})^2$$

$$+ p_3(\Sigma x_{i3})(2,454) \tag{6.8}$$

to find that $\Sigma x_{i3} = 11$ and $f_3(\Sigma x_{i3}) = 3,486$. We are down to only 11 units in the risky investment. By the same reasoning we can show that $\Sigma x_{i4} = 1$ and $f_4(\Sigma x_{i4}) = 4,487$.

We now show that with five or more periods to go, $\Sigma x_{it} = 0$. Not only don't you kill the goose that lays the golden egg, you don't even trim its feathers. To see that $\Sigma x_{i5} = 0$, consider the situation with five periods to go. One has:

$$f_5(\Sigma x_{i5}) = \max_{\Sigma x_{i5}} 5(200 - \Sigma x_{i5}) + 23\Sigma x_{i5} - .25(\Sigma x_{i5})^2$$

$$+ p_5(\Sigma x_{i5})(4,487). \tag{6.9}$$

The optimal solution is $\Sigma x_{i5} = 0$. Indeed, this will be the case for any Σx_{it}, $t \geq$ 5, since f_t is monotonic in t.

We can now calculate the optimal return to be extracted from the destructible resource, in expected value terms. During the first 16 periods, the resource is not exploited at all. Each period, all 200 tokens are invested in Market 1, yielding an aggregate return of $5(200)(16) = 16,000$ cents or $160.00. During the last four periods, investment levels are 1, 11, 23, and 36, respectively, with an expected return of 4,487. The overall expected return is therefore $20,487 = 204.87.

A Nash equilibrium prediction for this environment can be determined using similar reasoning.[4] Let x_{it} denote the investment decision of player i at time t, when there are t periods remaining: $0 \leq x_{it} \leq 25$. Let $x_t = (x_{1t}, \ldots, x_{8t})$ be the vector of individual investments of time t; $u_{it}(x_t)$, player i's one-period return at time t when the group strategy x_t is played; and $f_{it}(x_t)$, the value to player i from being in the game with t periods to play. The optimal return function for player i at time t, $f_{it}(x_t)$, is defined recursively as:

$$f_{it}(x_t) = \max_{x_{it}} u_{it}(x_t) + p_t(x_t)f_{i,t-1}(x_{t-1}), \tag{6.10}$$

where p_t is the probability that the resource survives. In the event that the resource is destroyed, no further value is obtained.

We begin the dynamic programming argument at $t = 1$, the last period. Since this is the last period, the equilibrium condition is that an equilibrium $x_{it}*$ satisfy

$$\frac{\partial u_{i1}(x_1^*)}{\partial x_{i1}} = 0, \text{ for all } i. \tag{6.11}$$

For these designs, equation (6.11) implies $x_{i1}* = 8$, for all i as discussed in chapter 5. Substituting into (6.10), one has $f_{i1}(x_1) = 141$ cents.[5] For the decision step in periods other than the last period, one differentiates the right-hand side of (6.10), for each time period t, to obtain:

$$0 = \frac{\partial u_{it}(x_t^*)}{\partial x_{it}} + f_{i,t-1}(x_{t-1})(-1/200) \tag{6.12}$$

---

4. The equilibrium we describe is symmetric and subgame perfect. It shares the backward induction logic of the optimum. There are other Nash equilibria, however, which are less compelling, due to their imperfection. There are also asymmetric equilibria that cluster around this symmetric equilibrium.

5. For ease of presentation, we will assume in this derivation that tokens are divisible. Working out the recursive equations for the case of indivisible tokens leads to quantitatively the same result, to the accuracy of 1 token invested, or 1 cent in payoff.

TABLE 6.1.   Dynamic Programming Paths, Design I

Periods Remaining	Optimum Path		Subgame Perfect Equilibrium Path	
	Aggregate Investment	Optimal Value Per Capita in Cents	Aggregate Investment	Equilibrium Value Per Capita in Cents
1	36.0	166	64.0	141
2	22.8	307	61.5	243
3	11.5	435	59.7	318
4	01.1	561	58.3	375
5	00.0	686	57.3	419
.	.	.	.	.
.	.	.	.	.
.	.	.	.	.
18	00.0	2,311	53.8	571
19	00.0	2,436	53.8	573
20	00.0	2,561	53.8	574

the last term arising from the effect of the probability of destruction on future earnings.

In table 6.1, we present the solution to (6.12) for the entire life of the resource, given that it lasts at most 20 periods, as well as the optimal solution.[6] Three features of this symmetric subgame perfect path should be noted. In contrast to the optimal path, where only in the last four periods is there a positive probability of destruction, here there is a positive and growing probability of destruction throughout the experiment. At the outset, the one-period destruction probability is approximately 27 percent, and it rises to 32 percent by the end. With one-period destruction probabilities this high, it is unlikely (probability less than .05) that the resource would last 10 periods along this equilibrium path. This increased probability of destruction accounts for the lower overall value of the resource to investors, slightly less than $6 each, or $46 aggregate (8x(574) cents), as opposed to over two hundred dollars at the optimum. Finally, individual value stabilizes at 574 for infinitely long experiments. Thus, 20 periods is long enough to approximate steady state equilibrium behavior.

Destruction Design II

Our Design I is unforgiving in the sense that any investment in the CPR leads to a positive probability of destruction. Our second design adds a safe zone for Market 2 investment in order to investigate whether subjects might focus on a

---

6. For periods 6–17, all values change monotonically except for optimal investment, which remains at 0.

clear-cut, safe investment opportunity. The announcement to subjects for Design II is summarized as follows.

> The subjects were notified that the experiment would continue up to 20 rounds. After each decision round a random drawing would occur that would determine if the experiment continued. If the group invested 40 tokens or less in Market 2, the experiment automatically proceeded to the next round. If the group invested more than 40 tokens in Market 2, the probability of ending the experiment increased by 0.5 percent for each token invested in Market 2 by any participant. For example: if the group invested *50* tokens total in Market 2, the probability of ending the experiment was *25 percent*. The drawing at the end of each round worked as follows: a single card was drawn randomly from a deck of 100 cards numbered from 1 to 100. If the number on the card was equal to or below the probability of ending the experiment for that round (as determined by the group investment in that round) the experiment ended. Otherwise, the experiment continued to the next round.

Thus, the parameterization was GLB = 40, LUB = 200, and the probability of continuation was given by (6.6) on the open interval (40,200). Design II gives subjects a large safe zone [0,40] in which to exploit the resource.[7] Since the safe zone includes the one-period optimal solution, a coordinating rational agent would play 36 tokens each period to maximize rents.

Subgame perfect Nash equilibria can be found by applying dynamic programming to (6.5). First, note that the Nash equilibrium path described for Design I remains an equilibrium path for Design II, since this path never enters the safe zone. There is, however, another equilibrium path in Design II that is better in payoff space. On this equilibrium path, each player invests 8 tokens in Market 2 (an aggregate of 64 tokens—the Nash equilibrium prediction for the constituent game with no probabilistic destruction) that yields each player a payoff of 141 cents. Now consider $f_{i2}(x_2)$, the payoff function for player i in the next-to-last period. Suppose all seven players, except player i, are investing a total of 35 tokens (their symmetric share of the safe aggregate investment of 40 tokens). If i invests 5 tokens, then they get a sure payoff of $u_{i2}(5) + 141$, leading to an overall two-period expected value of 306 cents. There is no threat of destruction in this case. Now suppose instead that player i makes the best response *in the destruction zone* to 35 tokens invested by the

---

TABLE 6.2. Dynamic Programming Paths, Design II

Periods Remaining	Optimum Path		Best Subgame Perfect Equilibrium Path	
	Aggregate Investment	Optimal Value Per Capita in Cents	Aggregate Investment	Equilibrium Value Per Capita in Cents
1	36.0	166	64.0	141
2	36.0	331	61.5	243
3	36.0	496	40.0	408
4	36.0	662	40.0	573
5	36.0	827	40.0	738
.	.	.	.	.
.	.	.	.	.
.	.	.	.	.
18	36.0	2,978	40.0	2,883
19	36.0	3,144	40.0	3,048
20	36.0	3,310	40.0	3,213

others. This turns out to be 17 tokens, leading to a 26 percent chance of destruction and an expected two-period payoff of 314 cents. Thus, with two periods to go, staying in the safe zone is not an equilibrium. Each player following this logic leads to an aggregate Nash investment of 61.5, with expected payoff to each player of 243. Repeating the above calculations for t = 3, the safe investment yields an expected payoff of 408 cents over the last three periods, while the investment of 17 tokens (still the best response in the destruction zone) yields a payoff of only 390 cents. Thus, with three periods remaining, the future value of preserving the resource is sufficient to justify staying in the safe zone as a noncooperative equilibrium. Since expected future value grows with time remaining, once this backward induction path enters the safe zone, it stays there.[8] Indeed, this equilibrium path with an efficiency of 97 percent is nearly as good as the optimum path for Design II. The optimal path and the best subgame perfect equilibrium path are shown in table 6.2. There is a dramatic difference in payoffs between the good equilibrium and the bad one; this environment gives a clear equilibrium focal point for behavior. By investing 40 tokens in every period, the group receives very close to optimal yield (97 percent) and runs no risk of ending the experiment.

---

8. Following Benoit and Krishna (1985), once we have a good and a bad subgame perfect equilibrium, we can construct many others. These two equilibrium paths, however, seem to us the most likely to be observed in the laboratory.

TABLE 6.3. CPR Investments in Destruction Experiments

Experiment	Average Tokens Invested	Number of Rounds before Destruction	Percentage of Optimal Income Earned[a]
Design I			
7	35.25	4	19
8	55.00	4	23
9	60.33	3	17
10	53.00	6	36
11[b]	65.00	2	11
Design II			
12	42.83	6	30
13	59.68	3	13
14	63.41	5	21
15[b]	61.34	6	25
16	37.94	17	84
17	37.93	15	74
18	52.50	2	10

[a]Actual income earned/income using optimal path.

[b]Subjects were experienced in a previous destruction experiment.

Experimental Results

Our experimental results are summarized by first examining aggregate investments. The aggregate results of all 12 experiments (numbers 7–18) are presented in table 6.3. Appendix 6.1 contains group Market 2 investment decisions for each round. All five Design I experiments (numbers 7–11) yielded investment efficiencies below 37 percent. The longest experiment lasted six decision rounds. The average efficiency over all Design I experiments was 21 percent. This result in the aggregate is very close to the prediction of subgame perfection.[9] These results are striking. In a decision environment with a well-defined probability and significant opportunity costs of destruction, efficiency is very low and the resource is quickly destroyed. Individual and group investments in Market 2 are well beyond optimum levels, with an average investment of 47.1 tokens per round. Thirty-two percent of all group outcomes lie in the interval (54–64) containing the subgame perfect equilibrium path. Fifty-three percent lie below 54 and 16 percent lie above 64.

In five of the seven Design II experiments (numbers 12–18), destruction occurred early, and efficiency was below 30 percent. Of these five experi-

---

9. Subgame perfection yields a prediction of 22 percent. This figure follows from the optimal and equilibrium payoff values shown in table 6.1.

ments, the longest lasted six rounds. In two Design II experiments, destruction did not occur until late in the experiment (rounds 15 and 17) and efficiencies were high (74 percent and 84 percent). Overall average efficiency was 37 percent in Design II, a significant increase over Design I. Average investment in Market 2 fell to 45.9 tokens per round. It appears that in Design II the large safe zone did serve as a focal point for many subjects. This is borne out by the data displayed in table 6.4. A Kolmogorov-Smirnov test shows a significant difference in the cumulative distribution of Market 2 investments in the two designs. The percentage of rounds where Market 2 investment is less than or equal to 40 nearly doubles in Design II. We can also see this effect in the individual data, although it is less pronounced.

At the individual level, the data for the two experiments that survived the longest present a mixed picture. There were numerous rounds in which (a) a subset of players played well beyond the safe strategy equilibrium and (b) aggregate investment in Market 2 was beyond the safe investment of 40 tokens. What is different about these two experiments is that in many rounds a sufficient number of players made small enough investments in Market 2 to offset the large investments by others. Further, in rounds in which the groups invested beyond 40, a "good" draw led to a continuation of the experiment. Subjects in these experiments made average Market 2 investments of 38 tokens, below the safe focal point of 40 tokens, but in no round did the groups reach the safe equilibrium of every player investing 5 tokens in Market 2.

These results are even more striking than those obtained in Design I. In a decision environment with a well-defined probability of destruction, with a safe zone in which optimum rents could be obtained (and which included a safe subgame perfect equilibrium path near the optimum): (1) in only two experiments did groups follow an investment pattern generally in the vicinity of the good subgame perfect equilibrium (17 of 32 rounds strictly in the safe zone); and (2) in the remaining five experiments, groups followed an investment pattern dispersed around the bad subgame perfect equilibrium.

Figure 6.1 summarizes first round individual behavior. The top panel displays observations pooled from the Design I experiments. Only 2 of 40 individuals play the safe strategy of investing 0 tokens in Market 2. Further,

TABLE 6.4. Cumulative Investments in Market 2

Aggregate	$\Sigma x_i \leq 40$	41 to 53	54 to 64	> 64	
Design I	21%	32%	32%	16%	
Design II	39%	35%	19%	6%	
Individual	$x_i \leq 5$	$6 \leq x_i \leq 10$	$11 \leq x_i \leq 15$	$16 \leq x_i \leq 19$	$20 \leq x_i \leq 25$
Design I	54%	30%	10%	2%	4%
Design II	66%	22%	8%	2%	2%

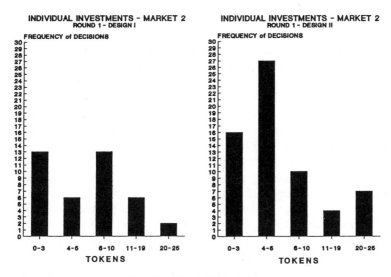

Fig. 6.1. Round 1 decisions

the frequency of players investing 6 or more tokens in Market 2 is high (21 of 40). In each of the five experiments, at least two players followed a strategy of investing 10 or more tokens. One might conjecture that, after an initial decision round with a significant probability of destruction, players would fall back to a safe strategy. In no experiment did all players fall back to cooperative strategies with very low levels of investments in Market 2. Experiment 7 resulted in the most significant drop, with investments falling from an aggregate of 80 in round 1 to 32 in round 2. Even in this experiment, however, investments began to increase after round 2.

The first round behavior of Design II is summarized in the lower panel of figure 6.1. Many players (43 of 64) did in fact play a strategy consistent with staying in the safe zone by investing 5 tokens or less in Market 2. However, each experiment had at least two players investing beyond the safe strategy. The resulting outcome led in subsequent rounds to an increase in Market 2 investments by many players who initially followed the safe strategy.

Conclusions

The results of these experiments are hardly cause for optimism with regard to CPR survival in environments where no institutions exist to foster cooperative behavior. In our experimental setting, when there is a nonnegligible probability of destruction, the CPR is in every case destroyed and, in most cases, rather quickly. The consequence of this destruction is a significant loss in yield from the resource. Even when there is a focal point Nash equilibrium that is completely safe and yields near optimal returns, subjects do not stabilize at this equilibrium. Thus, the results from this time-dependent environment reinforce the answer to question 1 from chapter 1. The inefficiencies observed in the appropriation decisions of chapter 5 are paralleled by the inefficiencies observed in this finitely repeated CPR demand-side provision dilemma. Aggregate predictions from noncooperative game theory continued to be supported by the evidence.

The time-dependence problem our subjects face is far simpler than those faced in naturally occurring renewable resources. In fisheries, for instance, not only is there a clear and present danger of extinction but also, the one-period payoff functions fluctuate wildly. As discussed by Allen and McGlade (1987), these fluctuations are driven by both economic and biological forces. On the economic side, input and output prices vary. On the biological side, population dynamics are much more complex than assumed in standard bionomic models. In such models, extinction is a limit that is approached slowly, while in reality, many biological species have a population dynamic that is characterized by sudden extinction. Our design captures this feature of sudden extinction, without recourse to other nonstationarities. In the presence of naturally occurring nonstationarities, the task of learning the payoff functions, much less best responses, is formidable. There will usually be considerable uncertainty surrounding the safe zone (whether one exists, how large it is, etc.). As a result, there will be uncertainty about the best policy to improve the extremely low efficiencies. In the time it takes to learn in natural settings (void of institutions designed to foster accumulation of accurate knowledge and cooperation), the resource may already be destroyed.

The behavior in this laboratory CPR environment adds additional evidence to field data regarding the need for well-formulated and tested institutional changes designed to balance appropriation with natural regeneration. Our laboratory setting offers one possible environment for investigating alternative institutions. One institutional change currently under discussion appears in Malik, Larson, and Ribaudo 1991. In deliberations over reauthorization of the U.S. Water Quality Act of 1983, one proposal involves the use of an environmental bond. Each period, appropriators post a bond of a determinate size, which they forfeit in the event that the CPR is destroyed (or some other well-defined measure of overuse). Otherwise, the bond is retained for another period. In our laboratory environment, one can show that posting a bond the size of the steady state value in our Design I is enough theoretically to induce appropriators to preserve the CPR. A somewhat smaller bond is sufficient to move appropriators to the safe zone in Design II. Behaviorally, the mere fact of having to post a bond could serve to focus subjects on the safe zone, even if their behavior is only limitedly rational.

Our initial laboratory investigation of an alternative type of institutional arrangement, face-to-face communication, is the topic of discussion in the next chapter. We show that subjects' appropriation levels are significantly reduced with the introduction of this institutional change.

APPENDIX 6.1. Across Period Behavior: Tokens Invested in Market 2

	Round																			
	1	2	3	4	5	6	7	8	9	10	11	12	13	14	15	16	17	18	19	20
Design I																				
7	36	36	44	25																
8	80	32	51	57																
9	49	60	52																	
10	47	45	54	51	61	60														
11X	70	60																		
Design II																				
12	45	40	41	44	36	51														
13	62	59	58																	
14	78	45	63	64	67															
15X	58	75	87	44	46	58	38	36	34	38	44	50	42	40	37	42	42			
16	50	21	28	45	30	28	43	28	30	41	36	40	37	36	43					
17	41	30	32	55	32	45														
18	55	50																		

CHAPTER 7

Communication in the Commons

In chapters 5 and 6, we investigated behavior and outcomes in CPR dilemmas embedded in minimal institutional configurations. The behavior of subjects in these settings generates suboptimal, aggregate outcomes. In particular, outcomes closely approximate the aggregate predictions derived from noncooperative game theory applied to finitely repeated CPR dilemmas and are thus grossly inefficient from the perspective of maximizing group income. As we shall see in chapters 10–14, data from field settings suggest this type of outcome is not inevitable in settings with a richer set of institutional options for fostering communication and/or allowing sanctioning of noncooperative behavior. In this and the next chapter, we begin to examine simplified versions of more complete institutions. In this chapter, we explore the effects of face-to-face communication on appropriation behavior. In chapter 8, we examine behavioral properties of sanctioning as an independent mechanism and in conjunction with communication.[1]

Communication: Theoretical Issues

The effect of communication in CPR situations, where individuals repeatedly decide on the number of resource units to withdraw from a common pool, is open to considerable theoretical and policy debate. Words alone are viewed by many as frail constraints when individuals make private, repetitive decisions between short-term, profit-maximizing strategies and strategies negotiated by a verbal agreement. Hobbes justified the necessity of a Leviathan on the frailty of mere words. For Hobbes, a contract that involves a promise by at least one of the parties to perform in the future is called a "covenant." When both parties promise future performance, it is a "covenant of mutual trust" (Hobbes [1651] 1960, 87, 89). A covenant of mutual trust in a state of nature is void in Hobbes's view if either has a reasonable suspicion that the other will not perform.

---

1. This chapter relies extensively on E. Ostrom and Walker 1991.

> For he that performeth first, has no assurance the other will perform after; because the bonds of words are too weak to bridle men's ambition, avarice, anger, and other passions, without the fear of some coercive power; which in the condition of mere nature, where all men are equal, and judges of the justness of their own fears, cannot possibly be supposed. (Hobbes [1651] 1960, 89–90)

On the other hand, a covenant made "where there is a power set up to constrain those that would otherwise violate their faith" is likely to be fulfilled (Hobbes [1651] 1960, 90). Thus, Hobbes argued for the necessity of a "coercive power, to compel men equally to the performance of their covenants, by the terror of some punishment, greater than the benefit they expect by the breach of their covenant" (Hobbes [1651] 1960, 94).

The weakness of mere words and the necessity of external agents to enforce contracts is also a foundation upon which the powerful edifice of noncooperative game theory has been constructed. John Nash (1950, 1951) was among the first to distinguish between cooperative and noncooperative games. In cooperative games, players can communicate freely and make *enforceable* agreements; in noncooperative games, they can do neither. Some theorists particularly stress the inability to make enforceable agreements:

> the decisive question is whether the players can make enforceable agreements, and it makes little difference whether they are allowed to talk to each other. Even if they are free to talk and to negotiate an agreement, this fact will be of no real help if the agreement has little chance of being kept. An ability to negotiate agreements is useful only if the rules of the game make such agreements binding and enforceable. (Harsanyi and Selten 1988, 3)[2]

Thus, much of contemporary, noncooperative game theory treats one of Nash's conditions as superfluous. In this view, the ability to communicate is inessential and unlikely to change results unless the individuals involved can

---

2. Harsanyi and Selten add that in real life, "agreements may be enforced externally by courts of law, government agencies, or pressure from public opinion; they may be enforced internally by the fact that the players are simply unwilling to violate agreements on moral grounds and know that this is the case" (1988, 3). To model self-commitment using noncooperative game theory, the ability to break the commitment is removed by trimming the branches that emanate from a self-commitment move to remove any alternative contrary to that which has been committed. In a lab setting, this would mean changing the structure of the alternatives made available to subjects after an agreement, which was not done.

call on external agents to enforce agreements.[3] Verbal promises to keep agreements lack credibility when individuals know they will face future choices
where sticking with an agreement would be costly. Theoretically, such promises are an insufficient basis for individuals to change strategies from a Nash
equilibrium to something more cooperative.[4] In the standard formulation of
the theory, the key is that verbal commitments do not change the formal game
structure. That is, if the games implemented in our laboratory setting accurately induce the valuations corresponding to the payoff function of the constituent game X, no strategic content is ascribed to nonbinding communication. More formally, when the symmetric constituent game X has a unique
symmetric equilibrium x^*, neither finite repetition nor communication creates
new symmetric equilibrium outcomes. Let c denote a communication strategy, in the communication phase C, available to any player. As long as saying
one thing and doing another has no payoff consequences, then any strategy of
the form (c, x^*) is an equilibrium of the one-shot game (C, X), and finitely
repeated x^* is a subgame perfect equilibrium outcome of one-shot communication (C, X, X, . . . , X) or repeated communication (C, X, C, X, . . . , C,
X). In this situation, subgame perfection is deaf to covenants. However, as we
show below, communication makes a big difference to behavior.

While the necessity of external enforcers is assumed necessary for cooperation in finitely repeatedly games, most theorists argue that stable and
efficient equilibria can be achieved by participants in infinitely repeated games
without the necessity of external enforcers.[5] These arguments rely on trigger
strategies (see chap. 3). Such strategies contain both a "stick and a carrot."
The carrot (or benefit) is the gains that accrue to players from cooperation.
The stick (or the punishment) is the credible threat to return to playing a one-
shot noncooperative equilibrium strategy. A "grim trigger" strategy involves
the threat to play the punishment strategy forever. Faced with the prospect of
an infinitely long punishment, the argument is that no one would deviate from
cooperative play. But, as we discussed in chapter 5, our games are not infi-

---

3. Self-commitment is also possible, but whether the agreement is backed by external
agents or self-commitment, the essential condition is that all branches of the game tree are
removed that correspond to moves violating the agreement that has been made (Harsanyi and
Selten 1988, 4). In the lab, this would mean that the experimenters would reprogram the experiment so that no more than the agreed upon number of tokens could be invested in the CPR. This
condition was never imposed in the laboratory experiments. In the field, this would mean that
some action was taken to remove the feasibility of certain types of activities. In a field setting, this
is an almost impossible task.

4. Considerable theoretical interest exists in various types of "cheap talk" options and their
role in helping players achieve cooperative outcomes.

5. This is based on the Folk Theorem of infinitely repeated games.

nite, and as we discuss in chapter 9, there is some doubt whether trigger strategies organize observed behavior.

Even though our games are finite, there are two alternative approaches for explaining observed patterns of cooperation. These approaches rely on notions of incomplete information. One source of incomplete information could surround the subjects' perception of the termination point of the experiment. For example, suppose the players approach the game as if it were repeated, but with only a vague notion of how many repetitions. Assuming a very low termination probability, subjects may realize there is more than one sensible way of playing the game and that there are group gains to some of these possibilities. That is, not knowing exactly when it ends, they form their own continuation probability and act as though the game might last forever. In this case, there are many other equilibria available to them besides those associated with grim triggers. Some of these have efficiencies higher than that implied by the one-shot Nash equilibrium being played repeatedly, but less than 100 percent. A second source of incomplete information concerns other players' types. For example, face-to-face communication (and resulting verbal commitments) may change subjects' expectations of other players' responses. In particular, if a subject believes that other subjects are of a cooperative type (that is, will cooperate in response to cooperative play) that subject may play cooperatively to induce cooperation from others. In this case, cooperating can be sustained as rational play in the framework of incomplete information regarding player types.[6]

Studies of repetitive CPR situations in field settings show that appropriators in many, but by no means all, settings adopt cooperative strategies that enhance their joint payoffs without the presence of external enforcers. Many situational factors appear to affect the capacity for resource users to arrive at and maintain agreed-upon limits to their appropriation activities.[7] The ability to communicate appears to be a necessary but not a sufficient condition. The presence of external monitors and enforcers appears to be neither necessary nor sufficient (Wade 1988b; Siy 1982; McKean 1992). In many natural settings, monitoring and enforcement activities are undertaken by participants themselves and often *without* external recognition and support. Rarely does

---

6. See McKelvey and Palfrey for a discussion of this argument for the case of the "centipede" game (1992, in particular pages 804–5).

7. Among the variables that have been identified as affecting the capacity of individuals to devise their own rules for limiting the use of a CPR are (1) net benefits from the restrictions; (2) discount rates of CPR users; (3) size of the appropriating group; (4) asymmetry of appropriations with regard to information, asset structure, leadership, and appropriation technologies; (5) the physical complexity of the resource; and (6) the institutional structure and incentives in place (see E. Ostrom 1990 and Libecap 1989).

one see behavior in field settings that would be consistent with the use of trigger strategies.[8]

In prior laboratory investigations, communication has been shown to be a very effective mechanism for increasing the frequency with which players choose joint income-maximizing strategies, even when individual incentives conflict with the cooperative strategies.[9] Hypotheses forwarded to explain why communication increases the selection of cooperative strategies identify a process that communication is posited to facilitate: (1) offering and extracting promises, (2) changing the expectations of others' behavior, (3) changing payoff structure, (4) the re-enforcement of prior normative orientations, and (5) the development of a group identity. Experimental examination of communication has demonstrated the independent effect of all five of these processes, but they also appear to re-enforce one another in an interactive manner.[10] Prior research that relied on signals exchanged via computer terminals rather than face-to-face communication has not had the same impact on behavior. Sell and Wilson (1991, 1992), whose experimental design allowed participants in a public-good experiment to signal a promise to cooperate via their terminals, found much less sustained cooperation than we report below based on face-to-face communication.

A deeper examination of the role of communication in facilitating the selection and retention of efficient strategies is thus of considerable theoretical (as well as policy) interest.[11] In this chapter, we focus primarily on the findings from a series of experiments in which we operationalize face-to-face communication (without the presence of external enforcement) in the CPR appropriation environment of chapter 5.[12] The role of communication and its success in fostering outcomes more in line with social optimality is investi-

8. Slade (1987), for example, concludes from her study of price wars among gas stations in Vancouver that they used small punishments for small deviations rather than big punishments for big deviations.

9. Among the studies showing a positive effect of the capacity to communicate are Bornstein and Rapoport 1988; Bornstein et al. 1989; Braver and Wilson 1984, 1986; Caldwell 1976; Dawes, McTavish, and Shaklee 1977; Dawes, Orbell, and van de Kragt 1984; Edney and Harper 1978; Hackett, Schlager, and Walker 1993; Jerdee and Rosen 1974; Kramer and Brewer 1986; van de Kragt et al. 1986; Isaac and Walker 1988a, 1991; Orbell, Dawes, and van de Kragt 1990; Orbell, van de Kragt, and Dawes 1991; and E. Ostrom and Walker 1991.

10. Orbell, van de Kragt, and Dawes (1988) summarize the findings from ten years of research on one-shot public good experiments by stressing both the independent and interdependent nature of the posited explanatory factors for why communication has such a powerful effect on rates of cooperation.

11. See Banks and Calvert 1992a, 1992b for an important discussion of the theoretical significance of communication in incomplete information games.

12. See E. Ostrom and Walker 1991 for a more detailed discussion of the role of communication and the experimental evidence summarized here.

gated in settings in which (1) the communication mechanism is provided as a costless one-shot opportunity, (2) the communication mechanism is provided as a costless opportunity and on a repeated basis, and (3) the subjects face a provision dilemma of having to provide the communication mechanism in a voluntary contribution decision environment.

One-Shot Costless Communication

We first turn to the simplest of all of our communication environments. The structure of the experiments in this design is:

$$X, X, \ldots, X, C, X, X, \ldots X, X.$$

That is, subjects were given a one-time opportunity to communicate followed by a series of repeated independent decisions. This environment allows for several insights into the role of communication. Subjects have a one-time opportunity to discuss the decision problem. If so desired, they can work at determining a joint income-maximizing strategy and agreeing to such a strategy. They have a one-time opportunity to impress on each other the importance of cooperation. But since the communication mechanism is not repeated, they have no opportunity to react jointly to ex post behavior.

Our first communication design paralleled that of the high-endowment (25-token) baseline game for the first 10 repetitions of the constituent game. The only difference was that subjects received information on all individual decisions after each round. As discussed above, the anonymity of subjects was retained since no subject knew the identity of the individuals identified as player 1, 2, . . . 8 on their computer screen. Each subject was identified by a tag with a letter from A to H when they communicated, but they were told (and, this was actually the case) that there was no connection between the order of the alphabetical tags and the order of the player numbers assigned in the computer. This added information had no impact on observed yields.[13] At the end of the tenth round, the subjects were informed that they would have a single opportunity of 10 minutes to discuss the decision problem. The instructions are summarized below.

> Some participants in experiments like this have found it useful to have the opportunity to discuss the decision problem you face. You will be given 10 minutes to hold such a discussion. You may discuss anything

---

13. This information condition is similar to the "reveal" condition of Palfrey and Rosenthal (1992). They did not find that added information about individual contributions made a consistent difference in strategies adopted in noncommunication, repeated-game experiments.

you wish during your 10-minute discussion period, with the following restrictions: (1) you are not allowed to discuss side payments (2) you are not allowed to make physical threats (3) you are not allowed to see the private information on anyone's monitor.

After this opportunity to communicate, the subjects returned to the constituent game, which was then repeated up to 22 more times.

The subgame consistent[14] and subgame perfect equilibrium outcome for the one-shot communication game was for each individual to invest 8 tokens in the CPR, the same as in the baseline. The maximum yield was obtained if a total of 36 tokens were invested. Players were not allowed to invest fractional tokens and the symmetric strategy to obtain the maximum return is half way between everyone investing 4 tokens and investing 5 tokens. Thus, discovering and agreeing upon a joint strategy was a cognitive, as well as a strategic, challenge in this environment. If the players were to decide to invest either 4 or 5 tokens each, they would obtain 99 percent of maximum net yield in either case.

Experimental Results

The transcripts of the discussion during the communication round reveal that subjects perceived their problem as involving two tasks: (1) determining the maximal yield available and (2) agreeing upon a strategy to achieve that yield. The one-shot communication results are summarized in table 7.1. This table displays information regarding *percentage of maximum net yield* actually earned by subject groups.

The results of our three one-shot communication experiments are mixed. In experiment 19, the group achieved over 82 percent of maximum net yield in all but 2 of 22 rounds following communication. In experiment 20, communication had little efficiency-improving effects. Finally, in experiment 21, the group improved net yield significantly following communication but could not sustain such behavior.

Experiment 19
The players agreed to invest 6 tokens each in the CPR. While this investment level is somewhat higher than optimal, the players still obtained 89 percent of the maximal return in rounds in which they complied with the agreement. The group complied perfectly until round 21, at which point compliance began to break down. In round 21, one subject invested 7 tokens. In round 22, three

---

14. An equilibrium is subgame consistent if it prescribes identical play on identical subgames (Selten 1971).

**TABLE 7.1. One-Shot Communication after Round 10, 25-Token Design
(Average Net Yield as a Percentage of Maximum)**

			Round			
	1–5	6–10	11–15	16–20	21–25	26+
19	−48	−20	89	89	85	83
20	−73	−16	45	−0	12	32
21	−2	−2	88	48	31	61
Mean	−41	−13	74	45	43	59

subjects invested 15, 7, and 7 tokens, respectively, producing a drop in yield to 59 percent. In round 23, one subject withdrew all tokens from the CPR, while the other 7 players returned to the agreed-upon 6 tokens. In all subsequent rounds, at least one player deviated from the agreement to invest 6 tokens. In round 28, the subject who had invested 15 tokens in round 22, invested 15 tokens again. Otherwise, all CPR investments ranged from 5 to 7 until termination in round 32.

Experiment 20
Communication had little effect on yields. In the communication period, the subjects immediately identified an investment strategy of 5 tokens each. The subjects noted that one of them had invested 25 tokens in each of the first 10 rounds. One subject surmised that this person could not be making too much, but little attention was paid to what they should do if this person persisted. Only one comment was made about their need to "stick to their agreement," and that comment was made by the 25-token investor (who remained anonymous throughout the experiment). In rounds 11 and 12, seven of the players invested the agreed-upon 5 tokens, but the "heavy" investor from the first 10 rounds continued to invest 25 tokens. Thus, instead of earning 99 percent of maximal yield, the group earned only 56 percent. In round 13, one of these seven players doubled their investment in the CPR. This dropped the group yield to 35 percent. From round 14 to round 17, the group fluctuated between 20 percent and 55 percent. In round 18, several players increased CPR investment and yield plunged to -93 percent. When the experiment stopped after round 32, only two subjects were still investing 5 tokens in the CPR. No subject punished a defector by choosing to invest heavily in the CPR, as called for by trigger strategies employed in the Folk Theorem for infinitely repeated games. In fact, some subjects reduced their own investment levels in response to heavier investment by others. In 28 out of the 176 choices (or 16 percent), individuals invested less than the agreed-upon level of 5 tokens.

Experiment 21

Communication had a positive but not a sustained impact on yields. The subjects wanted to adopt a strategy that would maximize yield, but had considerable difficulty identifying such a strategy. They finally decided upon a complex strategy to invest 3 tokens each in round 11 and one additional token each in rounds 12, 13, and 14. Depending on the information they obtained from these four rounds, their plan was that each player would continue to invest the number of tokens that had produced the highest return. Round 11 went according to plan. In round 12, seven subjects stuck with the plan, but one invested 21 tokens. In round 13, six did follow the plan and in round 14 all players invested 6 as agreed upon. In round 15, two players reduced investments to 3 and the other six invested 6 tokens—achieving a 97 percent yield. From round 16 onward, at least one person invested more than 6 in each round and the percentage of maximal returns plummeted to as low as -49 percent.

What is obvious from these three experiments is that a single communication period enables participants to begin the process of adopting a joint strategy and to gain higher yields. However, the incapacity to communicate repeatedly limits the long-run durability of their agreements.

Repeated Costless Communication

Our second design involves repeated communication in both the low- and high-endowment settings. The structure of the experiments in this design is:

$$X, X, \ldots, X, C, X, C, X, \ldots C, X, C, X.$$

That is, at the outset, the constituent game was repeated for 10 rounds. After round 10, the players read an announcement, informing them they would have an opportunity for discussion after *each* subsequent round. The first opportunity to communicate lasted up to ten minutes. Each subsequent session lasted up to three minutes. During discussion sessions the subjects left their terminals and sat facing one another.[15]

Experimental Results: Low Endowment

Summary data from the low-endowment 10-token series (experiments 22–25) is reported in table 7.2.[16] These repeated communication experiments provide

---

15. As in the one-shot communication setting, each person was identified with a badge that was unrelated to their player number. This facilitated player identification in our transcripts. If unanimous, players could forgo discussion.

16. These low-endowment communication experiments were conducted very early in our

TABLE 7.2.   Repeated Communication after Round 10, 10-Token Design (Average Net Yield as a Percentage of Maximum)

	Round				
	1–5	6–10	11–15	16–20	21–25
22	26	26	96	100	100
23	35	21	100	97	100
24	33	24	99	99	—
25	37	39	94	98	100
Mean	33	27	97	98	100

strong evidence for the power of face-to-face communication. Players successfully use the opportunity to (*a*) calculate coordinated yield-improving strategies, (*b*) devise verbal agreements to implement these strategies, and (*c*) deal with nonconforming players through verbal statements. When allowed to communicate repeatedly, subjects greatly enhanced their joint yield and sustained this enhancement. For analytical purposes, we define a defection as a Market 2 investment larger than agreed upon. In the low-endowment environment, we identified only 19 defections from agreements out of 368 total decisions (a 5 percent defection rate).

Experimental Results: High Endowment
The high-endowment CPR game is a more challenging decision environment than the low-endowment game. While the equilibrium of the two games is identical, the disequilibrium implications of the 25-token game change considerably. With 25 tokens, as few as three subjects investing all of their tokens can essentially ruin the CPR (bring returns below *w*), while with 10 tokens it takes seven out of eight subjects to accomplish this much damage. In this sense, the 25-token environment is much more *fragile* than the 10-token environment. We were interested in exploring whether subjects could cope with this more delicate situation through communication alone. In the field, this type of fragility is manifest in fisheries (all small boats versus all trawlers) and in forestry (individuals with chain saws versus bulldozers).

Further, we were interested whether varying the information players received about past actions of all players and joint outcomes affected patterns

---

research and used a modified 10-token payoff function for Market 2 ($15(\Sigma x_i) - .15(\Sigma x_i)^2$). Yields as a percentage of maximum from experiments without communication using this payoff function closely parallel the yields observed in our 10-token low-endowment baseline design. Across 20 decision rounds, the difference in mean yields between experiments using these two alternative payoff functions for market 2 was only 6.4 percent, slightly higher in the low-endowment baseline design presented in the text.

of behavior. In experiments 26–28, subjects received only aggregate information on actions and outcomes between rounds. This level of information was identical to that of the 10-token repeated information discussed above. In experiments 29–31, subjects received additional information on individual Market 2 investments between rounds. This information was by subject numbers only. Unless the subjects successfully used the discussion rounds to ascertain actual subject identity, this information treatment left subject identity anonymous.

Table 7.3 summarizes the data for the 25-token repeated-communication experiments under both information conditions. In all six experiments (numbers 26–31), joint yield increased dramatically over that achieved in the first 10 rounds. In experiments 26, 28, and 30, however, the fragile nature of nonbinding agreements in this high-endowment environment became especially apparent, particularly near the end of the experiment.

Experiment 26
The subjects disagreed about the best strategy—some arguing for investing 7 or 8 in the CPR and others arguing for 4 or 5. As the end of their first discussion period was announced, they rushed into a rapid agreement to "try 6 each and see what happens." All but one person kept to the agreement, with two extra tokens invested. After further discussion of whether 6 was the right amount, they again agreed upon this level of investment. One player ended the discussion by saying, "Let's not get greedy. We just got to start trusting."

Fourteen extra tokens were invested in round 12, which produced a drop in their yield from 85 percent to 48 percent of maximum. When they next communicated, player B announced

> This should be our last meeting—if we can't get some trust, we might as well go back and screw each other over. We could all make more

TABLE 7.3. Repeated Communication after Round 10, 25-Token Design (Average Net Yield as a Percentage of Maximum)

	Round				
	1–5	6–10	11–15	16–20	21+
26	35	−43	76	75	54
27	60	8	85	82	85
28	4	−8	61	68	68
29	−60	13	80	93	99
30	−24	−3	40	67	−15
31	36	−41	84	86	80
Mean	8	−13	71	79	62

money if we could stick together, but if some are going to do the others in, then, we just should go.

Rounds 13, 14, and 15 were close to the agreed-upon levels and yields were above 80 percent of maximum for each of these rounds. After round 15, the discussion period started off with:

> Player H: Not everyone is investing 6.
> Player B: Evidently not.
> Player C: Unless everyone keeps to it, it starts to get away from us.
> Player H: Let's say we invest 6 again. Obviously, somebody is cheating, but what can we do? But the rest of us can just continue to invest 6.

The players refused to talk after round 16. After yield dropped to 56 percent of maximum in round 17, the discussion started off with:

> Player E: Someone is getting a free ride, so I say that we should just dump whatever we want into 2.[17]
> Player H: But we screw ourselves too.
> Player B: I think we should just turn it loose.
> Player H: I am happy with continuing to invest 6. Yeah, someone is cheating, but that is the best we can do. Is it worth a dime or five cents?
> Player E: [Obviously upset, shakes head and does not say anymore.]

The group in this experiment never again had perfect compliance.[18] But the threats to dump all the tokens into the CPR—a trigger strategy—were not carried out either. For 5 rounds, yields wavered between 72 percent and 80 percent of maximum. On the other hand, on the (unannounced) final round 23, their net yield plummeted to 11 percent of maximum.

Experiment 27
The subjects mistook the optimal strategy. They adopted a group strategy of investing 50 tokens in the CPR (two subjects invest 7, six invest 6). They devised a complex rotation scheme and kept to it with only one exception throughout rounds 11 to 23. When one subject invested 11 rather than the

---

17. The player is referring to Market 2 (the CPR).

18. Players H and E had followed the agreement through round 17; player B had followed through round 16, but was one of the four individuals who invested more than the agreed-upon level in round 17. Player E invested 8 in round 18, but then returned to follow the agreement throughout the remaining rounds. Player H never deviated from the agreement. Player B alternated between 6 and 7 tokens in Market 2 after this discussion.

agreed-upon 6 tokens, no one knew who the errant person was or whether the additional investment came from a single player (because subjects had information only about total investments).[19] In the communication round following this defection, the dialogue went like this:

> Player A: Who did it?
> Player C: Did someone get a little greedy?
> Player E: We ended up with more tokens in Market 2.
> Player C: But still the person who did put in the extra, they would not have made anymore, would they have?
> Player E: Just a few darn cents above the rest of us.
> Player A: Let's go back and try it the old way.

After further discussion, player A urged, "We should be able to keep this going a little longer," and player F wondered whether the person who put in the extra tokens was "greedy or was it just an error." Player D responded that perhaps the person was not thinking about the consequences. Player A urged everyone to "go back to the way we were doing it." The subjects then returned to their terminals for 3 more rounds of perfect compliance with their rotation agreement.

The transcript reflects individuals who are puzzling why someone would break their agreement and their resolve to return to the rotation scheme they had devised. They achieved 84 percent of the potential yield rather than a higher percentage because they had miscalculated the optimum and not because they had difficulty keeping to their agreement.

Experiment 28

The participants again mistook the optimum strategy. They initially adopted a group strategy of investing 50 tokens (two subjects investing 25 each, six investing 0) together with a rotation scheme. Several subjects articulated concerns about whether the experiment would continue long enough for them to complete the rotation, but they did agree on the system. When one subject put in 25 tokens for 2 rounds in a row, the information that 75 tokens had been invested in the CPR went without comment for 1 round. Once the rotation had been completed, the subjects discussed what to do now and whether the extra 25 tokens had been placed in error. They adopted a symmetric strategy of all investing 7 tokens in the CPR (20 tokens greater than optimum) that they held

---

19. This defection occurred in round 20. Since the baseline experiment was 20 rounds, defections were more likely on the twentieth round. That some defections come in the twentieth round points to the bounded nature of the experimental setting. That more defections do not come at this point or soon thereafter in the communication experiments is hard to explain using backward induction.

to with two small exceptions. When discussing these defections, one player asked, "Why mess it up?" The implication was that small defections could lead to a worse outcome for all if they continued. The implied threats worked relatively well in sustaining this suboptimal but yield-improving strategy.

As noted above, in experiments 29, 30, and 31, we modified the information provided subjects after each round so that in addition to learning about the total tokens invested, group yield and individual yield, each subject also received information about the individual decisions of other subjects in previous rounds. Information was given by subject number, thereby preserving anonymity. The major difference between experiments 26–28, on the one hand, and 29–31, on the other, was that subjects could know whether excess tokens above their agreements had been invested by one or two individuals or by most of the subjects.

Experiment 29

The subjects first agreed to one rotation system for 4 rounds and a second rotation system for 2 rounds. They settled on a pattern of all investing 4 tokens in the CPR and obtained 99 percent of the yield for the rest of the experiment. During the repeated communication portion of their experiment, there was no defection from their agreement.

Experiment 30

Player F suggested that they all put in 1 or 2 tokens in the CPR. Surprisingly, the group agreed to invest 1 token in Market 2 (the CPR). Not only did they agree but they kept to their agreement for 7 rounds. During this time they received only 40 percent of the achievable net yield. In the eighteenth round, player F put in 25 tokens, while everyone else continued with their investment of 1 token. Needless to say, the discussion after round 18 was heated. Player F eventually "confessed" and indicated that "I had wanted to do that forever. . . . I thought I had to do it." She was asked how much she made and the amount of the payoff ($3.75) was a shock to everyone. She had, in fact, captured most of the feasible yield. During that round, total yield rose to 99 percent! But, the distrust that was engendered meant that the group could not achieve an agreed-upon level of investment. In the subsequent round, the total yield dropped from 98 percent to 80 percent, to 78 percent, to 52 percent, to −117 percent, finally pulsing back to 21 percent at the end of the experiment. It is somewhat perplexing to know how to count "infractions" in this case. The agreement basically broke down. After round 18, only one subject continued to invest 1 token. Thus, 39 decisions out of 104 opportunities (or 38 percent) of the decisions were not in conformance with their original decision. In summary tables we develop in chapter 9, we will not count these decisions as defections since the agreement broke down.

Experiment 31

The subjects had experienced group yields in the first 10 rounds that varied from −216 percent all the way to 96 percent. In their first discussion round (after the tenth round of play), they agreed to invest 6 tokens in the CPR. In the eleventh round, six subjects invested at the agreed level or below while one subject (player E) invested 10 and another invested 7. When the group sat down for a discussion, several participants urged the individuals who had gone over their agreement to put in 6. This seemed to work in round 12, as everyone complied with the agreement. Round 13 produced almost complete compliance with one player putting in 1 token more than agreed. But in round 14, player E put in 10 tokens and player A put in 7. This produced a bit of an explosion. Several players searchingly asked who was the person putting in 10. One player remarked, "Someone is sitting here thinking—those idiots— they are so gullible." After lots of stressful discussion, they returned to their terminals with a plea to "try it again. If it doesn't work, we need to try to find out who 4 and 5 are [the two overinvestors]."

In round 15, players E and A again invested one more token than agreed upon and everyone else conformed to the agreement. At this point, one subject suggested that they "go around the circle and tell our numbers." Several subjects indicated that they were perfectly willing to tell who they were, but no further efforts were made to identify the individuals who had invested more than their agreement. Round 16 produced perfect compliance, and the subjects clapped when the result was announced on the screen. But, in round 17, players E and A again put in 7 while the others put in 6. The subjects who had earlier indicated that they wanted to know who the individual was started to reveal their own player numbers and asked the others to do so. Player A correctly revealed his identity as number 5 on their screens, but player E told the group (falsely) that she was player 7 (someone who had consistently held to their agreement). Since the real player 7 was also claiming to be player 7, this act by player 4 was quite "problematic" for the group.

From then on, player E consistently overinvested 1 or 2 tokens, while several others began to join her. The group always achieved far more than they had prior to communication (never below 78 percent), but the minor overinvestment by one, and eventually by a few, players, was a source of considerable annoyance to the others.

At several points, they discussed initiating a trigger strategy. One player asked: "Now what are we going to do, are we going to go for a free-for-all?" Another replied: "Go for a free-for-all? Shucks no, we all lose." The first proposed the idea again: "I am just saying that if we all go for a free-for-all, the person with the highest amount in there may well lose the most." The response this time was: "Yeah, it is not worth it, if somehow we could all put in 6, we gain a lot. Some people are preying on us, poor, honest souls here."

The possibility of adopting a trigger strategy—throwing a free-for-all—was discussed several more times during the remainder of the experiment but never tried. The infraction rate for this experiment was 19 incidents out of a total of 104, or 18 percent.

In these repeated communication experiments, subjects were able to obtain consistently higher payoffs than in the one-shot communication design, particularly after round 15. As shown in table 7.3, subjects in the repeated, communication experiments obtained an average yield of 78 percent of maximum in rounds 16 to 20 as contrasted to 45 percent in the one-shot communication design. In the rounds after round 20, the yields were 62 percent and 43 percent, respectively.

Subjects in the repeated communication setting were also able to keep their defection rates lower than in the one-shot setting. In the one-shot design, players invested more tokens in the CPR than agreed upon in 133 out of 528 opportunities (a defection rate of 25 percent), while the defection rate was 13 percent (42 out of 312) with repeated communication. Repeated communication enabled subjects to discuss defections and to cut the defection rate in half. In all communication experiments, subjects offered and extracted promises of cooperation, thereby increasing their joint yield significantly above that obtained prior to communication. Only in repeated communication did subjects develop verbal sanctioning mechanisms that enabled them to sustain consistently higher yields. Communication discussions went well beyond discovering what investments would generate maximum yields. A striking aspect of the discussion rounds was how rapidly subjects, who had not had an opportunity to establish a well-defined community with strong internal norms, were able to devise their own agreements and verbal punishments for those who broke those agreements. These verbal sanctions had to be directed at unknown defectors, since subjects' decisions were anonymous. Subjects detected defection solely through aggregate investments. In many cases, statements like "some scumbucket is investing more than we agreed upon" were a sufficient reproach to change defectors' behavior. However, verbal sanctions were less effective in the 25-token environment. These results are similar to those obtained in previous research in different but broadly similar environments.

Costly Communication

In this series of experiments, subjects faced the joint task of providing the opportunity to communicate and, if provided, using the mechanism productively. The structure of the experiments in this design is

X, X, . . . , X, PC, X, PC, X, . . . PC, X, PC, X,

where P denotes the opportunity to provide the communication mechanism, but at a cost. Specifically, in each decision round after the tenth round of the constituent game with no communication, subjects faced a decision of whether to invest toward the provision of the communication mechanism. The subjects were placed in a decision situation parallel to the provision point experiments discussed in the appendix to chapter 5. The provision mechanism imposed on the right to communicate placed subjects in a second-order public-good dilemma situation (with a provision point). Second-order dilemma games exist whenever individuals must expend resources to provide a mechanism that may alter the strategic nature of a first-order dilemma game (Oliver 1980; Taylor 1987). The opportunity to communicate in a CPR dilemma situation can be viewed as a mechanism that enables individuals to coordinate strategies to solve the first-order CPR dilemma. In our other designs, the opportunity was presented to the players at no cost.

In this design, however, we increased the realism of the experimental setting by imposing a cost for communicating. In field settings, communication is not free. Some individuals have to bear the cost of organization. If communication is going to continue, these costs must be borne repeatedly. Without continuing provision of a mechanism for communication, the communication effort may collapse and with it the possibility of avoiding the suboptimal outcomes of the first-order social dilemma.

These communication experiments were conducted to investigate the properties of a mechanism in which provision of the right to communicate was costly. Since our goal was to examine the "pure" effects of the costly provision structure, we wanted to control for subjects' awareness of the impact (success) of communication itself. This design feature was captured by using subjects who had participated in our previous communication experiments. Thus, these subjects had experienced the efficiency enhancing characteristics of communication. No subject group was drawn intact from a previous experiment. To utilize this design feature, however, we had to ensure that subjects did not enter the decision environment with prior "implicit bargain" agreements. That is, we needed a decision environment parallel in structure to our previous design, but with a different cooperative equilibrium. The equilibrium properties of this design capture this characteristic.

Parallel to other designs, we conducted this investigation with a set of noncommunication baseline experiments and a set of parallel experiments where communication was allowed if the costs were provided by the participants. In the three baseline noncommunication experiments, subjects participated in a series of at least 20 rounds in which no form of oral or visual communication was allowed. The first 10 rounds of the "costly communication" experiments were conducted in a manner identical to the noncommunication experiments. Prior to round 11, however, the subjects received an announcement that can be summarized as follows.

> Subjects were informed they would be given the opportunity to purchase the right to discuss (as a group) their investment decisions. The rules on discussion were exactly the same as in the discussion sessions in which they participated in previous experiments, except now the subjects were informed that they must purchase the right to communicate with each other. Each round they were asked to privately decide whether they would contribute $.20 toward the opportunity. If at least five agreed to contribute, the entire group was to be allowed to meet in a discussion session.[20]

There are several key differences in the parameterizations of this design relative to our previous designs. In these experiments (1) the payoff function for Market 2 was increased (shifted upward) relative to that of our other designs, (2) the payoff from Market 1 was reduced to zero, (3) individual token endowments were equal to 15 tokens, and (4) subjects started the experiment with an initial capital endowment of $5.00. The reasons for the increased token endowments and the use of an up-front capital endowment will be made clear after we investigate the theoretical properties of this design.

Theoretical Predictions

Consider the specific parameterizations for Market 1 and Market 2. The strategy set for each player is $x_i \in \{0, 1, 2, \ldots, 15\}$, where x_i denotes the number of tokens player i invests in Market 2. The payoff for player i $h_i(x)$, in cents, is:

$$h_i(x) = 0 \qquad\qquad\qquad\qquad\qquad\qquad \text{if } x_i = 0$$

$$= 0(15 - x_i) + (x_i/\Sigma x_i)(25\Sigma x_i - .30(\Sigma x_i)^2) \quad \text{if } x_i > 0$$

---

20. It was explained verbally to the subjects that all contributions were final. If the group was not successful in funding the communication session, contributions were *not* refunded. The particular cost of $.20 per individual and the requirement that five of eight individuals must contribute to provide the mechanism were chosen to make the provision a nontrivial problem and yet not to make the provision so costly that provision would have been virtually impossible. One would like to be able to calculate the expected costs and benefits from provision. These are not well-defined terms, however, in this context. Some groups may require only one round of communication to coordinate a strategy that stays in place for the entire experiment. Other groups may require repeated rounds of face-to-face discussion. The fact that our groups struggled with the provision problem, but did eventually succeed, suggests that our parameterizations were reasonable.

where $x = (x_1, \ldots, x_8)$ is the vector of strategies of all players. This symmetric game has multiple Nash equilibria in pure strategies, with $\Sigma x_i = 74$ (approximately 40 percent of maximum net yield possible from Market 2). These are generated by having six players play $x_i = 9$ and two players play $x_i = 10$. The game also has a symmetric Nash equilibrium in mixed strategies, with $E(\Sigma x_i) = 74$. This equilibrium is generated by each player playing $x_i = 9$ with probability .74 and $x_i = 10$ with probability .26.[21] Note that the decision of whether to contribute in the provision stage (providing the opportunity to communicate) does not affect the Nash equilibrium prediction of the appropriation stage. Whether one contributed or not in the provision stage is a sunk cost once one moves to the appropriation stage.

A group investment of 42 tokens yields a level of investment at which MRP = MC and thus maximum net yield. Conversely, a group investment of 83.3 tokens yields a level of investment at which ARP = MC and thus 0 net yield from Market 2. For this design, note that this result would yield a 0 total return from investments in Market 2.

Given the possible payoffs for this design, one can see why we modified certain features of this design relation to our original 10-token baseline design. We increased individual token endowments to 15 (from 10) so that full dissipation of net yield would not be inhibited by a binding constraint on resource endowments. Further, with this design, it is possible for subjects to actually have negative returns for a decision period. For this reason, and to increase the likelihood of subjects earning some minimal experimental earnings, we added the up-front cash endowment.

Experimental Results

We begin our interpretation of the results with a summary of the level of inefficiency generated in the noncommunication baseline experiments (32–34). As with our other baseline experiments with the 15-token design (experiments 32–34), the resource allocations between the two markets are at very low levels of efficiency. From table 7.4, we see that (pooling across all experiments and the first 20 rounds) average net yield equaled only 39 percent of optimum. Further, as noted with other experiments, there was a tendency for net yield to decrease with repetition of the decision process. Again, it was the Nash prediction that most accurately describes the aggregate data.

In table 7.4, we also present summary information on net yield accrued across experimental decision periods for the three "costly communication"

---

21. This design was created to hold constant the parameters from a design we used early in our research program but with an alternative value for Market 1. Having marginal cost equal to zero yields a nonunique Nash equilibrium.

TABLE 7.4. Baseline Zero Marginal Cost and Costly Communication after Round 10 (Average Net Yield as a Percentage of Maximum)

	Round				
	1–5	6–10	11–15	16–20	21–25
Baseline Zero Marginal Cost					
Mean, experiments 32–34	42	45	36	35	—
Costly Communication					
Experiment 35	67	54	60	100	100
Experiment 36	41	35	83	56	47
Experiment 37	32	26	85	97	83
Mean, experiments 35–37	47	38	76	84	76

experiments (35–37). Recall that the ability to fund the communication mechanism was allowed only in rounds 11–20. From table 7.4, we see the aggregate effect of the communication opportunity. In the first 10 rounds of the communication experiments, the mean level of net yield is nearly identical to that observed in our baseline experiments (42 percent compared to 43 percent). In rounds 11–20, net yields shift significantly to an average of 80 percent. This compares to 35 percent in rounds 11–20 of the baseline experiments. Clearly the ability to communicate has translated into a shift in efficiency. Unlike the 14 experiments in which the right to communicate was provided without cost on a repeated basis, however, these subjects struggled to provide the communication mechanism and to coordinate strategies.

We turn now to a detailed account of the decision process in each of the 3 costly communication experiments.

Experiment 35

In the first 2 rounds of this experiment, the players did not achieve sufficient contributions to fund the right to communicate. Three players contributed 20 cents after round 10 and again after round 11, but they failed to gain the five contributions needed to provide a communication period. After round 12, the group was successful when six players made contributions. Player D (who was the only player not to make a contribution in any of the prior rounds) led the discussion with a suggestion that the group develop a rotation scheme for investments in Market 2. Player D was the major "verbal organizer" in both communication experiments in which he participated. Players D and G spent a minute or so calculating the optimal strategy. Player G then proposed that "we all put in 5, and that we rotate two people putting in 6. That looks pretty good, shall we do that?" It took some time to figure out how to coordinate the rotation system, but eventually a scheme was agreed upon. In this discussion, no reference was made to the problem of cheating or to the need to hold firm to the agreement so as to avoid paying the cost of communicating again.

After this single communication period, the players implemented the agreement perfectly for 4 rounds. When this first "rotation" was accomplished, Player A cast a solitary vote for a second communication period. Only minor deviations occurred during the next 5 rounds, and no further effort was made to communicate. Overall, the players in this group conformed to their agreed-upon strategies in 92 percent of their actual investment decisions.

Experiment 36

In this second costly communication experiment, five subjects contributed 20 cents at their first opportunity. Player G started the session with this statement:

> The reason we are here is to make a profit, so we need to lower the group investment down from 66 and 70, which we have been doing, down to say 42 or 40. And if we all agree to invest 5, then we would have 40 invested as a group. Ten in Market 1 and 5 in Market 2. We would get maximum profit out of this. Is that a reasonable decision?

Some further effort was made to calculate whether or not this was optimal. Relative to other groups, these subjects focused on calculations with very little discussion. Only seven statements were made during the communication period. Player G ended this period with the statement: "Everybody needs to do it—if you remember from last time, if everyone does not do it then someone sucks it."

Round 11 involved perfect coordination. In round 12, player A (who had said nothing in the discussion period) invested 15 tokens in Market 2, while the others held to their agreement to invest 5. In round 13, players E and D increased their investment in Market 2 by 1 token, and thus joined player A as defectors, even though their rate of defection was low. By round 14, there were five defectors and only three players holding to the agreement. Three players contributed 20 cents each after the fourteenth round in an unsuccessful attempt to regain the right to communicate. After round 15, a solitary player contributed 20 cents toward communication; that was the last contribution toward communication made in this experiment. Several of the players continued their low contribution rates while most of the players did not.

The players in this group conformed to their agreed-upon strategies in 45 percent of their actual investment decisions—the lowest percentage of any of the communication experiments. Although the players had achieved over 90 percent of the available net yield in the first 4 rounds after communication, the percentage fell steadily to 47 percent in the last 3 rounds of the experiment.

Experiment 37

In this experiment, four subjects contributed toward communication after the tenth round, falling one vote shy of the provision level. After the eleventh round, six individuals made the necessary contribution to obtain the right to communicate. Two of the players, who had been among the most active communicators in the earlier experiments, took the lead (as well as financially contributing toward the achievement of a communication period). After some hurried calculations, the group decided to invest 6 tokens in Market 2 and 9 in Market 1. They obtained 98 percent of the available net yield with this strategy. The players seemed concerned about making a quick decision and avoiding the need for further communication. As player E argued during the communication period: "Let's decide something so that we all know what we are doing so that we don't have to conference each time." On his debriefing form, player E indicated: "Instead of a complicated maximizing scheme, we chose a simple, easy-to-follow method to set relatively maximized profits."

For 10 rounds, the players observed perfect compliance to their agreement with no further discussion. In round 20, player A invested 9 instead of 6 tokens in Market 2. In round 21—the unannounced final round—player A continued the investment of 9 tokens while player D invested all 15 tokens in Market 2. Player D had invested 15 tokens throughout the noncommunication rounds, had not voted at any time to hold a communication period, did not say anything during their discussion, and had conformed to the agreement for 9 rounds. On his debriefing form he commented on his actions in the following way:

> I never purchased because I felt like the others would purchase it, consequently, I wouldn't lose $.20. I didn't feel like I was taking advantage of the group in this respect. I also felt like since I didn't purchase the opportunity, I did not have to abide by the group's decision because I really didn't want to meet.

The players in this group conformed to their agreed-upon strategies in 96 percent of their actual investment decisions. In the 10 rounds following successful provision of the opportunity to communicate, this group averaged 96 percent of optimal net yield from the CPR.

These experiments demonstrate the strength as well as the fragile nature of costly communication. Since it was costly to communicate, each group met only once. Two of the groups had to go several rounds before sufficient contributions enabled them to meet. What is striking, however, is that two of the groups achieved almost perfect compliance to their joint strategy after only a single opportunity to discuss the problem. The other group experienced cascading defections once it was clear that they could not mount the level of voluntary contributions needed to achieve a second or third "pep talk."

Conclusions

These experiments provide strong evidence for the power of face-to-face communication in a repeated CPR dilemma where decisions are made privately. When communication was provided as a costless institution that could be drawn upon on a systematic basis, players successfully used the opportunity (1) to calculate coordinated yield-improving strategies, (2) to devise verbal agreements to implement these strategies, and (3) to deal with nonconforming players. Considerable time and effort was expended during the communication periods simply trying to ascertain the optimal, joint strategy, since these experiments afforded considerably more choice than a dichotomy between a "cooperative" and a "noncooperative" strategy. On the other hand, our design in which communication was a one-shot institution and our high-endowment design, which allowed for greater appropriation power in the hands of individuals, demonstrated that words alone can be quite fragile.

In those experiments where players received only aggregate information about outcomes, the problem of dealing with cheating was potentially even more difficult to cope with than the problem of discovering the optimum. How subjects dealt with this problem is revealing, both in terms of what they did and did not do. Verbal criticism was a common ploy used against anonymous defectors. Evocative terms, such as *scumbucket* and *pimp*, were used as negative persuasion. At no time did they agree to adopt a trigger strategy. Several groups overtly faced the problem of small levels of nonconformance, discussed trigger strategies, and decided to keep as close to their agreement as possible as long as the level of deviation did not get too large. The potential threat of everything unraveling was clearly in view.

In field settings, it is rare that the opportunity to communicate is costless. Someone has to invest time and effort to create and maintain arenas for face-to-face communication. The costly communication experiments investigated the effort of costly provision of the communication mechanisms on (1) the ability of players to provide the mechanism and (2) the impact of the second-order dilemma in solving the first-order dilemma posed by the CPR experiment itself. The provision problems that players faced in the costly communication experiments were not trivial and did, in fact, create a barrier. In all three experiments, the problem of providing the institution for communication reduced the speed with which an agreement could be reached and the efficacy of dealing with players who broke an agreement. On the other hand, all groups eventually succeeded in providing the communication mechanisms (but only once) and in dealing (to some degree) with the CPR dilemma. On average, efficiency in these groups increased from 42 to 80 percent.

In general, these results are consistent with closely related research. Isaac and Walker (1988a, 1991) found similar results for costless and costly communication in a public-good environment with symmetric payoffs. In experiments similar to those discussed above for costly communication, they found that increasing the complexity of the environment reduced the success of face-to-face communication, but that, even with this reduction, the institution remained a successful mechanism for improving market efficiency. Further, in recent research Hackett, Schlager, and Walker (1993) examine the robustness of communication as an efficiency-enhancing mechanism in settings where appropriators differ in size, as measured in appropriation capacity. This heterogeneity creates a distributional conflict over the allocation of access to common-pool resources. They present findings from a series of experiments where heterogeneous endowments are assigned (1) randomly, and appropriators have complete information; (2) through an auction, and appropriators have complete information; and (3) randomly, and appropriators have incomplete and asymmetric information. In summary, their study demonstrated the robustness of this institution in situations of endowment heterogeneity. Heterogeneous appropriators, when allowed to engage in face-to-face communication, substantially increased the level of rents earned from the common-pool resource. In addition, yield enhancement remained substantial (although reduced) under relatively severe conditions of four endowment types with incomplete and asymmetric information.

Of the five hypotheses forwarded by others to explain the impact of communication (see the first section of this chapter), the evidence from our experiments clearly supports two:

1. Communication did provide an opportunity for individuals to offer and extract promises of cooperation for nonenforceable contracts.
2. Communication did facilitate the boosting of prior normative orientations.

Our experiments, however, cannot clearly differentiate between the various normative orientations that are evoked in such situations. We tend to agree with Orbell, van de Kragt, and Dawes (1988) that keeping promises appears to be a more fundamental, shared norm than "cooperation per se." It is, of course, difficult to sort these out. When a defector is called a "scumbucket," is the reproach being used because someone is breaking a promise, is being uncooperative, or is taking advantage of others who are keeping a promise? The strength of the reproaches used probably reflects the multiple offenses committed by those who did not keep to their prior agreements.

The evidence from these experiments demonstrates that external agents are not necessary to achieve high levels of conformance to verbal promises even when

1. players make repeated anonymous and private decisions and breaking the verbal agreement strongly dominates keeping the verbal agreement; and
2. players do not have an opportunity to establish a well-defined community with strong internal norms and established ways to enforce these norms.

On the other hand, the evidence from these experiments should not be interpreted as supporting arguments that communication alone is sufficient to overcome repeated dilemma problems in general. While many endogenous arrangements appear to evolve in experimental and field settings to overcome CPR dilemmas, many endogenous efforts have failed as well. The evidence from the high-endowment and one-shot communication experiments suggests why individuals in some natural settings do not rely solely on face-to-face communication. When the actions of one or a few individuals can be a strong disequilibrating force or frequent opportunities for communication are not feasible, individuals who have the capacity to agree to sanction one another as well as communicate with one another might well want to add the sword to a covenant. While the theoretical predictions are that individuals in such settings would not sanction one another, endogenous sanctioning is frequently observed in field settings. In the next chapter, we explore a range of questions involving the development of endogenous institutions, including the effects of various types of internal and external sanctioning mechanisms.

CHAPTER 8

Sanctioning and Communication Institutions

In chapter 7, we investigated decision behavior in an environment with face-to-face communication as a mechanism for coordinating appropriation behavior. We found that communication improves efficiency, but several factors consistently affect its success. In situations where subjects were provided only one opportunity to communicate, communication enabled subjects to begin the process of adopting a joint strategy. The inability to communicate on a repeated basis, however, limited the durability of their agreements. In a decision environment where subjects were given repeated opportunities to communicate, subjects offered and extracted promises of cooperation and chastised one another when conformance was not complete, thereby increasing their joint yield significantly above that obtained prior to communication.[1]

Discussions went well beyond discovering the level of investments that would generate maximum yields. Subjects used the communication periods to establish a well-defined community and internal norms, as well as to devise their own agreements and verbal punishments for those who broke those agreements. These verbal sanctions had to be directed at unknown defectors in the group, since subjects' decisions were anonymous. Subjects, who had to detect defection solely through aggregate investments, were still able to decrease defection rates substantially. However, verbal sanctions were less effective when the token endowment of each subject was increased, thus giving each subject the opportunity to exercise a greater impact in the CPR environment. In the low-endowment environment, net yields averaged 99 percent of optimum in the repeated-communication phase with a 5 percent defection rate. In the high-endowment environment, net yields averaged only 73 percent of optimum, with a 13 percent defection rate. Finally, when subjects were placed in a decision environment in which they must first pay for the opportunity to communicate, the efficiency-generating properties of this mechanism were shown to be further constrained. Understanding internally imposed monitoring and sanctioning behavior more thoroughly provides a key to under-

---

1. This chapter relies extensively on E. Ostrom, Walker, and Gardner 1992.

standing endogenous solutions to collective-action dilemmas. Using controlled laboratory experiments, we now examine more closely existing theories of CPR equilibrium in the absence of and presence of sanctioning and monitoring.

Sanctioning in the Constituent Game

Our sanctioning institution is built on the constituent game X in the following fashion. It can be represented formally using the following construction. Let s, the sanctioning matrix, be a matrix of 0's and 1's, where $s_{ij} = 1$ means that player i has sanctioned player j, and $s_{ij} = 0$ means that i has not sanctioned j. Row i of the matrix s codes all of player i's sanctioning behavior. As before, let x be a vector of individual investments in the CPR and $u_i(x)$ be i's payoff function in the game without sanctioning. Player i's payoff function in the game with sanctioning, $u_i(x,s)$, is given by

$$u_i(x,s) = u_i(x) - f1 \sum_j s_{ij} - f2 \sum_j s_{ji}. \qquad (8.1)$$

The parameters $f1$ and $f2$ represent the cost of fining and the cost of being fined, respectively.[2] The sum Σs_{ij} is the total number of fines j levied by player i, costing him or her $f1$ each; the sum Σs_{ji} is the total number of times player i is fined, costing him or her $f2$ each.

Adding this sanctioning mechanism to our constituent game X produces a game X-S with a unique symmetric subgame consistent equilibrium. In a one-shot game with a unique symmetric equilibrium x^*, any sanctioning activity is costly and cannot lead to higher payoffs. Thus, the symmetric equilibrium of the one-shot game with sanctioning is the pair $(x^*,S^*) = (x^*,0)$; that is, the equilibrium sanctioning matrix is the 0-matrix. At equilibrium, no one sanctions. Now suppose that the one-shot CPR game with sanctioning is to be repeated a finite number of times T. This finitely repeated game has a unique symmetric subgame consistent equilibrium given by (8.2):

In every round, play $(x^*,0)$.
In the event of any deviation from prescribed play,
resume playing $(x^*,0)$ after the deviation.   (8.2)

This equilibrium follows from backward induction. At the last round T, no deviation is profitable. At the next to last round $T-1$, given that no deviations

---

2. We use the word *fine* not in the context of redistribution. What is crucial here is that real resources are used up, and not merely redistributed, by efforts to sanction.

will occur in the last round, then no deviation is profitable, and so on. Repeating the game should not lead to sanctioning either.

Besides the unique symmetric subgame consistent equilibrium, there are many imperfect equilibria as well. Let $z_i < x_i^*$ be the same for all i. Consider the repeated game strategy (8.3):

> In every round except T, play $(z,0)$.
> In the event of any deviation, play $(x_i = e, s = I)$ for one round,
> then resume playing $(z,0)$.
> If no deviation took place in round $T-1$, play $(x^*,0)$ in round T.   (8.3)

Equation (8.3) represents a trigger strategy. All players agree to invest less than they would according to (8.2). If some player cheats, then every player dumps all their resources into the CPR ($x_i = e$) and every player issues one sanction for one round. Then play returns to normal. In the final round, everyone plays the one-shot Nash equilibrium. We claim that (8.3) represents an imperfect equilibrium. To show this, it suffices to show that no deviation from prescribed play pays. Let $F(ne)$ be a very large negative number. For $f1$ and $f2$ large enough, a player who deviated optimally for one round would lose some positive amount, depending on the level of z_i, but in the next round would lose $(1/n)F(ne) + f1 + f2$ due to punishment from overinvestment and sanctions, as in (8.3). This threat we call the *dire threat*, as it is the worst threat imaginable for one round in our design. Given such a threat, it does not pay to deviate, even for one round. Finally, if a punishment is not called for in the last round, the endgame equilibrium is played in that round. This shows that (8.3) is an equilibrium. The imperfection of (8.3) lies in the fact that the trigger punishment—dumping all tokens into the resource, everybody placing a fine—is too harsh to be credible at the end of the game.[3]

There is a large set of equilibria along the lines of (8.3), involving variation of the length of punishment (1 or more rounds), the base level of investments z_i, and the direness of the one-period threat (dump not quite all tokens in the CPR, levy fines with some probability). In particular, by varying $f1$ and $f2$, we hoped to allow the subjects to find equilibria of the family (8.3) that involve punishments of the form (z_i,I)—that is to say, reduced investment in the CPR, but sanctions for everyone if a deviation occurs (see Jankowski 1990).

---

3. Besides the symmetric imperfect equilibria given above, there are many asymmetric equilibria. Take any permutation of the identity matrix—for instance, 1 sanctions 2, 2 sanctions 3, and so on. Then these permuted sanctions also support the same outcome as (7) does. Notice that if mistakes are what cause deviations, then an equilibrium like (7) will generate n fines every time a mistake takes place, which is considerably more than the 0 fines generated by the subgame consistent equilibrium (6).

We investigate the combination of communication with sanctioning in two ways. Our first design allows for a one-shot communication period, which is then followed by a sequence of constituent games with a sanctioning mechanism imposed. In our second design, we impose a one-shot communication period in conjunction with an opportunity for the subjects to choose whether or not they want a sanctioning mechanism. In both designs, the payoff functions are still given by (8.1) since communication per se has no payoff consequences and sanctioning does. Without loss of generality, let c be a communication strategy. Then appending c to the strategy given by (8.2) yields a subgame consistent equilibrium, and every subgame consistent equilibrium has the same payoffs as does (8.2). In addition, as in repeated X-S, imperfect equilibria exist yielding higher payoffs than equilibria that are subgame consistent.

The Experimental Setting and Results

The parameters for all experiments reported in this chapter are identical to those for the high-endowment (25 tokens per subject) reported in chapter 5. Our presentation of the results will be organized around two major institutional configurations: (1) an imposed sanctioning mechanism and (2) an imposed communication mechanism with an imposed sanctioning mechanism or with an opportunity to choose a sanctioning mechanism. Figure 8.1 gives an overview of the experimental design. For the reader interested in a brief summary, table 8.1 presents results across designs, focusing on the average net yield from the CPR (Market 2) as a percent of maximum possible net yield.

Imposed Sanctioning—No Communication

Experiments in this design began like high-endowment baseline experiments with the exception that after each round, subjects received *individual* data on all decisions.[4] This information was given by subject number, thus maintaining anonymity. Our sanctioning mechanism required that each subject incur a cost (a fee) in order to sanction another. In our first sanctioning design, after round 10, subjects were given an announcement summarized below.

> Subjects were informed that in all remaining rounds each would be given the opportunity to place a fine. Each subject could levy one fine at a specified fee. The subject fined would pay a fine of a specified amount. It

---

4. Earlier experiments focusing on sanctioning mechanisms without communication include Yamagishi 1986, 1988.

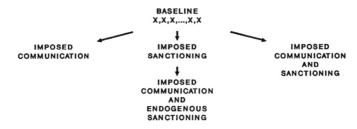

Fig. 8.1. Experimental design: institutions for facilitating gains in efficiency

was possible for a single subject to be charged multiple fines. After each round, each subject filled out a fining form. These forms were collected and tallied by the experimenter, who then reported the results privately to each subject. Note that any subject who was fined did not know the identity of those who imposed the fine. At the end of the experiment, the experimenters subtracted from subjects' total profits the total of all fees and all fines.

The actual fees ranged from 5 to 20 cents, and fines from 10 to 80 cents. The fee/fine ratio was either .25 or .50. After subjects read the announcement, questions regarding the implementation of the procedure were answered. No

TABLE 8.1. Baseline and Sanctioning, 25-Token Designs (Average Net Yield as a Percentage of Maximum)

Experimental Design	Round					
	1–5	6–10	11–15	16–20	21–25	26+
Baseline	−43	−12	10	32	—	—
Sanctioning	−36	−40	40	39	29	—
One-shot communication sanction	−1	−27	87	86	83	78
One-shot communication no sanction chosen[a]	46	41	92	62	15	—
One-shot communication sanction chosen[a]	−17	−5	93	92	90	94
One-shot communication sanction chosen[b]	—	—	97	97	97	90

[a]Communication and sanctioning choice occurred after round 10.

[b]Communication and sanctioning choice occurred after round 1; data displayed beginning in round 11 for comparison purposes.

discussion was held on why the subjects might want to use the procedure or its possible consequences. This created an experimental setting as close as possible to the noncooperative assumptions of no communication and no capacity to engage in enforceable agreements. The structure of the imposed sanctioning design is

X, X, . . . X-S,X-S,X-S, . . . , X-S, X.

The principal results from these experiments can be summarized as follows:

1. Significantly more sanctioning occurs than predicted by subgame perfection and the frequency is inversely related to cost.
2. Sanctioning is primarily focused on heavy Market 2 investors.
3. There is a nontrivial amount of sanctioning that can be classified as error, lagged punishment, or "blind" revenge.
4. Independent sanctioning as employed in this experimental context has a modest impact on net yield from Market 2 (the CPR).
5. When fining fees and sanctioning costs are included in measurements of net yield, the gains in net yield due to lower Market 2 investments are wiped out.

Our first principal finding is that subjects actually sanctioned each other at a much higher rate than the 0 rate predicted by subgame perfection. We observed 176 instances of sanctioning across the eight experiments. In no experiment did we observe fewer than 10 instances of sanctioning. The frequency of sanctions is inversely related to the cost of imposing the fine and dramatically increases with the stiffness of the fine. Further, our results, although reminiscent of equation (8.3), do not strictly support the conclusion that players were playing an equilibrium of this form. Except for experiment 43, where the degree of reduction in net yield was less than 5 percent, our experiments reveal patterns of investments in the CPR and levels of sanctioning that are too inefficient to be imperfect equilibria.

The second and third results relate to the reasons for sanctioning. From postexperiment interviews and personal observations, we offer four explanations for the higher-than-predicted level of sanctioning.

a. One-period punishment—the person fined was the highest or one of the highest investors in the previous period.
b. Lagged punishment—the person fined was one of the highest investors in Market 2 in either the no sanctioning rounds or in earlier rounds of the sanctioning rounds.

c. Blind revenge—the person fined was a low Market 2 investor and was fined by a person fined in a previous period.

d. Error—no obvious explanation can be given for the action (trembling hand).

In table 8.2, we summarize the frequency of fines falling in each category (we have combined blind revenge and error due to low frequency and difficulty in distinguishing between the two in the data). Several conclusions can be drawn from this very preliminary analysis. Seventy-seven percent of all sanctioning is aimed at investors who in the previous period were above-average investors in Market 2. An additional 7 percent were aimed at players who had been heavy investors in Market 2 in earlier (but not the most recent) rounds. We would classify an additional 5 percent in the blind revenge category and the remaining 11 percent as errors.

The fourth result focuses on the level of net yield obtained from the CPR when sanctioning is imposed. The results from the eight experiments in which the sanctioning mechanism was used are reported in figure 8.2. This figure contrasts the mean level net yield accrued as a percentage of optimum in the baseline experiments with the results from the experiments with sanctioning. Clearly, the first 10 rounds (when no sanctioning was in place) do not significantly differ between the two sets of experiments. This result suggests that the addition of anonymous information on individual decisions had no observable impact on investments. In rounds 11–20, one might argue that sanctioning had some effect in increasing the level of net yield earned and thus increasing efficiency. However, the effect on the level of net yield accrual is

TABLE 8.2. Reason for Sanctioning (Number of Instances)

	Experiment (Fee/Fine)			
Reason	52, 53 (5/10)	56 (5/20)	77, 88 (40/80)	79, 83, 84 (20/80)	Mean Per Experiment
One-period punishment[a]	50	33	23	29	16.9
Lagged punishment[b]	1	1	1	10	1.6
Blind revenge or error[c]	3	8	3	14	3.5
Mean total incidents per experiment	27	42	13.5	17.7	

[a]The person fined was one of the highest investors in the previous round.

[b]The person fined was one of the highest investors in either the no-sanctioning rounds or in one of the prior sanctioning rounds.

[c]The person fined was a low investor and was fined by a person fined in a previous period; or no obvious explanation can be given for the action (trembling hand).

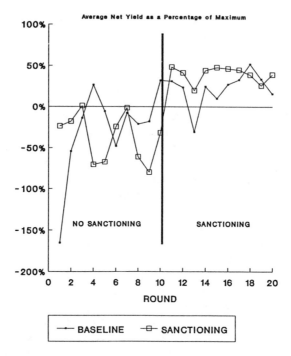

Fig. 8.2. Baseline (experiments 4–6) versus imposed sanctioning (experiments 38–45)

modest: average net yield over rounds 11–20 were 29 percent in the baseline and 39 percent in experiments with sanctioning.

In figures 8.3a–h, we report across period behavior within each of the sanctioning experiments. In the top panel of each figure the level of net yield accrued as a percentage of optimum is displayed. The lower panel summarizes period-by-period information on the number of fines that were placed each period and (above each bar) the number of individuals that were fined. Several features of these experiments stand out. In only one of the eight experiments do we see the sanctioning mechanism having a major impact on the level of net yield accrued (experiment 43). In this experiment, where the fee to fine ratio was 20/80, the level of net yield increased from an average of −60 percent in the first 10 rounds to 95 percent in the final 15 rounds. Fines were placed frequently (an average of 2.6 per period) and primarily on two subjects (28 of 37 fines) who tended to be relatively high Market 2 investors.

Our final result displayed in table 8.3 incorporates the impact of fees and fines on net yield. In summary, fining fees and sanctioning costs offset gains in efficiency arising from decreased investment in Market 2. In summary,

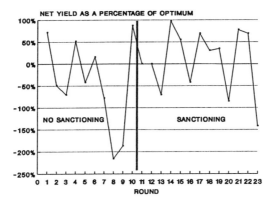

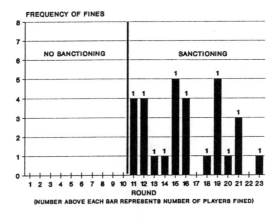

a) (experiment 38, 5/10)

Fig. 8.3. No communication with imposed sanctioning. (a) (experiment 38, 5/10). (b) (experiment 39, 5/10). (c) (experiment 40, 5/20). (d) (experiment 41, 40/80). (e) (experiment 42, 40/80). (f) (experiment 43, 20/80). (g) (experiment 44, 20/80). (h) (experiment 45, 20/80)

when fees and fines are accounted for, net yield drops from an average of 37 percent to 9 percent across rounds 11–20 or greater. Experiment 42 is an interesting case. During the sanctioning phase, net yield averaged 96 percent of optimum. Taking into account fees and fines, net yield was reduced to 17 percent of optimum.

One might conjecture that the lack of a significant improvement in net yield accrual with the introduction of a sanctioning mechanism in the design described above could be due to a hysteresis effect tied to the decisions in the first 10 rounds, rounds in which there was no sanctioning mechanism. Below,

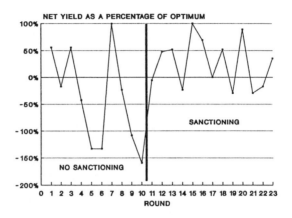

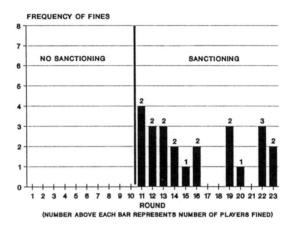

b) (experiment 39, 5/10)

Fig. 8.3. Continued

we report the results from three additional experiments (46–48) conducted in which the sanctioning mechanism was introduced prior to the first decision period. In all three experiments, the fee-to-fine ratio was $.40 to $.80. Subjects used fines repeatedly in all three experiments. On average, there were 17.3 fines placed per experiment, similar to the average of 13.5 (table 8.2) we observed in our first set of 40/80 experiments. The results from these three new experiments are summarized in figure 8.4. Plotted is the mean level of net yield accrual for each decision period. These measures are contrasted with the means from our baseline experiments in which no sanctioning mechanism was available to subjects. As one can see, the results are consistent with those

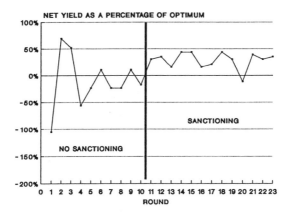

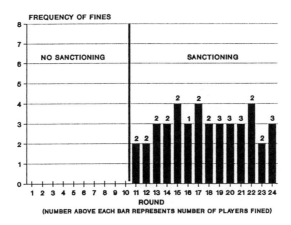

c) (experiment 40, 5/20)

Fig. 8.3.   Continued

for our first design. There is no persistent yield-improving behavior that can be tied to the introduction of the sanctioning mechanism. Examining net yield when costs of fees and fines are incorporated leads to the same conclusion. In fact, it points to the composite result that fees and fines had a negative impact on net yield in comparison to our baseline results.

Imposed and Endogenous Sanctioning with Communication

Our last two decision environments investigate the consequences of combining a one-shot opportunity to communicate with either (1) an experimenter-

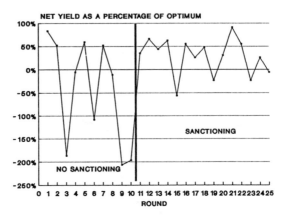

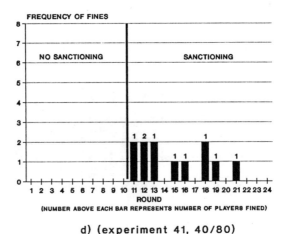

d) (experiment 41, 40/80)

Fig. 8.3.   Continued

imposed sanctioning mechanism or (2) an opportunity to decide whether or not to adopt a sanctioning mechanism endogenously. These experiments began like those in the design with sanctioning alone. After round 10, subjects were given an announcement that they would have a single 10-minute discussion period. In experiments with an imposed-sanctioning mechanism, subjects were also given an announcement (prior to discussion) similar to that of the sanctioning alone environment. In experiments where subjects had an opportunity to choose a sanctioning mechanism, the announcement informed them that at the end of 10 minutes they would vote (1) on whether to institute a sanctioning mechanism and (2) on the level of fines if they did institute one.

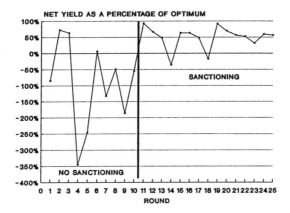

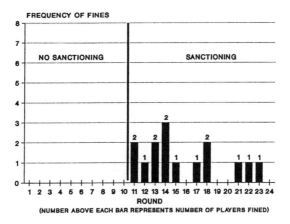

e) (experiment 42, 40/80)

Fig. 8.3. Continued

The only restriction on the sanctioning mechanism was that the fee to fine ratio was 1:2. The voting rule was strict majority, with the status quo being a repeated baseline experiment without a sanctioning mechanism.

Imposed Communication and Imposed Sanctioning
The structure of the three experiments in this design is

X, X, . . . , X, C, X-S, X-S, . . . X-S, X.

The results from the experiments conducted in this decision environment are summarized in table 8.4. In experiment 49, the participants rapidly focused

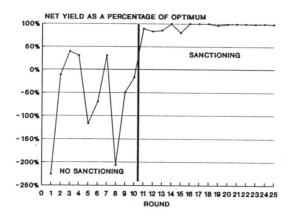

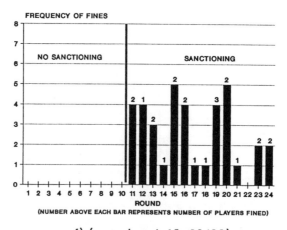

f) (experiment 43, 20/80)

Fig. 8.3. Continued

on the problem of deciding upon a joint investment strategy. They spent most of their 10 minutes calculating various options to ensure that they had discovered an optimal strategy. They decided to invest 4 tokens each in Market 2 and the remaining 21 tokens in Market 1. Further, they agreed to fine one another if anyone put more than 4 tokens in Market 2. One subject characterized their strategy in the following way: "If everyone puts in 4 tokens, we are going to be making 42 cents more money in the individual accounts. This is the highest." A second subject characterized their unanimous agreement: "Does everyone agree to this? OK, now we have agreed that everyone will put 4 tokens in and if anyone puts any more in, we are all going to fine them. Is that

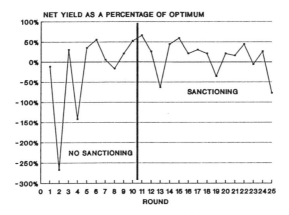

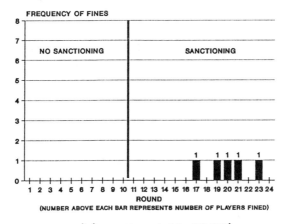

g) (experiment 44, 20/80)

Fig. 8.3. Continued

all agreed, now?" With this specific agreement to which everyone nodded assent, the subjects returned to their terminals and made investments for 16 more rounds without a single defection nor any use of the sanctioning mechanism. They obtained 98 percent of maximum net yield from the CPR and did not waste resources on fees or fines.

In experiment 50, the subjects did not find the optimal strategy but devised a complex rotation system to ensure that they all received what they thought would be maximal returns. They decided that each subject would invest 6 tokens in Market 2 and the right to invest 2 more tokens each round would be rotated first to subject 1, then to subject 2, on through subject 8. One

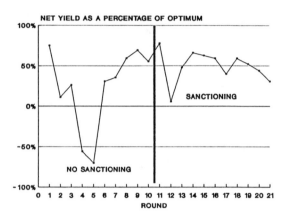

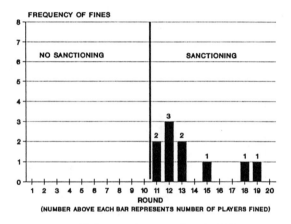

h) (experiment 45, 20/80)

Fig. 8.3. Continued

subject suggested that they not fine at all, but another argued: "No, let's fine anyone who breaks our rules. If they break our rules, then we should fine 'em!" After further discussion, the subjects agreed that they would use the sanctioning mechanism to fine anyone who deviated from "their rules." For 2 rounds they kept their agreement. On round 13, one subject invested 7 rather than 6 and was immediately fined by one of the other subjects. On round 19, two subjects invested one more token than agreed upon and were immediately sanctioned by one subject each. No more defections were attempted and no more fees were paid to assess fines. In this experiment, the subjects achieved

TABLE 8.3.   Average Percentage of Net Yield without and with Fees and Fines in Sanctioning Experiments without Communication

Experiment (fee/fine)	Average Percent of Net Yield	
	Without Fees and Fines Included	With Fees and Fines Included
38 (5/10)	50	24
39 (5/10)	13	3
40 (5/20)	26	18
41 (40/80)	7	−3
42 (40/80)	96	17
43 (20/80)	49	12
44 (20/80)	29	−0
45 (20/80)	28	6
Average	37	9

Notes: Sanctioning experiments had no sanctioning option in rounds 1–10. Sanctioning followed each round after round 11. Experiments were conducted from 21 to 25 decision periods.

86 percent of maximum net yield (since they had miscalculated the optimum). When fees and fines are incorporated, net yield drops to 79 percent.

In experiment 51, the subjects never discussed the possibility of devising a joint strategy even though they mentioned how the overinvestment of some of the subjects during the first 10 rounds had made it difficult for the rest of them. The closest they got to an agreement was to discuss fining those who were obviously overinvesting—for example, "those who invested over 21 tokens in Market 2." A considerable amount of their discussion time was wasted in awkward silence. They finally asked whether they had to sit there the entire 10 minutes. After verifying that no subject wanted to use the remaining two minutes of their time for further discussion, the experimenters let the subjects return to their terminals. Following the communication period, the subjects achieved an average of 70 percent of net yield from the CPR, up from −14 percent in prediscussion rounds. A total of 20 $.40 fees were paid to impose the same number of $.80 fines on other subjects. The fines were directed toward subjects who had invested heavily in Market 2 in the prior round. Net yield fell to 24 percent with fees and fines deducted from earnings.

Imposed Communication and Endogenous Sanctioning
In order to make the choice of a sanctioning mechanism meaningful, subjects in this decision environment were randomly drawn from the pool of subjects

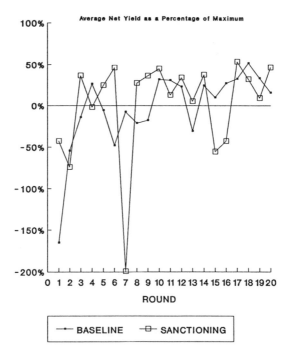

Fig. 8.4. Baseline (experiments 4–6) versus imposed sanctioning (experiments 46–48)

from our design with imposed sanctioning but *no communication*. The structure of the experiments in this design is

X, X, . . . , X, C, X, X, . . . , X or

X, X, . . . , X, C, X-S, X-S, . . . , X-S, X.

The results from the four experiments conducted in this decision environment are summarized in tables 8.5 and 8.6.

In experiments 52 and 53, the subjects agreed to an investment strategy and a sanctioning mechanism that led to near optimal yield. Further, there was very little waste of resources in implementing the sanctioning mechanism. In experiment 52, no sanctions were used. Net yield increased from an average of 26 percent in the first 10 rounds to an average of 90 percent in the rounds following communication and implementation of the sanctioning mechanism. In experiment 53, there were several rounds in which sanctions were employed. In nearly all cases, these fines were concentrated on players who,

TABLE 8.4. One-Shot Communication with Imposed Sanctioning (Average Net Yield as a Percentage of Maximum)

Experiment	Round					
	1–5	6–10	11–15	16–20	21–25	26
49	−14	−31	98	99	99	99
50	22	−36	86	86	86	91
51	−10	−14	77	75	63	44
Mean	−0	−27	87	86	83	78

given their CPR investments, were deviating from the agreed-upon strategy. Net yield increased from an average of 4 percent in the first 10 rounds to an average of 92 percent afterwards. With fees and fines incorporated, net yield still increased to 89 percent.

The subject groups in experiments 54 and 55 treated the opportunity to communicate and devise a sanctioning mechanism very differently from the subjects in the other two experiments with this design. Experiment 54 is an outlier. Out of more than a hundred experiments we have conducted, this is the only one where yields in the first 10 rounds were essentially optimal. When given the opportunity to discuss the decision problem and choose a sanctioning mechanism, the group (1) agreed that they did not need a mechanism and (2) agreed that no one should try to get "greedy"—that is, invest too much in the CPR. The group held together for a few rounds, after which yields began a gradual decline. This decline was due primarily to a gradual increase in CPR investments by two subjects. By round 25, yield had dropped to 56 percent of optimum.

TABLE 8.5. Sanctioning Agreements in One-Shot Communication with Sanctioning Option

Experiment	Communication Round	Agree to Use Fines	Fines Agreed Upon	Number of Tokens Agreed to Invest	Defection Rate	Fining Rate
52	After tenth round	Yes	$0.10	6	.00	no need
53	After tenth round	Yes	$0.20	5 or 6 is best, 8 too high	.04	1.0+
54	After tenth round	No	na	no agreement	na	na
55	After tenth round	No	na	4	.41	na
56	First round	Yes	$1.00	5	.00	no need
57	First round	Yes	$0.20	rotate 5 and 6	.04	1.0

**TABLE 8.6.   One-Shot Communication with Sanctioning Option
(Average Net Yield as a Percentage of Maximum)**

Experiment	Round				
	1–5	6–10	11–15	16–20	21–25
Design xx...xcsxsx...sxsx or xx...cxx...x					
52	−18	−35	89	89	89
53	−16	24	96	94	91
54	93	87	84	76	68
55	−0	−5	99	48	−39
Mean	15	18	92	77	52
Design cxsxsx....sxsx					
56	99	99	99	99	
57	95	95	95	82	
Mean	97	97	97	90	

The first 10 rounds of experiment 55 exhibit the standard pulsing pattern in yields, net yield averaging below 20 percent. When given the opportunity to communicate, most players in this group (not all) adamantly opposed the implementation of the sanctioning mechanism. The group discussed the optimal investment strategy; each subject agreed to invest 4 tokens in the CPR. The group members opposing the use of a sanctioning mechanism argued that (1) it was too stressful; (2) fines couldn't be focused sufficiently, and at times "snowballed" into players fining other players with "revenge" in mind; and (3) a system of fines took money away from the group as a whole.

After the discussion, this group successfully followed their near-optimal investment pattern for two rounds. In round 13, one subject increased their investment to 5 tokens. In round 14, this subject returned to 4 tokens but another subject invested 5 tokens. In round 14, both of these subjects marginally increased their CPR investments. The subsequent rounds showed a gradual increase in investments by virtually every player. By round 17 the group was back to a pattern of investments parallel to baseline conditions. Net yields reached levels as low as −322 percent of maximum yield. After the experiment ended, several of the subjects expressed the opinion that they should have established a sanctioning mechanism after all.

We have traced back to the specific sanctioning/no communication experiment in which each of these subjects participated. Of the 32 subjects in these four experiments, 18 voted for and 14 voted against the implementation of a sanctioning mechanism. Of the 14 who voted no, 11 had previously participated in a sanctioning experiment with a fee to fine ratio of $.20/$.80. Of the 18 who voted yes, only 3 had been in a $.20/$.80 design. We infer from this result that the high level of sanctioning activity in the $.20/$.80 design, the lack of overall efficiency gains, and the presence of blind revenge combined to impede the willingness of participants to choose a sanctioning mechanism.

It is possible that the experience of the first 10 rounds of the constituent game had an effect on mechanism choice. To examine this possible hysteresis effect, two additional experiments (56–57) were conducted. In these two experiments, the opportunity to communicate and to adopt a sanctioning mechanism was available at the outset. The structure of these two experiments is

C, X, X, . . . , X or C, X-S, X-S, . . . , X-S, X.

The results are presented in tables 8.5 and 8.6.

In both of these experiments, the subjects quickly agreed to an investment strategy and a sanctioning mechanism to punish defectors. In experiment 56, the subjects agreed to a strategy in which each invested 5 tokens in the CPR. The subjects in this experiment earned 99 percent of maximum net yields in every round. The adopted sanctioning mechanism was never used.

The subjects in experiment 57 adopted a sanctioning mechanism with a $.10/$.20 fee to fine ratio. The subjects mistook 46 tokens for the optimal solution (a solution that still earned them 95 percent of maximum yields). More importantly, however, investing 46 tokens meant the group had to work out a rotation scheme in which two subjects invested 5 tokens and the remaining six subjects invested 6 tokens. This strategy was followed for 2 rounds. In round 3, one subject deviated by investing 6 tokens instead of 5, and was promptly fined by two others. The group returned to compliance until round 14. At this time, the deviator from round 3 again deviated and was again fined twice. In round 19, a different subject deviated by investing 6 tokens. This subject was fined by one player. In this experiment, the subjects never explicitly agreed to a strategy that *all* players would fine a subject whose investment deviated from the agreed-upon strategy. In fact, most of the subjects did not impose a fine on those who deviated. It is worth noting, however, that the net benefit from investing 6 tokens instead of 5 is negative in the case in which there is at least one person fining.

The payoff consequences of selecting or not selecting a sanctioning mechanism were very different across the experiments in this design. The groups choosing some form of sanctioning institution earned average net yields of 93 percent in the postdiscussion phase. Indeed, yields this high suggest that this set of institutions, endogenously chosen, approximates the conditions necessary for a cooperative game. The groups not choosing some form of sanctioning institution earned average net yields of only 56 percent, with serious decay.

The results from this set of communication and sanctioning experiments suggest that some subjects can find yield-improving joint strategies, design a sanctioning mechanism, use the sanctioning mechanism, and achieve a high rate of conformance to their joint strategies. On the other hand, prior negative experience with institutions that individuals view as punitive and inefficient is not conducive to the design of better institutions nor to a willingness to use them.

Conclusions

The empirical evidence of this chapter is quite inconsistent with theoretical predictions. In experiments with an imposed sanctioning institution and no communication, as summarized in table 8.7, we find

1. subjects are willing to pay a fee to place a fine on another subject far more than predicted; and
2. average net yield increases from 21 percent with no sanctioning to 37 percent with sanctioning. When the costs of fees and fines are subtracted from average net yield, however, net yield drops to 9 percent.

Thus, subjects overuse the sanctioning mechanism, and sanctioning without communication reduces net yield.

In experiments where communication and sanctioning is combined in diverse ways, we find

TABLE 8.7. Aggregate Results, 25-Token Designs

Experimental Design	Average Percent Net Yield	Average Percent Net Yield (minus fees and fines)	Defection Rate (Percentage)
Baseline (experiments 4–6)	21	na	na
Sanction (experiments 38–45)	37	9	na
One-shot Communication, Sanction (experiments 46–48)	85	67	1
One-shot communication, no sanction chosen (experiments 54–55)	56	na	42
One-shot communication, sanction chosen (experiments 52–53, 56–57)	93	90	4

Note: All computations are for rounds in which the treatment was in effect. Nash equilibrium for all designs is 39 percent net CPR yield.

3. With an imposed sanctioning mechanism and a single opportunity to communicate, subjects achieve an average net yield of 85 percent. When the costs of fees and fines are subtracted, average net yield is still 67 percent. These represent substantial gains over baseline, where net yield averaged 21 percent.

4. With the right to choose a sanctioning mechanism and a single opportunity to communicate, subjects who adopt a sanctioning mechanism achieve an average net yield of 93 percent. When the costs of fees and fines are subtracted, average net yield is still 90 percent. In addition, the defection rate from agreements is only 4 percent.

5. With the right to choose a sanctioning mechanism and a single opportunity to communicate, subjects who do not adopt a sanctioning mechanism achieve an average net yield of only 56 percent. In addition, the defection rate from agreements is 42 percent.

Thus, subjects who use the opportunity to communicate to agree to a joint strategy and choose their own sanctioning mechanism achieve close to optimal results based entirely on the promises they make, their own efforts to monitor, and their own investments in sanctioning (Frohlich, Oppenheimer, and Eavey 1987 have similar findings). This is especially impressive in the high-endowment environment, where defection by a few subjects is very disruptive.

In no experiment where one or more subjects deviated from an agreed-upon joint strategy did the subjects then follow a strategy of substantially increasing their investments in the CPR.[5] In fact, in some experiments where one or more subjects deviated from an agreed-upon joint strategy, some subjects subsequently *reduced* their investments in the CPR. When subjects discussed the problem of how to respond to one or more defectors, they overtly rejected the idea of dumping all of their tokens into the CPR.

Two major implications follow from the results of this chapter. The first relates to policy analysis. Policymakers responsible for the governance and management of small-scale, common-pool resources should *not* presume that the individuals involved are caught in an inexorable tragedy from which there is no escape. Individuals may be able to arrive at joint strategies to manage these resources more efficiently. To accomplish this task they must have sufficient information to pose and solve the allocation problems they face. They must also have an arena where they can discuss joint strategies and perhaps implement monitoring and sanctioning. In other words, when indi-

---

5. Inducing trigger strategy behavior in experimental subjects is evidently extremely difficult. For a recent attempt, see Sell and Wilson 1991.

viduals are given an opportunity to restructure their own situation they frequently, but not always, use this opportunity to make commitments that they sustain, thus achieving higher joint outcomes without recourse to an external enforcer. We cannot replace the determinate prediction of "no cooperation" with a determinate prediction of "always cooperate." Our findings challenge the Hobbesian conclusion that the constitution of order is only possible by creating sovereigns who then must govern by being above subjects, by monitoring them, and by imposing sanctions on all who would otherwise not comply.[6]

The second major implication relates to behavioral theory. In finitely repeated social dilemma experiments, a wide variety of treatments that do not change the theoretically predicted subgame consistent equilibrium outcomes do change subjects' behavior. This raises a *substantive* question whether our subjects conceptualize their decision task in the way theorists do. For instance, if subjects believe the game is being repeated according to some exogenous probabilistic mechanism, then there are equilibria supporting more cooperative behavior if the subjective continuation probability is not too low. Or, it may be that subjects are acting as boundedly rational players in the sense of Selten, Mitzkewitz, and Uhlich 1988. In this case, the observed improvement in yield could be the result of boundedly rational behavior, as Selten, Mitzkewitz, and Uhlich observe in a duopoly context. This is an important question that we will address in the next chapter.

---

6. See V. Ostrom 1987, 1989, 1991 for an elucidation of an alternative theory to that of Hobbes.

CHAPTER 9

Regularities from the Laboratory and Possible Explanations

Our experiments have generated a series of empirical regularities. Let us briefly review these findings.

1. In the baseline experiments, the Nash equilibrium is the best predictor of aggregated outcomes for low-endowment experiments. In the high-endowment setting, aggregate behavior is far from Nash in early rounds but begins to approach Nash in later rounds. However, Nash is not a good predictor of individual strategies in either design. Further, subjects told us in debriefing interviews that they were investing more (less) in the CPR when the average rate of return on the previous round exceeded (fell below) the return from their other option. This type of heuristic helps to explain the pulsing patterns observed in baseline experiments, but is not consistent with predictions derived from noncooperative game theory.
2. The theoretically predicted outcomes are the same in low- and high-endowment environments. However, empirical results in the high-endowment design exhibited greater instability, less effective communication, lower joint outcomes, and higher defection rates.
3. Contrary to the theoretical prediction, subjects used the sanctioning mechanism even when they could not communicate. Subjects directed most of their sanctions toward those who overinvested in the CPR.
4. According to subgame consistency, past experience should not affect the decision whether or not to adopt a sanctioning mechanism. However, in our experimental designs with endogenous choice of a sanctioning mechanism, past experience affected subjects' choice. Two of the six groups presented with the choice to adopt sanctions decided against it. A high percentage of subjects in these two groups had experienced an environment in which a low cost, punitive sanctioning mechanism was imposed and used extensively.

195

One of the major questions left open by the series of communication experiments reported in chapters 7 and 8 is: Why is there so much cooperation in CPR dilemmas where subjects can communicate face to face? This question is of special importance given the findings from chapters 5 and 6. In experiments where subjects are not able to communicate, behavior at the aggregate level is consistent with predictions of suboptimality. Empirical regularities related to these communication experiments are as follows:

1. Subjects in repeated, high-endowment, CPR constituent games, with one and only one opportunity to communicate, obtained an average percentage of net yield above that which was obtained in baseline experiments in the same decision rounds without communication (55 percent compared to 21 percent—see table 9.1.).
2. Subjects in repeated, high-endowment, CPR constituent games, with *repeated opportunities* to communicate, obtained an average percentage of net yield that was substantially above that obtained in baseline experiments without communication (73 percent compared to 21 percent). In low-endowment games, the average net yield was 99 percent as compared to 34 percent.

TABLE 9.1.   Aggregate Results, All Designs

Experimental Design	Average Percent Net Yield in Experimental CPR after Round 10	Average Percent Net Yield in Experimental CPR (minus fees and fines)	Defection Rate
Baseline 10 tokens	34	na	na
Baseline 15 tokens	36	na	na
Baseline 25 tokens	21	na	na
One-Shot Communication 25 tokens	55	na	25
Costly Communication 15 tokens	80	na	20
Repeated Communication 10 tokens	99	na	5
Repeated Communication 25 tokens	73	na	13
One-Shot Communication Sanction 25 tokens	85	67	1
One-Shot Communication 25 tokens No Sanction Chosen	56	na	42

Note: All computations are for rounds in which the treatment was in effect. Nash equilibrium for all designs is 39 percent net CPR yield.

3. Repeated communication opportunities in high-endowment games led to higher joint outcomes (73 percent) than one-shot communication (55 percent), as well as lower defection rates (13 percent compared to 25 percent).
4. In no experiment where one or more subjects deviated from an agreed-upon joint strategy did the other subjects then follow a grim trigger strategy of substantially increasing their investments in the CPR.
5. Although communication agreements often came very close to near optimal yield, the subjects in these experiments frequently debated which strategy to adopt. Even with the high levels of information that we gave to subjects, it is obvious that subjects found the task of determining optimal strategies to be challenging. The agreements they adopted were frequently easy to remember and implement.

Assuming that individuals perceive the game as we have operationalized it in the laboratory setting, the subgame consistent equilibrium prediction for one-shot and repeated communication is the same as that for a finitely repeated constituent game without communication. Communication in any form should not make a difference, but it does. Repeating the opportunity for "mere jawboning" should not yield different results than one-shot communication, but it does. If communication were simply being used to agree upon a joint strategy, then one round of communication should suffice. Once individuals have made an agreement in the lab, much of the time spent communicating is devoted to establishing trust and verbally chastising unknown individuals if agreements are broken. These activities, when not backed up by enforceable agreements, do not yet play a theoretical role in explaining results within noncooperative game theory. These findings on the effects of face-to-face communication are supported by other experimental research (see discussion in chap. 7).[1]

For those who base predictions of higher levels of cooperation in repeated settings on the presumption that individuals will adopt grim trigger strategies, our evidence is contrary. Surprisingly, when one or more subjects deviated from an agreed-upon joint strategy in some experiments, a few subjects subsequently *reduced* their investments in the CPR. In all discussions of how to respond to individuals who broke agreements, subjects always rejected any proposal that they should invest all of their tokens in the CPR so as to punish the defector.

Thus, behavior of subjects in both communication and noncommunication experiments was inconsistent in a variety of ways with behavior predicated from the theoretical perspective of complete rationality. In the remain-

---

1. We focus on face-to-face communication. This institution may be quite different in both strategy space and behavior in comparison to highly limited nonverbal communication.

ing sections of this chapter, we explore possible explanations for the results obtained in our communication experiments.

Why So Much Cooperation in Communication Experiments?

We are not the first to observe high levels of cooperation in experimental social dilemmas with communication. The theory of infinitely repeated games is one explanation offered for this finding.[2] In infinitely repeated games, some of the many possible equilibria are fully efficient (Friedman 1990). In chapter 7, we discussed two alternative approaches for explaining observed patterns of cooperation, both of which rely on notions of incomplete information.

One of these approaches interprets the game as if it were infinitely repeated. This approach relies on incomplete information surrounding the termination point for the experiment. For example, suppose the subjects approach the game as if it were repeated, but with only a vague notion of the number of repetitions.[3] Further suppose that the subjects think the termination of the experiment is due to randomness, and that the probability of termination in any round is small. In these circumstances, subjects may recognize more than one sensible way of playing the game, some of which increase group gains. That is, not knowing exactly when it ends, the subjects act as though the game might last forever. If this were the case, there are many other equilibria available to them. All of these equilibria have efficiencies at least as great as that of the subgame perfect equilibrium of the finitely repeated game. Our data are not inconsistent with such an interpretation. Given the plethora of equilibria available to the subjects (if they were to perceive the game as infinite), they face a difficult coordination problem. We are, however, skeptical of this interpretation as being the sole explanation for these findings. For instance, it is well documented in public-goods experiments that even when the termination point is made explicit to the subjects, the results are strikingly parallel to those observed here (see for instance Isaac and Walker 1988a, 1991, and discussion in appendix 5.1). Also, in recent CPR experiments with an explicit termination point, our findings are strongly supported (Hackett, Schlager, and Walker 1993).

A second approach relying on incomplete information concerns other subjects' types. For example, face-to-face communication (and resulting verbal commitments) may change a subject's expectations of other players' responses. In particular, if a subject believes that other subjects are of a cooperative type (that is, will cooperate in response to cooperative play), that subject

---

2. If a game were to be repeated infinitely, there would be no last period and the logic of backward induction no longer applies in this form.

3. As mentioned in chapter 5, subjects are told that the experiment will last up to two hours and have already experienced training experiments that lasted no more than 20 rounds.

may play cooperatively to induce cooperation from others. In this case, cooperating can be sustained as rational play in the framework of incomplete information regarding player types. The cost of this approach is the incredible calculation processes involved in determining an equilibrium under incomplete information.

Given our reluctance to rely on these two approaches, we propose two principles based on the evidence we have gathered. The first principle is that agents use communication to reach an agreement.[4] The second principle is that agents will find and adopt a simple agreement. In a communication session, our subjects tend to do two things: (1) focus on an agreement approximating the group maximum and (2) formulate a simple symmetric plan of play for the repeated game. The principle of simplicity in the one-shot case carries over to the repeated case. Interestingly enough, these two principles are also consistent with arguments of bounded rationality.[5]

Game theory based on complete rationality requires that players have a strategy—a complete plan of play for every contingency. Selten, Mitzkewitz, and Uhlich (1988) argue that players are basically reactive in nature. Suppose that players in a communication phase have reached agreement on how play should proceed. As long as play proceeds according to the agreement, there is no need to react. Reaction is only called for when something unexpected happens, in particular, a defection from the agreement. The first principle that subjects use when communicating about equilibrium selection—find a simple symmetric solution—gives the subjects a reference point, their agreement, for reactions. The second principle—simplicity—reinforces the agreement as a reference point and suggests the form that reactions may take to deviations from the agreement. One possible type of "simple" reaction is a *measured reaction*.[6] There are other possible reactions, some of which we briefly discuss below.

Measured Reactions

In a measured reaction, a player reacts mildly (if at all) to a small deviation from an agreement. Defections trigger mild reactions instead of harsh punish-

---

4. This point is made forcefully by Banks and Calvert 1992a, 1992b.

5. Colleagues working with Reinhard Selten in the Department of Economics at the University of Bonn have developed and tested a series of behavioral strategies related to various types of games. See Rockenbach and Uhlich 1989 on two-person characteristic function games; Mitzkewitz and Nagel 1991 on ultimatum games with incomplete information; and Keser 1992.

6. Our use of this term was inspired by the concept of "measure-for-measure" introduced by Selten, Mitzkewitz, and Uhlich 1988. However, there are important differences in our application relative to theirs. Namely, their subjects do not have a communication phase, and they model their subjects using Selten's three-stage theory of bounded rationality. Our application makes use of only one of these three stages and substitutes communication for another stage.

ments. If defections continue over time, the measured response slowly moves from the point of agreement toward the Nash equilibrium. Thus, a measured reaction is very different from a grim trigger strategy. The intuition behind measured reactions is that, by keeping play near the agreement, it is easier to restore the agreement. Further, the risk of a complete unraveling toward the one-shot game equilibrium is reduced when players do not overreact to deviations. Since the payoff achieved from an agreement (or, play close to the agreement) dominates one-shot game payoffs, measured reactions represent a useful response to the problem of equilibrium selection.

Consider our designs with one-shot or repeated communication, where agents have agreed to contribute 6 tokens each to the CPR (this is the agreement reached in several of our experiments). Then a typical measured reaction would look as shown in the left panel of figure 9.1. The reaction shown in this figure has on the x-axis the average decision of all other players in the previous round ($t - 1$), and on the y-axis the decision of a given player in the current round (t). The measured reaction passes through the agreement: if all others kept to the agreement in $t - 1$, then this player keeps to it in round (t). Moreover, if others invest less than the agreed amount, this player sticks to the agreement. Finally, if others invest more than the agreement calls for, this player responds in a measured fashion by investing somewhat more or by sticking to the agreement in the hopes of getting others to return to the agreement. Measured reactions continue until the one-shot equilibrium is reached. At this point, no further reactions are called for. Play has now reached the one-shot equilibrium, and any further deviations reduce a player's payoff. If investments were to exceed the Nash equilibrium, eventually a player would do best to leave the CPR entirely and invest all tokens in the safe alternative.

The linear reaction shown in the left panel of figure 9.1 is simple but ignores the restriction that decisions have to be integer valued. We call any reaction function passing through the agreement point and the one-shot equilibrium a measured reaction. The right panel of figure 9.1 graphically presents the measured reaction box, which shows the limits within which all such reactions must be found. Note that the lower-left and upper-right corners of this box are defined by the agreement reached in an experiment, AGREEMENT, and the symmetric one-shot equilibrium (8,8), NASH. All integer-valued step functions lie within this box.

Besides measured reactions, there are many alternative reactions subjects might exhibit in our decision situation. At one extreme, they may make the same decision under all circumstances, constant play. We have observed behavior consistent with other possibilities as well. For instance, a subject who invests at a maximal rate while other subjects hold back their investment level to an agreed-upon level is playing "never give a sucker an even break." A

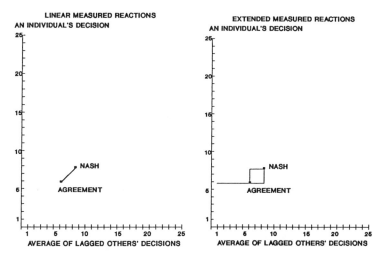

Fig. 9.1. Linear and extended measured reactions

variation on this strategy is observed when a subject convinces the others to invest at low levels and then proceeds to invest at a maximal level. This could be called "sandbagging the suckers."

Measured reactions appear to have improved cooperation in our communication experiments without sanctioning. There are 18 such experiments where subjects had at least one opportunity (15 costless, 3 costly) to communicate but no opportunity to use fines. In all these experiments, the anonymity of the subjects was maintained. In some of these experiments (all 25-token, one-shot communication and half of all 25-token repeated communication), subjects had information about the individual investments of each player. This information was anonymous, however, in respect to the actual identity of each player. An analysis of the responses made by subjects in these experiments is summarized in table 9.2 and discussed below.

High-Endowment Experiments with One-Shot
Communication

After the first 10 rounds of experiment 19, first reported in table 7.1, the subjects were given a single opportunity to communicate. In their discussions, they stressed that they wanted to obtain a fair outcome where everyone received the same outcome. The subjects agreed upon a strategy of investing 6 tokens each in the CPR. While the agreement was not at the optimum, if all participants followed this agreement, they earned 89 percent of the optimum yield. The experiment lasted 22 rounds after the communication round, leaving 21 rounds $\times$ 8 decisions to seek evidence of measured reactions.

TABLE 9.2. Measured Reactions in Communication Experiments

Type of Communication Experimental Design	First Reported in Table	Percentage Agreement	Percentage Extended Agreement	Percentage in the Box	Percentage Total Measured Reactions	Percentage Large Deviations	Average Percentage of Yield after Agreement
One-Shot							
19[b]	7.1	53	7	82	89	1	88
20[b]	7.1	0	3	31	34	15	23
21[b]	7.1	0	10	41	51	10	57
54[b]	8.6	1	3	31	34	4	76
55[b]	8.6	21	0	55	55	15	36
Costly Communication							
35	7.4	92	0	100	100	0	99
36	7.4	45	1	67	68	22	67
37	7.4	97	0	99	99	1	96
Repeated 10-Token[a]							
22	7.2	100	0	100	100	0	99
23	7.2	88	0	97	97	3	99
24	7.2	99	0	99	99	0	99
25	7.2	95	0	97	97	2	97
Repeated 25-Token							
26	7.3	0	0	93	93	0	70
27	7.3	99	0	99	99	0	84
28	7.3	97	0	99	99	1	65
29[b]	7.3	100	0	100	100	0	89
30[b]	7.3	57	0	75	75	3	37
31[b]	7.3	82	0	96	96	0	84

[a]In the 10-token design, a bounded investment decision of 10 tokens is considered as a large deviation.
[b]Subjects received information on Market 2 decisions for each individual subject by an anonymous identification number.

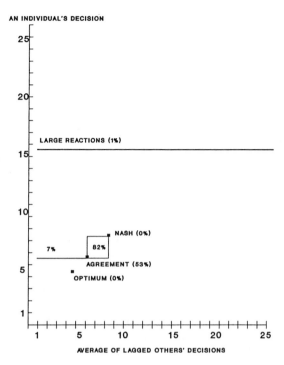

AN INDIVIDUAL'S DECISION

Fig. 9.2.   Measured reactions (experiment 19)

Figure 9.2 shows how the reactions appear in reaction space. In 53 percent of all decisions (89/168), a subject invested at the agreement in round t in response to an average investment equal to the agreement in $t - 1$. This can be interpreted to mean that the individual knows that on average the others kept to the agreement in $t - 1$, and so the individual keeps to the agreement in t. This 53 percent is represented in figure 9.2 in parentheses next to the word AGREEMENT.

Besides the 53 percent of all reactions at the agreement point, there were an additional 29 percent inside the measured reaction box. This is depicted in figure 9.2 by the number 82 percent within the measured reaction box, which includes the reactions at the agreement point, the Nash point, and interior to the box. There were no observations of one-shot Nash. This is represented by the 0 percent in parentheses next to NASH on the figure. Measured reactions are only defined between the AGREEMENT and one-shot NASH. In this experiment, and as we shall see in most one-shot communication experiments, a noticeable percentage of players stick to the agreement when the group average is less than the amount agreed upon. In this experiment, for example, 7 percent of all responses were of the form where "i's reaction is 6 in round t, when the other's average in $t - 1$ was less than 6." This is represented by the number 7 percent above the line extending leftward from the agreement point.

There are two other types of reactions worth emphasizing. One is the optimum. The second is what we refer to as a *large* reaction. In this experiment, we observed no reactions where the individual invested at the optimum in response to an investment in the previous round that averaged at the optimum. We define a *large* reaction as any reaction greater than or equal to the one-shot best response to the agreement. For instance, the one-shot best response to the agreement at 6 tokens is 15 tokens by the player breaking the agreement. In this experiment, there is only one large reaction (rounded to 1 percent), displayed next to LARGE REACTIONS. In this experiment, the measured reaction is very much in evidence.

In experiment 20, the participants again had only one opportunity to talk. After a short discussion, they agreed to invest 5 tokens each. They saw on their screens that one player had invested 25 tokens in each of the first 10 rounds. Only one player speculated about the payoffs that the all-25 player had obtained and mused that this player "could be coming up with real money if everyone else is pulling back." Unfortunately for the others, this player could make twice the money the others made by persisting in his behavior and was perfectly willing to exploit the reaction.[7] He had actively promoted the decision to select 5 rather than 6 tokens as their agreement. As his parting shot at the end of the round, he told the others, "So we all need to stick to it."

This player did not follow the same heuristic as the others. He adopted something closer to "never give a sucker an even break." With no further communication, the other seven players could see on their screens round after round that the same player invested 25 tokens. As shown in figure 9.3, 31 percent of the reactions were in the measured reaction box, while 15 percent were large reactions—most of which were the actions of this one player.

Let us examine in more detail what the others did. In figure 9.4, we have plotted the number of players who followed an almost measured reaction (investing at the agreement point, below the agreement, or 1 token above the agreement) for rounds 11 through 32. As shown, all of the other players kept close to the agreement in the first few rounds after discovering the blatant violation of their agreement. Over time, the number of individuals keeping to

---

7. When the other players contributed 5 tokens each, someone contributing 25 tokens could make 8 "experimental cents" on each token in the CPR and only 5 "cents" on the same tokens in the alternative investment. That meant that the individual investing 25 tokens made a total of 200 "cents" on any round when the others invested no more than 35 tokens in total. The others made 140 "cents." If everyone had followed the agreement, all would have made 185 "cents." Subjects were paid one half of the "experimental cents" they earned in the 25-token experiments.

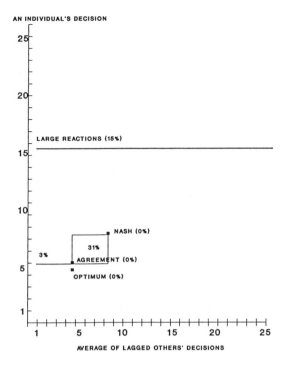

Fig. 9.3. **Measured reactions (experiment 20)**

the agreement slowly dropped. In the last 3 rounds, one-half of the participants continued to invest very near the agreement or somewhat less while the other half invested 7 or above. It appears that seven of the individuals wanted to adopt measured reactions and adhered to them as long as they felt there was any chance to keep their payoffs in Market 2 above those in Market 1. Absent one recalcitrant individual, the group would have followed a measured reaction and achieved a much higher joint return.

In experiment 21, the subjects disagreed on what the optimal investment was. They finally decided to invest 3 tokens each in round 11, 4 tokens each in round 12, 5 tokens each in round 13, 6 tokens each in round 14, and then to pick the best (independently). During this trial phase, there were two large deviations as well as one reaction out of sequence. Once the trial phase was completed, the modal subject choice from then on was 6 tokens. From this we infer that an implicit agreement at 6 had been reached. Since the group never had another chance to communicate, there is no way to check this inference. Clearly, the lack of a clear agreement point at the end of the communication period jeopardized the performance of any heuristic, such as measured reac-

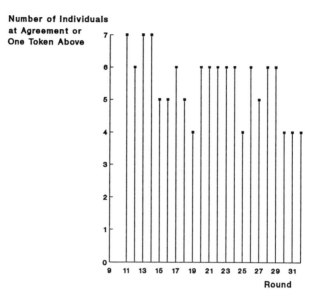

Fig. 9.4.   Limited measured reactions (experiment 20)

tions. As shown in figure 9.5, 41 percent of the reactions were in the measured reaction box, while 10 percent were large reactions.

In addition to these three one-shot communication experiments, there are two additional experiments with a comparable structure. As discussed in chapter 8, we ran six experiments in which groups had an opportunity to decide whether to impose a sanctioning mechanism on themselves or not. Two of the groups decided against adopting a sanctioning mechanism. These two experiments constituted a one-shot opportunity to communicate followed by a series of rounds without a sanctioning mechanism or any further opportunity to communicate. These subjects were very experienced players. To be in this experiment, they had to have had a prior experience with a sanctioning mechanism. Many of the individuals in these two experiments had been in sanctioning experiments where we had used a 20-cent fee to impose an 80-cent fine. The fining rate in these 20–80 experiments was much higher and more erratic than in the other sanctioning experiments. Many of the subjects expressed a strong aversion to the use of a sanctioning mechanism.

In experiment 54, the subjects did not come to a clear, explicit agreement as to the number of tokens they should invest. They said they wanted to continue doing the same as before. Since the average individual investment in the first ten rounds was 5.8 tokens, we interpret this desire as an implicit agreement to 6 tokens each. This group did not maintain the status quo,

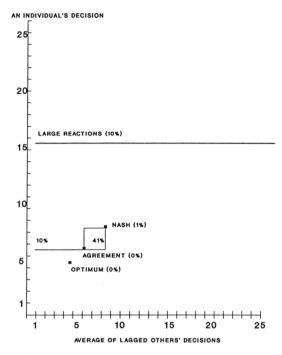

Fig. 9.5. Measured reactions (experiment 21)

however. In the 15 rounds following communication, there was a substantial decay of returns, as two subjects averaged over 10 tokens invested each. By the end of the experiment, this group was close to the one-shot Nash equilibrium, and its implicit agreement had collapsed. As shown in figure 9.6, 31 percent of the reactions were in the measured reaction box, while 4 percent were large reactions.

In experiment 55, the subjects clearly agreed on an investment of all 4s. The first few infractions were small and so were the reactions. Beginning in round 17, one player consistently invested 20 or higher tokens in each round until the end. The other players used great restraint for 3 rounds, at which time two players increased their individual investments beyond the Nash equilibrium. In round 22, a total of 110 tokens was invested and the group earned −322 percent of total yield. Four players still continued to use measured reactions throughout. Their efforts were futile, since the group earned only 36 percent of total yield after the communication round, but their measured reactions did help make performance after communication quite a bit better than it had been before (positive vs. negative yield). As shown in figure

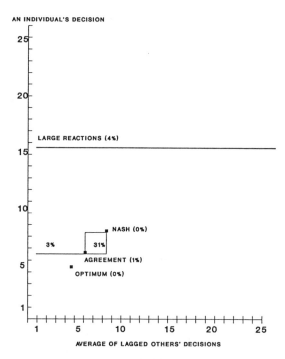

Fig. 9.6. Measured reactions (experiment 54)

9.7, 55 percent of the reactions were in the measured reaction box, while 15 percent were large reactions.

15-Token Experiments with Costly Communication
Chapter 7 describes three experiments (35–37) where subjects were given an opportunity to communicate if five out of eight of them contributed to the provision of the communication round. In two of these experiments (35 and 37), agreements were reached as soon as the provision of a communication round was accomplished and either 100 percent or 99 percent of the responses were in the measured reaction box. The average percentage of yield in both experiments also came close to optimal. In the second experiment of this series (36), the subjects immediately paid the cost of a communications round and agreed to invest 5 tokens in the CPR. After only 1 round of full agreement, one player invested all 15 tokens in the CPR and continued to do so until the game ended. The reaction of the other players in the next round was measured, to say the least. Five players kept with the agreement and the other two invested 1 token more than the agreement. When a second player began to invest all 15 tokens in the CPR, the other six players were indeed faced

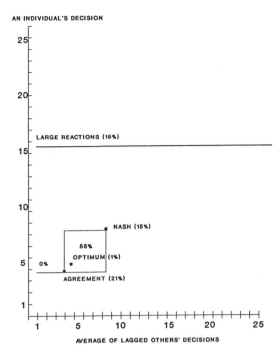

Fig. 9.7. Measured reactions (experiment 55)

with a puzzle. Over the life of the experiment, 22 percent of the responses were large reactions (in this case, all were 15 tokens). No one invested more than the Nash equilibrium, however, for the next 4 rounds. In fact, there were only three investments that exceeded the Nash equilibrium other than those of the two players who invested 15 tokens each round. With only 45 percent of the reactions on the agreement point and only 67 percent in the measured reaction box, the group achieved only 67 percent of total yield after their agreement, as contrasted to the two other costly experiments where a near-optimal response was sustained.

Low-Endowment Experiments with
Repeated Communication
In all four of the repeated communication, 10-token experiments, subjects followed their agreements with a high level of fidelity and responded to the few deviations in such a manner that one could safely argue that the subjects used measured reactions in these experiments (reported in table 9.2). The reactions diagrams for these four experiments all have higher than 97 percent of the reactions in the measured reaction box, and almost all of these are at the

agreement point. For this reason, we have not reproduced these reaction diagrams here.

High-Endowment Experiments with
Repeated Communication

As discussed earlier, the 25-token design is behaviorally a far more difficult situation than the 10-token design. We conducted six experiments with high endowments and repeated opportunities to communicate (from table 7.3). In all six experiments, subjects reacted consistently with measured reactions, with at least 75 percent of all reactions in the box. We now consider each experiment in some detail. In experiment 26, subjects agreed to invest 6 tokens each. Thus, the agreement point in reaction strategy space is the point (6,6). The big difference between this experiment and the previous ones is that not a single reaction of the form (6,6) was ever observed. This group was literally never at the agreed-upon point. Nevertheless, the group did achieve a reasonable net yield (70 percent), and stayed in the vicinity of the agreement. In the 12 rounds where reactions could be observed following the initial communication round, 93 percent (89/96) of the reactions lay within the measured reaction box (see fig. 9.8). There were only 7 reactions lying outside the box, and none of these were large. This is especially impressive given that there are no observations at (6,6).

The transcript of this experiment provides evidence about the expressed thoughts of the subjects as they coped with the continuing problem of defecting members. In the first rounds, seven subjects invested at the agreement and the eighth subject (player C) invested two tokens over the agreement. After considerable discussion about what to do, they finally agreed that "staying with 6 is the best." The last two comments made before they returned to their terminals were:

Player B: Let's not get greedy. We've just got to start trusting.
Player H: Let's everyone do 6.

In the next round, the 12th, player C increased investments in the CPR from 8 tokens, invested in round 11, to 19 tokens. This constituted a real challenge to their agreement and an affront to the other players. Player A invested 7 rather than 6 tokens (consistent with a measured reaction). All the others stayed with the agreement and invested 6 tokens. After this round, the discussion opened with

Player B: This should be our last meeting—if we can't get some trust, we might as well go back and screw each other over. We could all make more money if we could stick together, but if some are going to

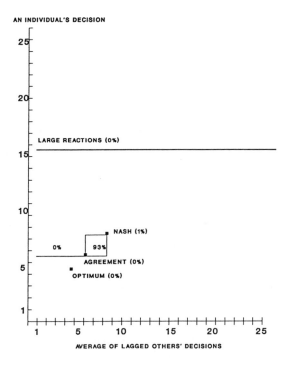

Fig. 9.8. Measured reactions (experiment 26)

do the others in, then, we just should go. Does *everyone* agree to do the same thing?

Player D: If there is any objection to this, can we just plain hear why not?

Player H: Well, it is obvious that someone is making a little more money.

Player B: Well, they know that they are going to make more money, they could probably make all of two bucks, but still, I mean, if we go back to the way we were, none of us will make as much.

Player E: Let's try it one more time.

Player H: No, let's go back to the way we were doing it.

Player D: If you do, you sure lose!

Player G: If you don't work together, you lose.

Player E: That person will do it, whatever we agree to.

Player H: Does anyone want to confess?

Player D: Let's try one more time.

Player G: If this doesn't work, then forget all about it.

Player H: Want to try to invest 6? Let's try it.

Player B: Let's go for 6. [Player B then looks at each and every one of the other 7, points to each one, and looks at each one directly in the eye.] It shouldn't take very long for anyone to put in 6 in Market 2!

After this dramatic close, player C dropped back to the agreed-upon 6 tokens in round 13, but player A invested 8. In the discussion following round 13, the players were so glad to be close to their agreement that they simply congratulated themselves on getting closer and asked to return to their terminals early. They had similarly short discussions from then on. After the fifteenth round, for example, they had the following exchange:

Player H: Not everyone is investing 6.
Player B: Evidently not.
Player C: Unless everyone keeps to it, it starts to get away from us.
Player H: Let's say we invest 6 again. Obviously somebody is cheating, but what can we do? But the rest of us can just continue to invest 6.

At a still later point, player E suggested that they dump whatever they wanted into Market 2. Player H disagreed and pointed out that "we screw ourselves too."

The transcript reflects a group of subjects trying to grapple with a situation on the brink of disaster. Instead of going over the brink, their measured reactions to the provocation sustained behavior close to their agreement, even though they never achieved perfect compliance.

In experiment 27, the participants miscalculated the optimum at 50 tokens (instead of 36) and devised a rotation scheme whereby six individuals invested 6 tokens and two individuals invested 7 tokens. They had perfect compliance to their rotation system through round 20, when one subject invested 11 rather than 6 tokens. Given past experience in experiments with 20 rounds, this may have been an "end effect." The discussion after round 20, reproduced in chapter 7, reflects individuals who are puzzled why someone would break their agreement. They resolved to return to their rotation scheme. They did return to their terminals and continued with perfect compliance from there on. They achieved 84 percent of the potential yield, rather than a higher percentage, because they had miscalculated the optimum and not because they had difficulty keeping to their agreement.

In experiment 28, the players again overestimated the number of tokens that was optimal and agreed to invest 50 each round for four rounds (with a rotation system) and then 49 tokens each round. They faced only three defections during the course of their experiment. In the discussion following these defections, the players stressed the importance of not "messing it up" by small deviations and never discussed the possibility of punishing those who deviated. The central focus was on keeping the agreement going still further.

In experiment 29, the subjects initially miscalculated the optimal investment level, but used their discussion to improve their agreement. By the last 5 rounds, they obtained 99 percent of the yield. Since they never faced a defection throughout the experiment, they never discussed a response for coping with this problem.

Experiment 30 was unique in one crucial respect. These subjects agreed to invest 1 token each in the CPR. This represents by far the worst agreement ever reached, with a potential group yield of only 40 percent. This agreement at the point (1,1) further implies the largest measured reaction box, with corners at (1,1) and (8,8). A large box is really easy to hit; indeed, 75 percent of all reactions in the 13 periods following the agreement landed in the box (see fig. 9.9). Despite this poor agreement, subjects held to it for 7 rounds. Then the *same* player who had suggested the agreement in the first place made the largest possible Market 2 investment, 25 tokens.[8] A lively discussion ensued, as reported in chapter 7. In the last 5 rounds of the experiment, there were 17 double-digit reactions, and the agreement clearly unraveled. The combination of poor agreement and unraveling meant an overall average yield of only 37 percent, by far the lowest of the set of repeated communication, 25-token experiments.

Experiment 31 also helps illuminate how individuals who use a measured reaction avoid the complete unraveling of an agreement when presented with small infractions by one or two individuals. In this experiment, the group agreed to invest 6 tokens each. While they did achieve some rounds of perfect compliance, they frequently faced rounds in which one or two persons invested 7 or 8 tokens rather than the agreed-upon 6. At several points in their discussions, the participants discussed the possibility of strategies that mimic trigger responses and always rejected the idea. Here is one exchange:

Player D: What can we do to lose the most?
Player A: Lose the most?
Player D: Yeah, to get back at her—points at E (who was suspected of having overinvested).
Player A: But that hurts us all as well.
Player D: We probably don't have that many rounds left to really worry about this stuff of putting one more penny than we have agreed on.

---

8. The heuristic this player may have been playing could be described as: "Set the suckers up for a preemptive strike."

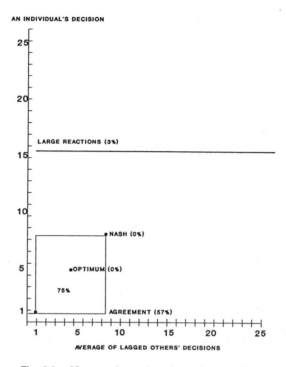

Fig. 9.9. Measured reactions (experiment 30)

> Let's just keep on putting in those 6s—and let them have the benefits
> of their stupid penny.

At a later juncture, one player commented that the set of reliable players is
even smaller (while only two people had defected, one of those individuals
had never defected before). This was followed with:

> Player E: What are we going to do, are we going to go for a free-for-all?
> Player B: Go for a free-for-all? Shucks no, we all lose.
> Player D: No, we all lose.

The discussion rounds in this experiment were quite heated, but by stressing
the fact that they would all lose if they moved too far away from the agreement point, the group was able to gain 84 percent of net yield even when
facing the problem of repeated but small defections.

Summarizing the results of the six repeated-communication, 25-token
experiments, we find high rates of measured reactions, at least 75 percent in

all cases and at least 93 percent in five cases. We find very low rates of large deviations, never higher than 3 percent, with no large deviations whatsoever in four cases. In the five experiments where the initial agreement promised a high average yield (at least 90 percent), measured reactions enabled groups to obtain on average 78 percent yield in a very challenging situation. Of course, measured reactions cannot salvage a very deficient agreement.

Bounded Rationality and Behavioral Heuristics

The above discussion of measured reactions provides part of an explanation of "Why so much cooperation in communication experiments?" but only part. Communication allows individuals to agree on a joint strategy and to begin a process of building trust in others to abide by that agreement. When sanctioning is not available, trust has to be built through communication and consequent changes in patterns of behavior. When behavior is relatively close to the agreed-upon level, most individuals respond to deviations in a very measured fashion. When most individuals use a measured reaction, even in challenging situations, they are able to gain joint returns close to the level agreed upon. Their closeness to optimality depends both on the yield potential of their agreement and on their rate of compliance. Individuals who exhibit measured reactions are able to sustain cooperation for an extended period and reap the benefits of doing so.

On the other hand, when one or a few individuals do *not* respond consistently with measured reactions and are able to deviate in an extreme manner from an agreement (by having sufficient resources to be very disruptive to attempts by others to form near optimal agreements), measured reactions are not very effective. Dealing with extreme deviations is especially problematic when players communicate only once. To prevent agreements from unraveling, the ability to chastise offenders verbally on a repeated basis is essential in laboratory experiments without sanctions. In the 12 experiments where individuals reacted in a measured fashion by sticking to their agreements or by keeping deviations small (greater than 85 percent in the box), yields averaged 89 percent of optimum. In the 6 experiments where this was not the case, yields averaged only 43 percent of optimum.

Even if measured reactions work, this still leaves unanswered why some groups exhibit them and others do not. Where do such reactions come from? One answer to this question starts with Selten's dictum that complete rationality is the limiting case of bounded or incomplete rationality (1975, 35). From this perspective, a behavioral response like measured reactions are heuristics used by individuals as problem-solving tools when complete analysis is difficult and short-term self-interest dictates unsatisfactory long-term outcomes, such as the case where the cognitive task is beyond the immediate scope of the individual, or game equilibria lead to suboptimal outcomes. Individuals learn to use a repertoire of heuristics depending upon their experience and their perception of the situation in which they find themselves, including the likely behavior of others.

In simple situations where short-term self-interest leads to near-optimal outcomes, individuals may very well exhibit behavior that closely parallels that predicted by a model of complete rationality. In simple situations where short-term self-interest leads to a highly suboptimal outcome, individuals may learn from experience or be taught by mentors that use of a heuristic may lead to better outcomes, as long as others follow similar behavior. In complex situations, individuals may adopt heuristics as a first approach to learning about the decision situation. Many terms are used for the concept of a heuristic including "rule of thumb," "standard operating procedure," and "standard of behavior."[9]

In a two-person, binary choice, repeated social dilemma where full information is available about the behavior of each person in the previous round, individuals who learn to play a tit-for-tat strategy, for example, can achieve high payoffs across many different encounters so long as there are a sufficient number of other individuals in the population prepared to play the same strategy (Axelrod 1984). Axelrod's and Selten's work on two-person decision settings shows that the best response depends not only on the game structure but also on the behavior of the other players (see also Taylor 1987; Bendor 1987; Bendor and Mookherjee 1987, 1990). Cooperating with those who cooperate enables individuals to obtain benefits not achievable by individuals following other strategies.

N-person situations are far more complex than 2-person situations. In a 2-person game of complete information, each person knows with certainty their own response and can infer the response of the other also with certainty. In an N-person setting, it is extremely hard to know whether a particular outcome is the result of many individuals cheating just a little or one person cheating a lot. No heuristic is as simple and straightforward as tit-for-tat is in the 2-person situation.

Individuals who come to a situation with a complete preprogrammed strategy may miss out on opportunities for mutual gain that are available to those who can respond somewhat more adaptively. A bounded rationality approach enables the theory to make less severe assumptions about individuals' calculation capabilities and shows that such individuals may do better in some environments than their completely rational counterparts. Instead of calculating all future contingencies and forming a complete plan of play, an individual uses rules of thumb sequentially as he or she learns about others'

---

9. See Groner, Groner, and Bischof 1983 for a general discussion of heuristics.

patterns of play. If all of the players are using measured responses, the evolving pattern of play will lead them to much higher outcomes than other types of reactions.

Those following measured reactions, however, are no more likely than others to cope effectively with the problem presented by the presence of individuals who adopt entirely different types of heuristics—particularly some of the nastier ones involving either complete unconcern for keeping agreements, or even worse, luring others into an agreement where they are set up for a strike. Individuals who cannot draw on some form of sanction are all relatively exposed to the predatory actions of those who are perfectly willing to unilaterally take advantage of others.

In a situation without communication and with more than two individuals, it is extremely difficult to initiate a process by which individuals learn a measured heuristic. Similarly, if groups only communicate once, and if some individuals adopt less cooperative strategies than measured reactions, it is harder to sustain cooperation over time than when groups are able to discuss their joint behavior and outcomes continuously. As we see in our experiments, individuals who might use a measured reaction when communication is possible may not use it when communication is impossible.

But once individuals communicate (especially if they can communicate with one another repeatedly), they can build up trust through their discussions and through achieving better outcomes. If individuals come to these situations with a willingness to devise sharing rules and to follow a measured reaction, then communication facilitates agreement selection and the measured reaction facilitates agreement retention. The measured reaction heuristic prevents the full unraveling of an agreement when minor deviations first start to occur but is not effective when major deviations occur. In the latter event, no response other than a sanction directed at a large deviation is likely to be effective. In CPR situations, individuals come armed with an array of previously learned heuristics. With communication, these individuals have a chance to discover the approaches others are using to the game. Without communication, they do not know what to do in the situation they face and adopt strategies that vary tremendously.

Many individuals utilize heuristics learned from childhood experiences. On playgrounds around the world,[10] children arguing about the allocation of toys, space, or the use of facilities are taught, depending on the situation, to use principles such as

---

10. Piaget's theory of moral development is based on his observations of how children learn to play the game of marbles (Piaget [1932] 1969). The playground is where many individuals learn the heuristics that they will use for the rest of their lives in orienting themselves to diverse situations (V. Ostrom 1994).

- share and share alike (equal division);
- first in time, first in right;
- take turns;
- share on the basis of need; and
- flip a coin (use a randomizing device).[11]

Most of the agreements developed in the lab setting were based on the first principle—share and share alike. The basic symmetry of the specific series of symmetric experiments apparently evoked this principle frequently.[12] Once a sharing principle is devised (and a conception of the size of the joint good to be shared), individuals can agree to follow the sharing principle even without enforcement if they presume that most of the individuals with whom they are relating will reciprocate their trust. The adoption of a measured reaction heuristic enables individuals to start on a productive path toward higher joint outcomes without outside enforcers.

So long as the population of individuals sampled for laboratory experiments has a sufficient proportion of individuals who know and use a measured reaction heuristic, individuals can use this shared knowledge or social capital as a resource for gaining substantially better outcomes than they would otherwise have gained. Even when groups discover individuals within their midst playing entirely different strategies, the restraint shown by the remaining individuals keeps their joint returns higher than they were when pursuing completely independent strategies.

Conclusions

We have now addressed in some depth the first and second core questions that we posed in chapter 1. At the aggregate level, predictions derived from noncooperative game theory are given considerable measure of support in situations that most closely approximate a barren institutional setting involving no capacity to make binding agreements as well as no capacity to commu-

---

11. We are indebted to Vincent Ostrom for his persistent stress on these universal types of sharing principles. In chapter 4, we use several of these sharing principles as allocation rules and examine what difference they make in the structure of an assignment rule. Specifically, we compare a first in time, first in right, a priori announcement, and a rotation system with the default condition that fishers are permitted to take any amount of fish they would like.

12. In experiments where asymmetric endowments were distributed randomly or using an auction mechanism, Hackett, Schlager, and Walker (1993) found that subjects chose and successfully maintained allocation rules that were consistent with approximate rent maximization. In the treatment design in which token endowments were allocated randomly, subjects most frequently adopted rules that called for equal withdrawal. In the treatment design in which larger token endowments were purchased through an auction mechanism, subjects explicitly sought to adopt rules to achieve maximum rents and equalize payoffs net of auction prices.

nicate. Even in these environments, however, behavior at an individual level does not conform to theoretical predictions and does not appear to settle down to an equilibrium. The type of pulsing behavior that we observe is not predicted by any variant of noncooperative game theory. We do, however, find behavioral regularities that can initially be explained as a consequence of the type of heuristics that players adopt in these situations.

We now turn more overtly to the relationship of institutional variables to an explanation of the level of cooperation found in CPR dilemmas and begin to explore how these findings are related to the effect of rules on games. In the laboratory setting, the rules that govern situations are largely preset by the experimenters. Different experimental designs can be viewed as the imposition of different sets of rules or institutional arrangements. In our baseline experiments, for example, subjects were told that they could not verbally communicate and that the game would end if they tried to verbally communicate.[13] In our one-shot communication experiments, subjects were told they had one and only one opportunity to communicate. The instructions given to the subjects and the way the experiments were programmed were, in essence, the rules of the game. In a one-shot communication experiment, subjects could develop a sharing agreement, but had no way to develop sanctioning mechanisms. In repeated communication experiments, subjects could agree on a sharing rule and could also use jawboning as a crude method of sanctioning those who did not keep to an agreement. Jawboning is most successful when most individuals want to cooperate—so long as others do. Jawboning alone is not very effective against those who do not care what others think. In most of our experiments, subjects were not given the opportunity to devise sanctioning mechanisms to be used against those who did not rely on measured responses.

In two experimental designs, however, subjects were given an opportunity to decide upon the fundamental rules they would use in organizing a future series of decision rounds. In one series, they could decide (using majority rule) whether they wanted to provide a communication arena. In the other, they could decide (again, using majority rule) whether they wanted to use a sanctioning mechanism in future rounds and how much they were willing to charge themselves to implement a fine on someone else. Of the three groups presented with the option of providing the communication institution, all three eventually chose the option. Of the six groups who were presented the opportunity to decide whether or not to have a sanctioning mechanism, four decided to change their operating rules and adopt a sanction-

---

13. For a subject who is interested in earning money, ending the game is a strong punishment. It is also a credible threat given two experimenters in the lab. While we were prepared to stop a game if someone started to communicate, we never had to do so.

ing mechanism. The groups that did opt to change their rules and impose a sanctioning system upon themselves were able to achieve the highest average net yield (93 percent) of all experimental groups facing the high-endowment situation. These groups used their one-shot communication opportunity to agree to a well-defined set of investments and backed this agreement with an agreed-upon sanctioning system.

The results from these experimental designs replicate a core part of our essential findings from the field. When substantial benefits can be gained by arriving at a joint plan of action for a series of future interactions, individuals may have in their repertoire of heuristics simple sharing rules to propose, backed up by a presumption that others will use something like a measured response. If in addition, individuals have learned how a monitoring and sanctioning system enhances the likelihood that agreements will be sustained, they are capable of setting up and operating their own enforcement mechanism. It is now time to turn to a discussion of our findings from the field.

Part 3
Field Studies

In the next five chapters, we shift from the laboratory setting of part 2 to an empirical analysis of data obtained in field settings. These chapters provide an overview of some of the forms of self-organization observed in CPR field settings in four sectors: irrigation, inshore fisheries, forestry, and groundwater. The first four chapters describe settings where CPR appropriators have relied to some extent on patterns of reciprocity but have also devised rules backed by sanctions to cope with the problem of punishing noncooperators. These chapters illustrate the capabilities of appropriators facing CPR problems to craft rules that change the structure of the situations they face, fostering more effective use of the CPR. On the other hand, examples are also given where self-organization has clearly not been successful.

Evidence from previous field studies can be classified into four broad categories.

1. Clearly suboptimal outcomes—appropriators' behavior has led to high levels of conflict, overuse, and, in some cases, to the destruction of the resource upon which appropriators' livelihood depends.[1]
2. Long-lived, endogenous monitoring and sanctioning systems— appropriators have designed rules regulating the entry and appropriation from a CPR that are enforced by the appropriators themselves.[2] Outcomes may not achieve optimality, but come close enough for appropriators to continue investing in costly monitoring and sanctioning.
3. Short-lived, endogenous monitoring and sanctioning systems— appropriators cease to monitor and sanction after an exogenous shock, such as a major change in factor prices, a dramatic increase in popula-

---

1. See Christy and Scott 1965; Bell 1972; McHugh 1972; and Sandberg 1991a.
2. See Netting 1974, 1981; Berkes 1986; Siy 1982; McKean 1992; Libecap 1990; E. Ostrom 1990, 1992; E. Ostrom et al. 1993; Curtis 1991; McCay and Acheson 1987; Pinkerton 1989; and Bromley 1992.

tion, or declaration by an external government of its jurisdiction over the resource.[3]

4. Short-lived, exogenous monitoring and sanctioning systems—external authorities impose rules regulating entry and appropriation but fail to enforce these rules.[4]

Evidence from the first category is not surprising. This evidence is consistent with predictions derived from widely accepted theories of collective action, particularly applied to natural resource settings.

The evidence from the other three categories is, on the other hand, surprising, but for different reasons. Evidence from the second category illustrates the capability of appropriators to design their own institutions and willingness to invest time and effort in monitoring and sanctioning. This is the type of behavior exhibited in most of the experimental CPRs where a choice of rules was made available to subjects. This is not, however, the typical result predicted by most current theories. Evidence from the third category illustrates that endogenously designed systems can collapse. This is not so surprising, given the catastrophic nature of the shocks involved in many of these settings. What is surprising from a theoretical perspective is that such endogenous institutions existed without external enforcers for substantial periods of time prior to collapse. Evidence from the fourth category illustrates that the remedies so often prescribed for solving CPR problems are frequently ineffective.

The results in the next four chapters are consistent with evidence from categories 1, 2, and 4 above. In chapters 12 and 13, respectively, Agrawal and Blomquist identify CPRs where appropriators do not cope effectively with CPR dilemmas (category 1). All four chapters, however, document the existence of long-lived monitoring and sanctioning systems (category 2). In chapter 10, Tang's analysis of the difference in performance between farmer-owned and government-owned irrigation systems strongly finds that rules devised by external authorities are frequently ineffective (category 4). None of the chapters identify short-lived endogenous monitoring and sanctioning systems (category 3). However, there is no doubt that such systems exist in field settings. We now provide a short preview of the next four chapters.

In chapter 10, Shui Yan Tang focuses attention on the CPR problems faced by those who provide, maintain, and utilize irrigation systems around the world. He develops a performance measure related to both the provision

---

3. See Alexander 1982; Cordell 1978a, 1978b; W. Cruz 1986; Baines 1989; Blaikie and Brookfield 1987; and Messerschmidt 1986.

4. See A. Davis 1984; Feeny 1988, 1993; Thomson 1977; Thomson, Feeny, and Oakerson 1992; Arnold and Campbell 1986; Messerschmidt 1986; Gadgil and Iyer 1989; Cordell and McKean 1992; W. Cruz 1986; Dasgupta 1982; Panayoutou 1982; and Pinkerton 1989.

and appropriation of CPRs. He uses this measure to evaluate the effectiveness of different boundary and allocation rules used by government-owned and farmer-owned irrigation systems. He also investigates the provision of rules, the monitoring of rules, and the enforcement of rules. He finds that irrigation systems where farmers have provided their own rules tend to perform better than systems owned and operated by central government authorities.

In chapter 11, Edella Schlager examines three types of problems faced by inshore fishers. She develops a conceptual argument for why endogenous solutions to assignment problems and technological externality problems are more likely to develop than endogenous solutions to appropriation externalities. She examines the types of rules used by 33 organized subgroups of fishers, illustrating how most of them relate to the allocation of *space* rather than to the allocation of *quantity* of fish. She also finds strong evidence that fishers monitor rules they themselves create.

In chapter 12, Arun Agrawal explores self-organization in the context of several Indian forests. He focuses primarily on the problem of time-independent appropriation externalities and assignment problems. Documenting several different institutional arrangements that have evolved, he shows how successful arrangements involve a very major investment in sanctioning and monitoring. In contrast, those villages not investing heavily in monitoring and sanctioning have forests that are characterized by a higher level of degradation.

In chapter 13, William Blomquist focuses on single-period and time-dependent appropriation externality problems in the context of four groundwater basins in southern California. These appropriation externality problems are ever present in the use of a groundwater basin when the demand for water approaches or exceeds the average natural recharge of water to the basin. Blomquist illuminates the process of crafting new rules in a complex setting where large groups cope with complex CPRs. Here, the design of new institutions is facilitated (but not guaranteed) by the presence of government agencies that can provide reliable information and arenas for the enforcement of contracts.

The final chapter in this section identifies the commonalities that occur in the self-organized CPRs described in chapters 10–13. Most of these commonalities relate to the presence or absence of key rules, in particular boundary rules and authority rules. This chapter explores the crucial interaction between physical and institutional variables that affects the ability of CPR appropriators to devise and maintain their own rules.

CHAPTER 10

Institutions and Performance in Irrigation Systems

In the past three decades, the total irrigated area in the world has almost tripled, amounting to around 250 million hectares in 1986 (Postel 1990, 40). Many countries and donor agencies such as the World Bank and United States Agency for International Development have invested billions of dollars in irrigation development and are planning to invest billions more (Sampath and Young 1990). Irrigated agriculture is now and will continue to be the major source of income for millions of farmers around the world.

Operating irrigation systems is more than a technological issue. In the past few decades, many technologically sophisticated, large-scale irrigation projects have failed to meet operational targets or have deteriorated rapidly soon after their construction. A major source of these failures is a lack of institutional arrangements that can effectively resolve common-pool resource (CPR) problems faced by irrigators. Resolving CPR problems through effective institutions is crucial for productive irrigation development (Tang 1991, 1992, 1993).

Irrigation systems share two features with other CPRs. First, exclusion is nontrivial. In some cases, the high cost of exclusion is due to the size of the water delivery facilities and the flow nature of water. In others, legal doctrines or government policies mandate that whoever cultivates land within certain areas is entitled to water. Second, water is subtractable and the flow of water available at any one time in an irrigation system is scarce in an economic sense. These two features—nontrivial exclusion and nonsubtractability—define a CPR (see chap. 1).

In many irrigation systems, irrigators face both appropriation and provision problems. Appropriation problems arise when the amount of water is insufficient to satisfy everyone's cultivation needs. Water needs to be allocated in some fashion to ensure effective use. The allocation of water may be based on the number of shares held, the amount of farmland cultivated, or many other criteria. Regardless of the bases of allocation, the need to adopt rules implies that some irrigators will obtain less water than they want. As the availability of water decreases, temptation increases for irrigators to break rules that limit water allocations.

Provision problems arise when substantial resources are needed to construct and maintain water retention and diversion facilities such as dams, canals, and pumps. Because it is often difficult to exclude other irrigators from enjoying the benefits of an operating system, each irrigator has an incentive to refrain from investing in the construction and maintenance of irrigation facilities. To coordinate provision efforts, rules are needed to specify the amounts of contributions (labor, money, etc.) required of each irrigator for constructing and maintaining physical facilities.

To understand the action situations that give rise to appropriation and provision dilemmas in irrigation, one must systematically analyze underlying contextual factors. According to the Institutional Analysis and Development (IAD) framework introduced in chapter 2, three sets of factors affect an action arena—the rules that individuals use to order repetitive relationships, the states of the physical world and their transformations, and the nature of the community in which the arena occurs. These three sets of factors combine to create different incentives and constraints for irrigators in different action arenas. As irrigators react according to these incentives and constraints, their strategic interactions produce different patterns of outcomes.

This chapter examines how different contextual factors affect interactions among irrigators and their abilities to solve appropriation and provision dilemmas in field settings. The evidence is based on a systematic examination of 47 cases. The chapter first discusses the characteristics of the cases and the method of collecting and comparing them. Second, it discusses a method of evaluating performance of irrigation systems and how performance is related to problem resolution in multiple action arenas. Third, it examines the patterns of operational rules found in the sample of cases and the need to match these rules to underlying physical domains. Fourth, it examines how multiple levels of institutional arrangements can be used to solve various collective-action problems in irrigation. Lastly, it examines how performance is related to the way rule conformance is monitored and sanctioned.

Comparing Irrigation Systems

Comparing irrigation systems requires a consistent way of identifying their boundaries. One way of conceptualizing such boundaries is to consider the water delivery processes. These processes are divided into four stages or distinct resource parts—production, distribution, appropriation, and use (see Plott and Meyer 1975). Water is produced, for example, by damming a river. The dam is the *production resource* of the irrigation system. From the production resource, water may be distributed through a canal to the irrigated area; the canal is the *distribution resource*. In the irrigated area, water may be appropriated from the local ditches, tanks, or pumps; these physical structures are the *appropriation resource*. The water appropriated is then used to irrigate crops in the fields; the fields and crops together constitute the *use resource*.

With these distinctions, two kinds of irrigation systems can be identified. In a simple system, the production and distribution resources supply water to only one appropriation area. In a complex system, the production and distribution resources deliver water to multiple appropriation areas. This chapter analyzes activities and attributes related to the entire appropriation resource of a simple system and selected appropriation areas (i.e., watercourses) within a complex system.

The data for this chapter were collected through the CPR project conducted by the Workshop in Political Theory and Policy Analysis at Indiana University. A series of coding forms, containing mostly closed-ended questions, was used to code information provided by in-depth case studies in irrigation systems. For each case, information about key physical, community, and institutional attributes and about collective outcomes was coded.

Extensive efforts have been undertaken by members of the project to identify theoretical and case studies in irrigation systems. Over one thousand items, including books, dissertations, journal articles, monographs, and occasional papers have been identified in the area of water resources and irrigation (F. Martin 1989). Over 450 documents describing irrigation resources and institutions have been collected by the research project. Cases were selected from these documents for coding only if they contain detailed information about (1) participants in the resource, (2) strategies used by participants, (3) the condition of the resource, and (4) rules-in-use for the resource. Cases were also selected in such a way as to include in the sample as much diversity in terms of physical, community, and institutional attributes and collective outcomes as possible.

The sample of cases used in this study consists of 47 cases: 29 farmer-owned systems that are governed entirely by irrigators; 14 government-owned systems whose production resources are governed by a national or regional government agency or enterprise; and 4 other systems whose production resources are governed by local governments. Twenty-nine of the cases are simple systems; 18 are complex ones. The major irrigated crop in most of the systems is rice. The systems are located in the following countries: Bangladesh (1 case), Indonesia (5), India (4), Iran (2), Iraq (1), Laos (1), Mexico (1), Nepal (5), Pakistan (4), Peru (3), Philippines (13), Tanzania (1), Thailand

(4), Taiwan (1), and Switzerland (1). The detailed profile of these cases is reported in appendix 10.1.[1]

Performance Measures and Linkages among Action Arenas

As discussed in chapter 2, most social reality involves multiple action arenas that are linked sequentially or simultaneously to one another. To govern and manage a CPR, individuals must be involved in a complex series of processes that are related to many simultaneous and sequential action arenas (see also discussion in chap. 13). The extent to which an irrigation system can effectively serve the needs of irrigators depends on the simultaneous resolution of problems in multiple action arenas.

One way to measure the performance of an irrigation system is to first measure the outcomes from several different arenas. Information on three outcomes is generally available in case studies on irrigation systems whether (1) a system is well maintained, (2) most irrigators regularly follow operational rules, and (3) the water supply is adequate for all irrigators.[2] Because each of these three outcomes is affected by the extent to which farmers succeed in solving various provision and appropriation problems, they can potentially be used, in combination with one another, to measure the performance of an irrigation system.

The first outcome, the proper maintenance of an irrigation system, depends on coordinated inputs from irrigators. Given its initial construction and physical environments, whether an irrigation system is well maintained reflects the extent to which farmers succeed in coordinating their *provision* activities. The second outcome, the extent irrigators follow rules, affects the coordination of various maintenance and water allocation activities. The viability of rules as coordinating devices depends on whether appropriators regularly follow them. The third outcome, the adequacy of water supply in an irrigation system, depends partly on whether its water retention and transportation structures are properly maintained and whether the existing water flow is efficiently allocated. The degree of water adequacy in an irrigation system partly reflects the extent to which problems in provision and appropriation are solved.

---

1. All the cases were coded by Tang. The coding of each case was reviewed by E. Ostrom. Disagreements on the proper way of coding were discussed and resolved in regular meetings of the project. Since the cases are the basic evidence of the study, the generalizations derived from the study pertain to what has been reported in the cases. For a discussion on the strengths and weaknesses of this method, see Yin and Heald 1975.

2. See Tang 1992 for discussion of how these three variables were coded with dichotomous responses and examples of typical responses for each value.

Within the sample of 47 cases examined here, these three outcomes occur in a pattern that forms a Guttman scale. In a Guttman scale, the component items can be arranged in a systematic and cumulative fashion so that there is "a continuum that indicates varying degree of the underlying dimension" (Nachmias and Nachmias 1987, 475). As shown in table 10.1, these three outcomes can be arranged cumulatively along a continuum in which some outcomes are less likely to occur than others. Within the sample of cases, an adequate supply of water occurs with least frequency. Only 21 out of the 47 cases attain adequate or better rating in regard to the adequacy of the water supply. A somewhat higher number of cases attains conformance to rules. There are 30 out of 47 cases where most farmers follow the rules of their system. And, lastly, there are 33 systems out of 47 where the maintenance of canals can be rated as good or higher. Forty-six out of 47 cases conform perfectly to the scalable pattern. The coefficient of reproducibility, which measures the degree of conformity to a perfectly scalable pattern, is 99 percent.

If the scalable pattern were perfect, an irrigation system with a high degree of rule conformance would also be well maintained; a case with an adequate supply of water would have both a high degree of rule conformance and good maintenance. All 21 cases with adequate supplies of water are characterized by both high degrees of rule conformance and good maintenance. The scale also illustrates that even in cases characterized by good maintenance and a high degree of rule conformance, the supply of water may still be inadequate. Out of the 29 cases with a high degree of rule conformance and good maintenance, 8 of them are characterized by an inadequate supply of water. These cases illustrate that even if appropriators cooperate in rule enforcement and maintenance, an appropriation resource may still have an inadequate supply of water. Water scarcity may be a result of constraining factors

TABLE 10.1. Three Outcomes in Irrigation System on a Guttman Scale

Good Maintenance	Rule Conformance	Adequate Water Supply	Number of Cases
yes	yes	yes	21
yes	yes	no	8
yes	no	no	4
no	no	no	13
no	yes	no	1
Total			47
CR (coefficient of reproducibility = $1 - (1/(47 \times 3)) = 0.99$			

Source: Adapted from Tang 1992, 56.

unrelated to appropriators' failure to enforce rules and to maintain appropriation resources.

Nayband, for example, is an oasis on the Plateau of Iran that has plenty of land but a limited supply of water from nearby springs. Water inadequacy is an environmental constraint beyond the irrigators' immediate control. Other examples are Kottapalle and Sananeri (in India) and Nam Tan Watercourse (in Laos), all of which are located in complex, government-owned irrigation systems. In these systems, the amount of water available to an appropriation area is affected by such factors as the location of the area within the larger system and decisions by the officials who are responsible for releasing water from the main canal to the area. These factors are beyond the immediate control of the irrigators in the appropriation area.

For analytic purposes, the sample of cases can be divided into two sets: one consisting of cases that are rated as positive in both rule conformance and maintenance; the other consisting of cases that are negative in either rule conformance or maintenance, or both. The first group (29 cases) thus represents those in which farmers are relatively successful in solving their provision and appropriation problems; the second group (18 cases) represents those in which farmers have failed to solve some of their provision and appropriation problems. This composite performance measure provides a way of evaluating the extent to which some CPR problems are solved in different irrigation systems. For the analyses presented in this chapter, the first group is classified as high-performance cases and the second group as low-performance cases.

Matching Rules to Physical Domains

As demonstrated in chapter 4, the structure of a game and its equilibria depend on both the underlying institutional rules and physical domain. Depending on the underlying physical constraints, a particular set of institutional rules may produce similar or divergent incentives and thus similar or divergent outcomes. Only when institutional rules are congruent with particular physical domains can games with nonoptimal equilibria be transformed into games with better equilibria.

The need to match institutional rules to physical domains can be illustrated by the pattern of operational rules reported in the sample of cases. Operational rules define the constraints and guidelines for coordinating daily appropriation and provision activities. To be effective, operational rules need to create enough predictability among individuals yet permit enough flexibility to deal with various contingencies. In *irrigation*, three types of operational rules are particularly important for solving collective-action problems.

These are boundary rules, authority rules regarding allocation,[3] and authority rules regarding input requirements.[4]

Boundary Rules

Boundary rules specify the requirements one must fulfill before appropriating water from a system. Boundary rules may constrain how much water is appropriated by limiting the number of irrigators eligible to receive water from a system. If the boundary rules authorize more irrigators to take more water than the system can make available, substantial conflict and difficulties related to water allocation can still occur. A boundary rule that successfully limits the number of appropriators, holding other factors constant, can enable the irrigators to achieve an adequate supply of water for their agricultural needs.

Four types of requirements appear most frequently in the case studies.

1. *Land*: ownership or leasing of land within a specified location
2. *Shares*: ownership or leasing of shares, transferable independently of land, to a certain proportion of the water flow or water delivery facilities
3. *Membership*: membership in an organization
4. *Fee*: payment of certain entry fee each time before appropriating water

The variety of boundary rules used in irrigation systems appears to be more limited than the variety in boundary rules for inshore fisheries. In chapter 11, Schlager finds 12 different types of boundary rules. Only 2 rules are used in both fisheries and irrigation systems: the requirement that an appropriator own or lease land in a specified area and membership in a particular organization.[5] The variety is reduced further when one examines the rules that are used in the 14 government-owned systems for which data

---

3. Authority rules regarding allocation specify the procedure and basis for withdrawing units from a CPR.

4. The analysis in the rest of this chapter focuses on two types of irrigation systems—those that are owned by farmers and those owned by national or regional governments. The four systems that are owned by local governments are excluded from the analysis because they are substantially different in regard to many variables. Given that we have information about only four of these municipal irrigation systems, the analysis is clearer when limited to farmer-owned and those systems owned by national or regional governments.

5. A comparison can be made between the variety and type of rules used in these two sets of cases since both are based on the same structured coding form.

TABLE 10.2. Boundary Rules and Performance

Level of Performance	Land as the Sole Boundary Requirement	Other Types or Combinations of Boundary Requirements	Total
	Government-Owned Irrigation Systems		
High	6	0	6
Low	8	0	8
Total	14	0	14
	Farmer-Owned Irrigation Systems		
High	3	15	18
Low	6	1	7
Total	9	16	25

about rules are available:[6] All of them use land as the sole boundary requirement (see table 10.2). Among the 25 farmer-owned systems for which data
about boundary rules are available, land is used as the sole boundary requirement in only 9 of the cases. The other 16 use other types or combinations of
boundary requirements.[7]

A boundary rule may be sufficient for allocation purposes if it limits the
number of appropriators to the extent that the amount of water needed for
efficient irrigation is less than the amount available. Collective-action problems, however, may remain if the boundary rule allows more water appropriation than the system can support. Many irrigation systems that use land
as the sole boundary requirement appear to have difficulty in keeping the
number of irrigators within limits. As shown in table 10.2, among the 15 low-
performance cases, 14 use land as the sole boundary requirement.

In these 14 cases, water is supposed to be available to all plots within a
certain service area. Problems, however, often arise when more land is included than the source of water can support. A formal policy goal of many
government-owned irrigation systems, especially in India and Pakistan, is to
deliver water to as much land as possible in order to justify their construction
and maintenance costs. Increasing the number of beneficiaries of irrigation
projects is also a common way for politicians in these countries to gain
electoral support (Repetto 1986). As a result, the official service areas in many

6. From case descriptions, it is difficult to code reliable information on the rules being
used. Thus, only cases that report detailed information about the specific rules are analyzed in this
chapter.

7. The distribution among these 16 cases is shares (4 cases); shares plus membership (1
case); land plus other requirements (5 cases); and different requirements applied to different
subgroups (6 cases).

of these irrigation systems are much larger than can be supported by the water sources. Irrigators in these systems face a high degree of water scarcity and various allocation and maintenance problems.

Authority Rules Related to Allocation

Three types of authority rules are frequently used for water allocation:[8]

1. *Fixed percentage*: the flow of water is divided into fixed proportion by some physical device.
2. *Fixed time slots*: each individual is assigned fixed time slots during which he or she may withdraw water.
3. *Fixed orders*: individuals take turns to get water.

Some forms of authority rules related to allocation are reported to be in use in all but 3 of the cases. Although allocation procedures, per se, do not guarantee success, various kinds of water allocation and maintenance problems are reported in the 3 cases where no allocation procedures are in use. In these 3 cases, where water supplies are scarce, conflicts over water allocation arise frequently among irrigators.[9] As shown in table 10.3, among the three types of procedures, fixed time slots are the most commonly used: 19 out of 37 cases (for which data are available) use fixed time slots as the sole allocation procedure. They are used in 10 out of 12 government-owned systems and 9 out of 25 farmer-owned systems.[10]

Why are fixed time slots used more frequently than other water allocation procedures? One possible explanation is that they are relatively easy to enforce. If each irrigator knows his or her time slot, the irrigator will show up at the right spot and divert water to the field when his or her time slot begins. Since each farmer has an incentive to guard his or her own time slots against

---

8. Each of these procedures may be based on different premises such as amount of land held, amount of water needed to cultivate existing crops, number of shares held, location of field, or official discretion. An allocation procedure, for instance, may require each irrigator to appropriate water in specific time slots. The length of the slot assigned to each irrigator may be determined by the number of water shares he or she holds, that is, the greater the number of shares, the longer the time slot to which one is appointed.

9. Where there is an abundant supply of water, however, allocation procedures may not be necessary. One example is an irrigation system in the Philippines, Nazareno-Gamutan, where water is so abundant that appropriators can have a continuous supply of water and no allocation procedure is needed (see Ongkingko 1973).

10. In an irrigation system, more than one set of allocation procedures may be used for different occasions. In many irrigation systems, a more restrictive set of allocation procedures is used during a certain period in a year and a less restrictive set is used during another. The allocation procedures reported here are the most restrictive ones reported in the case studies.

TABLE 10.3.   Allocation Procedures and Performance

Level of Performance	Fixed Time Slots as the Sole Allocation Procedure	Other Types or Combinations of Allocation Procedures	No Allocation Procedure	Total
	Government-Owned Irrigation Systems			
High	3	2	0	5
Low	7	0	0	7
Total	10	2	0	12
	Farmer-Owned Irrigation Systems			
High	7	11	0	18
Low	2	2	3	7
Total	9	13	3	25

water theft the arrangement may be self-enforcing and require minimal supervision. This appears to be true in 3 of the cases in the sample: Nayband and Deh Salm in Iran, and Felderin in Switzerland. Even though there is no specialized enforcement arrangement in these three communities, irrigators regularly follow allocation procedures. It should, however, be noted that all of these systems are small in scale: Nayband has a population of around 80 families; Felderin irrigates 19 hectares of fields; and Deh Salm serves 50 families. Irrigators can monitor one another easily because of the small number of individuals or the small area involved.

Assigning irrigators fixed time slots, however, has a potential problem: If the water flow in the system is erratic, an irrigator owning a share for a particular time slot is still uncertain about supply. Dhabi Minor Watercourse, for example, is located in a government-owned irrigation system in India where irrigators are assigned time slots in different water distribution cycles within a watercourse (Reidinger 1980). At the system level, water supplies to various watercourses are determined by yet another water distribution cycle. Because of a lack of coordination between distribution cycles at the two levels, an irrigator assigned a particular time slot may fail to get any water if no water flows into the watercourse during that time. Irrigators in the watercourse therefore face a high degree of uncertainty about their water supplies, which in turn affects their willingness to cooperate in water allocation and maintenance. The Dhabi Minor Watercourse is characterized by a high frequency of rule violations and poor maintenance.

Allocating water by fixed time slots may require less administrative costs than other allocation procedures. Serious problems may, however, arise if the procedure is used without considering its compatibility with other institutional and physical attributes of the appropriation resource. The example of Dhabi Minor Watercourse is a case in point. Within the sample, this kind of incompatibility appears to happen mostly in irrigation systems governed by national or regional agencies: Of the 10 government-owned systems that use time slots as the sole allocation procedure, 7 are low-performance cases; of the 9 farmer-owned systems that use time slots as the sole allocation procedure, only 2 systems are low-performance cases.

Combined Configurations of Boundary Rules and Allocation Procedures

As shown in the preceding discussion, farmer-owned irrigation systems are characterized by a wider diversity of boundary rules and allocation procedures than systems governed by government bureaucracies. The contrast between the two types of systems becomes more apparent when one examines the combined configurations of the two types of rules. As shown in table 10.4, of the 12 government-owned systems for which data about both types of rules are available, 10 use one particular configuration, that is, land plus fixed time slots. Seven out of these 10 cases are low-performance cases. On the other hand, a greater diversity of rule configurations exists among farmer-owned systems. High-performance cases are associated with almost every possible configuration of the two types of rules. The only exception is the one configuration that includes no allocation procedures, where all 3 cases have low performance.

Table 10.4 illustrates that land and fixed time slots are not inherently ineffective rules. They may be appropriate in some situations, as is the case in some high-performance systems that use both rules together. Problems, however, arise if these rules are applied to every situation, no matter whether the rules are appropriate to the specific institutional and physical environments. This kind of problem seems to exist in many government-owned irrigation systems that rigidly use one particular configuration of operational rules, regardless of their specific environments.[11] This contrasts with many farmer-owned systems that are able to tailor their operational rules to their specific circumstances.

---

11. It should be noted that the government-owned systems analyzed in this chapter refer to those whose production resources are governed by national or regional agencies. These agencies are usually large bureaucratic organizations that are not directly accountable to the local constituencies in which the irrigated areas are located. Irrigation systems governed by these external bureaucratic organizations may function very differently from those governed by local governments. It is possible, for example, that local governments are more flexible and responsive to irrigators' needs than national bureaucratic organizations because local governments tend to be smaller in size and more directly accountable to local constituencies.

TABLE 10.4.   Combined Effect of Boundary and Allocation Rules on Performance

Level of Performance	Land as Sole Boundary Rule			Other Boundary Rules			Total
	Fixed Time Slots	Other Allocation Procedures	No Procedure	Fixed Time Slots	Other Allocation Procedures	No Procedure	
	Government-Owned Irrigation Systems						
High	3	2	0	0	0	0	5
Low	7	0	0	0	0	0	7
Total	10	2	0	0	0	0	12
	Farmer-Owned Irrigation Systems						
High	1	2	0	6	7	0	16
Low	1	2	3	1	0	0	7
Total	2	4	3	7	7	0	23

Authority Rules Related to Input Requirements

The need to tailor operational rules to the underlying physical domain can be further illustrated by examining the authority rules related to input requirements. Input rules specify the types and amounts of contributions required of each participant. A major type of contribution required of irrigators is labor for regular maintenance. There are two major types of rules for regular labor input. One simply requires equal contribution from all irrigators. The other requires contributions roughly in proportion to the benefit each obtains from the system, for example, proportional to one's share of the water, or the amount of land one irrigates.

Maintenance intensity appears to be a factor affecting performance and the choice of labor input requirements. Maintenance intensity can be roughly measured by dividing the total number of person-days of labor per year mobilized in an appropriation area to maintain the irrigation system by the total number of irrigators in the appropriation area. Only 11 of the cases (8 owned by farmers and 3 owned by local governments) report information about both maintenance intensity and labor input requirements for maintenance (see table 10.5).

Two observations can be made with respect to this limited amount of information. First, systems with very low maintenance intensity (an average of less than two days per irrigator per year) are among those that have low performance. A possible explanation for this is that a low degree of labor mobilization often results from the lack of effective cooperation among irrigators.

TABLE 10.5. Maintenance Intensity and Regular Labor Input Requirements (Person-Days of Labor per Cultivator per Year)

Level of Performance	Equal-Contribution Rule	Proportional Rule
High	3.8 (2)[a]	17.7 (4)
Low	1.7 (5)	

[a]Figures in parentheses give number of systems for which data are available.

Second, maintenance intensity affects the choice of labor input requirements: Systems with higher maintenance intensity tend to adopt the proportional rule for labor inputs, while those with lower maintenance intensity tend to adopt the equal-contribution rule. Administrative costs appear to be a factor that affects the choice between proportional and equal-contribution rules. To enforce the proportional rule, resources are needed for recording and organizing different contributions from various appropriators. For systems that require only two or three days of work from each irrigator every year, the potential benefits of proportional rules could easily be offset by the costs of enforcing the proportional rule, whereas for systems with higher maintenance intensity, the gain from the proportional rule may be higher than the administrative costs.

The above discussion illustrates that rules, to be effective, must be compatible with underlying physical domains. Operational rules may work well in one physical domain but fail in others. The search for one best rule for solving all CPR problems is doomed to failure.[12] A more realistic strategy is to develop an institutional framework in which operational rules can be adopted, changed, and enforced in response to variations in the physical environments. To understand the structure and process for generating operational rules that are compatible with the underlying physical domains, one must use multiple levels of analysis, which are discussed in the following section.

Multiple Levels of Institutional Arrangements

As discussed in chapter 2, besides there being multiple and nested action arenas, rules are nested in another set of rules that define how the first set of rules can be enforced and changed. Operational rules specify what is allowed, required, and forbidden in making day-to-day operational decisions. In irrigation, the most important kinds of operational rules include boundary rules and

---

12. See E. Ostrom (1990, chap. 1) for a discussion on the intellectual root of the one best prescription for CPR problems.

authority rules that specify how water is allocated and how much input (labor, money, etc.) is required of each irrigator. Collective-choice rules specify the terms and conditions for interpreting, enforcing, and altering operational rules.

Different sets of collective-choice rules and different communities of participants may be involved in creating and enforcing operational rules. Depending on the size of the irrigation system, the number of irrigators involved, and other physical attributes of the system, different collective-choice entities may be involved in governing an irrigation system. In some government-owned systems, all operational rules are created and enforced by one government agency. In many farmer-owned systems, the collective-choice entity is constituted solely by irrigators themselves, who adopt and enforce their own collective-choice and operational rules.

In other government-owned systems, multiple collective-choice entities are involved. In this kind of system, one community of irrigators is subject to two or more sets of operational rules adopted by different collective-choice entities—one at the system level and one or more at various subsystem levels. In some large, government-run irrigation systems, for example, irrigators are expected to follow a set of operational rules adopted by a government agency. The same group of farmers has also constituted their own farmer associations that adopt and enforce their own operational rules within their own appropriation area.

Local collective-choice entities are important for the effective operation and maintenance of large irrigation systems for several reasons. First, as discussed earlier, operational rules have to match different physical domains to be effective. In many large irrigation systems, different watercourses vary in terms of such physical attributes as soil type, field topography, cropping pattern, and amount of water available. If there is only one collective-choice entity to create and enforce a single set of operational rules for an entire system, the set of rules is unlikely to match the physical domains of all appropriation areas equally well. Local collective-choice entities at the watercourse level are more likely to utilize knowledge about local conditions in formulating and enforcing operational rules and choices. Their proximity to the appropriation area also enables them to act quickly in solving problems. This contrasts with many bureaucratic agencies in which the responsible officials live far away from the irrigated area and possess little knowledge about local environments.

Besides being compatible with the underlying physical domains, rules can be effective only if participants share a common understanding of the rules. Rules developed in local collective-choice arenas often result from extensive trial and error by the appropriators. Appropriators are more likely to share a common understanding of the rules developed by themselves than those handed down from distant government agencies.

Furthermore, individuals who have lived together for some time may be able to develop various social networks and reciprocal relationships with one another in various social arenas. Knowledge about these networks and relationships is shared by members of the community. It is often difficult for outsiders to identify these networks and relationships. Members of the community know when and how they can utilize this social capital (Coleman 1990) to develop and enforce various institutional rules.

Large-scale irrigation systems that are governed solely by national or regional government agencies are unlikely to solve most water allocation and maintenance problems at the watercourse level. Within the sample of cases, all six of the cases governed solely by national or regional government agencies are characterized by low performance (see table 10.6). In these cases, operational rules handed down from bureaucratic agencies often turn out to be incompatible with the special circumstances of individual irrigated areas.

The involvement of irrigators in the formulation and enforcement of operational rules facilitates the adaptation of operational rules to the specific environments of different appropriation areas. In some of the large government-owned irrigation systems, local appropriators have constituted additional collective-choice mechanisms that adopt and enforce their own operational rules at the watercourse level. Operational rules developed and enforced by these local collective-choice entities are usually more effective in meeting local needs. Among the government-owned systems in the sample, those with local collective-choice entities are characterized by a higher level of rule conformance and maintenance than those without.

Local collective-choice entities, however, may not be effective in all circumstances. Irrigators' organizations are more likely to perform relatively effectively when (1) they are able to secure extra benefits for the community of irrigators and (2) members of these organizations are also relatively free to

TABLE 10.6. Rule Conformance by Local Collective-Choice Entity: Government-Owned Irrigation Systems

Level of Performance	With Local Collective-Choice Entity	Without Local Collective-Choice Entity	Total
High	6	0	6
Low	2	6	8
Total	8	6	14

Source: Adapted from Tang 1992, 116.

develop their own collective-choice rules and processes that directly affect their own welfare.

Whereas collective-choice entities at the subsystem level facilitate adaptation to the specific needs of various irrigated areas, a collective-choice entity at the system level is necessary to deal with broader problems such as the allocation of water among different irrigated areas and the maintenance of diversion works for the entire system. The collective-choice entities at the subsystem level, however, can still maintain their autonomy in relation to water allocation and maintenance within their respective areas. If different levels of collective-choice entities are constituted to deal with problems of different scopes, many coordination problems associated with large-scale irrigation can be avoided.[13]

Monitoring and Enforcement Arrangements

Not only may the type of collective-choice entities affect performance but also the way rule conformance is monitored and sanctioned. Effective rule enforcement often depends on guards that are proactive and willing to impose sanctions whenever rule violations are found.

Data are available for 44 of the systems in the CPR database about the type of guards employed.[14] Among the 29 farmer-owned systems, local farmers are hired as guards in 17 of them, while no guards are used in the other 12. Among the 15 government-owned systems, guards are hired in 12 of them, and most of these guards are employees of the central or regional government instead of local farmers (see table 10.7).

While most of the guards hired by the farmer-owned irrigation systems are part-time, and many are not even paid, these local guards are more likely to impose sanctions on rule violations than guards hired by the government-owned irrigation systems. In 15 of the 16 farmer-owned systems that employ guards (and for which data are available), the guards are proactive and likely to impose sanctions on rule violations. Proactive guards exist in only 4 of the 11 government-owned systems that employ guards. In all of the farmer-owned systems, the local guard is authorized to take action on the spot. This is not the case in many of the government-owned systems. As Harriss reports regarding a government-owned system in Sri Lanka:

> Prosecutions have to be carried out by the police, who have usually treated water offenses as trivial, and who do not have the same incentives

---

13. For a more detailed discussion on the coordination between different levels of collective-choice entities in irrigation, see Tang 1993.

14. The data reported in this section were compiled by E. Ostrom.

TABLE 10.7. Monitoring, Sanctioning, and Rule Following in Farmer-Owned and Government-Owned Irrigation Systems

	Farmer-Owned Irrigation Systems	Government-Owned Irrigation Systems
Presence of Guards		
External guards	0	9 (60%)
Local guards	17 (59%)	3 (20%)
No guards used	12 (41%)	3 (20%)
Total	29 (100%)	15 (100%)
Full-time Guards**		
Yes	2 (12%)	8 (73%)
No	14 (88%)	3 (27%)
Total	16 (100%)	11 (100%)
Payment of Guards*		
Money or in-kind	2 (15%)	9 (82%)
Reduced obligations	8 (52%)	2 (18%)
Not at all	5 (33%)	0
Total	15 (100%)	11 (100%)
Likelihood of Guards**		
Imposing Sanctions		
Very likely or unlikely	15 (94%)	4 (36%)
Unlikely	1 (6%)	7 (64%)
Total	16 (100%)	11 (100%)
Irrigation Rules Followed		
Systems with guards:		
Yes	13 (93%)	7 (64%)
No	1 (7%)	4 (36%)
Total	14 (100%)	11 (100%)
Systems without guards:		
Yes	5 (45%)	0
No	6 (55%)	3 (100%)
Total	11 (100%)	3 (100%)

*$p < 0.05$.
**$p < 0.005$.

to tackle them as in other cases. Further, delays over court proceedings and the very light fines, which have been imposed on those who have been found guilty of irrigation offenses, have made the legal sanctions ineffectual. (1984, 322)[15]

The presence of guards is an important factor affecting the level of rule conformance in farmer-owned systems: While routine rule conformance is

---

15. See Wade 1987 and Hunt 1990 for further descriptions of the problems related to guards on government-owned irrigation systems in India.

reported in 13 out of the 14 farmer-owned systems *with* guards, it is reported in only 5 out of 11 farmer-owned systems *without* guards. Among government-owned systems, the presence of guards also appears to be important: All three of the government-owned systems *without* guards are characterized by a lack of routine rule conformance. The presence of guards, however, does not guarantee routine rule conformance in government-owned systems: 4 out of the 11 government-owned systems *with* guards are characterized by a lack of routine rule conformance.

Conclusions

This chapter has illustrated four related themes discussed in this volume. First, different CPR problems are related to one another through an interactive series of action arenas. Concerted efforts are needed to tackle related problems in order to ensure productive uses of a common-pool resource. To determine whether CPR problems are effectively solved in an irrigation system, one needs to develop a performance measure that is based on outcomes generated in multiple action arenas.

Second, institutional rules, to be effective, must be compatible with the underlying physical domains. Different configurations of rules and physical domains lead to different types of games which in turn lead to higher or lower performance. A more realistic strategy than to search for one best rule for solving all CPR problems is to develop institutional frameworks that can facilitate the direct involvement of appropriators in governing CPRs. Irrigators' organizations are likely to be more effective than large bureaucratic organizations in adopting, changing, and enforcing various configurations of operational rules in response to physical diversities.

Third, multiple levels of rules may be adopted and enforced by more than one collective-choice entity. Effective coordination among different collective-choice entities is essential for the effective governance of many large-scale common-pool resources.

Fourth, monitoring mechanisms are important in regard to the performance of irrigation systems. What is surprising is that even though (or, perhaps because) farmer-owned systems tend to employ local farmers on a part-time basis and frequently do not pay them a monetary wage, these guards are more proactive and rule conformance is more predictable than when full-time external government agents are the guards.

TABLE 10.1A. Farmer-Owned Irrigation Systems: Cases Coded

Country	System Name	System Type	Service Area (in hectares)	Major Crop	Documentation
Bangladesh	Nabagram	Simple	29	—	Coward and Badaruddin 1979
Indonesia	Bondar Parhudagar	Simple	4	Rice	Lando 1979
Indonesia	Takkapala	Simple	95	Rice	Hafid and Hayami 1979
Indonesia	Saebah	Simple	100	Rice	Hafid and Hayami 1979
Indonesia	Silean Banua	Simple	120	Rice	Lando 1979
Iran	Deh Salm	Simple	300	Other grains	Spooner 1971, 1972, 1974
Iran	Nayband	Simple	—	Rice	Spooner 1971, 1972, 1974
Nepal	Raj Kulo	Simple	94	Rice	E. Martin and Yoder 1983a, 1983b, 1986
Nepal	Thulo Kulo	Simple	39	Rice	E. Martin and Yoder 1983a, 1983b, 1986
Nepal	Char Hazar	Simple	200	Rice	Fowler 1986
Nepal	Chhahare Khola	Simple	20	Other grains	Water and Engineering Commission 1987
Nepal	Naya Dhara	Simple	55	Rice	Water and Engineering Commission 1987
Philippines	Agcuyo	Simple	9	Rice	de los Reyes 1980a
Philippines	Cadchog	Simple	3	Rice	de los Reyes 1980a
Philippines	Calaoaan	Simple	150	Rice	de los Reyes 1980a
Philippines	Mauraro	Simple	15	Rice	de los Reyes 1980a
Philippines	Oaig-Daya	Simple	100	Rice	de los Reyes 1980a
Philippines	Sabangan Bato	Simple	94	Rice	de los Reyes 1980a
Philippines	Silag-Butir	Simple	114	Rice	de los Reyes 1980a
Philippines	San Antonio 1	Simple	23	Rice	de los Reyes et al. 1980
Philippines	San Antonio 2	Simple	7	Rice	de los Reyes et al. 1980
Philippines	Tanowong T	Simple	—	Rice	Bacdayan 1980
Philippines	Tanowong B	Simple	—	Rice	Bacdayan 1980
Philippines	Pinagbayanan	Simple	20	Rice	F. Cruz 1975
Tanzania	Kheri	Simple	260	Other grains	Gray 1963
Thailand	Na Pae	Simple	64	Rice	Tan-kim-yong 1983
Philippines	Zanjera Danum Sitio	Complex	45/1500[a]	Rice	Coward 1979
Switzerland	Felderin	Complex	19/—	Meadow	Netting 1974, 1981
Thailand	Chiangmai	Complex	—	Rice	Potter 1976

Source: Adapted from Tang 1992, 43.

N = 29

— = Missing in case.

[a]Service area of the appropriation area/service area of the entire system.

TABLE 10.2A. Government-Owned Irrigation Systems: Cases Coded

Country	System Name	System Type	Service Area (in hectares)	Major Crop	Documentation
India	Kottapalle	Complex	500/—[a]	Rice	Wade 1988a, 1992
India	Sananeri	Complex	173/1,172	Rice	Meinzen-Dick 1984
India	Dhabi Minor Watercourse	Complex	21/—	Other grains	Gustafson and Reidinger 1971 Reidinger 1974, 1980 Vander Velde 1971, 1980
India	Area Two Watercourse	Complex	33/229,000	Other grains	Bottrall 1981
Indonesia	Area Three Watercourse	Complex	115/33,000	Rice	Bottrall 1981
Iraq	El Mujariin	Complex	307/208,820	Other grains	Fernea 1970
Laos	Nam Tan Watercourse	Complex	100/2,046	Rice	Coward 1980b
Pakistan	Dakh Branch Watercourse	Complex	152/—	Other grains	Mirza 1975
Pakistan	Gondalpur Watercourse	Complex	200/628,000	Rice	Merrey and Wolf 1986
Pakistan	Punjab Watercourse	Complex	96/—	Rice	Lowdermilk, Clyma, and Early 1975
Pakistan	Area One Watercourse	Complex	50/628,000	Other grains	Bottrall 1981
Thailand	Kaset Samakee	Complex	28/12,000	Rice	Gillespie 1975
Thailand	Amphoe Choke Chai	Complex	125/12,000	Rice	Gillespie 1975
Taiwan	Area Four Watercourse	Complex	150/67,670	Rice	Bottrall 1981

Source: Adapted from Tang 1992, 44.

$N = 14$

— = Missing in case.

[a]Service area of the appropriation area/service area of the entire system.

TABLE 10.3A. Other Irrigation Systems: Cases Coded

Country	System Name	System Type	Service Area (in hectares)	Major Crop	Documentation
Peru	Hanan Sayoc	Simple	—	Other grains	Mitchell 1976, 1977
Peru	Lurin Sayoc 1	Simple	—	Other grains	Mitchell 1976, 1977
Peru	Lurin Sayoc 2	Simple	—	Other grains	Mitchell 1976, 1977
Mexico	Diaz Ordaz Tramo	Complex	2/150[a]	Other grains	Downing 1974

Source: Adapted from Tang 1992, 45.

Note: The production resource of Lurin Sayoc 1 is governed by barriowide rural political officials. The production resources of the other three cases are governed by municipal governments.

$N = 4$

— = Missing in case.

[a]Service area of the appropriation area/service area of the entire system.

CHAPTER 11

Fishers' Institutional Responses to Common-Pool Resource Dilemmas

In 1982, fishers of Caye Caulker, Belize, harvested record amounts of lobster. The increase was attributed to a red tide, a presence in the water of small plantlike organisms that killed the predators of young lobster, permitting dramatic growth in lobster populations (Sutherland 1986, 36). In 1990, Maine fishers harvested a record 28 million pounds of lobster.[1] While the lobstermen of Belize and of Maine experienced abundance, fishers at other times and places face scarcity due to declining fish populations or fish failing to appear at expected times of the year (K. Martin 1979; Shortall 1973). As K. Martin explains in discussing the cod fishers of Fermeuse, Newfoundland,

> Until very recently, Fermeuse fishermen have seldom thought of any-one's fishing activities, perhaps least of all their own, as having an appreciable effect upon fish populations. "Queer things" happen, as in years when fish do not appear, but this is explained in terms of natural factors (e.g., a change in water temperature) over which man has no control. (1979, 285)

Fluctuating stocks of fish are a major source of uncertainty about the physical environment confronting fishers, but so too are weather and determining the location of fish. Physical uncertainty pervades fishers' lives.

Coastal Fisheries as Common-Pool Resource Dilemmas

Human behavior in the context of coastal fisheries, a type of CPR, compounds physical uncertainty creating complex situations for fishers to address. Human behavior compounds a CPR situation because more than a single fisher or team of fishers harvests fish from the resource. Consequently, the fish that are

---

1. "For A Lot of Mainers, the Lobstering Life Is Losing Its Allure," *New York Times*, 1 May 1991, sec. B.

harvested by one fisher are not available for other fishers to catch. Thus, the outcome a single fisher achieves depends not only on his or her own actions but also on the actions of the other fishers using the same grounds.

Multiple fishers interacting within a single fishery may create a CPR dilemma. For a coastal fishery to be characterized as a CPR dilemma, fishers must pursue strategies that result in suboptimal outcomes and alternative strategies must exist that are more efficient than current strategies. For instance, early in this century, fishers of Valença, Brazil, pursued suboptimal strategies as they developed their estuarian fishery (Cordell 1972). The Valença fishers used a variety of technologies within their estuary, interfering with each other as they harvested fish. In addition, different areas within the estuary were more productive than others, and fishers competed for the best fishing spots. Gear interference and competition for productive spots resulted in the destruction of gear and in physical violence among the fishers. As Cordell explains:

> From my conversations with older fishermen it was apparent that long ago they recognized the chance of interference, even if unintentional, was fairly high, especially during spawning seasons. Because of the difficulty in establishing exclusive long-term control over net fishing areas, considerable violence was characteristic of canoe fishing in its earlier phases. However, as fishermen noted, the more violence-prone participants in fishing had gradually abandoned it. . . . The reasons for this were clear: loss of equipment due to retaliatory acts, canoes sunk, nets burned or stolen, and in some cases people shot while attempting to take a *lanco* by force. (1972, 105)

Developing a base of information concerning the physical environment can provide the basis for addressing commons dilemmas. The Valença fishers, over a period of time, acquired an intimate knowledge of their estuary, determining relationships between phases of the moon, tides, and the consequent location of fish. But information, in and of itself, does not address conflict among fishers using a shared resource. In order to address problems that arise through interactions among individuals using a common resource, information about the physical environment must be used to coordinate harvesting activities. Coordination occurs through the use of rules defining acceptable or unacceptable behavior. The fishers of Valença addressed problems that arose among themselves by changing the rules they used.

Over time, the Valença fishers developed new rules to prevent interference among each other and to allocate choice spots. For instance, the fishers divided their estuary into various areas and assigned a different technology to each area.

The mangrove fence and barricade net are always located highest on the shore, succeeded by the dragged nets, encircling nets, and tidal flat fish corrals. Finally, moving out to the channel are positioned the fish traps, trotlines and gillnets. In any case, the distribution of techniques in a wedge of water is always such that they do not overlap. (Cordell 1972, 42)

In gaining access to a spot within a particular technological zone fishers used a prior announcement rule to claim a spot for a day (see chap. 4). "When someone wishes to fish in a particular spot at a particular tide level, he may announce his intentions several days in advance. This . . . serves to establish his claim to a designated water space. The place set aside for this purpose is a local bar where fishermen congregate" (Cordell 1972, 98). In addition, if several boats arrived at a specific spot simultaneously, the fishers of each boat would often draw lots to determine the order of use of the spot. If a fisher violated these rules and caused harm to another fisher, he or she could expect to be punished by that fisher. The fishers "recognize a definite danger in letting a competitor get away with harmful acts, and consider it up to whoever has been wronged to 'get back' at the violator so he won't *ficar viciado* (become addicted to wrongdoing)" (Cordell 1972, 106).

The Valença fishers experienced problems common to most coastal fishers who do not coordinate their harvesting of fish—technological externalities and assignment problems (see chap. 1). And just like many other coastal fishers who have coordinated their harvesting, the Valença fishers adopted self-governing arrangements carefully crafted to the exigencies of their particular situation. This is not to say that coastal fishers only experience dilemmas that involve technological externalities and assignment problems. They may face others, such as appropriation externalities, which affect the stock of fish and the cost per unit of fish caught. However, when coastal fishers adopt self-governing arrangements, such arrangements are typically designed to directly address technological externalities and assignment problems; they may only indirectly address appropriation externalities.

This chapter provides an explanation for why fishers tend to adopt particular types of rules and not others. The chapter begins with a discussion of typical dilemmas that fishers face. The likelihood of fishers addressing such dilemmas is affected by the physical environment of coastal fisheries. The unpredictable fluctuations in fish flows prevent fishers from gaining control over such flows. However, there are other aspects of the physical environment that are much more predictable and regular, for instance, the physical structure of coastal fishing grounds. By accumulating information on the physical structure of their grounds, fishers can utilize that information to coordinate their harvesting activities and reduce or resolve particular types of CPR dilemmas.

In the sections that follow, an analysis of the impact of the physical environment on the complexity of fishery dilemmas leads to a hypothesis concerning the types of dilemmas fishers are more likely to attempt to resolve through the use of rules. This hypothesis is tested using data collected about the rules in use from 30 in-depth case studies of coastal fisheries located around the world. The types of rules fishers often adopt suggest that they directly attempt to reduce particular types of dilemmas.

CPR Dilemmas, Complexity, and Coastal Fisheries

Coastal fisheries experience CPR dilemmas, which include appropriation externalities, technological externalities, and assignment problems. Appropriation externalities arise because fishers are withdrawing fish from a common stock without taking into account the effects of their harvesting upon each other. When a fisher harvests fish, he or she subtracts from the amount of fish available to be harvested, increasing the marginal costs of appropriating additional fish and lowering the marginal product of additional fishing effort. Thus, the increased costs of harvesting due to reducing the stock not only affect the fisher who harvested the fish—the fisher who generated the costs—but all fishers who fish that stock.[2]

Technological externalities emerge when fishers physically interfere with each other in harvesting fish. Wilson defines technological externalities as "gear conflicts or other forms of physical interference which arise because fishermen often find it advantageous to fish very close to one another" (J. Wilson 1982, 423). Technological externalities also emerge by indirect physical interference. Gear does not become entangled or destroyed, but it is set so close together that the flow of fish among gear is obstructed. As Smith explains, "Externalities may also enter via crowding phenomena: If the fish population is highly concentrated the efficiency of each boat may be lowered by congestion over the fishing grounds" (1968, 413).

The physical environment of coastal fisheries often times promotes assignment problems. Fish unevenly distribute themselves across fishing

---

2. Lee Anderson defines these externalities as follows: "The individual fishermen do not consider the effect that their production will have on the production of all others in the current period. . . . At the same time, however, the stock is being nonoptimally depleted because individual operators do not consider the user cost they are imposing on harvesters in future periods" (L. Anderson 1986, 47). Smith states that these externalities occur because "no individual competitive fisherman has control over population size as a private decision variable yet it enters as a parameter in each fisherman's cost function" (Smith 1968, 413). Gordon argues that these externalities arise because "it is not the relative *marginal* productivities of the two grounds but their *average* productivities. The fisherman does not ask what allocation of effort will maximize the aggregate production of the fishing fleet but what action will give him, individually, the greater yield" (H. Gordon 1953, 451).

grounds, congregating in areas that provide food and shelter. Consequently, particular areas or spots of fishing grounds are more productive than others, with fishers desiring to fish the most productive spots. Assignment problems occur when fishers, in their uncoordinated choice of a fishing spot, do not allocate themselves efficiently across spots. Problems arise over who should have access to the most productive spots and how access should be determined. As illustrated in chapter 4, failure to solve assignment problems can lead to conflict among fishers and increased production costs.

In the context of the physical environment of coastal fisheries, appropriation externalities, technological externalities, and assignment problems vary in their complexity. This complexity affects the likelihood of fishers designing institutional arrangements to address specific externalities. J. Wilson argues that dilemmas meeting three criteria are likely candidates for solution. These three criteria are as follows:

1. Repeated encounters under roughly similar circumstances in which opportunistic individual behavior is seen to destroy the possibilities for collective gain
2. An information network—arising from trading, competition, or other interactions—that forms the basis for the identification and negotiation of possible rules
3. A collective means for the enforcement of these rules (1982, 420)

In other words, according to Wilson, if fishers are to voluntarily address CPR dilemmas, fishers must first recognize that their actions negatively affect each other. Such recognition is more likely to emerge in repeated situations. But simple recognition is not enough. Fishers must also regularly interact within a community that provides them with opportunities to discuss their common problems and to propose collective solutions. Finally, if solutions (i.e., rules) are adopted, they must be enforced to be effective.

Whether these criteria are met, however, depends critically upon the aspects of the physical environment of coastal fisheries most closely intertwined with the CPR dilemma. As discussed below, dilemmas that are based upon the flow of fish are less likely to meet Wilson's three criteria, whereas dilemmas that are based upon the physical structure of fishing grounds are more likely to meet his criteria.

Appropriation Externalities

On the basis of the criteria, fishers are less likely to engage in institutional change in efforts to directly resolve appropriation externalities. This dilemma, which arises because numerous fishers harvest from shared stocks, is one of the most complex for fishers to directly resolve due to the nature of fish stocks. Fishers harvest from multiple stocks whose populations fluctuate unpredictably and whose population dynamics are not well understood (Dickie 1979; J. Wilson 1982). Consequently, it is extremely problematic for fishers to determine whether a decrease in the fish population is due to harvesting, environmental circumstances, or both. In addition, because coastal fishers lack information concerning the population dynamics of fish stocks, determining how many fish constitute the stock, how many are withdrawn, and therefore, the effect that each fisher's catch has upon the catches of other fishers is also difficult, if not impossible. Since fishers cannot measure with sufficient accuracy the magnitude of the problem, nor the exact causes, they are unlikely to devise arrangements that would directly address appropriation externalities, such as individual transferable quotas. Appropriation externalities do not meet Wilson's first criterion of repeated encounters under similar conditions.

Wilson's second criterion, that the dilemma be confined primarily to fishers who harvest from shared grounds, also is frequently not met in relation to appropriation externalities. Numerous communities of fishers often harvest from the same stocks of fish, compounding the problem of determining the production effects fishers have upon each other. In order to address appropriation externalities, fishers would have to determine the costs generated by all other fishers utilizing a common stock. All communities of fishers harvesting from a single stock would have to coordinate their activities to eliminate appropriation externalities. Having failed to meet Wilson's first two criteria, considerations concerning the third criterion—enforceability of agreements—are moot.

Technological Externalities

Unlike appropriation externalities, technological externalities may be more amenable to solution because they are not based on fluctuating flows of fish. Direct physical interference, that is, entangling of gears, is immediately noticeable, and the causes of it understood. Indirect physical interference is not immediately apparent, although through "repeated encounters under roughly similar circumstances" it may become so. Over time, fishers may realize the effects upon their catches of fish when other fishers set their gear close by (K. Martin 1979; Raychaudhuri 1980; Shortall 1973). By possessing knowledge of the causes of technological externalities, fishers can consider alternative sets of rules to address these problems. Technological externalities appear to meet Wilson's first criterion.

Second, unlike appropriation externalities that may span numerous communities of fishers, technological externalities often arise within a single "information network" or community of coastal fishers utilizing common grounds. As fishers engage in harvesting within a finite space, they can interfere with each other's activities. Mobile gears can be dragged through an area where fixed gears are set, damaging both technologies. The effects of technological externalities may be localized to a few fishers or a group of coastal fishers, meeting Wilson's second criterion.

The ease and costliness of monitoring rules affects the likelihood and extent to which rules will be enforced—Wilson's third criterion. The costliness of monitoring is affected by the type of behavior upon which the rules focus, the design of the rules used, and the ability of fishers to monitor as a by-product of harvesting fish. In relation to technological externalities, rules typically constrain the types of gear that may be utilized as well as the spacing of gear (Berkes 1977; Cordell 1972; A. Davis 1984). Such required behavior is relatively easy to monitor. In many instances, one need only look at a boat to determine the type of gear utilized and whether it is located in an appropriate area. Thus, monitoring is easily accomplished by fishers as they engage in harvesting. In fact, it is often in their direct self-interest to do so. If a fisher notices another boat utilizing gear in an area forbidden to that gear, the fisher, in either reporting the violation or confronting the transgressor, acts to protect his or her own gear. In many instances, technological externalities meet Wilson's third criterion.

Assignment Problems

Assignment problems are defined by the physical structure of fishing grounds and often meet the first two criteria established by Wilson. Fish consistently congregate to those areas and spots that provide food and shelter from predators (Grossinger 1975; D. Miller 1989). Since those areas and spots of fishing grounds remain stable across time, choice fishing spots also remain stable. The stability of the spots permits fishers to determine their location, which is oftentimes common knowledge to a community of fishers (Berkes 1986, 1992; A. F. Davis 1975; Forman 1966).

The stability of choice fishing spots meets Wilson's first criterion. In competing for productive fishing spots, fishers experience repeated encounters under similar circumstances. Day after day, and possibly year after year, fishers compete to gain the best spots. As the result of conflict and possible escalation of conflict, fishers are made aware that opportunistic individual behavior results in suboptimal outcomes. These problems are immediately noticeable. In addition, because choice spots arise in relation to the physical structure of fishing grounds, assignment problems arise among the community of fishers who are utilizing those grounds. Because these problems are restricted to a geographic area, they often meet Wilson's second criterion.

The difficulty and costliness of monitoring and enforcing rules designed to address assignment problems may, in many instances, be relatively low. In relation to assignment problems, rules typically allocate spots for a specified period of time (Berkes 1986, 1992; K. Martin 1979). Such required behavior is relatively easy to monitor. One need only look at the positioning of a boat to determine whether it is located in its specified area. This can easily be accomplished by fishers as they engage in harvesting. In fact, it is often in their direct self-interest to do so. To avoid being foreclosed from harvesting fish, fishers face strong incentives to ensure that their assigned spots are not utilized by others. Wilson's third criterion is often met in relation to assignment problems.

Given Wilson's criteria and the physical environments in which fishers operate, when confronted with appropriation externalities, technological externalities, and assignment problems, fishers are more likely to attempt to mitigate technological externalities and assignment problems than they are appropriation externalities. When confronted with technological externalities and assignment problems, a group of fishers can reduce such problems by changing the structure of their situation by adopting rules that coordinate their use of a shared fishing ground. That is, they can manage the use of space within their fishing ground. In contrast, a group of fishers are less likely to reduce appropriation externalities by adopting a set of rules, since the cause of such externalities extends beyond the boundaries of a single group of fishers, and, consequently, beyond their ability to resolve.

Fishers' Responses to CPR Dilemmas

In this section, the above assertion will be given an initial examination. First, the data set will be introduced. Next, the rules that organized fishers have adopted to coordinate their use of shared fishing grounds will be presented and discussed. Finally, the performance of the rules adopted by the fishers is examined. The rules are generally successful in assisting fishers in resolving technological externalities and assignment problems. Fishers, however, appear to be more adept at reducing assignment problems than they are at reducing technological externalities.

Data from the Field

Data was collected from case studies of coastal fishing grounds located around the world (see table 11.1). The data were extracted from these case studies using a set of detailed coding forms containing mostly closed-ended questions that captured the physical, institutional, and community attributes of coastal fishing grounds and the fishers who utilize them (see Schlager 1990; Tang 1992). In choosing particular case studies two criteria were used. First, the

TABLE 11.1. Description of Case Studies

Country	Location	Harvested	Subgroups	Periods	Number of Appropriators Harvesting	Documentation
Belize	Caye Caulker	Lobster	1	1	297	Sutherland 1986
Belize	San Pedro	Lobster	2	1	165	E. Gordon 1981
Brazil	Arembepe	Mixed	1	1	178	Kottak 1966
Brazil	Coqueiral	Mixed	1	1	85	Forman 1966, 1970
Brazil	Valença	Mixed	5	3	500	Cordell 1972, 1974, 1978b, 1983, 1984
Canada	Baccalaos Cove	Cod	2	1	81	Powers 1984
Canada	Cat Harbour	Cod	2	1	72	Faris 1972
Canada	Fermeuse	Cod	2	1	56	K. Martin 1973, 1979
Canada	James Bay	Whitefish	1	1	387	Berkes 1977, 1987
Canada	Petty Harbour	Cod	2	1	104	Shortall 1973
Canada	Port Lameroon Pagesville	Lobster	1	1	29	A. F. Davis 1975 and A. Davis 1984
Canada	Port Lameroon Pagesville	Mixed	1	1	33	A. F. Davis 1975 and A. Davis 1984
Greece	Messolonghi Etolico	Mullet/Seabrea	2	1	370	Kotsonias 1984

(*continued*)

TABLE 11.1.—*Continued*

Country	Location	Harvested	Subgroups	Periods	Number of Appropriators Harvesting	Documentation
India	Jambudwip	Mixed	2	1	243	Raychaudhuri 1968, 1980
Jamaica	Fraquhar Beach	Mixed	1	1	94	Davenport 1956
Japan	Ebibara	Shrimp	1	1	missing	Brameld 1968
Korea	Kagoda	Anchovy	1	1	missing	Han 1972
Malaysia	Kampong Mee	Mixed	1	1	missing	E. Anderson and Anderson 1977
Malaysia	Perupok	Mixed	1	1	245	Firth 1966
Mexico	Andres Quintana Roo	Mixed	1	1	missing	D. Miller 1982
Mexico	Andrea Quintana Roo	Lobster	1	1	65	D. Miller 1982
Mexico	Ascension Bay	Lobster	1	1	110	D. Miller 1982, 1989
Nicaragua	Tasbapauni	Turtle	2	1	80	Nietschmann 1972, 1973
Sri Lanka	Gahavalla	Mixed	3	3	284	Alexander 1982
Thailand	Rusembilan	Mackerel	1	1	200	T. Fraser 1960, 1966
Turkey	Alanya	Mixed	1	1	100	Berkes 1986
Turkey	Ayvalik-Haylazli	Mixed	1	1	103	Berkes 1986
Turkey	Tasucu Pagesville	Mixed	1	1	140	Berkes 1986
Venezuela	Chiguana	Lisa	1	1	48	Breton 1973
U.S.A.	Mount Desert Island	Lobster	1	1	72	Grossinger 1975

study had to describe a coastal fishing ground that had been or was a CPR dilemma as defined in chapter 1. Second, the study had to contain information on the rules that fishers used to organize their harvesting activities. After searching through hundreds of documents, 30 in-depth coastal fishery case studies were identified where substantial information existed about the rules-in-use. These case studies are not a random sample from the population of coastal fishing grounds located throughout the world. Consequently, one must be cautious in generalizing these findings. On the other hand, a consistent set of variables were collected across the cases, permitting controlled comparisons.

The unit of analysis used is the subgroup. A subgroup is a group of fishers who harvest from the same fishing ground and who are relatively similar in relation to the following five characteristics:

1. Their legal rights to appropriate fish
2. Their withdrawal rate of fish
3. Their exposure to variation in the supply of fish
4. Their level of dependency on fish withdrawn from the resource
5. Their use of the fish they harvest

This definition of a subgroup depends on the sharing of similar characteristics and not on the presence or absence of an organization of fishers. More than one subgroup of fishers may utilize the same fishing grounds simultaneously. In the sample of 30 fisheries, the analysis identifies 44 unique subgroups. These 44 subgroups are the units of analysis that form the basis for this study.

Organized Fishers

One response to a fishery dilemma is to do nothing. By assumption, each fisher makes his or her best response to the fishing strategies adopted by others. This is the response that many theorists and policymakers expect from fishers caught in a dilemma. Another response, however, is to attempt to organize so as to change the structure of the rules affecting fishing activities. As stated above, one could hypothesize that fishers are more likely to organize to address technological externalities and assignment problems than they are to address appropriation externalities.

In examining this assertion, one is immediately faced with the question of how one knows whether fishers are organized, since many fishers' organizations are quite informal. They may involve meeting in the local coffeehouse to discuss common problems at the end of the day rather than creating a formal organization that is somehow recognized from the outside. Christy (1982) argues that for fishers to organize and gain control over their grounds, they must be able to use a boundary rule that requires something in addition to simple residency in a locality, such as the purchase of a license or a required type of technology. This is the first criterion used here to determine whether fishers are organized—the presence of a boundary rule with more provisions than simply local residence. The second criterion used to determine whether some form of organization is present relates to the existence of authority or scope rules that place limits on the actions that can be taken or on the outcome achieved. Of the 44 subgroups for which data is available, 33 meet these two criteria and are considered organized. Eleven of the subgroups do not have restrictive boundary, authority, or scope rules and are thus not considered to be organized.

Boundary Rules

Established boundary rules reveal attempts on the part of fishers to limit the number of fishers who can access fishing grounds and the types of technology that can be utilized (see table 11.2). Fourteen different types of boundary rules are utilized among the 33 organized subgroups. Each of the 33 subgroups use combinations of rules. That is, no subgroup uses just a single boundary rule. The rules used by most subgroups (30 out of 33) are residency rules that require fishers to reside in a particular village or region of a country to gain access to particular grounds. The second most common rule is a technology

TABLE 11.2.   Required Boundary Rules

Type of Rule	Number of Organized Subgroups Using Rule ($N = 33$)	Percentage of Subgroups Using Rule
Residency-local	30	91
Use of particular technology	22	67
Membership in an organization	13	39
License	7	21
Ownership of limited property related to harvesting (i.e., fishing berths)	7	21
Lottery	5	15
Race	5	15
Registration on eligibility list to participate in lottery	4	12
Continuing usage of access rights	3	9
Ethnicity	3	9
Ownership or leasing of land in area	3	9
Caste	2	6

rule. Twenty-two subgroups (67 percent) limit access to their fishing grounds on the basis of the type of technology used. Boundary rules based on gear assist in alleviating technological externalities. By limiting the types of gear that can be brought into the grounds, interference among gears is minimized. Note further, that boundary rules can have an effect upon appropriation externalities. Limiting both the number of individuals who can access a ground and the type of technologies they can utilize reduces the amount of fishing effort applied in harvesting, thereby possibly affecting the magnitude of appropriation externalities.

Authority and Scope Rules

A frequency count of the authority and scope rules used in the 33 organized subgroups is shown in table 11.3. Five different types of rules are used in these groups: location rules, size rules, season rules, order rules, and time-slot rules. Subgroups frequently rely on more than one authority or scope rule. The most often used rule is a scope rule that limits harvesting activities to specific locations or spots. Every subgroup in the sample used a location rule to determine how choice fishing spots are distributed. Access to fishing spots is dependent on meeting any of a variety of requirements. The gear that a fisher uses may affect which fishing spots are available to a given fisher (A. F. Davis 1975). Or a fisher may gain access to a choice spot through a lottery (Faris 1972).

The second most frequently used rule is a size rule requiring that fishers harvest fish greater than a minimum size. This rule is typically used to ensure that fish achieve maturity and have a chance to spawn before being harvested. Nine of the 33 subgroups utilize this rule. In all but one instance an external authority imposed the size rule on the fishers.[3]

The third most frequently used rules are seasonal restrictions and harvesting in a fixed order. Seasonal restrictions forbid the harvesting of fish during specific times of the year, typically when fish spawn. In the case of seasonal restrictions, all but one of the rules was devised by a government authority. Harvesting in a fixed order defines how choice spots on the grounds can be accessed and harvested. Oftentimes the rule requires that fishers take turns in accessing particular spots. All of the order rules were devised by fishers.

The fourth most frequently used rule is a fixed time-slot rule. This rule is often combined with a fixed-order rule or a location rule. It limits the amount of time that a boat can remain on a choice fishing spot. Typical limits involve one casting of a net, or one day (Alexander 1982; Cordell 1972).

---

3. That exception is the Cree Indians in northern Canada as reported by Berkes 1977, 1987.

TABLE 11.3.   Required Authority and Scope Rules

Type of Rule	Number of Subgroups Using Rule ($N = 33$)	Percentage of Subgroups Using Rule
Withdraw at specific locations/spots	33	100
Withdraw fish of at least a specific size	9	27
Withdraw in a fixed order	7	21
Withdraw only during specific seasons	7	21
Withdraw at a fixed time slot	4	12

The types of boundary, authority, and scope rules that fishers utilize to organize themselves provide evidence concerning the types of dilemmas fishers are attempting to resolve. The rules utilized by the 33 organized subgroups demonstrate attempts to resolve technological externalities and assignment problems, but not appropriation externalities, at least, not directly. Boundary rules demonstrate an attempt on the part of fishers to close access to their fishing grounds, allowing only local fishers to have access. In addition, in many cases not only must a fisher meet residency requirements, but he or she must also meet technological requirements. Only particular types of technology may be used in local fishing grounds.

Once access is gained to fishing grounds, fishers are not free to engage in harvesting of fish in any manner they desire; rather, a host of authority and scope rules coordinate their use of fishing grounds. In particular these rules allocate space. Choice spots are allocated through a variety of mechanisms such as lotteries or first in time, first in right rules. In other cases, whole areas of fishing grounds are divided among different types of technologies. Fishers, in organizing, adopt configurations of rules that define access to and use of fishing grounds. These rules directly address assignment problems and technological externalities by allocating space within fishing grounds. These rules may only indirectly affect appropriation externalities.

Commons Dilemmas and Organized Fishers

As well as examining the types of rules fishers adopt, we may explore the types of dilemmas fishers are more likely to address by examining whether fishers, when confronted with technological externalities, assignment problems, and appropriation externalities, are equally likely to address each dilemma, or if instead they are more likely to attempt to address particular ones. While it is possible to conduct such an inquiry in relation to technological externalities and assignment problems, because data on such problems is available, it is not possible to do so in relation to appropriation externalities.

Obtaining a measure of appropriation externalities is highly problematic. Not only do fishers lack sufficient information concerning stock dynamics and the effects of their actions upon each other's harvest, researchers also have inadequate measures of stock dynamics in field settings. Thus, direct measures of appropriation externalities are not reported in the case studies. Consequently, only data on technological externalities and assignment problems will be presented. Such data suggest that fishers often attempt to address technological externalities and assignment problems when confronted with them.

Table 11.4 arrays the presence of technological externalities and/or assignment problems at the beginning of the case history by whether fishers had organized harvesting activities. The expected relationship that subgroups who have experienced either or both of the dilemmas will have organized their harvesting activities holds. Among all 44 subgroups comprising this data set, 31 subgroups initially experienced moderate to high levels of assignment problems or technological externalities. Of those 31, 27 have organized their harvesting activities, while 4 have not.[4]

---

4. Recall from the previous section that of the 44 subgroups in total, 33 have organized their harvesting activities. Of those 33, 27 have organized in response to technological externalities and/or assignment problems. In considering the six subgroups who had organized but who had not experienced assignment problems (or, for whom insufficient information exists to determine whether they have experienced technological externalities), two very closely related processes appear to be occurring that may explain why they have organized. Members of two of the six subgroups were required by law to organize before they could access fishing grounds and withdraw fish. Members of the remaining four subgroups organized for some other purpose and later extended their existing organization to cover harvesting activities. For instance, the fishers constituting one of the subgroups that was required to organize, reside in Turkey and harvest from a lagoon. As reported by Berkes (1986, 1992), Turkish fishers who organize themselves into cooperatives can apply to the Turkish government for exclusive rights to harvest from specific lagoons. Turkish law gives preference to fishers' cooperatives over other organizations in granting such rights. As Berkes states:

> This successful fishery is run by a cooperative established in 1974 to make a bid for the lease of Camlik lagoon, which had previously been operating under a private company. A few of the members had been employed as laborers by the company. Taking advantage of a provision under the Aquatic Resources Act to give priority to cooperatives in the leasing of lake and lagoon fisheries, the Ayvalik-Haylazli Cooperative was successful in its bid. (1992, 172)

Thus, the Turkish fishers were required to organize before they could gain access to their fishing ground.

The other subgroup that was required to organize resides in Ebibara, Japan (Brameld 1968). In 1950, the Japanese federal government adopted a law placing coastal waters under the control of local cooperatives. Coastal waters were divided among local communities and fishers from each community were required to belong to their co-op and to fish in their waters only (Brameld 1968, 26).

Of the four subgroups who organized for some other purpose, two are located in Belize (E. Gordon 1981); one in Malaysia (Firth 1966); and one in Thailand (T. Fraser 1960).

TABLE 11.4.   Technological Externalities and/or Assignment Problems by Organization

	Moderate to High Technological Externality and/or Assignment Problem	Minimal Technological Externality and/or Assignment Problem	Indeterminate	Total
Organized	27	0	6[a]	33
	(87%)	(0%)	(75%)	
Not Organized	4	5	2	11
	(13%)	(100%)	(25%)	
Total	31	5	8	44
	(100%)	(100%)	(100%)	

Lambda = .45

[a]Of these 6, none experienced assignment problems. There was insufficient information to determine whether any of the 6 experienced technological externalities.

All 27 subgroups that have organized their harvesting activities in response to technological externalities or assignment problems require that fishers engage in harvesting activities in specific areas, or spots. In some instances, different types of gear are relegated to different areas of the fishing ground in order to reduce technological externalities. For example, the cod fishers of Fermeuse, Newfoundland, described by K. Martin (1973, 1979), have "divided their own fishing grounds, as have many inshore fishing communities, by setting aside certain fishing areas (usually the most productive) for the exclusive use of certain technologies" (1979, 285). The fishers of Port Lameroon Harbour, Nova Scotia, have done the same. "A rectangularly shaped area stretching from the Gate Rocks to the Half Moons and out to the Fairway Buoy is reserved primarily for herring and mackerel gillnets" (A. Davis 1984, 141–43), whereas the area around Brazil Rock is reserved for handling for cod.

In other instances, rules requiring fishers to harvest from specific spots within a fishing ground are used to resolve assignment problems. Often specific spot rules will be combined with other rules such as "harvest in a specific order" or "harvest during a fixed time slot," so that all fishers have equal opportunities of harvesting from the most productive spots over the course of a year. For instance, one of the most elaborate arrangements for assigning productive spots has been devised by the fishers of Alanya, Turkey (Berkes 1986, 1992, and briefly described in chap. 4). Prior to 1960, there were 15 fishers and 15 productive spots. After 1960, the number of fishers increased and severe conflict erupted as fishers competed for a limited number of spots. Over a period of 15 years, the fishers developed a lottery and rotation system to allocate the best fishing spots. At the beginning of the season, a list of fishers wanting to participate and a list of the named fishing spots are drawn up. Fishers gather at the coffeehouse to draw lots for the named spots. Since the number of fishers exceeds the number of spots, some fishers draw blanks. That does not mean they cannot fish; rather, they are rotated into the system.

> During the period September to May, each participating fisherman moves each day to the next location to the east. This gives each fisherman an equal opportunity at the best sites. The stocks are constantly migrating through the area, east to west between September and January, and reversing their migration from January to May. (Berkes 1992, 170)

Thus, the fishers of Alanya combine spot rules with time and turn rules to create an intricate system in which each fisher has an opportunity to fish from all of the productive spots over the course of a season.

Performance of Fishers' Organizations

Do the rules that fishers utilize to coordinate their use of fishing grounds reduce technological externalities and assignment problems? That is, by changing the rules that govern the situations that fishers find themselves in, are incentives appropriately changed so that fishers change their behavior and achieve some success in reducing commons dilemmas? The evidence suggests that rules adopted by the fishers do reduce the severity of technological externalities and assignment problems. Considering just the 31 subgroups that experienced technological externalities or assignment problems, table 11.5 examines whether fishers who adopted rules were more likely to have reduced the severity of those dilemmas by the end of the case study. The evidence clearly suggests that those who organized were generally successful in reducing the severity of technological externalities and assignment problems.

Among the 31 subgroups of fishers, 10 experienced only assignment problems, 12 experienced only technological externalities, and 9 experienced both. The top half of table 11.5 examines the 19 subgroups that experienced assignment problems. Of those 19, 16 are organized. Of those 16, 81 percent experienced minimal assignment problems, while 19 percent experienced moderate assignment problems. All 3 unorganized subgroups experienced high levels of assignment problems. Clearly, fishers who have organized themselves have succeeded in reducing assignment problems.

The bottom of table 11.5 examines the 21 subgroups that have initially experienced technological externalities. Of those 21 subgroups, 17 are organized. Of those 17, 53 percent experienced minimal levels of technological externalities, and 47 percent experienced moderate to high levels of technological externalities.

TABLE 11.5. Performance of Fishers' Organizations

	Organized	Not Organized	Total
Assignment Problems			
Minimal assignment problems	13	0	13
	(81%)	(0%)	
Moderate assignment problems	3	0	3
	(19%)	(0%)	
High assignment problems	0	3	3
	(0%)	(100%)	
Total	16	3	19[a]
	(100%)	(100%)	
Technological Externalities			
Minimal technological externalities	9	0	9
	(53%)	(0%)	
Moderate technological externalities	7	1	8
	(41%)	(25%)	
High technological externalities	1	3	4
	(6%)	(75%)	
Total	17	4	21[b]
	(100%)	(100%)	

[a]Of these 19, 9 experienced technological externalities.
[b]Of these 21, 9 experienced assignment problems.

All 4 subgroups who have not organized experienced moderate to high levels of technological externalities. Fishers who have organized have been more successful in addressing technological externalities, although they have not been as successful as those fishers who have reduced assignment problems. Clearly, fishers who have been able to devise and adopt rules that change the structure of their situation have achieved better outcomes than fishers who have failed to coordinate their harvesting activities.

Conclusions

Fishers organize to coordinate their harvesting activities in order to address assignment problems and technological externalities. Most of the rules used govern the type of technologies that can be utilized in fishing grounds rather than the quantity of fish harvested. In addition, fishers allocate space within their fishing grounds either to particular technologies or to fishers to be used for a given period of time. These rules are successful in reducing technological externalities and assignment problems.

Little evidence suggests that coastal fishers themselves attempt to directly address appropriation externalities. It is surprising that there is *no* instance among this sample of coastal fishing grounds where fishers developed and used a quota rule allocating a quantity of fish to each fisher or fishing boat based on an estimate of the sustained yield of fish. Thus, in this sample, no attempt has been made by the fishers involved to directly regulate the quantity of fish harvested based on an estimate of the yield.[5] This is particularly surprising given that the most frequently recommended policy prescription made by fishery economists is the use of individual transferable quotas based on estimates of the economically optimal quantity of fish to be harvested over the long run (see L. Anderson 1986; Copes 1986; and discussion in chap. 14).

Fishers are capable of responding to some types of CPR dilemmas but not necessarily to others. In responding, fishers devise rules that are highly dependent upon time and place information, especially as it relates to the particular physical environment of their fisheries. Government officials, or virtually any outsiders to these fishing communities, would be hard-pressed to devise as effective rule configurations as have these fishers. Fishers who have devised these arrangements not only gain the benefit of them but also bear the cost of monitoring and enforcing them. For all of these reasons, self-governing organizations devised by fishers deserve to be studied and incorporated into policy decisions rather than presumed to be nonexistent and ignored. While appropriation externalities are more difficult for fishers to directly reduce through rules limiting quantity of fish harvesting, all of the problems facing fishers who might try to cope with this CPR problem also face officials located far away from a local fishing ground.

---

5. There are instances of fishers devising quotas in order to affect market prices, rather than attempting to address appropriation externalities (see Sturgess, Dow, and Belin 1982; McCay 1980).

CHAPTER 12

Rules, Rule Making, and Rule Breaking: Examining the Fit between Rule Systems and Resource Use

This chapter examines institutions that guide fodder and fuelwood use in community forests. The community forests discussed are called *panchayat* forests. They are managed by local institutions called *van panchayats*—literally, councils of five individuals who are responsible for making collective choices about the rules to be used in a particular forest. The forests and van panchayats all lie in the middle Himalayan ranges in Almora district. Almora is one of the eight mountainous districts that together comprise the Uttarakhand in Uttar Pradesh (see fig. 12.1). The analysis focuses on the effects of institutional rules on common resource use—particularly rules related to enforcement. The chapter is based on intensive fieldwork conducted during 1990 in six villages located in the Almora district.

Successful institutional solutions to the governance and management of forests depend on rules that can solve appropriation and provision problems related to the use of community resources. Among the more important rules are (1) boundary rules that limit who can use a forest, (2) authority and scope rules that specify how much of what type of forest product can be extracted or the condition of the resource after harvesting, and (3) the authority and payoff rules that empower monitoring, sanctioning, and arbitration.

The creation and enforcement of these rules constitute a collective-choice problem as described in chapter 2. If the collective-choice problem is solved successfully, institutional arrangements are created that support sustainable use of a resource. Those engaged in collective choice may design rules that are too lax or overly restrictive in regard to the amount of resource units that can be harvested. If too lax, the capability of the resource to continue generating resource units is threatened. If too restrictive, users may be forced to violate prescribed rules due to their extreme need for forest products. Behavior in violation of prescribed institutional rules creates higher-

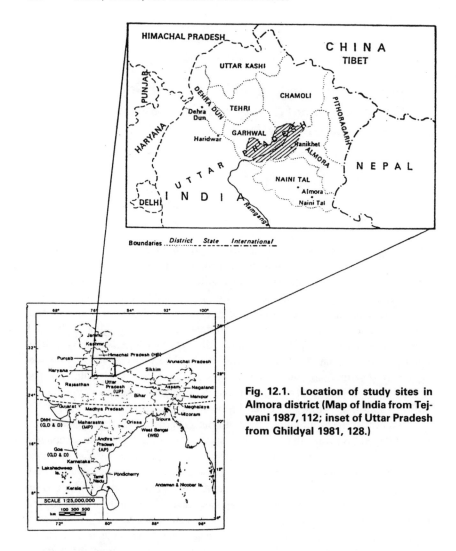

Fig. 12.1. Location of study sites in Almora district (Map of India from Tejwani 1987, 112; inset of Uttar Pradesh from Ghildyal 1981, 128.)

order CPR dilemmas that require a solution to problems associated with monitoring and sanctioning (see chap. 1).

It is, of course, also possible for those who undertake collective choice (the van panchayats) to design rules that advantage some users over others. The costs of monitoring and enforcing rules that are not perceived to be equitable are higher than enforcing rules that participants consider to be equitable. In addition, failure to sanction rule violators, or mistakenly sanctioning those who did not violate the rules, encourages further rule violations or promotes resentment among users against existing institutions. The analysis of different rule configurations in the six villages shows that constraints on the capacity of village officials to enforce rules are associated with unsuccessful institutions and degraded panchayat forests.

The Historical Context

The institutional rules in the van panchayats in Almora are powerfully influenced by the Van Panchayat Act of 1931. This statute forms the framework for the rules that villagers devise to manage forests. The British government passed the act after prolonged resistance offered by the hill villagers in Kumaon and Garhwal.[1] Almora is one of the three districts in Kumaon Division. The other two are Nainital and Pithoragarh.

From the 1840s, the British government asserted its absolute rights over all land and forests in Kumaon and Garhwal and brought more than 60 percent of the land in Kumaon under its control between 1840 and 1910 (Atkinson [1882] 1973; Pant 1922). The primary motivation was economic. In the 1830s, forest revenues were low, less than four thousand rupees a year. Over the next 30 years they grew enormously, surpassing agricultural revenues in some years.[2]

The state was able to extend its rights over forests only by limiting villager access and use rights to the resource. The Imperial Forest Department protected state forests from trespassing, unauthorized tree felling, grazing, and firing.[3] Villagers protested incessantly against encroachments by the state on their traditional rights in the forests. They employed what J. Scott (1985, 1986, 1990) has called "everyday forms of resistance," as well as more active resistance. Guha (1989) describes and traces in detail the more active and militant forms of protest by the peasantry in Kumaon. Faced with the prospect of unceasing and unmanageable peasant protest, the government was forced to look into the demands of the peasants (Pant 1922).

On the recommendations of the Forest Grievances Committee, set up in 1921, the government reclassified forests into class 1 and class 2 forests. Class 1 forests were transferred to the Revenue Department, and the class 2 forests were retained by the Forest Department. Under the provisions of the

---

1. Kumaon and Garhwal are the names of the two ancient hill kingdoms in Uttar Pradesh province.

2. In 1872, forest revenues were about Rs 267,000 to agricultural revenues of about Rs 164,000. In the next year, forest revenue rose to over Rs 365,000 while agricultural revenues remained the same. By 1876, however, forest revenues fell below those of agriculture and remained there for some time.

3. Villagers fired the grasses and undergrowth before monsoons to get a good grass crop. Such fires prevented forests from growing and regenerating.

Van Panchayat Act, villagers could create community-managed forests from the forests controlled by the Revenue Department. The provisions of the act were simple and facilitated collective action by villagers. Any two villagers could apply to the deputy commissioner of the district to create the panchayat forest out of revenue department forests that were located within the village boundaries.[4]

The Van Panchayat Act also prescribes the process of forming van panchayats and imposes certain duties on village forest councils. Officials must be elected regularly to the van panchayat. The elected officials (the council for managing forests—the van panchayat *samiti*, and the head of the council— the *sarpanch*) must meet three to six times every year. Villagers must protect forests from illegal tree felling, fires, encroachments, and cultivation. They must demarcate the boundaries of the panchayat forest. In addition, 20 percent of the area of the forest must be closed to grazing every year. Villagers feel that through the act, the bureaucracy exercises excessive control over forest panchayats. Bureaucrats, on the other hand, believe that in the absence of central control, villagers would clear-cut the entire forest. It is certain, however, that the act facilitated the efforts by residents of nearly four thousand villages to create local institutions that would permit them to use and manage a significant proportion of local forests.

The Local Context

The day-to-day management of panchayat forests was observed in six villages where the author did fieldwork in 1990. Daily operation is chiefly governed by rules that villagers have crafted. In most instances, the panchayat officials elected by the villagers designed the rules. In others, they were aided by government officials or villagers. As table 12.1 shows, in the first three villages the forest is in excellent, or excellent to good condition. In the other three, the resource condition is poor to fair.[5] Since the six study villages are

---

4. Currently, at least a third of the village residents must apply to form the village panchayat, as required by the law authorizing the creation of forest panchayats.

5. In the cases studied, market and population pressures do not help to explain the differences between successful and unsuccessful cases of forest management. The first three villages, where the forest is in good condition, are located 3.1 kilometers away from the market on the average. The latter three, where the resource condition is poor to fair, are 2.8 kilometers distant. In the first three villages, there is .57 hectare of panchayat forest land per household; .14 hectare per livestock unit. In the other three villages, the corresponding figures are .41 hectare and .14 hectare. These differences are not important. If we consider total forest and pasture land available to households and livestock, in the first three villages there is .86 hectare available per household and .22 hectare per livestock unit. In the remaining three villages, the same figures are 1.0 hectare and .36 hectare. In sum, no systematic relationships exist between the condition of the resource and market or population pressures on the resource system.

TABLE 12.1. Basic Statistics on the Six Villages Studied

Village	Resource Condition	Households	Livestock	Panchayat Forest (in ha.)	Other Pastures (in ha.)
1	8	37	220	14	55
2	7	13	52	16	9
3	7	124	424	70	86
4	4	38	194	10	39
5	3	79	228	39	83
6	2	108	305	27	66

Note: The resource condition is denoted by numbers ranging from 0 (degraded) to 8 (excellent). Thus, the higher the number, the better the condition of the resource. See Agrawal 1992 for a description of the methods used to evaluate resource condition.

all situated in Almora district, their resource management institutions have been subject to the same administrative and bureaucratic rules. Government regulations, we can therefore infer, are not responsible for variations among the study villages. The variation in the resource condition of the two sets of villages can be explained best by examining local rules for (1) using the resource, (2) monitoring the use, (3) sanctioning violations, and (4) arbitrating disputes.[6]

Authority Rules Related to Allocation

The first set of operational rules we consider are rules for taking fodder from the community forests. These rules specify who can withdraw benefits from the forest, how much fodder can be extracted, the manner in which fodder can be extracted, and the obligations users must fulfill to remain beneficiaries. In all but one of the cases, boundary rules specify that users must be residents of the village where the forest is located. In the exceptional case, the family of an individual who aided in creating the panchayat forest is allotted rights to harvest benefits from the resource.

In most of the villages, allocation rules specify how fodder is to be extracted from the resource system. Animals cannot graze in the forest for most of the year. Villagers can harvest fodder only for 2–12 weeks. When cutting leaves from trees for fodder, villagers must leave behind at least two-thirds of the leaf cover on the tree.[7] In different villages, rules also vary in the type of rights they confer on users. In some of the villages, users have equal

---

6. Most of the data on rules is culled from records of the forest panchayat meetings (which in some instances go back more than 60 years) and records kept by the village revenue officials (the *patwari*).

7. The main fodder tree in this region is oak.

rights—without regard to their contributions in maintaining the resource. Villagers can buy and sell rights among themselves.[8] In others, their rights to the resource are a function of the effort they have invested in the maintenance of the resource (by paying the salary of the guard or by helping in planting trees); in yet others, their rights are a function of their ability to make high bids in auctions where benefits from the forest are sold to the highest bidder.

In some cases, institutional rules not only specify who has the rights and how these rights can be used, they also state how much fodder can be withdrawn from the resource. Fodder from forests constitutes a renewable resource. To ensure regular annual supplies and the continued health of the forest, it is therefore essential to match extraction levels to regeneration. Villagers who designed rules have attempted to match regeneration levels and withdrawal levels by assessing fodder growth during the year, fixing extraction levels below the annual regeneration, and metering fodder extraction using simple measures. To assess regeneration, panchayat officials visit forest compartments prior to opening them to the villagers. The officials make an eyeball estimate of the total amount of fodder bundles available and then open the forest for limited grazing or grass harvesting. The total number of animals that can graze or bundles of grass that can be extracted depends on the initial estimates made by the panchayat officials. Forest guards, selected by the panchayat officials from among villagers, monitor (and enforce) the panchayat's decision. Bundles of grass are measured with the help of uniform lengths of rope that are used to tie the fodder bundles. In villages 1, 2, and 3, users can cut grass from the forest only for a specified number of days in the year. The panchayat officials carefully meter the amount of grass extracted. Passes entitle holders to cut a specified number of fodder bundles from the forest. All users are provided with a rope that they must use to make a bundle out of the grass they have cut. All villagers, therefore, can extract only specified levels and equal amounts of fodder.

There are also villages where panchayats have not designed rules to match withdrawn regeneration. In villages 4 and 5, rules fail to facilitate the metering of withdrawal from the resource. The grass in these village forests is sold primarily through auctions. The auction winner is free to cut grass from that section of the community forest for which he or she has successfully bid. This means that the winning bidder has little incentive to stint in his or her behavior when cutting the grass. He or she may cut too close to the ground, damaging roots and harming the growth for the next year. In auctions involving leaf fodder, he or she may harvest too many leaves, damaging the capacity of the tree to produce fodder. In village 6, users are

---

8. Users mainly buy or sell rights to bundles of fodder rather than rights to use the forest for the entire year.

allocated spaces on the commons where they must harvest grass. Although this prevents disputes among the users by solving an assignment problem, users still attempt to harvest as much as they can from the area allocated to them. As pointed out in chapter 3, solving assignment problems may eliminate some of the costs associated with suboptimal allocations, but the incentives to overextract are not necessarily countered by clear rules assigning individuals to a spatial location on the commons.

Two factors may explain why the right to harvest fodder is auctioned in some villages. Auctions reduce the management effort that the panchayat must expend in extracting and distributing benefits from the resource. Once the auction has been held, the panchayat officials need no longer worry about regulating and supervising the removal of fodder from the forest.[9] To create institutional mechanisms that would distribute benefits among a large number of small users might improve equity, but at the cost of greater management and supervision effort on the part of the owners or managers.

A second, possibly more important factor prompting auctions is that auctions effectively concentrate the fodder harvested from the forest in the hands of just a few users. In villages that use auctions, panchayat records document that the same three or four individuals repeatedly make successful bids for the rights to harvest fodder from panchayat forests. In villages 4 and 5, the upper and lower castes (Brahmins and Harijans) have a history of simmering hostility. The Brahmins, who are also the richer individuals in the two villages, were instrumental in the creation of the forest panchayats. They designed the rules that guide fodder extraction from the panchayat forests. Although the panchayat elects officials every five years, the numerical superiority of the Brahmins in the two villages has guaranteed them effective control over the panchayat.

We can draw the following conclusions. At the local level, there are cases of successful rule designs to use resources sustainably and equitably. Village panchayats have demonstrated their capacity to craft rules that limit the extraction of fodder and that distribute it equally among villagers. Local users and managers have many advantages over centralized governments and bureaucracies in creating appropriation rules that can match demands on a resource with its regenerative capability. They have greater information about themselves, about their needs, and about the resource.[10] Such information is

---

9. A similar procedure for distributing resources is followed by the Uttar Pradesh government, which auctions grass in the Himalayan foothills. In the foothills, the rights to harvest grass from large areas (up to a hundred square miles) are sold to the highest bidder. The government interacts with just a few persons who then create their own systems for harvesting the grass.

10. A large number of authors have extolled the virtues of local management. I do not survey this literature. See E. Ostrom, Schroeder, and Wynne 1993 for a thorough discussion and for relevant literature citations.

crucial if rules guiding extraction levels are to match regeneration and mitigate appropriation externalities. Central governments seldom have requisite
capacity to gather necessary information regarding variations in productive
capacities of different fodder plots. It is almost axiomatically true, therefore,
that central governments cannot achieve "congruence between rules and physical reality."

Simply because local governance structures possess the capacity to carefully craft rules to match withdrawal levels with sustainable yields, it does not
follow that they will necessarily create rules that solve the resource problem.
Therefore, even if forest management is delegated to the local level, local
managers[11] may not (be able to) use resources efficiently, sustainably, or
equitably. In three of the cases above, van panchayat officials failed or chose
not to exercise their capacity to create rules that would promote sustainability
and equity. Local factional struggles played a role in generating behavior that
led to suboptimal rules. Issues of ensuring compliance to rules, however,
remain equally pivotal in our explanation, since the rules that villagers created
were not self-enforcing.

Monitoring

The problem of ensuring compliance to rules is acute. In all the villages
studied, violations of allocation rules occurred routinely, even if they were not
always reported. In the two villages that maintained detailed records on rule
violations (villages 3 and 6), minor violations occurred almost every day (see
table 12.2). Villagers illegally entered the panchayat forests, cut grass and
leaf fodder from trees, grazed their animals, collected twigs and branches,
and in some instances even felled trees. Their activities occurred in violation
of the rules, and in spite of the presence of guards who could discover and
report them to the panchayat, which would then try to force them to pay fines.
The records, while documenting high levels of abuse, underestimate the extent of illegal grazing and cutting. The guards are often absent from the forest
and even when at their posts cannot monitor all compartments of the panchayat forest simultaneously. The community forest is too large and
dispersed.

To detect all rule violations, all behavior must be monitored—a prohib-
itively expensive proposition. A resource system need not deteriorate, however, if the infractions are minor and a significant proportion of rule breakers
are discovered and sanctioned (Tsebelis 1990a). In the forest panchayats,
officials monitored user behavior, but not perfectly; and users broke rules, but

---

11. Local managers in my cases are the panchayats; in other cases they would be the
relevant community organizations.

TABLE 12.2. Detected Rule Violations in Panchayat Forests

Year	Village 3[a]	Village 6[b]
1977	—	138
1979	40	91
1980	—	2
1981	354	—
1982	—	26
1983	389	95
1985	114	—
1987	87	—
1988	—	30
1989	40	—

[a]Data is for the fiscal year ending in the year posted.
[b]Data is for the calendar year.

not always. The exact frequency of rule violations and probability of detection depended upon the benefits from breaking rules, the incentives to monitor, the costs of getting caught, and the cost of monitoring. Therefore, it is only when rules are not enforced or monitored and violations not sanctioned that formal rules become meaningless as guides to behavior.

In the first three cases of sustainable resource use, the panchayats took great pains to monitor. Panchayat officials recognized the higher-order CPR dilemma involved in monitoring and realized that unless resource use is effectively monitored, rules serve no purpose. Not only did they understand that monitoring is necessary, they also recognized and solved the problem of monitoring the monitor (see chap. 1; Elster 1989, 40–41). They employed two methods. First, they linked the monitor's performance to the rewards he or she received. Second, they untangled the Gordian knot of monitoring the monitor by closing the loop between monitors and users.

In the first three cases, the guards were monitored by panchayat officials. Guards were assigned different compartments of the forest. It was easier then to monitor the guards than to monitor the villagers. To monitor villagers and assign blame, individuals must be discovered in the act of violating rules. But freshly cut grass or tree branches in the forest provide evidence that the guard had not been guarding. Further, the panchayat could easily sanction the guard since the panchayat controlled the purse strings. In some cases, the panchayat paid the guard a lower salary when high levels of rule violations occurred. In others, panchayats dismissed guards and refused to pay them a salary if they found rule violation levels to be very high. Panchayat officials would resume the guard's salary and reinstate him or her only when he or she promised to improve his or her performance. Thus, officials created institutional incentives for the guards to monitor users assiduously.

The panchayat in village 3 solved the problem of who would monitor the monitor by involving all the villagers. The panchayat officials monitored the guard who monitored the users who monitored the officials. At each level, incentives were created for reporting violations. When a *panch*[12] or his or her family members were discovered in the forest, illegally grazing cattle or cutting fodder, an open meeting of the whole village could be summoned where the panch would confess his or her crime and pay a fine. The confession in front of the assembled village was as potent a deterrent as the fine. By creating a closed loop, and providing monitoring incentives to all the links in the loop, the problem of who would monitor the monitor was successfully solved.

In none of the cases did villagers use trigger strategies to force individuals to reduce their levels of rule violations. When the panchayat or the villagers discovered that rule infractions had increased (as in village 3), their response was not to step up their own level of infringements to punish the infractors for their rule breaking (as in a trigger strategy). Instead, the panchayat and the users took other steps to ensure that the level of rule violations would be reduced. They attempted to improve the efficiency of monitoring, increased the hours spent on monitoring, and tried to innovate graded sanctions (see next subsection). The behavior of the panchayat officials in village 3 exposes a problem in suggesting trigger strategies as solutions to collective-action problems generally. Trigger strategies work best when none of the individuals in a group actually defect. Defection by one individual triggers defection by all. Trigger strategies by themselves can create cooperation only as threats, not after an individual has initiated defection. Panchayat officials used other mechanisms, discussed earlier, to ensure rule compliance. These mechanisms, once in place, helped villagers follow rules.

In contrast to villages 1, 2, and 3, panchayat officials in villages 4, 5, and 6 did not emphasize monitoring. In village 4, the panchayat did not employ a guard for most of the year. In village 5, panchayat records mentioned few instances of rule violations. Most recorded instances were connected with intercaste disputes in the village. It seems that the panchayat, dominated by Brahmins, used its control over the panchayat forest as a way of dominating the Harijans. Instances of rule breaking by Harijans were mentioned in panchayat records with regularity. But from the records, it appeared as if Brahmins never broke rules. Such prejudiced reporting and enforcement could only increase rule violations and resource degradation. The Brahmin residents in the village, if never reported and sanctioned, would get a license

---

12. A panch is an elected official of the panchayat. Five panches make up the panchayat.

to break rules; the resentment against the Brahmins would goad Harijans to break rules as often as possible. In village 6, the community forest was highly dispersed. The panchayat considered monitoring important but was unable to devise a system of salary payments to guards that could allow it to employ two guards for the dispersed panchayat forest compartments. It seems, then, that in contrast to villages 4, 5, and 6, the first three panchayats not only realized the importance of monitoring user behavior but also successfully devised mechanisms to ensure compliance by users.

Finally, rule violations occur in successful as well as unsuccessful village institutions. As table 12.2 shows, in just two panchayats (in villages 3 and 6) is the detected number of rule violations relatively high. If villagers are to be believed, the actual incidence of rule violations may be much higher.[13] Casual walks with panchayat officials in community forests revealed villagers illegally collecting fodder and fuelwood almost each time we took a walk. For just two villages,[14] possibly a thousand rule violations occurred every year in the panchayat forests. Almora, which has more than three thousand inhabited villages, probably has three million rule violations occurring every year. Given such high levels of rule violations, it seems safe to infer that in unsuccessful village panchayats, a very large gap exists between actual rule breaking and reported incidents of it. The lack of reported incidents of rule breaking reflects not that villagers do not break rules. Rather, it reveals that monitoring arrangements are lax or nonexistent.

Although village panchayats seem lax or slow to detect rule violations, the government bureaucracy is even less capable. Guha (1989) reports that for the entire Kumaon region, between 1926 and 1933,[15] the forest department detected a total of 16,805 violations[16]—that is, less than three thousand violations per year, a thousand times less than what may actually have been

---

13. I interviewed more than 40 individuals who had been sanctioned by the panchayat officials for rule breaking. With remarkable regularity, these villagers asserted that the panchayat had been too hard on them, was not even aware of offenses by their neighbors and friends, and was too lax in controlling fuel and fodder theft by "other" villagers. Villagers who had not recently been sanctioned by the panchayat also pointed the finger at numerous village families whose rule-breaking behavior often went undetected. According to them, the panchayat discovered no more than 20 to 30 percent of rule violations.

14. The nature of rule violations is similar in both villages. In both village 3 and 6, guards detected villagers in the act of cutting grass and leaf fodder, collecting twigs and branches, and grazing animals.

15. Kumaon circle at this time included most of the present-day Nainital district, Almora district, and Pithoragarh district. So the population in Kumaon Circle in the 1930s and in Almora today is probably roughly similar, making the figures on rule violations in Kumaon Circle then somewhat representative of rule violations in Almora district today.

16. Violations detected by forest department officials are for the most part quite similar to those that guards employed by panchayats detect. They include illegal grazing, tree felling, fodder and fuelwood collection, and firing.

occurring. Although these are figures from the past, they indicate a general failing of central authorities to enforce rules. Even if the forest department increased the number of guards (at present it employs one guard for 15–20 villages), it would not be able to accurately monitor rule violations. Any increase in the size of the bureaucracy would increase expenses on salary and infrastructure and at the same time either promote collusion between the forest guards and unscrupulous villagers, or force villagers to pay bribes to the guards in exchange for extracting basic means of subsistence from the forest.

Sanctioning

In all the village institutions, villagers have created rules for sanctioning rule breakers whose activities caught the attention of the panchayat. The panchayats employ a variety of mechanisms to increase the effectiveness of the sanctions they imposed. They ask offenders to render written or public apologies, confiscate cutting implements such as scythes, strip villagers of use rights, impose fines, report villagers to government officials, and sometimes, seek redress in courts. The sanctions they impose depend on a number of factors: the severity and nature of the offense, the economic status of the offender, whether the person is known to be a troublemaker, the attitude that the rule breaker displays towards the panchayat and its authority, and so forth. The purpose of the sanctions is as much to punish somebody for a crime that was committed as to uphold the authority of the panchayat in issues of resource use.

Upholding authority is very important in the context of the forest panchayats, because they have no formal or legal powers to automatically impose sanctions on rule breakers. If the users openly flout panchayat authority by breaking use rules and disregarding panchayat directives to pay fines, the panchayats will be hard put to create any kind of management system for the panchayat forests. Thus, the panchayats often excuse even repeat violators from paying fines imposed on them, if the offender is willing to render a written or public apology.[17] Such an apology reinforces the authority of the panchayat to manage the forest and to punish other individuals who commit rule infractions.

Given the fact that the panchayats have no legal authority to impose sanctions on villagers who break rules, it may seem puzzling that many of the villagers pay the fines, especially in view of the fact that none of the panchayats invoke social boycotts or ostracize offenders as punishment. If we examine the income and expenditure statements of the different panchayats in table 12.3, the proportion of income from fines is significant for all the suc-

---

17. Of course, if a person is found to continue infringing rules even after rendering a written apology, the panchayat is more strict in imposing sanctions on the individual.

TABLE 12.3. Income and Expenditures of Van Panchayat by Village

Income	Percentage	Expenditure	Percentage
Village 1			
Fines/collections	29	Stationery	2
Tree sale	55	Guard's salary	90
Fodder sale	7	Miscellaneous	8
Minor forest produce sale	8		
Total income for the panchayat for the period was Rs 3,722.00			
Total expenditure for the panchayat for the period was Rs 2,777.00			
Village 2			
Fines	39	Stationery	14
Fodder sale	11	Guard's salary	33
Wood sale	51	Legal expenses	43
		Donations	9
Total income for the panchayat for the period was Rs 1,188.00			
Total expenditure for the panchayat for the period was Rs 2,335.00[a]			
Village 3			
Resin sale	48	Guard's salary	72
Fodder sale	49	Stationery	1
Fines	3	Legal expenses	2
		Public donations	25
Total income for the panchayat for the period was Rs 20,443.00			
Total expenditure for the panchayat for the period was Rs 21,671.00[a]			
Village 4			
Tree sale (contractor)	70	Tree planting	48
Tree sale (villagers)	5	Fertilizers	40
Grass sale	24	Stationery	2
Fines	1	Legal expenses	9
Total income for the panchayat for the period was Rs 5,636.00			
Total expenditure for the panchayat for the period was Rs 5,337.00			
Village 5			
Resin royalties	23	Stationery	2
Grass sale	22	Tree planting/fencing	68
Grass auction	53	Guard's salary	15
Tree sale	2	Legal expenses	14
Total income for the panchayat for the period was Rs 4,425.00			
Total expenditure for the panchayat for the period was Rs 8,181.00			
Village 6			
Tree sale	44	Stationery	9
Grass sale	19	Guard's salary	19
Fines	32	Legal expenses[c]	9
Miscellaneous	5	Public donations	43
		Tree planting	21
Total income for the panchayat for the period was Rs 3,779.00			
Total expenditure for the panchayat for the period was Rs 4,974.00			

[a]The excess of expenses over income was met through income accrued in other years.

[b]The panchayat has deposited a large sum, earned from resin sales, with the district magistrate. Rs 16,000 of this amount have been used to lay a water pipeline for the village.

[c]The legal expenses were incurred in a lawsuit with villagers from a neighboring village.

cessful panchayats (except for the panchayat in village 3—where the total income is very high), and quite low for all the unsuccessful panchayats.

Arbitration

All the panchayats also act as arbiters over disagreements that arise about the imposition of sanctions on rule breakers, and for interpretations of rules and disputes over the creation of rules. In this capacity they often reduce or excuse fines, allow villagers to influence the dates when the different forest compartments may be opened for grazing by animals or for removal of fodder, resolve disputes between village users and forest guards, and so forth.

The puzzle of their continued authority, despite the lack of formal powers, lies in the relative power positions of different actors if the panchayat chooses to take any of the users who break rules to court. Even if the panchayat does not have formal legal powers to extract fines from rule breakers, in courts of law its word carries greater weight than that of an ordinary villager. Since it has been created by a statute of law, its mere existence has the support of law. Further, in major disputes with users, there are a number of villagers who will support the interpretation of events presented by the panchayat—the guard who is appointed and paid by the panchayat, and the panches who are official members of the panchayat. The rule breaker, on the other hand, is unlikely to have any witnesses who will attest to his or her innocence. Finally, the panchayat is likely to have more funds available to fight lawsuits in comparison to an ordinary user.

The above factors imply that unless the user who violated rules is influential and wealthy, he or she will find it worthwhile to pay the small fine rather than go to court. It is this ultimate loading of the dice in the favor of the panchayat that drives the outcomes in the intermediate stages in its favor. Thus, we find that many of the users pay their fines, appear before the panchayat when summoned, render apologies, and promise not to break rules in the future.

Still, not all panchayats are equally willing to take matters to court, or to apply rules with equal strength. We find that for panchayats in villages 1, 2, and 3, there is strong evidence that the panchayats expend effort and funds in monitoring and enforcing their rules. The income and expenditure statements of the panchayats shown in table 12.3 indicate that in village 1, the panchayat spends 90 percent of its expenses on monitoring; in village 2, 76 percent of the panchayat expenditure is on monitoring and legal expenses; and in village 3, 74 percent of the panchayat expenses are monitoring and legal expenses. In contrast, villages 4, 5, and 6 spend a much smaller proportion of their expenses on these tasks. In village 4, just 9 percent of the expenses are spent on legal expenses, none on monitoring; in village 5, a total of 29 percent of

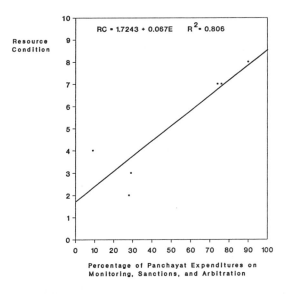

RC = resource condition
E = expenditures on monitoring, sanctions, and arbitration

Fig. 12.2. Resource condition and attention to monitoring, sanctions, arbitration: six villages

expenses are incurred on these heads; and in village 6, again, only 28 percent of the expenses are towards enforcement. These figures tell a clear story about the importance of ensuring monitoring and sanctioning to create effective institutions.

We can examine the importance of expenditures by panchayats on monitoring, sanctioning, and arbitration (see fig. 12.2).[18] Using proportions of panchayat expenditures on monitoring, sanctioning, and arbitration as the independent variable, we find that a significant relationship exists between enforcement and resource condition.[19] The Beta coefficient is statistically significant at the .001 level[20] (*t*-statistic is 4.1); and the adjusted R^2 equals

---

18. The regression in this case needs to be taken with even greater caution since we have only six data points.

19. For explanation of the numbers signifying resource condition, see table 12.1.

20. I must sound a note of caution here. Since the dependent variable is categorical, it can be argued that OLS is not the most appropriate technique to demonstrate the relationship between resource condition and the attention panchayats pay to enforcement. However, there are three points in defense. The observed values of the dependent variable are distributed over the range of the different categories—from poor to excellent. Second, we possess information on only six cases. Using Logit, while more appropriate, may be similar to using a cannon to demolish an

.76. The statistical evidence would thus seem to bear out our proposition that institutions that commit substantial resources to monitor and sanction rule breakers are more likely to be successful. Conversely, institutions paying little attention to either monitoring or sanctioning are less likely to be successful in governing and managing forest resources.

Conclusions

In this chapter, I have suggested that to explain resource degradation and conservation successfully, we must examine the institutional design that guides resource use. Successful institutional design must solve four distinct problems of collective action: (1) creation of boundary and authority rules determining who can use how much from a resource, (2) effective monitoring of rules, (3) sanctioning of violators who break rules, and (4) arbitration of disputes among monitors, users, and managers.

Alternative allocation rules affect whether communities are able to restrict resource use to levels below sustainable yield. Unlike the other villages, villages 4 and 5 used rules that implicitly treated different caste groups unequally. Monitoring rules provide information that is necessary to punish rule breakers. We find that while the first three villages successfully attempted to monitor the monitor, in villages 4, 5, and 6, there were not even institutionalized mechanisms through which adequate information on rule breaking could be collected. In fact, in villages 4 and 5, monitoring seemed to be prompted by a desire to persecute the Harijans. In the absence of accurate information about rule breaking, sanctions could not be imposed in the latter three villages, nor could panchayat officials assert their authority as arbiters. Thus monitoring and sanctioning, which the first three villages emphasized, were almost ignored by the three unsuccessful village institutions. Similarly, arbitration, which is important to reinforce sanctions, was ineffective in the latter three villages.

Thus, villagers in villages 4, 5, and 6 did not successfully create appropriation rules that could prevent users from overexploiting and degrading resources. They also failed to solve the dilemmas involved in designing suitable monitoring and sanctioning rules. The failure of these three panchayats to create adequate institutions explains resource degradation in these villages. Local political struggles and social factions within villages, as indicated above, explain why villagers may fail to create rules that distribute benefits efficiently and/or equitably.

---

outhouse. Finally, the purpose of using the regression is simply to provide a numerical estimate on the strength of the relationship, not to demonstrate it. The data, even observed visually, are clear enough in their implications.

CHAPTER 13

Changing Rules, Changing Games: Evidence from Groundwater Systems in Southern California

Renewable local water supplies are limited in semiarid southern California. Precipitation is unpredictable from season to season, and surface water flow is erratic. Agricultural development on the coastal plain and in the inland valleys exhausted the base flows of the area's main surface streams by the turn of the century. Thereafter, continued agricultural development as well as urbanization of southern California depended heavily on the impoundment and controlled release of storm flows, the importation of water from other watersheds, and the use of groundwater. For most landowners and public or private water suppliers, groundwater use was the easiest and cheapest option, so its use increased rapidly during this century throughout southern California. Eventually in each basin underlying developed areas, annual groundwater use exceeded renewable yields, producing common-pool resource problems.

Groundwater Basins as Common-Pool Resources

A groundwater basin is literally a common pool. Exclusion of multiple pumpers is difficult and costly (unless the basin is so small that an individual can control access to it). Consumption is rival. As water withdrawals from a basin exceed the amount replenished (due to any combination of more pumpers, greater withdrawals by each, or declining replenishment), pumpers visit appropriation externalities upon each other. Underground water levels within the basin decline, lengthening pumping lifts (the distance water must be drawn to the surface). Longer pumping lifts impose increased costs on pumpers. If basin water levels decline far enough, wells go dry and must either be deepened or replaced, at even more cost to pumpers.

In special circumstances, even more dire consequences may result from falling water levels. Depending on the amount of underground water in storage and the composition of soil materials, overlying lands may subside or even split, damaging overlying structures and endangering residents. In a coastal basin, if groundwater levels drop below sea level, saltwater may intrude into the basin and degrade the quality of the freshwater supply to the point where it is no longer usable for many important purposes, including human consumption.

At the same time that their actions result in these externalities, pumpers can face provision problems of at least two kinds. The first involves the generation of a collective good: increasing water replenishment in order to stabilize the basin. Under normal circumstances, any success at improving replenishment raises basin water levels. As water levels rise, all users benefit from reduced costs of pumping water. The second kind of provision problem involves resisting a collective "bad," such as intrusion of saltwater into a coastal basin. Familiar collective-action problems may be expected to hinder the implementation of a replenishment program or the successful organization of an effort to hold back the sea.

If not overcome, these appropriation externality and provision problems could have produced disastrous consequences for southern California. The region's economic development and population depended crucially on the availability of dependable water supplies. Human health and welfare and tremendous economic assets would be at risk if water became unavailable, or even undependable. At a minimum, destruction of the area's local water supplies would mean total reliance upon imported water supplies that are both more variable and more expensive. Replacing the water supplies, and the storage capabilities, of southern California's groundwater basins could have cost several times more than their preservation (Blomquist 1992) and visited severe economic hardship on the area.

Water users and their representatives tried to alleviate these CPR problems and stave off disaster by changing institutional arrangements. This chapter examines attempts to change rules in three southern California groundwater systems in an effort to illuminate the connections between rules and games in CPRs. These three cases present the least complicated basin governance and management arrangements of eight that have been studied intensively (Blomquist 1992), allowing the analysis here to focus on the levels of action, the resulting operational rule configurations, and their effects on strategies, behavior, and outcomes.

The Levels of Action

Actions by individuals have been defined as occurring at three levels: an operational level, a collective-choice level, and a constitutional level (Kiser and Ostrom 1982). Actions at each level are affected by corresponding sets of rules: operational-level rules, collective-choice-level rules, and constitutional-level rules. The levels of action, their relation to each other, and their relation to rules, are illustrated in chapter 2.

In the context of a groundwater system, action at the operational level might include water users withdrawing water from wells; action at the collective-choice level might include the adoption or modification of well-spacing regulations; and action at the constitutional level might include the establishment and authorization of the entity making the well-spacing regulations. This example comports with the identification of operational-level action with appropriation, collective-choice-level action with management and policy-making, and constitutional-level action with governance (E. Ostrom 1990).

It is not presumed that the individuals acting at all three levels are the same, nor is it presumed that they are not. It is possible that water users themselves constitute a governing body (e.g., a water users' association) authorized to take collective decisions that apply to all users. It is equally possible that a separate set of officials authorizes the creation of an administrative board and appoints its members, who in turn develop regulations that apply to water users.

The possibility that the same individuals act at all three levels complicates the task of analysis. Among a set of participants within an action arena, "choices of actions *within* a set of rules as contrasted to choices *among* future rules are frequently made without recognizing that the level of action has shifted" (E. Ostrom 1991, 2). Nevertheless, to apply the Institutional Analysis and Design (IAD) framework to actual CPR settings, we must maintain analytic separations of participants' actions among the multiple levels.

In the CPR settings represented by the Raymond, Orange County, and Mojave River basins, water users took or initiated actions at multiple levels. Constitutional-level actions established and authorized governance structures; collective-choice-level actions set and modified groundwater management policies and programs (including operating rules for appropriation, provision, monitoring, and enforcement); and the operational-level actions of pumpers, monitors, and the staff and officials of basin governance organizations resulted in actual resource use and the execution of management practices. Actions at all levels in the three cases are described briefly below. For ease of comparison, tables 13.1, 13.2, and 13.3 summarize those constitutional, collective-choice, and operational-level actions.

Raymond Basin

In 1937, action by the city of Pasadena, the largest pumper from Raymond Basin, led to an adjudication of pumping rights among the 30 pumpers throughout the basin. In the shadow of the court, the pumpers negotiated a

TABLE 13.1. Constitutional-Level Actions in the Three Cases

Raymond Basin
- Establishment of stipulated judgment, with continuing jurisdiction retained by the court, establishing the original distribution of pumping rights in the basin, and authorizing the creation of a watermaster service for Raymond Basin with costs paid by pumping rights owners, the creation of a Water Exchange Pool, a system for determining water spreading credits, a system for determining changes in the pumping rights in the Eastern Unit of the basin based on water levels at designated wells
- Modification of judgment, creating the Raymond Basin Management Board (RBMB) as a representative body of pumpers from the basin, with authorization of RBMB to act as watermaster, acquire staff services and basin studies as needed, recommend adjustments in pumping patterns
- Creation of Foothill Municipal Water District (FMWD) to import water for basin communities not already annexed to MWD or under contract with the State Water Project

Orange County
- Creation of the Orange County Water District (OCWD), by act of the state legislature, to be governed by a board of directors elected from divisions by voters residing within the district, with authority to acquire and defend water and water rights on behalf of residents, and to increase water storage and water storage capacity in the basin, but forbidden to participate in an intrabasin determination of pumping rights
- Amendments to the Orange County Water District Act, adopted by the state legislature, authorizing the district board to impose pump taxes, including differential pump taxes (basin equity assessments), to raise revenue for acquisition of supplemental water supplies

Mojave River
- Creation of the Mojave Water Agency (MWA) by act of the state legislature, to be governed by a board of directors representing divisions (and existing municipalities and water districts) within the agency, with authority to acquire and defend water rights on behalf of the residents, to enter into contacts for and raise revenue to acquire supplemental water supplies, and to initiate an intra-agency determination of water rights
- Amendments to the Mojave Water Agency Law, adopted by the state legislature, reorganizing and reducing the size of the agency board of directors

---

near-unanimous stipulated judgment. Upon its acceptance by the judge in 1945, the judgment became the constitution for Raymond Basin governance (see table 13.1).

The Raymond Basin judgment defined and protected the groundwater rights of the pumpers, limiting their aggregate rights to the determined basin safe yield. It also designated the Southern District office of the California Department of Water Resources (DWR) as watermaster to monitor and report on the administration of the judgment. And it retained for the court continuing jurisdiction to enforce the judgment and to modify its provisions.

In 1984, the judgment was modified to create the Raymond Basin Management Board (RBMB), composed of pumpers' representatives, and to authorize it to take over from the DWR as watermaster and serve as a basin policy-making body. Other constitutional-level action in Raymond Basin entailed the formation of the Foothill Municipal Water District (FMWD) in 1952 under the terms of the state's municipal water district enabling legislation.

Within this basin governance structure, several collective-choice actions

TABLE 13.2.   Collective-Choice-Level Actions in the Three Cases

Raymond Basin
- Modification of basin safe yield determination, with adjustment of pumping rights
- Choice of watermaster (first, DWR, later RBMB)
- Choice of FMWD to provide staff support to RBMB
- Contracting out of data collection, analysis, and report preparation to DWR
- Decisions by RBMB on voluntary adjustments to pumping patterns in basin
- Authorization of watermaster expenditures and actions, and assignment of charges to pumpers to finance those expenditures and actions
- Authorization of spreading credits, and of changes in Eastern Unit pumping amounts
- Operation of Water Exchange Pool
- Establishing requirements for metering and monitoring of wells
- Authorization of basin studies and cooperative agreements

Orange County
- Adoption by OCWD board of basin management policies, including targets for replenishment water purchases and basin pumping as a percentage of total water production
- Establishing requirements for metering and monitoring of wells
- Acquisition and operation of spreading grounds and basin replenishment program
- Construction and operation of injection barrier projects to halt saltwater intrusion along the coast
- Approval of OCWD budget and authorization of OCWD expenditures
- Annual determination of pump tax rates
- Authorization of basin studies and cooperative agreements

Mojave River
- Approval of MWA board of agency expenditures, and payments to DWR under provisions of State Water Project contract
- Setting property tax rates to cover agency expenditures
- Authorizing basin studies and cooperative agreements
- Authorizing lawsuit to determine pumping rights
- Authorizing purchases of surplus water from DWR
- Authorizing pipeline projects
- Initiating legal actions against upstream development and diversions
- Adopting land use guidelines as recommendations for communities within MWA

have been taken in Raymond Basin (see table 13.2). The court's continuing jurisdiction was used in 1955 to alter the determination of basin safe yield and adjust pumping rights accordingly, and in 1984 to change the watermaster designation from the DWR to the RBMB. Policy initiatives and policy changes have authorized water spreading and storage programs, modified provisions concerning pumping activities in the basin's Eastern Unit, and established contracts for staff support and services between the RBMB and FMWD and between the RBMB and DWR. Operational-level actions by pumpers, monitors, and others are summarized in table 13.3. Since the rules developed in Raymond Basin are similar to those developed in five other neighboring basins, I do not attempt to describe the rules that evolved in these other settings (see Blomquist 1992 for a detailed analysis of these systems).

TABLE 13.3.   Operational-Level Actions in the Three Cases

Raymond Basin
- Actions of pumpers: water withdrawals, metering of wells, reporting of production, payment of charges for basin administration, water spreading and storage by some
- Actions of importers: FMWD, Pasadena, and others import water for direct delivery or wholesaling to others
- Actions of DWR staff: monitoring wells, gathering data on water pumping, importing, spreading, storage, and so on within the basin, preparation of reports on basin conditions and operation under the judgment
- Actions of FMWD staff: assistance to RBMB members, distribution of annual basin reports to pumpers and other interested parties, financial accounting
- Actions of RBMB members: attending meetings, reviewing reports, monitoring basin conditions, reporting to court

Orange County
- Actions of pumpers: water withdrawals, metering of wells, reporting of production, payment of pump taxes for basin administration, replenishment, and barrier programs
- Actions of importers: Anaheim, Santa Ana, Municipal Water District of Orange County, and others import water for direct delivery or wholesaling to others
- Actions of OCWD staff: operation of the basin replenishment and barrier programs, monitoring wells, gathering data on water pumping, importing, spreading, etc. within the basin, preparation and distribution of reports on basin conditions and operation, assistance to OCWD board members, financial accounting
- Actions of OCWD Board members: attending meetings, reviewing reports, monitoring basin conditions

Mojave River
- Actions of pumpers: water withdrawals
- Actions of MWA staff: monitoring and reporting on basin conditions, assistance to MWA board members, financial accounting
- Actions of MWA members: attending meetings, reviewing reports

Orange County

Constitutional-level actions in the Orange County basin occurred primarily in legislative rather than judicial arenas and resulted in a different governance structure. Orange County water users and their representatives obtained state legislative approval of the Orange County Water District Act in 1933. It authorized the formation and powers of the Orange County Water District (OCWD), governed by a board of directors elected by district residents (see table 13.1).

In 1953, a set of amendments developed by a committee of water users was submitted to and approved by the California legislature, substantially reconstituting the OCWD—enlarging its territory to cover parts of the basin not originally included, and adding the power to tax pumping directly to cover the costs of basin replenishment programs. In 1968, the OCWD's basic charter was amended again, authorizing the district to charge differential pump tax rates in order to more effectively discourage pumping and adjust pumping patterns.

The OCWD's governing board is the authorized policy-making and management entity in the Orange County basin. Its management and policy-making activities are listed in table 13.2. They include both the provision of a basin replenishment program and a freshwater barrier against saltwater intrusion. Operational-level activities of the board members, staff, pumpers, and others are summarized in table 13.3.

Mojave

In 1959, water users along the Mojave River drafted legislation that was approved by the state legislature, authorizing the formation of the Mojave Water Agency (MWA) and defining and limiting its powers (see table 13.1). The MWA was to be governed by a board of directors chosen by resident voters and by existing local governments.

Unlike the situations in the cases above, significant and continuing groundwater overdraft problems had not developed along the Mojave River by the time of this constitutional-level action. The original intention in constituting the MWA was to create an entity to contract with the state for future deliveries of supplemental water from the soon-to-be-constructed State Water Project. Partly as a result, the MWA covers a territory much larger than the groundwater system along the Mojave River, encompassing several other adjacent basins. Nevertheless, the Mojave Water Agency Law and amendments to it granted the MWA extensive authority to engage in groundwater policy-making and management activities.

By 1964, the MWA board and staff had decided to attempt an adjudication of pumping rights for the groundwater system along the Mojave River. A complaint was filed in 1966, but efforts to achieve a stipulated judgment failed, and the action was dismissed in 1976. Without control of pumping, and without authority to tax pumping, the MWA has been unable to effectively operate any basin replenishment or management programs. Collective-choice actions in the Mojave River area have been essentially limited to those listed in table 13.2. Operational-level actions of pumpers and others in the Mojave River groundwater system are indicated in table 13.3.

Linked Action Arenas

In addition to leaving out details of how the actions in the cases occurred, this abbreviated description of the levels of action also leaves out their many connections to other action arenas to which the actors and their water supply problems are linked. As emphasized in chapter 2, collective action in CPR settings frequently transpires in multiple, linked action arenas, as well as at multiple levels within an action arena.

The governance and management of groundwater systems in southern California were and are closely connected with the development of imported water supplies. Several southern California cities, including some in the Raymond and Orange County basins, were original members of the Metropolitan Water District of Southern California (MWD), which constructed and operates the area's aqueduct from the Colorado River. Most communities in the Raymond Basin have annexed to MWD, and all member agencies have representation on MWD's Board of Directors. Later, MWD contracted with the California Department of Water Resources for northern California water via the State Water Project, as did the Mojave Water Agency. MWD is now the largest supplier of water to southern California communities, including water for groundwater basin replenishment. Decisions and actions taken concerning the Colorado River Aqueduct and the State Water Project bear importantly upon the use and conditions of the groundwater basins.

Closer to home, the Raymond and Orange County basins are embedded within river systems that have governance arrangements to represent the interests of upstream and downstream areas. Water users in Raymond Basin are indirectly represented on the San Gabriel River Watermaster, and those in Orange County are indirectly represented on the Santa Ana River Watermaster and the Santa Ana Watershed Project Authority.

Actors and actions in the three cases also are linked with the actions of flood control agencies in Los Angeles, Orange, and San Bernardino counties. Those agencies operate flood-control impoundments, from which accumulated storm flows can be released into spreading grounds for groundwater replenishment. The U.S. Army Corps of Engineers operates Prado Dam and Flood Control Reservoir, which controls flows into the Orange County basin, and the Forksite Dam below the headwaters of the Mojave River.

Issues of wastewater collection, reclamation, and reuse—including use for basin replenishment—link basin governance and management systems to county sanitation districts, municipal and regional wastewater treatment facilities, and the California Department of Health Services. Water quality concerns involve the Department of Health Services, Regional Water Quality Control Boards, the U.S. Environmental Protection Agency's Superfund program, and so on. Responses to water quality problems can affect pumping patterns and replenishment options.

Operational-Level Rule Configurations

Operational-level actions in CPR settings are defined by operational-level rules. Operational-level rules require, authorize, or forbid certain actions, affecting the incentives and choices of operational-level actors. Their operational-level actions interact with physical attributes of the CPR to yield outcomes ranging from sustained development and more efficient use to resource exhaustion and destruction. Therefore, to examine the effects of the collective actions described above on CPR conditions in the three cases, we first examine operational-level rules and their effects on operational-level actions.

Following the IAD framework, rules are assigned to seven categories: position, boundary, scope, authority, information, aggregation, and payoff (see chapter 2). Where working rules governing particular actions have not been established or modified, the rules in that category are presumed to remain at default settings; in the analysis below, operational-level scope and aggregation rules are left at default settings.

Table 13.4 presents a side-by-side comparison of some operational-level rules in the three cases. The figure does not include every operational-level rule in use; it emphasizes operational-level rules that were explicitly adopted or modified in at least one of the three cases. For simplicity of presentation, the presence or absence of a particular rule in each case is indicated by a yes (Y) or no (N) answer to a question, although this limits the presentation of details and qualifications of particular rules.

Even with these limitations, table 13.4 illustrates several features of the operational-level rules that resulted from the constitutional-level and collective-choice-level actions of participants in the three cases. First and most obviously, the operational-level rules in use differ noticeably across the cases; pumpers and monitors in the three basins do not operate under identical institutional arrangements. Second, the Mojave River case stands out from the others; virtually no rules regulating pumpers' activities have been adopted there (the rule requiring large pumpers to report extractions is a state law applying to several southern California counties). The operational-level rules in the Mojave River case are essentially the same as those *prior to* the collective actions taken in the other cases, and therefore provide a useful comparison.

Third, the operational-level rules for the Raymond and Orange County cases reveal different approaches to basin management. In Orange County, pumpers' rights to water withdrawals are not defined or transferable or restricted to specific quantities; in the Raymond Basin, they are. In Raymond Basin, new pumpers are barred from use of the basin unless they acquire rights from existing pumpers. In Orange County, overlying landowners who are not currently withdrawing water for use on their lands cannot be barred from doing so in the future. Orange County has imposed a pump tax to support a basin replenishment program; in the Raymond Basin, individual parties with access to supplemental water may spread and store it under-

TABLE 13.4. Partial Configurations of Operational-Level Rules in the Three Cases, 1990

Rule Type and Rule	Raymond	Orange	Mojave
Position Rules			
Does position of authorized pumper exist?	Y	N	N
Does position of monitor exist?	Y	Y	N
Boundary Rules			
Can any overlying landowner pump from the basin?	N	Y	Y
Are new pumpers required to obtain rights from existing pumpers?	Y	N	N
Authority Rules			
Are pumpers restricted in amount pumped?	Y	N	N
Are all pumpers required to install meters?	Y	Y	N
Can monitors enter onto pumpers' property to check wells and meters?	Y	Y	N
Are pumpers authorized to elect representatives?	Y	N	N
Can pumpers acquire rights from each other (apart from transferring land)?	Y	N	N
Can pumpers store water in basin for later recapture?	Y	N	N
Information Rules			
Are large (> 25 after/year) pumpers required to report pumping?	Y	Y	Y
Are small pumpers required to report pumping?	Y	Y	N
Are pumpers entitled to receive regular reports on basin conditions?	Y	Y	N
Are monitors required to report their activities and findings to pumpers?	Y	Y	N
Do reports list each pumper's water production?	Y	N	N
Payoff Rules			
Is pumping taxed to pay for administrative costs of basin management?	Y	Y	N
Is pumping taxed to pay for basin replenishment?	N	Y	N
Can fines or penalties be assessed for over-pumping?	Y	N	N
Can pumpers be offered incentives to adjust pumping patterns?	Y	Y	N

ground, but there is no basinwide replenishment program. And, in the Raymond Basin, each pumper's annual water withdrawals are published in a report distributed to all pumpers.

That information rule—that every pumper is entitled to see every other pumper's production data—underscores a point made in chapter 2 about the configurational nature of rules. At any level of action and in any action situation, rules operate configurally, meaning that the *effect* of a change in one rule depends on the other rules in use (E. Ostrom 1991, 7). By itself, the effect of the authority-rule change in the Raymond Basin restricting each appropriator to a specific quantity of water per year would be relatively unclear. When that rule change is taken together with other rules in use, a clearer picture emerges. If pumpers are restricted to a specific quantity of withdrawals *and* are required to install and maintain meters on their wells *and* monitors are employed to check on pumpers' wells and meters *and* monitors report each pumper's withdrawals to all other pumpers *and* fines can be imposed on pumpers who exceed their allotted withdrawals or fail to install or maintain accurate meters, then the effect of the pumping restrictions can be anticipated with greater confidence. With such a configuration of rules, one would anticipate that pumping restrictions would likely result in restraint by pumpers.

Operational-Level Rules and Game Structure

We may now address directly the relation of operational-level rule configurations to the structure of games, examining in our groundwater context the claim in chapter 1 that "rules can change the games that appropriators play." As stated in chapter 4, many analysts have argued that the incentives and choices for appropriators in CPR settings where there are no restrictions on access and use are very similar to those facing players in a Prisoner's Dilemma (PD) game. Each appropriator's dominant strategy is to exploit the resource without constraint, or to decline to contribute to its preservation and maintenance, *regardless of what other appropriators do*. Figure 13.1a depicts this situation.

Among the southern California cases, the operational-level rule configuration for the Mojave River case is characterized by very few rules restraining access and use, and virtually no regular arrangements for monitoring use. Given the value of water supplies in a rapidly developing desert region like the Mojave River area, we would anticipate ceteris paribus that pumpers would respond to the lack of enforceable restraints on access and use by taking actions that are individually rational, placing ever-increasing demands upon the resource. Doing so, they collectively realize a deficient equilibrium. This has been the case in the Mojave River area, and in the other groundwater systems of southern California prior to collective actions (E. Ostrom 1990, 108).

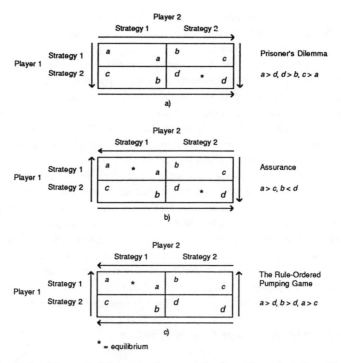

Fig. 13.1. Prisoner's Dilemma, the assurance problem, and the rule-ordered pumping game

The Mojave River case adds another empirical example to the often-noted connection between a relatively open-access CPR and a PD game. But developing the connection between operational-level rules and game structures entails moving beyond this CPR-PD equation and examining how changes in operational-level rules can change game structures. "The task of crafting institutions is to change the incentives so that free riding is no longer the dominant strategy" (E. Ostrom 1992, 64n).

One alternative conception of the game structure of a CPR has been offered by Runge (1984a, 1992). He has stated that most actual CPR situations more closely resemble the Assurance Problem (AP) than the PD, because of the potential joint benefits as well as the joint harms facing users of a valued common resource. In the AP (fig. 13.1b), there are two equilibria and no dominant strategies. Individuals' strategy choices depend on their expectations of others' strategy choices. In this structure, Runge 1984a identifies strong incentives for developing institutional arrangements that will coordinate appropriators' expectations about each other's behavior.

Quick examination of the payoff structures reveals a key difference between the AP and the PD. The AP reduces the PD's temptation to "defect" (strategy 2) when the other player "cooperates" (strategy 1). In the AP, the preferred choice of strategy if the other player cooperates (strategy 1) is to cooperate (strategy 1). The *possibility* of defecting when others cooperate is not blocked (the strategy 2–strategy 1 combination still exists), but the payoff from this combination is less than the payoff from the strategy 1–strategy 1 combination.

The different characterizations of CPR problems as resembling PD or AP game structures is useful to a point, but our interest is in the effects of rule changes on incentives and behavior. As a first step in this inquiry, then, we are not as interested in whether a PD or AP characterization of a CPR problem is the correct one, but in how a change *from* a PD structure *to* an AP structure could be brought about.

Like Runge (1984a, 161), we do not wish to ascribe altruistic behavior to appropriators of a common resource. Altruism solves too much, since altruistic individuals would cooperate even if others defected. Rather, we are interested in the change of incentives that could encourage rational and self-interested appropriators to cooperate when others do the same.

A rule change that established sufficient sanctions for noncooperative behavior, coupled with institutional arrangements authorizing monitoring activities, could lower the payoff from noncooperative behavior. It might even be lowered to just below the benefits from cooperating when others cooperate. Thus, it is at least feasible that changes in operational-level rules can alter the payoff structure of a PD game in the direction of an AP game. (Note: the defecting option is not blocked, but the choice of this option results in a smaller payoff than before.)

Is there any empirical support for this proposition? Returning to the configuration of operational-level rules in use in the Raymond and Orange County cases, we find pumpers subject to sanctions if they engage in noncooperative behavior such as overpumping, failing to report production, and failing to pay assessments based on their pumping rights or their actual withdrawals. Those sanctions include fines and (in the Raymond case) potential loss of rights to use. Furthermore, pumpers are required to meter and report their production, and monitors can check meters and wells. Under these circumstances, one would anticipate that a typical pumper in a given time period would find the payoff from attempting to free ride sinking below the payoff from cooperating as long as others do.

In the AP, although the temptation to defect while others cooperate is curtailed, the risk of being a "sucker" remains. The payoff from cooperating while others defect remains lower than the payoff from defecting while others defect. Suppose that monitoring and enforcement could reduce the chances of being a "sucker" and raise the chances of being caught and sanctioned for defecting. Suppose further that the payoff for cooperating now exceeds the payoff from defecting. Appropriators' best response would then be to cooperate even if others defect. The AP could be transformed into something like the "rule-ordered pumping game" shown in figure 13.1c.

This transformation is more difficult to imagine, but Runge 1984a, 1992, and Wade 1987 supply some rationale for its feasibility. Runge (1992, 27) raises the possibility that appropriators of a common resource might take into account more than the individual benefits and costs they receive from following or breaking the rules that coordinate resource use. If they include the opportunity costs of foregone joint benefits and the expected costs of developing new rules if defecting behavior leads to the breakdown of existing arrangements, appropriators may recognize incentives to maintain those arrangements by adopting a cooperative strategy over numerous iterations.

The key institutional arrangements to be supplied and maintained, then, provide information to appropriators about each other's actions and the level of compliance with the rules. This includes the knowledge that one's own actions are known to others: "The more information player 1 has about player 2 and others' ability to predict his actions, and vice versa, the more mutual confidence or assurance exists" (Runge 1984a, 164). In an irrigation context, Wade (1987) refers to the degree of "transparency" of CPR arrangements, and articulates somewhat more specifically how such operational-level institutional arrangements might work:

> in many situations individual irrigators will restrain their water rule breaking if they are confident that others will also refrain and if they are confident that they will still get as much water as they are entitled to (even if not as much as they would like). They will more likely refrain from cheating if they are confident that by doing so they will not be the "suckers." Where people are motivated by an "I'll restrain if you restrain" calculation, then an institution (such as an irrigation department) that convinces them that these expectations are justified can promote voluntary compliance with the rules. (Wade 1987, 178)

Empirical evidence from the Raymond Basin case illuminates Runge's reasoning about the incentives to cooperate when information is available to all participants. The empirical evidence also supports Wade's reasoning about the role of institutional arrangements in promoting voluntary compliance with rules by raising participants' confidence in each other's rule-following behavior. Raymond Basin pumpers not only institutionalized rules restricting quantities of water withdrawn, requiring well meters to determine quantities withdrawn, mandating contributions to basin administration on the basis of quantities withdrawn, and authorizing monitors to check on wells and meters, but also entitling each pumper to an annual report on basin conditions and the water withdrawals of every other pumper. Pumpers receiving such reports become the monitors of each other's behavior *and* know that their own behavior is equally visible to others. Under those circumstances, the possibility of being played for a "sucker" (at least more than once) by other pumpers is reduced, confidence that noncomplying behavior by any pumper will be caught and sanctioned is raised, and if available sanctions are nontrivial, the payoff for cooperating exceeds the payoff from defecting.

In this rule-ordered pumping game, it makes sense to follow rules and contribute to provision even if someone else defects or free rides. Runge adds, however, that widespread noncompliance by others could still lead an individual appropriator to drop his or her cooperative strategy: "where noncompliance is the rule, it does not seem fair to many that they pay as part of a minority" (1984a, 161). This is an important point, if it is meant to suggest that institutional arrangements can erode over time if not maintained. However, it remains unclear how widespread noncompliance emerges in any given time period if each individual faces greater incentives to cooperate and contribute than to defect and free ride.

Rules, Actions, and Outcomes: Evidence from the Cases

In the Raymond and Orange County cases, the relatively transparent institutional arrangements developed by pumpers and others over time have produced something like a rule-ordered pumping game, where pumpers respond to the incentives and choices available by selecting a strategy of cooperation. Although the institutional arrangements have been in effect in Raymond Basin for nearly 50 years and in Orange County for 40 years, sanctions have never been applied for noncompliance. When instances of noncompliance with rules requiring meter installations, meter repairs, payment of contributions, or restrictions on water withdrawals have occurred, reporting of the violation has sufficed to bring about compliance in the next time period without the application of sanctions. Although the rule-ordered pumping game with its dominant strategy of cooperation seems unlikely in the context of the literature on CPRs, the operational-level rule configurations put in place in the Raymond and Orange County cases appear to have created something approaching it.

Our final inquiry is whether and how the operational-level rule configurations in these cases appear to be linked to outcomes, that is, changed CPR conditions. Table 13.5 briefly summarizes the status of basin conditions in the three cases as of 1990; greater detail on institutional performance is available in Blomquist (1992). The first two questions in table 13.5 address whether the

TABLE 13.5. Comparison of Basin Conditions in the Three Cases

Conditions	Raymond	Orange	Mojave
Has imported water use increased relative to basin water use?	Yes	Yes	No
Is basin water relied on to a greater extent for emergency and "peak" supplies?	Yes	Yes	No
Is the basin in continuing overdraft condition?	No	No	Yes
Are basin water levels rising, stable, or falling?	Stable	Stable	Falling
Are water consumers charged roughly the replacement cost of water supplies?	Yes	Yes	No
Is total water use in the basin rising, stable, or falling?	Stable	Stable	Rising
Is per capita water use in the basin above or below the state average?	Below	Below	Above
Is per capita water use in the basin rising, stable, or falling?	Falling	Falling	Stable

groundwater system is now used more efficiently, as part of a conjunctive-use system in which imported water is used for average daily requirements and the groundwater storage capacity is relied upon primarily for peaking and emergency supplies. The next two questions address overt measures of groundwater conditions—the presence of persistent overdraft and the status of underground water levels. The remaining questions address whether the institutional arrangements governing water use have encouraged rational water pricing that provides water consumers with incentives to conserve water in this relatively dry region, and whether water consumers have responded to those incentives.

As mentioned above, the operational-level rules governing access to and use of the Mojave River groundwater system have remained very near the structure of a PD game. Accordingly, in light of previous theory and research on CPRs under such circumstances, we would expect basin conditions to be deteriorating. Table 13.5 illustrates that in the Mojave case, basin overdraft continues, water levels are falling, total water use is rising, and per capita water use is above the state average and holding steady despite substantial statewide efforts to encourage water conservation.

Table 13.5 shows a clear contrast between the Mojave case and the Raymond and Orange County cases on these outcome criteria. The groundwater systems in those cases are relied upon to a greater extent for storage and peak use while imported water is used to greater degree for direct use. Overdraft has not continued, and underground water levels have stabilized. Moreover, in Orange County, an extensive program of artificial basin replenishment has operated for nearly 30 years and freshwater barriers against saltwater intrusion have functioned successfully for 20 years. In both basins, water consumers are charged prices for water that approximate its replacement cost (i.e., the marginal cost of additional imported water), and their total and per capita water consumption has responded by falling below the state average and declining.

As discussed in chapter 4: "When rules . . . are changed, the resulting games may produce incentives leading to the same, improved, or worse outcomes for the participants." The comparison of the cases in table 13.5 offers evidence of rule changes in two cases leading to a changed game that yields improved outcomes for the participants, and of a failure to make rule changes in the remaining case leading to a perpetuation of a game that yield deteriorating outcomes for the participants. In the Raymond and Orange County cases, the institutional changes correspond with Elinor Ostrom's general characterization that "in all cases in which individuals have organized themselves to solve CPR problems, rules have been established by the appropriators that have severely constrained the authorized actions available to them" (1990, 43). Even so, judging from the extent of rule compliance by pumpers in those two cases, the institutional changes also appear to represent or approximate rule reforms, defined in chapter 4 as rule changes yielding outcomes preferred by all players. Based on the outcomes summarized in table 13.5, they also meet the definition of a welfare improvement, where the aggregate payoff of a rule configuration is greater than that of its predecessor.

Conclusions

As stated in chapter 2, "The substantive questions of this book relate to how and when individuals using [CPRs] establish enforceable rules that enable them to use these resources relatively efficiently. The theoretical questions of this book relate to how rules are linked to strategic behavior within well-structured, repetitive situations that can be analyzed as games." Empirical evidence from groundwater systems in southern California bears upon both sets of questions and relates directly to the following propositions advanced in chapters 1 and 2.

1. Rules shape action situations, including situations that can be represented as games (chap. 1).
2. Rules shape action situations by affecting the incentives and choices available to individual actors, to which rational actors respond by adopting certain strategies and behaviors, which affect outcomes (chap. 2).
3. Changing rules can therefore change action situations in ways that motivate individuals to adopt different strategies and behavior, potentially yielding different outcomes (chap. 1).

4. Rule changes can be developed and deliberately chosen by the actors in an action situation, as well as imposed from outside (chap. 2).
5. Actors in an action situation change the rules shaping that situation by taking actions at multiple levels (chap. 2).
6. Actions frequently occur not only at multiple levels within a particular action arena but also in linked action arenas (chap. 2).

In these groundwater systems, water users took or initiated constitutional-level actions to create and modify collective-choice institutions and authorized actors in positions in those institutions to establish and enforce groundwater management policies and programs. In two of the three cases, those collective-choice institutions were employed effectively to establish or change rules guiding operational-level activities of pumpers, persons engaged in resource provision and maintenance, and persons engaged in monitoring and enforcement. This evidence supports three of the above propositions, namely that rule changes can be developed and deliberately chosen by the actors in an action situation, through actions taken at multiple levels and in linked arenas.

In two of the cases, the operational-level rule configurations resulting from processes of institutional change appear to be associated with changes in pumpers' strategies and behaviors, and with improved use of common resources. Elinor Ostrom's characterization of the West and Central basins applies equally well to the Raymond and Orange County cases: "After several decades of institutional change, the resulting institutional infrastructure . . . represented a major investment that dramatically changed the incentives and behaviors of participants and the resulting outcomes" (1990, 141). In the Mojave case, failure to change substantially the operational-level rule configuration appears to be associated with the perpetuation of pumpers' strategies and behaviors, and with continued deterioration of the condition of the common resource. This evidence supports the other three propositions, namely that rules shape action situations by affecting actors' incentives and choices and thus their adopted strategies and behaviors, and that rule changes can therefore result in actors' adoptions of different strategies and behaviors, yielding different outcomes.

Empirical evidence from the southern California experience cannot be read as prescribing a formula for the sustainable development and efficient use of all CPRs. Even in the relatively successful Raymond and Orange County cases, the constitutional and collective-choice actions produced operational-level rule configurations that differed substantially. The evidence from the southern California experience does, however, reinforce the close relationship between rules and games.

CHAPTER 14

Regularities from the Field and Possible Explanations

Chapters 10–13 clearly demonstrate that in some instances CPR appropriators are able to organize themselves when facing CPR dilemmas. When they do organize, appropriators use linked action arenas to solve second-order public-good problems by providing new rules and by monitoring and enforcing these rules. In light of this evidence, this chapter is devoted to exploring the institutional and physical variables that affect self-organization. We return to the third core question we posed in chapter 1: What type of institutional and physical variables affect the likelihood of successful resolution of CPR dilemmas?[1]

We first identify the commonalities that occur in the self-organized CPRs of chapters 10–13. Most of these commonalities relate to the presence of key rules. After examining these commonalities, we identify physical characteristics that tend to hinder or help self-organization. While prior empirical work has tended to focus on a limited number of cases from a single sector and region, we draw on results from four sectors and from many regions.

Commonalities across Organized CPRs

The commonalities that we identify as existing in all of the self-organized CPRs described in the previous four chapters are as follows:

- presence of boundary rules
- presence of authority rules related to allocation
- active forms of monitoring and sanctioning
- the absence of grim trigger strategies

---

1. This chapter draws on a paper by Blomquist, Schlager, and Tang 1991.

Presence of Boundary Rules

The adoption of boundary rules specifying who can appropriate from a CPR is accomplished in *all* of the organized CPRs. Devising boundary rules is a challenging task, given that one of the defining characteristics of a CPR is the difficulty of excluding potential beneficiaries. A wide diversity of appropriator characteristics—residence, land ownership, organizational membership, share ownership—form the basis for boundary rules. These rules vary in their official status. Some are fully recognized and backed by formal, governmental authority (the California groundwater cases). Some are recognized as legitimate by participants but not by formal, governmental authorities (some of the inshore fisheries).

Many policy prescriptions are based on the presumption that all CPRs are open access. What chapters 10–13 document is that many CPRs are limited access rather than open access. The set of individuals who have access to a CPR is frequently defined by a boundary rule created by the participants themselves. While boundary rules make precise the set of individuals who might be party to an efficiency-enhancing agreement, such rules do not specify the content of such agreements. Thus, the establishment of boundary rules alone is not sufficient to solve most CPR problems.

As discussed in chapters 3–9, suboptimality can be a prediction for both limited- and open-access CPRs even though the degree of suboptimality is less for limited access. Thus, one should view the provision of boundary rules as an essential first step, but no more than this. The next step is the creation of authority rules that directly address the allocation problem.

Presence of Authority Rules Related to Allocation

Authority rules allocate the flow of resource units or the access to resource units through the allocation of space, time, and technological capabilities. Authority rules that enhance efficiency are similar to the agreements from the experimental lab, where subjects reduce their investment of tokens in the CPR. In irrigation systems, authority rules limit time and location of withdrawal; in fisheries, location and technology employed; in forests, location, quantity and product type; in groundwater basins, quantity. Thus, authority rules address different allocation issues in different CPR environments. Some of these differences are crucial as we discuss later in this chapter.

Active Forms of Monitoring and Sanctioning

All of the self-organized CPRs also developed ways to monitor and enforce their rules. Relative to inshore fisheries and groundwater basins, however, endogenous monitoring on irrigation systems and in forests is more frequent, often by hired guards who regularly patrol the terrain. Further, given the standard presumption that monitoring and sanctioning must be performed by external agents, it is important to note that Tang finds the least effective monitoring occurs on government-owned irrigation systems that rely on external enforcement. Guards working for government irrigation bureaucracies are notorious for their inattention to major infractions, except in circumstances where opportunities exist to earn side payments.

Monitoring arrangements in regard to fisheries are rarely as formal as those related to other sectors, but considerable self-monitoring occurs as fishers watch each other as they fish. Agrawal finds that Indian villages that devote substantial resources to monitoring and imposing sanctions are the ones whose forests are in much better condition than those that do not. Blomquist finds that successfully organized California pumpers rely on very specific information rules. These rules inform users of individual and aggregate pumping levels and regularly report on the condition of the basin.[2]

Not all of the sanctions administered are easily recognized by outsiders. Peer disapproval may represent a substantial cost in terms of willingness to extend trust in future dealings.[3] Many of the sanctioning systems used in field settings involve only minor sanctions for first infractions or for continued small infractions. Larger sanctions are invoked only in cases of major infractions. In fact, minor sanctions that escalate for repeat offenders appear to work in many cases. In some fisheries, those who initially violate rules may simply find their fishing gear tied up in a distinctive manner—hardly an overt cost at all. But the knot tied on their gear signifies that their infraction has been duly noted by others and that mutually productive dealings in the future depend on an absence of further infractions. Fishers who ignore the message of early warnings are apt to find their gear destroyed rather than simply marked with a knot.

No Grim Trigger Strategies Observed

Grim trigger strategies, a form of punishment posited in many theoretical arguments, were absent from the field settings. Irrigators on a farmer-owned system immediately sanction a rule breaker with name calling, fines, or extra work, but they do not immediately go out and begin to break their own rules.

---

2. Interestingly, Agrawal reports high level of rule violations, while Blomquist reports high levels of rule compliance.

3. We draw on a rich literature beyond the specific cases studied in chapters 10–13 that has studied how communities of individuals develop trust and social capital on which to build new rules related to sharing agreements, monitoring arrangements, sanctions, inducements, and other rules (see Coleman 1990; Ellickson 1991; Gambetta 1988; Hechter 1987; and Taylor 1982).

Fishers gang up on a rule breaker to destroy nets and other equipment, but they don't go overboard in their punishment, nor do they punish forever. Forest users rely on social sanctions, monetary fines, or confiscation of ill-gotten forest products. The level of information about small rule infractions in the groundwater basins has been sufficient enough that minor infractions have not continued beyond a single year and formal sanctions have not been needed. Thus, as in the lab, grim trigger strategies do not appear to organize behavioral data from the field.

We can now offer part of an answer to what type of institutional and physical variables affect the likelihood of successful resolution of CPR dilemmas. When appropriators monitor and enforce boundary and authority rules they consider to be legitimate and effective, they are likely to improve performance in the CPR. While legitimate and effective rules can come from external sources, our studies suggest that a more effective source is the appropriators themselves. The rules used in a self-organized CPR are often tailored to the specific characteristics of the CPR. Rules imposed by external authorities may fail to draw on knowledge of the time and place characteristics of a specific CPR. In fact, such rules may be less effective, or even counterproductive, compared to those designed locally.

Differences across Organized CPRs

In addition to the commonalities observed across the organized CPRs in the four sectors, some notable differences also exist. The first relates to the diversity of boundary rules in inshore fisheries compared to the lack of diversity of boundary rules in regard to irrigation. A second difference relates to the specific types of authority rules related to appropriation.

Types of Boundary Rules

Among the farmer-owned irrigation systems analyzed by Tang, the variety of boundary (as well as authority) rules adopted is greater than on government-owned systems. Government-owned systems tend to rely entirely on land as a boundary rule, while farmer-owned systems include share ownership and other user requirements for access. The diversity of boundary rules in fisheries is even greater. Schlager shows that most of the organized inshore fisheries use multiple boundary rules in addition to a minimal requirement that fishers live near where they fish. A similar diversity exists in regard to forestry resources in India. Users of each of the organized groundwater basins in southern California adopted a different blend of boundary rules. Historical use patterns establishing initial rights to a marketable share of the flow, however, are common for those relying on some form of litigation.

Types of Authority Rules Related to Appropriation

Authority rules related to appropriation vary systematically across the four sectors. Tang examines the types of allocation rules used on government-owned and farmer-owned irrigation systems. Most government-owned systems rely on the assignment of a fixed time slot to an irrigator, as do about a third of the farmer-owned systems. The variety of allocation rules used by farmer-owned systems is greater than on government-owned systems or in the other sectors. Most rules, however, focus principally on assigning the order and timing of rights to withdraw water, rather than the actual quantity of water to be appropriated.[4] A few farmer-owned systems devise ingenious physical structures that divide the flow of water to each farmer in a well-defined and marketable way. The comparison of two neighboring systems in Nepal by E. Martin and Yoder (1983a, 1983b)—one based on share ownership and the other based on land ownership—illustrates how share ownership can be more efficient than land ownership as the basis for water rights. Finally, farmer-owned systems that devise boundary and allocation rules to fit their local circumstances are more likely to perform better than government-owned systems relying on a limited set of rules.

Tang's study also illustrates how provision activities can be related to appropriation rights. The most challenging problem faced in managing irrigation systems is provision of the system itself. On many government-owned systems, little investment is made in maintenance. These systems are allowed to deteriorate at a grossly inefficient rate (see Ascher and Healy 1990; Chambers 1988). The proportion of farmer-owned systems where the resource has been maintained effectively is much higher than the proportion of government-owned systems, indicating that farmers have devised ways of creating internal incentives to invest substantial time and effort cleaning their canals. While based on data from only a few systems, Tang finds, in those systems where farmers invest significantly in maintenance, appropriation rights are closely correlated with the level of maintenance inputs. In other words, a degree of fiscal equivalence (Olson 1969) is achieved. The organized groundwater basins in Blomquist's study also engage in supply-side provision activities that are tied to fiscal equivalence. Specifically, revenues from pumping taxes (based on units pumped) are used for maintenance.

Appropriation rules devised by self-organized inshore fishers, on the other hand, appear to be oriented to solving assignment and technological externality problems. Use rights to space are common enough that fishery

---

4. Some irrigation systems have devised rules that allocate specific quantities of water to specific farmers and highly specialized water markets have evolved. See Maass and Anderson 1986 and E. Ostrom 1990.

economists have devised a term for them. They are called TURFs or "territorial use rights in fisheries" (see Christy 1982). These appropriation rules are different from those frequently recommended by policy analysts who argue for annual quotas similar to those devised in the groundwater systems studied by Blomquist. While various types of permanent or nonpermanent quota systems have been established by national governments in several countries,[5] Schlager's set of cases does not contain a single instance of an indigenous quota system.[6]

Schlager argues that inshore fishers devise rules to reduce the inefficiencies that would occur from assignment problems and technological externalities. The TURFs established by such rules give fishers the right to appropriate in a particular location for a specified period of time. Thus, they reduce conflict over who can fish where and reduce the costs of trying to accommodate mutually harmful technologies in the same space. TURFs can be inherited, auctioned, or assigned by lottery. Other rules typically adopted in conjunction with a TURF system (such as size of net or the establishment of a fishing season) also protect the stock needed for regeneration. Interestingly, such rules, as well as restrictions on technology, are often criticized as being inefficient in the resource economics literature.[7]

Agrawal finds a diversity of rules used to allocate forest products. In regard to the grasses growing in forested areas, many of the villages use rules that assign specific quantities to individuals based on (1) their contributions to the maintenance of the forest, (2) the price they are willing to pay in an auction, or (3) their per capita or per household share of the total annual yield. In villages that have maintained sustainable forests, Agrawal notes that village officials first estimate the total amount of fodder available. They then "carefully meter the amount of grass extracted" by giving each person a premeasured rope that they must use for bundling during authorized harvesting periods.

The groundwater pumpers described by Blomquist have access to state agencies who provide reliable, technical information and a court system that provides arenas for negotiating enforceable contracts. All but the pumpers in Mojave and Orange County devise variants of rules that assign transferable rights to a specified quantity of water. The quantity rights are based on information about sustainable yield of the basins. If this information is accurate, limiting the total quantity of water pumped solves the demand-side

---

5. New Zealand in 1980; Australia for specific fisheries; Iceland in 1984; and in Canada at different times for different fisheries (Hannesson 1988, 14–15).

6. Nor have these efforts to establish individually transferable quotas been equally successful. One of the first efforts was to set up a total allowable catch system in the Canadian Bay of Funday herring fishery. One of the major problems of implementing this and other systems is that associated with monitoring (see discussion in Hannesson 1988).

7. See, for example, the argument made by Crutchfield 1961 against gear restrictions.

provision problem created by time-dependent appropriation externalities discussed in chapter 1.[8]

The estimates of average sustainable yield, originally made by an independent agency of the State of California, have proven to be relatively accurate.[9] Once transferable rights to a proportion of joint yield were assigned, active water markets emerged. Water rights have been extensively traded ever since. There is considerable evidence that the ownership of these rights has consistently moved to pumpers with the highest valued uses—particularly municipal water suppliers who use the water to meet peak demand levels, thus saving the exorbitant costs of building more surface reservoirs in an urban area.

Thus, for the CPR dilemmas studied in chapters 10–13, self-organized appropriators using groundwater and forests develop rules that authorize transferable rights directly to *quantities* of resource units. On the one hand, groundwater rights are assigned permanently, based on an agreed-upon estimate of the sustainable yield of the resource. On the other, the rights to forest products in organized CPRs tend to be allocated annually based on a yearly estimate of sustainable yield. In self-organized inshore fisheries and irrigation systems, appropriation rules focus only indirectly on quantities. Rights are assigned in both inshore fisheries and irrigation systems, but they concern spatial and temporal attributes of the resource rather than the quantity of resource units.

Given the limited nature of the samples involved, these patterns can only be taken as suggestive, not definitive. Each of these studies has its unique elements. The irrigation systems studied by Tang do not include any systems where farmers have substantial input into decisions about the release of water from large storage reservoirs.[10] The inshore fisheries studied by Schlager do not include any cases where large-scale governments have experimented with

8. Technological externalities are involved in groundwater basins to the extent that the effluent of chemical plants and other industrial firms are allowed to enter the groundwater. Such problems are only now beginning to occur in the groundwater basins that were the focus of Blomquist's study and new regulations are in the process of being crafted to cope with these new problems.

9. Since many of the holders of rights employ well-trained technical staff, there are many participants fully capable of challenging data that they do not think is accurate. The amount of detailed data made available publicly every year allows for a close monitoring of the reasonableness of each year's information. Estimates of yield have been updated in light of better information over time. In one case, the estimate of the sustainable yield was increased enough that the initial agreement was amended and all pumpers received a somewhat larger allotment.

10. See Maass and Anderson 1986 for a description of the Alicante system, where the farmers control the water to be released from a major dam and thus control the quantity available during any period of time. In this system, the rights are to a specified time period rather than to a specified quantity of water. But when the quantity of water to be released in the canal is known, a farmer has a much better idea how much water is being bought when the unit is 5 minutes, 10 minutes, or an hour.

transferable quota systems or aquaculture. Agrawal studies a broader sample, but is able to obtain detailed information about enforcement patterns from only six Indian villages.[11] The California pumpers have access both to very good technical information provided by overlapping state and national agencies, and to arenas where enforceable contracts can be negotiated. Findings from other studies of organized, inshore fisheries, irrigation systems, and forest institutions, of which we are aware, are consistent with the findings reported above. Definitive findings related to the distribution of various types of allocation rules will require, however, a much larger, cross-sectoral sample.

Knowledge accumulates more effectively if scholars willingly offer their conjectures about their observations for further testing. In this spirit, we offer some conjectures about the importance of two physical variables on the types of allocation rules adopted in self-organized CPRs.

Physical Characteristics That Make a Difference

While many variables may help to account for the above differences in rules, two physical variables in CPRs appear to have a considerable influence on the kinds of appropriation and provision problems faced and the capabilities of appropriators to solve them.[12] These physical variables are *stationarity* and *storage*. The physical characteristics of stationarity and storage are linked to systematic differences in users' strategies and in the institutional arrangements developed to overcome appropriation and provision problems. Resource users face a number of interacting constraints. One would not want to contend that institutional arrangements are "determined" by physical characteristics. Rather, the physical characteristics of stationarity and storage shape the opportunities and constraints that appropriators face in attempting to resolve CPR problems, as well as the kind of information they have about these problems.

By *stationarity* we mean that resource *units* yielded by the resource (usable amounts of water, oil, fish, grasses, forest products, etc.) remain spatially confined prior to harvest, or at least travel so slowly as to be fixed for all practical short-term purposes. Examples of stationary resource units include water in a groundwater basin or lake, shellfish, and most forest products.[13] Nonstationary resource units include water moving in a surface stream or canal, wild animals, and most fish. Stationarity is thus an attribute of the

---

11. His evidence is quite consistent with that of Arnold and Campbell 1986, Messerschmidt 1986, Blaikie, Harriss, and Pain 1992.

12. See Blomquist, Schlager, and Tang 1991 for a more detailed discussion of these arguments.

13. Many constructed CPRs have stationary units. Parking garages and mainframe computers both are so characterized. On the other hand, one might think of bridges as having a constant flow of nonstationary units through them.

Resource Units

	Stationary	Nonstationary
Available Storage	groundwater basins, lakes	irrigation canals with reservoirs
Not Available	shellfish, grazing lands, annual forest products	migratory fish, run-of-the- river irrigation systems

Fig. 14.1.   A typology of CPRs

resource units yielded by a particular resource system. Clearly, stationarity is not bivariate. It may vary continuously across physical environments.

By *storage* we mean the existing physical capacity of a resource to collect and hold resource units. Storage is obviously related to stationarity, since storage can be used to retain resource units that would otherwise be mobile. Stored units can be appropriated as needed, rather than being appropriated only when available. Thus, storage allows appropriators to bank resource units for use when they are the most valuable. Resources with storage capability include surface and underground water reservoirs and irrigation systems connected to reservoirs. Examples of resources for which storage is far more problematic include fisheries, forest products other than timber, and grazing areas. As with stationarity, the presence of storage clearly varies across classes of CPRs.[14]

Stationarity and storage, when dichotomized, can be combined to create the typology of CPRs in figure 14.1. Individual CPRs can be classified according to whether particular resource units are stationary and whether storage is present. The cells in figure 14.1 contain relevant examples of types of CPRs illustrating each type. All other things being equal, appropriators of CPRs that lack storage and/or yield nonstationary resource units face greater difficulty in devising allocation rules that reduce appropriation externalities.

Stationarity and Appropriation Problems

The degree of stationarity affects the types of appropriation problems appropriators are likely to address. It is with regard to appropriation externalities

---

14. Of course, common-pool resources differ on other physical characteristics, as well: renewability, fragility of the resource, the length of time for resource units to become mature, the distribution of valued flow units throughout the resource, the visibility of the resource, and so on. In this analysis, we explore the implications of stationarity and storage, but do not imply that they are the only physical characteristics that affect the prospects for resolution of CPR dilemmas.

that the difference that stationarity makes is most apparent, and the problems created by nonstationarity are most acute. Appropriation externalities arise more from the current and over-time availability of resource units from a CPR than from the resource itself. Excessive harvesting creates time-independent appropriation externalities, leading to increased harvesting costs per unit of output. An excessive harvest in one year may also reduce or destroy the availability of resource units in future years. Holding constant resource maintenance, in order to resolve appropriation externalities, the quantity of resource units harvested must be regulated.

Appropriators of resources that naturally produce stationary resource units—such as the grasses and leaves produced in a forest or grazing area—have a substantial advantage over appropriators of a resource that naturally produce mobile units such as a fishery. Even though the annual yield may vary dramatically from one year to the next, the costs of assessing the quantity of units available to be harvested are less if the units remain in one place where they can be measured at a lower cost. As described by Agrawal, experienced officials can assess at a relatively low cost the safe fodder yield during a particular year, still protecting the regenerative capacity of the resource.[15] When the cost of assessing the availability of resource units is relatively low, it is easier to develop allocation rules that assign quantities to individuals. Consequently, we find the use of *annual* quotas in some of the Indian villages related to the amount of fodder that can be extracted. Sometimes these quotas can even be auctioned. Unless one has a relatively accurate measure of the quantity available, conducting an auction is problematic.[16]

In a CPR with nonstationary resource units, on the other hand, appropriators are more likely to address problems arising from the resource facility, rather than from the resource units. Appropriators possess more information, face less uncertainty, and can exert greater control over the resource facility than over the nonstationary units flowing through it. As illustrated by Schlager and Tang in their respective chapters, self-organized fishers and irrigators on run-of-the-river irrigation systems rarely use quota systems for allocating resource units.

Technological externalities and assignment problems can be more readily solved by spatial allocations that rely primarily on knowledge of the resource facility, as distinguished from the resource units. These problems are caused when multiple appropriators attempt to harvest within a resource's finite space—interfering with each other's appropriation efforts, or fighting over

---

15. Netting 1981 and Glaser 1987 describe similar systems in the Swiss Alps, where local officials make annual assessments of the fodder available and are thus able to regulate the amount harvested with some high degree of accuracy.

16. It is, of course, always possible to auction spatial locations without knowing the quantity of resource units that can be obtained from the use of this space.

access to the better locations. Even in a CPR with nonstationary resource units, appropriators possess (or through experience can gain) information about the incidence and causes of these two types of assignment and technological externality problems. Because these problems are experienced repeatedly under similar conditions, their diagnosis is a relatively straightforward process (J. Wilson 1982, 1990).

In a CPR with nonstationary resource units, it is less clear whether a decline in their availability is merely a temporary aberration or evidence of a longer-term phenomenon. Even if appropriators are convinced that the decline is permanent, diagnosis of its cause is problematic. The magnitude of the effect of appropriation activities in one period on the flow of units in future periods cannot be accurately predicted. Other plausible hypotheses present themselves. Perhaps some migratory patterns or precipitation patterns have shifted. Perhaps some infestation or pestilence is at work. Perhaps someone or something outside the resource has affected the flow, and so on.[17] When the cause of reduced CPR flows cannot be clearly determined, appropriators have greater incentives to reject, or cheat upon, agreements.

These difficulties in understanding and addressing appropriation externalities are compounded if the nonstationary resource units actually flow through multiple resources, as do migratory wildlife or aquatic species. This phenomenon aggravates the appropriation externality problem in four ways: (1) appropriators in any of the resources sharing a common nonstationary flow are likely to attribute flow declines to the behavior of appropriators elsewhere in the system; (2) appropriators in any one CPR cannot control the flow even if they act collectively; (3) because no one group can control the flow and capture the benefits of collective action, appropriators in any one resource are less likely to provide benefits for appropriators elsewhere by restraining their own appropriation activities; and (4) coordinating activities with appropriators from other resources in other locations raises transaction costs.

Stationarity and Provision Problems

Parallel observations apply to the effect of stationarity on provision problems. Supply-side provision problems are not as adversely affected by a lack of

---

17. Shortall describes a situation in which fishers experience both declining numbers and quality of fish available for harvest. The fishers harvest cod out of Petty Harbour, Newfoundland, and they believe that the causes of both problems lie elsewhere:

> the main migration has been observed by the fishermen to enter the Petty Harbour area before mid-June and to consist of smaller fish schools and of fish of reduced average size. . . . The smaller size of the fish schools and the reduced average size of the fish, however, are attributed to the growth of the offshore fishing fleets and to the introduction of gillnets in the inshore fishery elsewhere. (1973, 92)

stationarity as demand-side provision problems. Appropriators relying on both stationary and nonstationary types of fish may engage in supply-side activities, but of a slightly different variety. In one of the more stationary marine species—lobster—fishers are known to invest in such supply-side provision activities as the construction of hatcheries that release small lobsters after they have passed through the early stages of life where mortality is highest (Acheson 1989, 213). Since these lobsters will not migrate vast distances, hatcheries have been enthusiastically supported along the Maine coast. In many mountain commons, appropriators spend time and effort enhancing the productivity of the commons by weeding out undesirable species and transplanting and caring for more desirable species (McKean 1992).

Several options to enhance supply may be feasible even when the resource units are nonstationary. Fishers may place fish shelters in a fishing ground or protect the feeding or spawning areas of mobile fish species even when there is uncertainty regarding the stock. Irrigators may line irrigation canals or maintain diversion ditches even when the quantity of water available during the forthcoming year is unknown.

On the other hand, appropriators are less likely to commit to or engage in demand-side provision activities related to resources with nonstationary resource units. Nonstationary flows mean that the units not appropriated today are available to someone else tomorrow. The incentives for appropriators to take actions or make contributions to protect a nonstationary flow—whether to protect the quality of water in a surface stream or a migratory species habitat—are sharply attenuated relative to those incentives when resource units in a CPR are stationary. The negative consequences of degradation are (from an individual appropriator's viewpoint, literally) passed on to others. All other things equal, we would anticipate that appropriators of a CPR with nonstationary resource units are substantially more likely to pursue "first capture" ("use it or lose it") strategies.

Further, appropriators are less likely to engage in either supply-side or demand-side provision activities where they harvest nonstationary flows that migrate through surrounding CPRs. Appropriators are more likely to make provision efforts if they are able to capture the full benefits from such investments. The presence of appropriators who will harvest in surrounding locations before or after the mobile units come to a particular location reduces the incentive to invest or conserve since the benefits may simply be captured by others who did not contribute. Further, multiple resources sharing a common nonstationary flow compounds the uncertainty about the incidence and causes of flow declines.

Storage and Appropriation Problems

Because the availability of storage in a CPR allows appropriators to capture and contain resource units, at least temporarily, storage can help appropriators of CPRs with nonstationary flows overcome some of their appropriation problems. Among appropriation problems, the possibility of storing resource units within a CPR most clearly affects appropriation externalities.

Storage lessens the uncertainty that aggravates appropriation externalities. Storage can smooth flow variations in a CPR, deferring surpluses for later use. Appropriators may be able not only to understand better the relationship of current appropriation activities to future flows but to exercise a greater degree of control over that relationship. Storage also reduces the incentive to follow "first capture" or "use it or lose it" strategies that drive appropriation externalities in many CPRs. If appropriators can store flows, cycles of depletion may be interrupted before they pass a critical threshold and move toward extinction.

Without storage, even determining what a quota allocation scheme means can be difficult. As Hannesson (1989b, 467) points out, "Fluctuations in the abundance of fish stocks would appear to cause problems when the stocks are being managed by catch quotas. Such fluctuations are likely to make it necessary to vary annual catch quotas, and variations in annual catch quotas, one suspects, are economically disadvantageous." Hannesson reviews the different formulas considered by a government agency intending to set up a total allowable catch system. One method is for an agency to determine the total allowable catch and then assign individual quotas as a percentage of it. A second method is to assign fixed and unchanging quantities over time. If this is done, some agency must be set up that buys quotas in "bad" years and sells quotas in "good" years (Hannesson 1989a). Instead of physical storage, the agency would have to buy and sell rights to smooth the natural fluctuations that occur in most fishery stocks. Careful theoretical work has shown that the best formula to use for allocation depends on many situational factors and cannot be determined in a general way for all fisheries (Hannesson 1989b).

It is thus easy to see why appropriators may be more reluctant to accept allocation schemes based on individual quotas or quantity restrictions when their resource facility lacks storage. In a resource with storage, quantity assignments may not only be feasible, but may even be made variable, depending on the availability of stored units—for example, quantity assignments may be increased at time t to draw down the number of units in storage, and decreased at time $(t + 1)$ to replenish the number of units in storage. In resources with storage, appropriators may be less likely to fight over each other's appropriation activities. They may be more willing to defer or relocate their appropriation activities if they do conflict. In large-scale irrigation systems, storage tanks at the watercourse level help to reduce the coordination load of the system-level management (Wade and Seckler 1990). With these tanks, irrigators are able to match water supplies to local irrigation needs more precisely, which may not be possible if the system-level management has to bear all the information and transaction costs needed to fine-tune water supplies to various watercourses.

Storage and Provision Problems

Storage affects appropriators' willingness to contribute to development and maintenance by increasing the certainty that appropriators will be able to capture the benefits of their efforts. In resources with storage, appropriators can be more certain that actions taken to augment or maintain the resource and the flows it generates will provide them with greater availability of valued resource units in the future. Absence of storage means that appropriators cannot "bank" units in the resource.

On the other hand, while storage enhances appropriators' prospects for overcoming some maintenance failures, it also adds to the number of aspects of the system that must be maintained. Storage facilities (natural or human made) must themselves be maintained, which increases the possibility for maintenance failure to occur. *A priori* estimation of whether the maintenance benefits of storage in a typical CPR will outweigh the additional maintenance costs is difficult.

Stationarity, Storage, and Information

For appropriators to overcome higher order dilemmas, achieve agreements, and enforce rules, they need information about the structure of the problems they encounter. Most CPRs that occur in field settings are sufficiently complex to make obtaining reliable information problematic. The boundaries, capacity, yield, and other properties of such a CPR (including the identities of those appropriators whose actions must be coordinated) are known imperfectly at best. Obtaining reliable information is costly.

Physical attributes, such as stationarity and storage, significantly affect appropriators' incentives and capabilities to devise rules because of their impact on the type of information available to appropriators. Both attributes affect the level of reliable information and the costs of obtaining information. All other things equal, adequate information about the quantity and quality of resource units, and about patterns or trends in quantity or quality, is more costly to obtain in CPRs without storage and with mobile resource units. Other things equal, agreement among appropriators about the incidence and causes of problems, and the appropriate means of resolving those problems, may be attained more easily in CPRs with stationary and/or stored resource units.

Of course, appropriators of CPRs with storage capability must learn about that capability in order to take advantage of it. Acquiring information about storage capability and its relation to the flow depends on the type of storage involved. When farmers build a surface reservoir to cover one acre of land with a rim that will allow up to a known depth of water, they can install markers at low cost and compute exactly how much water is stored. The cost of computing the amount of water stored in a large dam is higher. Once computed, simple algorithms can be used to translate water height into water volume. The cost of computing the amount of water stored in a groundwater basin is even greater and depends on the availability of a geologic survey and good data about precipitation and water levels over time. The presence or feasibility of storage may reduce some information costs but raise others.

Stationarity and Information about Quantities Appropriated

When resource units are confined to a given location, it is not only easier to obtain accurate information about sustainable harvests, it is frequently easier to meter individual appropriation.[18] The cost of metering depends on the size of the resource itself, the number of entry points, whether resource units are sold in one market or many markets, and many other factors. In cases where resource access is limited to relatively short "harvesting seasons," however, it may be efficient to establish relatively costly metering systems. The enforcement cost per harvested unit is relatively low because of the concentration of effort during the limited harvesting period. Clearly any limits on appropriation (whether they are on quantity harvested or length of the harvesting season) can imply that capital used in harvesting sits idle. If the tools used in harvesting are not overly expensive, however, the gains from limiting the harvest season, in terms of preserving the regenerative capacity of the resource and keeping enforcement costs low, can offset the losses from idle capital.[19]

Conclusions

The answer that we can now give to the third core question posed in chapter 1 is that many institutional and physical variables are indeed important in affecting the behavior of appropriators and the outcomes achieved. On the institutional side, we expect appropriators to be more successful in solving CPR dilemmas when they can (1) define access conditions; (2) regulate appropria-

---

18. Although our work is exclusively concerned with renewable resources, this same observation holds with even greater force in the case of nonrenewable resources.

19. When the costs of metering and enforcement are taken into account, some of the rules adopted by self-organized appropriator groups might well turn out to be among the more efficient rules given the lower costs of monitoring and enforcing compliance with these rules. See the argument made by Andersen and Sutinen 1984 and by A. Scott 1979.

tion in terms of quantity, space, or technology; and (3) monitor and enforce these rules. Further, when boundary, authority, monitoring, and sanctioning rules are defined and enforced internally, the outcomes achieved are likely to be more efficient than those achieved when the rules are imposed externally.

On the physical side, we can expect local appropriators to be able to solve their own CPR problems more effectively when the costs of obtaining relevant information about both the resource facility and the flow of resource units are relatively low in comparison with the benefits that can be achieved through successful institutional design. We have focused specifically on the effect of storage and stationarity on the costs of gaining reliable information needed to design effective rules. Obviously the size of a CPR is also relevant. In our initial studies of small-scale CPRs, the size of the CPR facility has not varied substantially enough to demonstrate the importance of pure size. This was a conscious strategy to keep the systems we studied relatively comparable. We conjecture that the costs of ascertaining key information needed to design more effective institutions (as well as the likelihood of heterogeneous interests) rises as the size of a CPR rises. Future research in which larger CPRs are included should provide more insight into the relationship between CPR size and effectiveness of rules.

Part 4
Conclusion

CHAPTER 15

Cooperation and Social Capital

We began this book with a discussion of the fishers of Brixham Harbor and the power companies using The Geysers. We contrasted their unresolved CPR dilemmas with the improved situations of several groundwater basins in southern California, where users were involved in the design of new institutions. Thus, our first concern was with individuals facing problems in field settings. In order to grapple successfully with that concern, however, we have had to focus on issues that are of more theoretical than immediate policy interest. Some readers looking for general solutions to CPR problems may be disappointed with what they have found so far in this book. We hope, instead, that the reader has recognized the importance of theoretical issues for the development of policy analysis that is grounded on empirically supported theory. A policy is only as good as the theory underlying it.

Theoretical Choices in Doing Policy Analysis

In the empirical sections of this volume, we have found some support for theoretical predictions derived from the theory of fully rational individuals in finitely repeated, complete information CPR games. In CPR dilemmas where individuals do not know one another, cannot communicate effectively, and thus cannot develop agreements, norms, and sanctions, aggregate predictions derived from models of rational individuals in a noncooperative game receive substantial support. These are sparse environments and full rationality appears to be a reasonable assumption in them.

We would advise anyone in field situations closely matching these conditions to expect others to select strategies that generate aggregate outcomes close to Nash equilibrium and to act accordingly. In large-scale CPR dilemmas where communication opportunities for all parties are extremely limited, such an expectation means that others are likely to overappropriate, underprovide, and/or engage in high levels of conflict about assignment and technological externality problems. If faced with the necessity of acting in such situations ourselves, we would follow this advice. We would also try hard to find a way to get out of such unproductive situations or to change their structure.

In richer environments that vary from the institutionally sparse homeland of noncooperative game theory in ways that do not affect the strategic structure of the modeled game, some predictions based on the same theoretical foundations are not supported by our empirical investigations. Simply allowing individuals to talk with one another is a sufficient change in the decision environment to make a substantial difference in behavior, even though promises made without external enforcers are considered to be theoretically irrelevant. Individuals in many field settings not only come to agreements but craft their own rules and enforce these rules without relying extensively on external authorities. Even in the southern California groundwater cases where formal courts and government officials were an important part of the institutional facilities used by participants, the importance of external authorities lay more in the reliable technical information and in the arenas for negotiation they provided than in their design of rules. Designing rules was largely left to the participants themselves. Once the groundwater producers designed their own rules, external authorities assisted in monitoring and enforcing those rules in conjunction with local users.

Readers of chapter 9 will have a variety of reactions to our appeal to bounded rationality as an explanation of the empirical anomalies we have encountered. Some will see that appeal as an indictment of the use of rationality in game-theoretic models of CPR situations. This is not our intention, and we hope to dissuade anyone from drawing such a conclusion. Others will see this appeal as an unwarranted attack on rational choice theories. Again, this is not our intention, and we hope to dissuade anyone from drawing that conclusion. We conclude from our work that assuming fully rational play in a noncooperative game gives us useful and powerful tools to analyze CPR dilemmas. We will continue to assume rational play in noncooperative games as important theoretical tools relevant to our future work. The structure and analytical fabric of this book would not be possible without these tools. Still, all tools have limits. All artisans should know how to use their tools.

It is because we find complementarity in diverse theories and models that we need the IAD framework presented in chapter 2. This framework provides a set of paradigmatic questions to ask, a metalanguage in which to ask them, and a spectrum of variable types for analyzing any microsetting. In order to use tools, one has to have a language about tools—their uses, strengths, and limits. To talk about any particular theoretical language, one needs a metalanguage to engage in the discourse. Game theory provides tools for solving games. To solve a game, one has to develop a model of that game. To puzzle, evaluate, and change that model, one uses game theory as a metalanguage. The IAD framework is a metalanguage for discussing various questions about theories—game theory, economic theory, rational choice theory, bounded rationality, and public choice theory. These are our essential theoretical tools, and we are responsible for using them properly and treating them with respect.

Thus, we search for the appropriate conjunction of theories of bounded rationality and full rationality. Both provide tools that can be used to understand how individuals act in diverse situations. In simple situations, full rationality models will continue to be the most economic and powerful tools we have for predicting and explaining human behavior. In complex situations, however, it is often unreasonable to assume that individuals can undertake complete analyses and adopt unchanging strategies for a long series of repeated games. Efforts to explain cooperation in such settings based on full rationality have had to make assumptions that we do not find appropriate for explaining behavior of real decision makers with limited analytical abilities. Assuming that individuals, who are making decisions in a time frame that cannot exceed two hours, face an infinitely long sequence of decisions is rather dubious. Assuming that individuals would actually employ grim trigger strategies if someone were to break an agreement is not empirically supported. Assuming that individuals undertake incredible feats of calculation that are required under assumptions of incomplete information seems to us to go in the direction of assuming even higher levels of calculating skills rather than the lower levels we observe in empirical settings.

For scholars who are interested in understanding human behavior in field settings and in developing better polices—ones that are genuine reforms—there are reasons to employ assumptions of both full and bounded rationality selectively. The former is especially useful for the development of tight theoretical models. If an analyst wants to know what rational, self-interested individuals, without normative connections to one another, would do in a particular physical and institutional setting, game equilibrium models based on full rationality are essential techniques to provide an initial answer to this question. The series of games illustrated in chapter 4, created by changing rule configurations, would be difficult to analyze without the tools used in that chapter. Since the rules analyzed were stylized versions of rules discovered in empirical settings, the analysis provides an understanding of why such rules work in practice, even in environments where individuals may not be communicating or sharing much sense of community other than a willingness to abide by these rules.

For understanding human behavior in settings where complexity and uncertainty swamp the limited calculation capabilities of normal humans, however, bounded rationality is a more appealing assumption. In these settings, individuals do not appear to perform a complete analysis of all future moves and then decide—once and for all—on a strategy of how to play the entire game facing them. Instead, they take shortcuts, and sometimes detours, to arrive at their actual play. The more remote is a behavioral assumption from observed behavior, the less likely is it that the assumption will be useful for policy purposes. In some cases, game equilibrium models of rational play lead to an outcome set where players can do almost anything and still be consistent with the theory. The prediction that individuals might do anything from a large set of feasible strategies is neither useful nor precise.

Assuming that individuals adopt heuristics and learn from past experience enables one to come much closer to predicting and explaining human behavior and outcomes in complex situations. For example, we predict that in most settings where individuals have a chance to communicate effectively with one another and develop joint agreements, they will use measured responses to cope with potential deviations. We specify a distinct reaction space that we expect to see used if individuals use measured-response heuristics. The subspace that counts as a measured response is a small box theoretically carved out of the large space of feasible outcomes. We predict that if most early responses are in the "measured response box" and few responses are "large," subjects will achieve outcomes that approach optimality. The prediction is sustained by our initial evidence. Obviously, further work is needed to increase confidence in these predictions.

The difference between the type of heuristics we propose and traditional game analysis is important. As mathematical objects, games have solutions and game theorists find them. Ordinary players are another matter. The play of even the simplest games usually involves an initial sense of an ambiguous situation and some kind of characteristic orientation toward ambiguity (V. Ostrom 1994). In field settings, individuals have to learn from mistakes and acquire insight into the strategic structure of the situation. The heuristic for a good poker player, as opposed to the theory of poker, differ. Small changes in the "rules of the house" can make a major difference in the strategic structure of a game. When one moves from parlor games to CPRs in natural settings, the number of potential game structures that could be involved in a CPR situation is astronomical. We can never expect to know all of the games that could be constructed by real players in real settings. As we have seen in the experimental laboratory, small changes can make a major difference in the behavior of those involved. Given this variety, it is no wonder that human behavior approaches, but only approaches, full rationality. Models based on full rationality assumptions will be the most useful when applied to simple, repeated situations that are not subject to easy reconstitution by the participants themselves.

Thus, we think it is important when analyzing complex empirical settings to recognize that individuals have both less and more capabilities than assumed in full rationality models. In such situations, individuals are less capable of making complete analyses than would rational individuals. This leads them to make decisions sequentially in light of what they learn about the situation, rather than in a once-and-for-all calculation of a complete strategy. On the other hand, individuals may be more capable of changing their situations and of adopting workable heuristics (norms) than is typically presumed. Individuals who start as strangers with no normative relationship to one another may soon begin to discuss a problem with one another and eventually acquire a sense of community and moral responsibility. The capability of humans to agree upon rules that structure their own games has not been taken sufficiently into account in traditional analysis. We hope this book will help change that in the future.

In an empirical setting where individuals have at least some autonomy to decide on their own rules, we can also develop useful predictions. If the interests of the individuals involved are relatively symmetric, face-to-face communication is possible, and the situation is relatively simple, we expect individuals to select rules that are

1. already known to them, either by experience or by reputation;[1]
2. easy to learn, follow, and monitor;
3. likely to reduce the complexity of the situation; and
4. perceived as likely to improve joint outcomes.

For example, if individuals face an assignment problem, such as the one we discuss in chapter 4, we expect that they will draw on their prior experience to devise ways of allocating space or time to participants. If many assignment problems with which they are familiar are resolved by using "first in time, first in right" rules, it comes as no surprise that such a rule is proposed and adopted by participants anxious to improve upon the status quo. Alternatively, if they are more familiar with rotation systems rather than "first in time, first in right" rules, it is likely that individuals will develop a rotation system of some sort.

Rules do not operate by themselves. To be implemented successfully, participants must be able to understand rules and know how to make them work. This knowledge is part of the social capital that individuals develop over time when they have the autonomy to do so. Like all forms of capital, social capital takes a long time to develop and can be destroyed rapidly. Shared understandings about rules that tend to improve outcomes in some settings may be more important in enabling individuals to achieve higher outcomes through cooperation than extensive, written mandates that can never be fully understood or implemented.

Rules are used at times as tools for reducing the complexity of the

---

1. Borrowing rules to use in one setting from others is a time-honored practice. Many localities in Europe, for example, adopted the charters of other localities perceived to be relatively similar and to be successfully governed.

situations that individuals face. As we show in chapter 3, the more actions that participants can take, the more complex the strategic calculation for all participants. In very complex settings, it is difficult for participants to gain sufficient understanding of the transformations linking individual actions to outcomes. Simply reducing the number of authorized actions available to all participants may enable them to understand more fully the consequences of various strategies in the reduced subspace.

Individuals appropriating from the same resource and dealing with each other over a long period of time have many opportunities to make small adjustments in the rules they initially adopt. As they learn more and more about the structure of their resource, the strategies used by other participants, and joint outcomes achieved, they can change rules so as to experience improvement over time. Lack of conformance to their agreed-upon sharing and assignment rules will be seen as evidence either that these rules are not well suited to local circumstances or that incentives to cheat overwhelm current monitoring and sanctioning efforts.

Just as verbal agreements in the lab may be undone by a few individuals who engage in large deviations, verbal agreements in the field may be undone by a few individuals who do not follow agreed-upon strategies. Boundedly rational individuals with heuristics that involve cooperation and extending trust are often able to reach and sustain agreements. Boundedly rational individuals without such heuristics are not. The latter are prisoners of their own deep (and under some circumstances, justified) distrust of others. Adding modest self-monitoring and self-sanctioning capabilities to verbal agreements, however, helps prevent many agreements from unraveling. Such arguments can withstand the predations of a few or the temptations that all may face over the course of time. Measured response heuristics backed with moderate sanctioning capabilities appear to be used by participants in many different types of field situations, including establishing and sustaining international agreements (Keohane 1984, 1986; L. Martin 1992; Oye 1986).

Prior studies of robust CPR institutions have found that self-organized systems tend to rely on graduated sanctions starting with small fines or verbal rebukes that constitute hardly more than a symbolic deterrent (E. Ostrom 1990).[2] Nevertheless, such small sanctions appear to be very effective in

---

2. A very recent study of indigenous forest institutions in Nepal provides several instances of these kinds of graduated rules. In the village of Seli, for example, the villagers have devised rules related to harvesting from a community governed forest. Violators of these rules are fined in cash. Chhetri and Pandey describe the penalty system as follows:

> Someone violating the regulation for the first time generally pays a penalty of five rupees which goes up to Rs 50 and Rs 150 for the second and third violations respectively. A fourth-time violator is tried in front of all the user members and they may fix any amount of fine deemed appropriate depending on the seriousness of the violation. (1992, 25)

The researchers mention that they were told that almost everyone in the village has been penalized

showing that rule infractions have been detected and in foretelling the promise of stronger sanctions, if necessary, in the future. Thus, it appears that sanctions often developed in field settings use a similar approach to punishment as the measured responses observed for players in our CPR communication experiments.

We do not claim that the rules adopted by boundedly rational individuals during a learning process achieve optimality. In laboratory settings with all necessary information for finding an optimal solution, subjects frequently came tantalizingly close to, without actually reaching, the optimum. Very few field settings generate the quality of information that laboratory subjects have at their disposal. There is also a question of how individuals in field settings process the information they do have. Field settings are so wrapped up in complexity and uncertainty that *satisfactory* rules-in-use are a significant achievement, regardless of whether such individuals can actually achieve the optimal solution.

It is also possible that initial decisions to adopt a particular rule reduce the possibility of ever achieving a fully optimal outcome. When rules are used in part to reduce complexity so learning can occur, the best outcome may exist in a subspace that was cut off early in the process of crafting rules. One can expect that the efforts of individuals to constitute and improve their own rule systems are likely to improve the outcomes they achieve. They may even discover local optima. Whether global optima are ever discovered by participants (or, for that matter by external officials) in highly complex field settings is far less probable. One can expect path dependence to be as important a constraint in the design of institutions as it is in the design of technology (see Arthur 1989; North 1990). As we point out in chapter 14, the CPR problems faced in many field settings—characterized by resources that lack stationarity and storage—are particularly difficult for participants, observers, government officials, or anyone else to solve. More theoretical and empirical work is needed to identify those types of empirical settings where the individuals involved are most likely to develop satisfactory rules-in-use and those where perverse incentives or lack of relevant and accurate information make it extraordinarily difficult for self-organization to achieve satisfactory results.

Further, rules that are easy to learn, to follow, and to monitor are not always the rules that lead to the optimal return derived from a model that assumes away uncertainty, monitoring, and sanctioning costs. Many farmer-owned and governed irrigation systems, for example, use simple rotation systems where farmers with adjacent land are assigned sequential rights to

---

at least once because the rules are strictly interpreted. The fines go into a common fund used to buy utensils and equipment for communal work in the forest and are loaned to villagers at "reasonable" rates of interest. The exchange rate at the time of this study would have been about $1.00 = Rs 40.

water. These systems are extremely easy to operate. The sequence is frequently repeated. No one farmer really needs to know the entire sequence (Netting 1974). All each farmer needs to know is which day of the week and which hour is assigned to a particular plot, or alternatively, who are the two or three farmers whose turns come immediately prior in the sequence. Based primarily on technical grounds, water engineers have frequently pointed out that higher crop yields could be obtained by using more complex mechanisms to allocate water. Since these proposals do not take into account the added transaction costs involved in administering, monitoring, and sanctioning violators under a more complex rule system, it is not clear whether the theoretical gains in efficiency are operationally feasible.

Our evidence suggests that individuals with considerable experience crafting their own rules acquire a larger repertoire of satisfactory rules than those without such experience. Individuals in relatively simple systems are apt to develop rules more nearly optimal than individuals in more complex systems, especially systems involving substantial asymmetries of interest. Individuals facing complex systems may have a much harder time learning what works and what does not work. If such individuals are also participants in overlapping organizational arrangements that help generate information about successful efforts to govern CPR institutions, then they have a better chance at testing, modifying, and improving their rules.

Policy prescriptions based solely on models that generate deficient equilibria are likely to recommend either that external authorities impose and enforce rules or that no external help is needed. The prescription that external authorities must impose change leads to attempts to impose uniform national or regional laws. In any country where the attributes of the physical world vary substantially across locations, the same set of rules that engender positive outcomes in one physical location can engender negative outcomes in other locations. The imposition of uniform rules can lead to dramatic differences in outcomes or to extreme discretion on the part of officials who adjust the uniform rules to fit local circumstances. Such discretion opens the door to corruption. Those who are adversely affected are tempted to bribe officials to look the other way.[3] Encouraging federations of self-organized CPR users to exchange information about their experiences may be more important in enhancing the efficiency and equity of CPR use patterns than attempting to design and enforce uniform rules devised by an external authority.

By the same token, the broad policy prescription that no intervention is ever necessary, since individuals will always solve these problems, is equally suspect. Once one recognizes how difficult it is to obtain information about

---

3. Robert Wade (1988a) carefully documents how local villagers may engage in collective action to obtain funds to bribe government officials just to stay away.

the structure and flow from a CPR in the field, the importance of agencies that provide reliable information about local CPRs (such as the United States Geological Survey and the California Department of Natural Resources) is immediately obvious. Assuming that individuals have the information to calculate optima diverts attention from the importance of providing accurate, reliable information as part of the institutional arrangements that facilitate improved outcomes. Further, it is important to recognize that individuals can develop endogenous sanctioning systems when they are dealing with a well-developed community of understanding, but that these systems may need to be complemented by external authorities. Self-organized CPRs may need access to external enforcement of their agreements from time to time to ensure that common understandings are shared and enforced. Appropriate policies involve the provision of fair and inexpensive conflict resolution and back-up enforcement mechanisms, rather than the imposition of rule making and rule enforcement by external officials, on the one hand, or complete neglect on the other.

Surmounting CPR Dilemmas

The capacity to change the structure of a situation is a variable in field settings, not a constant. In most enduring relationships, participants have the capability to call "time out—it's time we talked about this situation and tried to change it for the better." In many CPR situations, it is necessary to examine the process of rule change. While playing short-term games within the existing institutional and parametric structure, we often find participants engaged in a long-term process of redefining their institutional structure.[4] Indeed, it is precisely this process that gives us renewed hope in the sustainability of CPRs the world over. Even the most degraded CPR may yet be saved by changes in the behavior of its appropriators.

In this book, we have examined how individuals behave in a multiplicity of CPR dilemmas. In many of these, but not all, individuals overcome the temptations present to overuse the CPR. They do this by communicating their desires to reach acceptable sharing agreements. They build trust in these agreements by extending reciprocity through the use of personal heuristics like measured reactions. In difficult settings, they use measured reactions to bolster their agreements as well as imposing sanctions on those who violate agreements. Individuals who extend reciprocity to others and who learn to

---

4. Chapter 4 of this book is an example of a formal treatment of how diverse rules affect the structure of a CPR assignment problem. Milgrom, North, and Weingast (1990) overtly analyze the evolution of court institutions and the effect of these changes on trade patterns. Calvert 1993 addresses the importance of making rule changes endogenous rather than treating rules always as exogenous. See also E. Ostrom and Gardner 1993.

craft their own effective rules can accomplish more than individuals who do not, especially when they can identify others following the same heuristics.[5] Such individuals achieve more than predicted by noncooperative game theory as currently understood.

Our analysis of successful self-organized CPR institutions makes us optimistic about human capacities to overcome the "social dilemmas" they face. It also makes us pessimistic about the likelihood of self-organized improvements in three types of settings. The first is where individuals have no expectation of mutual trust and no means of building trust through communication and continued interaction. The second is where mistrust is already rampant, and communication and continued interactions do not reduce the level of distrust. The third is where many, but not all, individuals are willing to extend reciprocity to others but lack authority to create their own self-governing institutions. Without the capacity to create rules and establish the means of monitoring and sanctioning these rules, reciprocity alone is frequently insufficient to cope with individuals who succumb to the temptations to cheat. If those who are preyed upon cannot develop sanctions against their predators, the likelihood of achieving higher outcomes through their own efforts is low.

Our findings from field studies also alert us to the differences among CPR situations and to the problems involved in crafting appropriate rules in complex situations. These difficulties may be overcome when external authorities facilitate the acquisition of reliable information, the development of long-term contracts, and enforcement mechanisms to complement internal mechanisms. The difficulties do not simply disappear by presuming that larger governmental units must impose solutions on those facing complex, highly variable settings. Finding solutions of any sort in these turbulent environments is a difficult and costly task. Efforts to establish one set of rules to cover large territories, which include significantly different types of local environments, are as problematic as the presumption that those involved may find adequate solutions entirely on their own.

The capacity of CPR users to govern themselves is often a necessary condition for overcoming the temptations involved in a CPR dilemma. The capacity to design and enforce one's own rules, however, is not a sufficient condition to ensure the resolution of difficult and complex dilemmas. Without some willingness to extend reciprocity to others, while building trust and better rules, initial agreements can rapidly unravel. Without access to reliable information about complex processes, participants may not understand the

---

5. In a very interesting paper, Charles F. Sabel (1993) discusses the extent of constitutional ordering in many different private and public settings and how these developments are overlooked by scholars using standard theories of decision making *within* already created settings.

ambiguous situations they face. The likelihood of crafting and sustaining rules in situations involving many exogenous changes is dramatically reduced. The capacity to design their own rules will not enhance the outcomes achieved by the nontrusting and narrowly selfish individuals of the world, but will enhance the outcomes of those who are prepared to extend reciprocity to others and interact with others with similar inclinations.[6] Those who have developed forms of mutual trust and social capital can utilize these assets to craft institutions that avert the CPR dilemma and arrive at reasonable outcomes.

6. See the insightful recent book by Robert D. Putnam, with Robert Leonardi and Raffaella Nanetti, which explores the question of why new democratic institutions are effectively used by citizens in some parts of Italy and not others.

Bibliography

Abel, Martin. 1977. "Irrigation Systems in Taiwan: Management of a Decentralized Public Enterprise." In *Water Resources Problems in Developing Countries*, ed. K. William Easter and Lee R. Martin, 29–45. Minneapolis: University of Minnesota, Economic Development Center.

Acheson, James M. 1989. "Where Have All the Exploiters Gone? Co-Management of the Maine Lobster Industry." In *Common Property Resources: Ecology and Community-Based Sustainable Development*, ed. Fikret Berkes, 199–217. London: Belhaven.

Advisory Commission on Intergovernmental Relations (Ronald J. Oakerson). 1987. *The Organization of Local Public Economies*. Washington, D.C.: U.S. Advisory Commission on Intergovernmental Relations.

——— (Ronald J. Oakerson, Roger B. Parks, and Henry A. Bell). 1988. *Metropolitan Organization: The St. Louis Case*. Washington, D.C.: U.S. Advisory Commission on Intergovernmental Relations.

——— (Roger B. Parks and Ronald J. Oakerson). 1992. *Metropolitan Organization: The Allegheny County Case*. Washington, D.C.: U.S. Advisory Commission on Intergovernmental Relations.

Agnello, Richard, and Lawrence Donnelly. 1975. "Property Rights and Efficiency in the Oyster Industry." *Journal of Law and Economics* 18:521–33.

Agrawal, Arun. 1992. "Risks, Resources, and Politics: Studies in Institutions and Resource Use from India." Ph.D. diss., Duke University.

Alexander, Paul. 1982. *Sri Lankan Fishermen: Rural Capitalism and Peasant Society*. Canberra: Australian National University.

Allen, P. M., and J. M. McGlade. 1987. "Modelling Complex Human Systems: A Fisheries Example." *European Journal of Operational Research* 30 (2): 147–67.

Andersen, Peder, and John G. Sutinen. 1984. "The Economics of Fisheries Law Enforcement." In *Papers Presented at the First Meeting of the European Association for Law and Economics*, ed. Göran Skog, 1–15. Lund: University of Lund.

Anderson, Eugene N., Jr., and Marja L. Anderson. 1977. "Fishing in Troubled Waters: Research on the Chinese Fishing Industry in West Malaysia." *Asian Folklore and Social Life Monographs*, vol. 100. Taipei: Orient Cultural Service.

Anderson, Jay M. 1977. "A Model of the Commons." In *Managing the Commons*, ed. Garrett Hardin and John Baden, 38–41. San Francisco: W. H. Freeman.

Anderson, Lee G. 1986. *The Economics of Fisheries Management*. Rev. ed. Baltimore: Johns Hopkins University Press.

Anderson, Terry L., and Peter J. Hill. 1975. "The Evolution of Property Rights: A Study of the American West." *Journal of Law and Economics* 12:163–79.

Andreoni, James. 1988. "Why Free Ride? Strategies and Learning in Public Goods Experiments." *Journal of Public Economics* 37:291–304.

Arnold, J. E. M., and J. Gabriel Campbell. 1986. "Collective Management of Hill Forests in Nepal: The Community Forestry Development Project." In *Proceedings of the Conference on Common Property Resource Management*, National Research Council, 425–54. Washington, D.C.: National Academy Press.

Arrow, Kenneth. 1966. *Social Choice and Individual Values*. 2d ed. New York: Wiley.

Arthur, Brian. 1989. "Competing Technologies, Increasing Returns, and Lock-In by Historical Events." *Economic Journal* 99:116–31.

Ascher, William, and Robert Healy. 1990. *Natural Resource Policy Making in Developing Countries: Environment, Economic Growth, and Income Distribution*. Durham, N.C.: Duke University Press.

Asian Development Bank. 1973. *Regional Workshop on Irrigation Water Management*. Manila, Philippines: Asian Development Bank.

Atkinson, Edwin T. [1882] 1973. *The Himalayan Gazetteer*. Vols. 1–3. New Delhi: Cosmo Publications.

Aumann, Robert J. 1987. "Correlated Equilibrium as an Expression of Bayesian Rationality." *Econometrica* 55:1–18.

Axelrod, Robert. 1984. *The Evolution of Cooperation*. New York: Basic Books.

Bacdayan, Albert S. 1980. "Mountain Irrigators in the Philippines." In *Irrigation and Agricultural Development in Asia*, ed. E. Walter Coward, Jr., 172–85. Ithaca, N.Y.: Cornell University Press.

Bagnoli, Mark, and Michael McKee. 1991. "Voluntary Contribution Games: Efficient Private Provision of Public Goods." *Economic Inquiry* 29 (2): 351–66.

Baines, Graham B. K. 1989. "Traditional Resource Management in the Melanesian South Pacific: A Development Dilemma." In *Common Property Resources: Ecology and Community-Based Sustainable Development*, ed. Fikret Berkes, 273–95. London: Belhaven.

Banks, Jeffrey S., and Randall L. Calvert. 1992a. "A Battle-of-the-Sexes Game with Incomplete Information." *Games and Economic Behavior* 4:1–26.

———. 1992b. "Communication and Efficiency in Coordination Games." Working paper. University of Rochester, Department of Economics and Department of Political Science.

Barrett, Gene. 1991. "'The Fish Pot Ban': Artisanal Overfishing and State Mismanagement in Bermuda." Paper presented at the Annual Meeting of the International Association for the Study of Common Property, Winnipeg, Canada, September.

Barro, Robert J., and Paul M. Romer. 1987. "Ski-Lift Pricing, with Applications to Labor and Other Markets." *American Economic Review* 77:875–91.

Barzel, Yoram. 1968. "Optimal Timing of Innovations." *Review of Economics and Statistics* 50:348–55.

———. 1974. "A Theory of Rationing by Waiting." *Journal of Law and Economics* 17:73–95.

Becker, Gary S. 1976. *The Economic Approach to Human Behavior*. Chicago: University of Chicago Press.

Bell, Frederick W. 1972. "Technological Externalities and Common Property Resources: An Empirical Study of the U.S. Lobster Industry." *Journal of Political Economy* 80:148–58.

Bendor, Jonathan. 1987. "In Good Times and Bad: Reciprocity in an Uncertain World." *American Political Science Review* 31:531–58.

Bendor, Jonathan, and Dilip Mookherjee. 1987. "Institutional Structure and the Logic of Ongoing Collective Action." *American Political Science Review* 81:129–54.

———. 1990. "Norms, Third-Party Sanctions, and Cooperation." *Journal of Law, Economics, and Organization* 6:33–63.

Benoit, J., and V. Krishna. 1985. "Finitely Repeated Games." *Econometrica* 53:905–22.

Berkes, Fikret. 1977. "Fishery Resource Use in a Subarctic Indian Community." *Human Ecology* 5 (4): 289–307.

———. 1986. "Local-Level Management and the Commons Problem: A Comparative Study of Turkish Coastal Fisheries." *Marine Policy* 10 (July): 215–29.

———. 1987. "Common Property Resource Management and Cree Indian Fishermen in Subarctic Canada." In *The Question of the Commons: The Culture and Ecology of Communal Resources*, ed. Bonnie McCay and James Acheson, 66–91. Tucson: University of Arizona Press.

———, ed. 1989. *Common Property Resources: Ecology and Community-Based Sustainable Development*. London: Belhaven.

———. 1992. "Success and Failure in Marine Coastal Fisheries of Turkey." In *Making the Commons Work: Theory, Practice, and Policy*, ed. Daniel W. Bromley, 161–82. San Francisco: Institute for Contemporary Studies.

Bianco, William T., Peter T. Ordeshook, and George Tsebelis. 1990. "Crime and Punishment: Are One-Shot, Two-Person Games Enough?" *American Political Science Review* 84:569–86.

Blaikie, Piers M., and Harold Brookfield. 1987. *Land Degradation and Society*. London: Methuen.

Blaikie, Piers M., John C. Harriss, and Adam N. Pain. 1992. "The Management and Use of Common-Property Resources in Tamil Nadu, India." In *Making the Commons Work: Theory, Practice, and Policy*, ed. Daniel W. Bromley, 247–64. San Francisco: Institute for Contemporary Studies.

Blomquist, William. 1987a. "Getting Out of the Trap: Changing an Endangered Commons to a Managed Commons." Ph.D. diss., Indiana University.

———. 1987b. *The Performance of Institutions for Groundwater Management, Volume 1: Raymond Basin*. Bloomington: Indiana University, Workshop in Political Theory and Policy Analysis.

———. 1988a. *The Performance of Institutions for Groundwater Management, Volume 2: West Basin*. Bloomington: Indiana University, Workshop in Political Theory and Policy Analysis.

———. 1988b. *The Performance of Institutions for Groundwater Management, Vol-*

ume 3: Central Basin. Bloomington: Indiana University, Workshop in Political Theory and Policy Analysis.

———. 1988c. *The Performance of Institutions for Groundwater Management, Volume 5: Orange County*. Bloomington: Indiana University, Workshop in Political Theory and Policy Analysis.

———. 1988d. *The Performance of Institutions for Groundwater Management, Volume 6: The San Fernando Valley*. Bloomington: Indiana University, Workshop in Political Theory and Policy Analysis.

———. 1989. *The Performance of Institutions for Groundwater Management, Volume 8: The Mojave River Basin*. Bloomington: Indiana University, Workshop in Political Theory and Policy Analysis.

———. 1990a. *The Performance of Institutions for Groundwater Management, Volume 4: The San Gabriel Valley*. Bloomington: Indiana University, Workshop in Political Theory and Policy Analysis.

———. 1990b. *The Performance of Institutions for Groundwater Management, Volume 7: The Chino Basin*. Bloomington: Indiana University, Workshop in Political Theory and Policy Analysis.

———. 1990c. "Groundwater Management through Interjurisdictional Coordination." Paper presented at the Annual Donald G. Hagman Commemorative Conference, University of California, Los Angeles, March.

———. 1992. *Dividing the Waters: Governing Groundwater in Southern California*. San Francisco: Institute for Contemporary Studies.

Blomquist, William, and Elinor Ostrom. 1985. "Institutional Capacity and the Resolution of a Commons Dilemma." *Policy Studies Review* 5 (2): 383–93.

Blomquist, William, Edella Schlager, and Shui Yan Tang. 1991. "All CPRs Are Not Created Equal: Two Important Physical Characteristics and Their Relation to the Resolution of Commons Dilemmas." Paper presented at the Annual Meeting of the American Political Science Association, Washington, D.C., 29 August–1 September.

Bornstein, Gary, and Amnon Rapoport. 1988. "Intergroup Competition for the Provision of Step-Level Public Goods: Effects of Preplay Communication." *European Journal of Social Psychology* 18:125–42.

Bornstein, Gary, Amnon Rapoport, Lucia Kerpel, and Tani Katz. 1989. "Within- and Between-Group Communication in Intergroup Competition for Public Goods." *Journal of Experimental Social Psychology* 25:422–36.

Bottrall, Anthony. 1981. "Comparative Study of the Management and Organization of Irrigation Projects." World Bank Working Paper no. 458. Washington, D.C.: World Bank.

Brameld, Theodore. 1968. *Japan: Culture, Education, and Change in Two Communities*. New York: Holt, Rinehart and Winston.

Braver, Sanford L., and L. A. Wilson. 1984. "A Laboratory Study of Social Contracts as a Solution to Public Goods Problems: Surviving on the Lifeboat." Presented at a meeting of the Western Social Science Association, San Diego.

———. 1986. "Choices in Social Dilemmas: Effects of Communication within Subgroups." *Journal of Conflict Resolution* 30 (1): 51–62.

Brechner, Kevin. 1976. "An Experimental Analysis of Social Traps." *Journal of Experimental Social Psychology* 13:552–64.

Breton, Yvan D. 1973. "A Comparative Study of Rural Fishing Communities in Eastern Venezuela: An Anthropological Explanation of Economic Specialization." Ph.D. diss., Michigan State University.

Bromley, Daniel W. 1982a. "Improving Irrigated Agriculture: Institutional Reform and the Small Farmer." World Bank Staff Working Paper no. 531. Washington, D.C.: World Bank.

———. 1982b. "Land and Water Problems: An Institutional Perspective." *American Journal of Agricultural Economics* 64:834–44.

———, ed. 1992. *Making the Commons Work: Theory, Practice, and Policy.* San Francisco: Institute for Contemporary Studies.

Bromley, Daniel W., and Michael Cernea. 1989. "The Management of Common Property Natural Resources: Some Conceptual and Operational Fallacies." World Bank Discussion Paper no. 57. Washington, D.C.: World Bank.

Brookshire, David, Don Coursey, and Douglas Redington. 1989. "Special Interests in the Voluntary Provision of Public Goods." Typescript.

Buchanan, James M., and Gordon Tullock. 1962. *The Calculus of Consent.* Ann Arbor: University of Michigan Press.

Caldwell, Michael D. 1976. "Communication and Sex Effects in a Five-Person Prisoners' Dilemma Game." *Journal of Personality and Social Psychology* 33 (3): 273–80.

Calvert, Randall L. 1993. "Rational Actors, Equilibrium, and Social Institutions." In *Explaining Social Institutions*, ed. Jack Knight and Itai Sened. New York: Cambridge University Press, forthcoming.

Cass, Robert C., and Julian J. Edney. 1978. "The Commons Dilemma: A Simulation Testing the Effects of Resource Visibility and Territorial Division." *Human Ecology* 6 (4): 371–86.

Cernea, Michael M. 1985. *Putting People First: Sociological Variables in Rural Development.* New York: Oxford University Press.

Chambers, Robert. 1977. "Men and Water: The Organization and Operation of Irrigation." In *Green Revolution? Technology and Change in Rice-Growing Areas of Tamil Nadu and Sri Lanka*, ed. Bertram H. Farmer, 340–63. Boulder, Colo.: Westview.

———. 1980. "Basic Concepts in the Organization of Irrigation." In *Irrigation and Agricultural Development in Asia*, ed. E. Walter Coward, Jr., 28–50. Ithaca, N.Y.: Cornell University Press.

———. 1988. *Managing Canal Irrigation: Practical Analysis from South Asia.* New York: Cambridge University Press.

Chambers, Robert, and I. D. Carruthers. 1986. "Rapid Appraisal to Improve Canal Irrigation Performance: Experience and Options." Research Paper no. 3. International Irrigation Management Institute, Digana Village, Sri Lanka.

Cheung, Stephen N. S. 1970. "The Structure of a Contract and the Theory of a Non-Exclusive Resource." *Journal of Law and Economics* 13:45–70.

Chhetri, Ram Bahadur, and Tulsi R. Pandey. 1992. *User Group Forestry in the Far-*

Western Region of Nepal. Kathmandu, Nepal: International Centre for Integrated Mountain Development.

Chomsky, Noam. 1980. *Rules and Representations*. New York: Columbia University Press.

Christy, Francis T. 1982. "Territorial Use Rights in Marine Fisheries: Definitions and Conditions." FAO Fisheries Technical Paper no. 227. Food and Agriculture Organization of the United Nations, Rome.

Christy, Francis T., and Anthony Scott. 1965. *The Common Wealth in Ocean Fisheries: Some Problems of Growth and Economic Allocation*. Baltimore: Johns Hopkins University Press.

Ciriacy-Wantrup, Siegfried V., and Richard C. Bishop. 1975. "'Common Property' as a Concept in Natural Resource Policy." *Natural Resources Journal* 15: 713–27.

Clark, Colin. 1976. *Mathematical Bioeconomics: The Optimal Management of Renewable Resources*. New York: Wiley.

————. 1980. "Restricted Access to Common-Property Fishery Resources: A Game-Theoretic Analysis." In *Dynamic Optimization and Mathematical Economics*, ed. Pan-Tai Liu, 117–32. New York: Plenum.

Clugston, M. 1984. "Nova Scotia's Lobster Wars." *Maclean's* 84:14–18.

Coase, Ronald H. 1937. "The Nature of the Firm." *Economica* 4:386–405.

Coleman, James S. 1990. *Foundations of Social Theory*. Cambridge, Mass.: Harvard University Press.

Commons, John R. 1957. *Legal Foundations of Capitalism*. Madison: University of Wisconsin Press.

Copes, Parzival. 1986. "A Critical Review of the Individual Quota as a Device in Fisheries Management." *Land Economics* 62 (3): 278–91.

Cordell, John C. 1972. "The Developmental Ecology of an Estuarine Canoe Fishing System in Northeast Brazil." Ph.D. diss., Stanford University.

————. 1974. "The Lunar-Tide Fishing Cycle in Northeastern Brazil." *Ethnology* 13:379–92.

————. 1978a. "Carrying Capacity Analysis of Fixed Territorial Fishing." *Ethnology* 17:1–24.

————. 1978b. "Swamp Dwellers of Bahia." *Natural History* 87:62–74.

————. 1983. "Social Marginality and Sea Tenure in Brazilian Fishing." Occasional Papers in Latin American Studies Association no. 7. Joint Center for Latin American Studies, Stanford, Calif.

————. 1984. "Traditional Sea Tenure and Resource Management in Brazilian Coastal Fishing." In *Management of Coastal Lagoon Fisheries*, ed. James M. Kapetsky and George Lasserre, 429–38. GFCM Studies and Reviews no. 61. Rome: Food and Agriculture Organization of the United Nations.

Cordell, John C., and Margaret A. McKean. 1992. "Sea Tenure in Bahia, Brazil." In *Making the Commons Work: Theory, Practice, and Policy*, ed. Daniel W. Bromley, 183–205. San Francisco: Institute for Contemporary Studies.

Cornes, Richard, and Todd Sandler. 1986. *The Theory of Externalities, Public Goods, and Club Goods*. Cambridge: Cambridge University Press.

Coward, E. Walter, Jr. 1979. "Principles of Social Organization in an Indigenous Irrigation System." *Human Organization* 38 (1): 28–36.

———. 1980a. "Management Themes in Community Irrigation Systems." In *Irrigation and Agricultural Development in Asia*, ed. E. Walter Coward, Jr., 15–27. Ithaca, N.Y.: Cornell University Press.

———. 1980b. "Local Organization and Bureaucracy in a Lao Irrigation Project." In *Irrigation and Agricultural Development in Asia*, ed. E. Walter Coward, Jr., 329–44. Ithaca, N.Y.: Cornell University Press.

———. 1985. "Technical and Social Change in Currently Irrigated Regions: Rules, Roles, and Rehabilitation." In *Putting People First: Sociological Variables in Rural Development*, ed. Michael M. Cernea, 27–51. New York: Oxford University Press.

Coward, E. Walter, Jr., and Ahmed Badaruddin. 1979. "Village, Technology, and Bureaucracy: Patterns of Irrigation in Comilla District, Bangladesh." *Journal of Developing Areas* 31:431–40.

Cox, James, Vernon Smith, and James M. Walker. 1984. "Theory and Behavior of Multiple Unit Discriminative Price Auctions." *Journal of Finance* 34:983–1010.

———. 1988. "Theory and Individual Behavior of First Price Auctions." *Journal of Risk and Uncertainty* 1:61–99.

Crawford, Sue, and Elinor Ostrom. 1993. "A Grammar of Institutions." Working paper. Indiana University, Workshop in Political Theory and Policy Analysis.

Crawford, V. P. 1985. "Learning Behavior and Mixed Strategy Nash Equilibria." *Journal of Economic Behavior and Organization* 6:69–78.

Cross, John G. 1983. *A Theory of Adaptive Economic Behavior*. Cambridge: Cambridge University Press.

Cross, John G., and Melvin Guyer. 1980. *Social Traps*. Ann Arbor: University of Michigan Press.

Crutchfield, James A. 1961. "An Economic Evaluation of Alternative Methods of Fishery Regulation." *Journal of Law and Economics* 4:131–41.

Cruz, Federico A. 1975. "The Pinagbayanan Farmers' Association and Its Operation." In *Water Management in Philippine Irrigation Systems: Research and Operations*, ed. International Rice Research Institute, 243–58. Los Banos, Philippines: International Rice Research Institute.

Cruz, Wilfrido D. 1986. "Overfishing and Conflict in a Traditional Fishery: San Miguel Bay, Philippines." In *Proceedings of the Conference on Common Property Resource Management*, National Research Council, 115–35. Washington, D.C.: National Academy Press.

Curtis, Donald. 1991. *Beyond Government: Organisations for Common Benefit*. London: Macmillan.

Cushing, D. H. 1981. *Fisheries Biology: A Study in Population Dynamics*. 2d ed. Madison: University of Wisconsin Press.

Dahl, Robert A., and E. R. Tufte. 1973. *Size and Democracy*. Stanford, Calif.: Stanford University Press.

Dasgupta, Partha S. 1982. *The Control of Resources*. Cambridge, Mass.: Harvard University Press.

Dasgupta, Partha S., and Geoffrey M. Heal. 1979. *Economic Theory and Exhaustible Resources*. Garden City, N.J.: J. Nisbet.

Davenport, William H. 1956. "A Comparative Study of Two Jamaican Fishing Communities." Ph.D. diss., Yale University.

Davis, Adam F. 1975. "The Organization of Production and Market Relations in Nova Scotian Inshore Fishing Community." Ph.D. diss., University of Manitoba.

Davis, Anthony. 1984. "Property Rights and Access Management in the Small Boat Fishery: A Case Study from Southwest Nova Scotia." In *Atlantic Fisheries and Coastal Communities: Fisheries Decision-Making Case Studies*, ed. Cynthia Lamson and Arthur J. Hanson, 133–64. Halifax: Dalhousie Ocean Studies Programme.

Dawes, Robyn M. 1973. "The Commons Dilemma Game: An N-Person Mixed-Motive Game with a Dominating Strategy for Defection." *Oregon Research Institute Research Bulletin* 13:1–12.

Dawes, Robyn M., Jeanne McTavish, and Harriet Shaklee. 1977. "Behavior, Communication, and Assumptions about Other People's Behavior in a Commons Dilemma Situation." *Journal of Personality and Social Psychology* 35 (1): 1–11.

Dawes, Robyn M., John M. Orbell, Randy Simmons, and Alphons van de Kragt. 1986. "Organizing Groups for Collective Action." *American Political Science Review* 80:1171–85.

Dawes, Robyn M., John M. Orbell, and Alphons van de Kragt. 1984. "Normative Constraint and Incentive Compatible Design." University of Oregon, Department of Psychology. Typescript.

Dawson, Richard E., and James A. Robinson. 1963. "Inter-party Competition, Economic Variables, and Welfare Policies in the American States." *Journal of Politics* 25 (2) (June): 265–89.

de los Reyes, Romana P. 1980a. *Forty-seven Communal Gravity Systems: Organization Profiles*. Quezon City, Philippines: Ateneo de Manila University, Institute of Philippine Culture.

de los Reyes, Romana P. 1980b. *Managing Communal Gravity Systems: Farmers' Approaches and Implications for Program Planning*. Quezon City: Ateneo de Manila University, Institute of Philippine Culture.

de los Reyes, Romana P., S. Borlavian, G. Gatdula, and M. F. Viado. 1980. *Communal Gravity Systems: Four Case Studies*. Quezon City, Philippines: Ateneo de Manila University, Institute of Philippine Culture.

de Vries, Sjerp. 1991. *Egoism, Altruism, and Social Justice: Theory and Experiments on Cooperation in Social Dilemmas*. Amsterdam: Thesis Publishers.

Dickie, L. M. 1979. "Perspectives on Fisheries Biology and Implications for Management." *Journal of the Fisheries Research Board of Canada* 36:838–44.

Dorsey, Robert E. 1992. "The Voluntary Contributions Mechanism with Real Time Revisions." *Public Choice* 73 (3): 261–82.

Downing, Theodore E. 1974. "Irrigation and Moisture-Sensitive Periods: A Zapotec Case." In *Irrigation's Impact on Society*, ed. Theodore E. Downing and McGuire Gibson, 113–22. Tucson: University of Arizona Press.

Downs, Anthony. 1957. *An Economic Theory of Democracy*. New York: Harper and Row.

Dudley, Dean. 1993. "Essays on Individual Behavior in Social Dilemma Environments: An Experimental Analysis." Ph.D. diss., Indiana University, Department of Economics.

Dye, Thomas R. 1966. *Politics, Economics, and the Public*. Chicago: Rand McNally.

Easter, K. William, and Delane E. Welsch. 1986. "Priorities for Irrigation Planning and Investment." In *Irrigation Investment, Technology, and Management Strategies for Development*, ed. K. William Easter, 13–32. Boulder, Colo.: Westview.

Eavey, C. L., and G. J. Miller. 1982. "Committee Leadership and the Chairman's Power." Paper presented at the Annual Meeting of the American Political Science Association, Denver, 2–5 September.

Edney, Julian J., and Christopher S. Harper. 1978. "The Commons Dilemma: A Review of Contributions from Psychology." *Environmental Management* 2 (6): 491–507.

Eggertsson, Thráinn. 1990. *Economic Behavior and Institutions*. New York: Cambridge University Press.

El-Gamal, Mahmoud, Richard D. McKelvey, and Thomas R. Palfrey. 1991. "A Bayesian Sequential Experimental Study of Learning in Games." Social Science Working Paper no. 757. California Institute of Technology.

Ellickson, Robert C. 1991. *Order without Law: How Neighbors Settle Disputes*. Cambridge, Mass.: Harvard University Press.

Elster, Jon. 1983. *Explaining Technical Change*. Cambridge: Cambridge University Press.

———. 1989. *The Cement of Society: A Study of Social Order*. Cambridge: Cambridge University Press.

Epstein, Richard A. 1986. "Past and Future: The Temporal Dimension in the Law of Property." *Washington University Law Quarterly* 64 (Fall): 667–722.

Eshel, I. 1982. "Evolutionarily Stable Strategies and Viability Selection in Mendelian Populations." *Theoretical Population Biology* 22:204–17.

Eshel, I., and E. Akin. 1983. "Coevolutionary Instability of Mixed Nash Solutions." *Journal of Mathematical Biology* 18:123–33.

Faris, James C. 1972. *Cat Harbour: A Newfoundland Fishing Settlement*. Toronto: University of Toronto Press.

Feeny, David. 1988. "Agricultural Expansion and Forest Depletion in Thailand, 1900–1975." In *World Deforestation in the Twentieth Century*, ed. John F. Richard and Richard P. Tucker, 112–43. Durham, N.C.: Duke University Press.

———. 1993. "The Demand for and Supply of Institutional Arrangements." In *Rethinking Institutional Analysis and Development: Issues, Alternatives, and Choices*, ed. Vincent Ostrom, David Feeny, and Hartmut Picht, 159–209. San Francisco: Institute for Contemporary Studies.

Feeny, David, Fikret Berkes, Bonnie J. McCay, and James M. Acheson. 1990. "The Tragedy of the Commons: Twenty-Two Years Later." *Human Ecology* 18 (1): 1–19.

Fernea, Robert A. 1970. *Shaykh and Effendi: Changing Patterns of Authority among the El Shabana of Southern Iraq*. Cambridge, Mass.: Harvard University Press.

Field, Alexander J. 1979. "On the Explanation of Rules Using Rational Choice Models." *Journal of Economic Issues* 13 (1): 49–72.

Field, Barry. 1986. "Induced Changes in Property Rights Institutions." Research Paper Series 86–1. University of Massachusetts, Amhurst, Department of Agricultural and Resource Economics.

Fiorina, Morris P. 1981. "Universalism, Reciprocity, and Distributive Policy-Making in Majority Rule Institutions." *Research in Public Policy Analysis and Management*, vol. 1, ed. John P. Crecine, 197–221. Greenwich, Conn.: JAI Press.

Firth, Raymond. 1966. *Malay Fishermen: Their Peasant Economy*. 2d ed. London: Routledge and Kegan Paul.

Forman, Shepard L. 1966. "Jangadeiros: Raft Fishermen of Northeastern Brazil." Ph.D. diss., Columbia University.

———. 1967. "Cognition and the Catch: The Location of Fishing Spots in a Brazilian Coastal Village." *Ethnology* 6:417–26.

———. 1970. *The Raft Fishermen: Tradition and Change in the Brazilian Peasant Economy*. Bloomington: Indiana University Press.

Fowler, Darlene, ed. 1986. "Rapid Appraisal of Nepal Irrigation Systems." Water Management Synthesis Report no. 43. Colorado State University.

Fraser, G. Alexander. 1979. "Limited Entry: Experience of the British Columbia Salmon Fishery." *Journal of the Fisheries Research Board of Canada* 36:754–63.

Fraser, Thomas M., Jr. 1960. *Rusembilan: A Malay Fishing Village in Southern Thailand*. Ithaca, N.Y.: Cornell University Press.

———. 1966. *Fishermen of South Thailand: The Malay Villagers*. New York: Holt, Rinehart and Winston.

Freeman, David M., and Max L. Lowdermilk. 1985. "Middle-Level Organizational Linkages in Irrigation Projects." In *Putting People First: Sociological Variables in Rural Development*, ed. Michael M. Cernea, 91–118. New York: Oxford University Press.

Freeman, Milton M. R. 1989. "Graphs and Gaffs: A Cautionary Tale in the Common-Property Resources Debate." In *Common Property Resources: Ecology and Community-Based Sustainable Development*, ed. Fikret Berkes, 92–109. London: Belhaven.

Friedman, Daniel. 1989. "Evolutionary Economic Games." Working paper. University of California, Board of Studies in Economics.

Friedman, James W. 1990. *Game Theory with Applications to Economics*. 2d ed. New York: Oxford University Press.

Friedman, James W., and R. W. Rosenthal. 1986. "A Positive Approach to Non-Cooperative Games." *Journal of Economic Behavior and Organization* 7:235–51.

Frohlich, Norman, Joe A. Oppenheimer, and Cheryl L. Eavey. 1987. "Choices of Principles of Distributive Justice in Experimental Groups." *American Journal of Political Science* 31:606–36.

Fudenberg, Drew, and Eric Maskin. 1986. "The Folk Theorem in Repeated Games with Discounting or with Incomplete Information." *Econometrica* 54:533–56.

Gadgil, Madhav, and Prema Iyer. 1989. "On the Diversification of Common-Property

Resource Use by Indian Society." In *Common Property Resources: Ecology and Community-Based Sustainable Development*, ed. Fikret Berkes, 240–72. London: Belhaven.

Gale, David, and Lloyd S. Shapley. 1962. "College Admission and the Stability of Marriage." *American Mathematical Monthly* 69:9–15.

Gambetta, Diego, ed. 1988. *Trust: Making and Breaking Cooperative Relations*. Oxford: Basil Blackwell.

Ganz, Joan S. 1971. *Rules: A Systematic Study*. The Hague: Mouton.

Gardner, Roy. 1983. "Variation of the Electorate: Veto and Purge." *Public Choice* 40 (3): 237–47.

Gardner, Roy, and Elinor Ostrom. 1991. "Rules and Games." *Public Choice* 70 (2): 121–49.

Gardner, Roy, Elinor Ostrom, and James M. Walker. 1990. "The Nature of Common-Pool Resource Problems." *Rationality and Society* 2:335–58.

Ghildyal, B. P. 1981. "Soils of the Garhwal and Kumaun Himalaya." In *The Himalaya: Aspects of Change*, ed. J. S. Lall, 120–37. Delhi: Oxford University Press.

Gillespie, Victor A. 1975. "Farmer Irrigation Associations and Farmer Cooperation." East-West Food Institute Paper no. 3. Honolulu.

Glaser, Christina. 1987. "Common Property Regimes in Swiss Alpine Meadows." Paper presented at the Conference on Comparative Institutional Analysis, Inter-University Center of Postgraduate Studies, Dubrovnik, Yugoslavia, 19–23 October.

Glick, Thomas F. 1970. *Irrigation and Society in Medieval Valencia*. Cambridge, Mass.: Harvard University Press, Belknap Press.

Gordon, Edmund T. 1981. "Phases of Development and Underdevelopment in a Caribbean Fishing Village: San Pedro, Belize." Ph.D. diss., Stanford University.

Gordon, H. Scott. 1953. "An Economic Approach to the Optimum Utilization of Fishery Resources." *Journal of the Fisheries Research Board of Canada* 10:442–57.

———. 1954. "The Economic Theory of a Common-Property Resource: The Fishery." *Journal of Political Economy* 62:124–42.

Gray, Robert. 1963. *The Sonjo of Tanganyika*. Oxford: Oxford University Press.

Grether, David M., R. Mark Isaac, and Charles R. Plott. 1979. "Alternative Methods of Allocating Airport Slots: Performance and Evaluation." Report prepared for the Civil Aeronautics Board.

Groner, Rudolf, Marina Groner, and Walter F. Bischof. 1983. *Methods of Heuristics*. Hillsdale, N.J.: Lawrence Erlbaum Associates.

Grossinger, Richard S. 1975. "The Strategy and Ideology of Lobster Fishing on the Back Side of Mt. Desert Island, Hancock County, Maine." Ph.D. diss., University of Michigan.

Guha, Ramachandra. 1989. *The Unquiet Woods: Ecological Change and Peasant Resistance in the Himalayas*. New York: Oxford University Press.

Gustafson, W. Eric, and Richard B. Reidinger. 1971. "Delivery of Canal Water in North India and West Pakistan." *Economic and Political Weekly* 6 (52): A157–62.

Hackett, Steven, Edella Schlager, and James M. Walker. 1993. "The Role of Communication in Resolving Commons Dilemmas: Experimental Evidence with Hetero-geneous Appropriators." *Journal of Environmental Economics and Management*, forthcoming.

Hackett, Steven, and James M. Walker. 1993. "Laboratory Experimental Research on Common-Pool Resources: A Methodological Discussion with Application to Wa-ter." In *Resolution of Water Quantity and Quality Conflicts*, ed. Ariel Dinar and Edna Loehman. Westport, Conn.: Greenwood Publishing Group, forthcoming.

Haddock, D. D. 1986. "First Possession versus Optimal Timing: Limiting the Dissipa-tion of Economic Value." *Washington University Law Quarterly* 64 (Fall): 775–92.

Hafid, Anwar, and Yujiro Hayami. 1979. "Mobilizing Local Resources for Irrigation Development: The Subsidi Desa Case of Indonesia." In *Irrigation Policy and the Management of Irrigation Systems in Southeast Asia*, ed. Donald C. Taylor and Thomas H. Wickham, 123–42. Bangkok: Agricultural Development Council.

Han, Sang-Bok. 1972. "Socio-Economic Organization and Change in Korean Fishing Villages: A Comparative Study of Three Fishing Communities." Ph.D. diss., Michigan State University.

Haney, Patrick J., Roberta Herzberg, and Rick K. Wilson. 1992. "Advice and Con-sent: Unitary Actors, Advisory Models, and Experimental Tests." *Journal of Conflict Resolution* 36 (4): 603–33.

Hannesson, Rögnvaldur. 1985. "Inefficiency through Government Regulations: The Case of Norway's Fishery Policy." *Marine Resource Economics* 2 (2): 115–41.

———. 1988. "Studies on the Role of Fishermen's Organizations in Fisheries Man-agement: Theoretical Considerations and Experiences from Industrialized Coun-tries." FAO Fisheries Technical Paper no. 300. Food and Agriculture Organiza-tion of the United Nations, Rome.

———. 1989a. "Catch Quotas and the Variability of Allowable Catch." In *Rights Based Fishing*, ed. Philip A. Neher, Ragnar Arnason, and Nina Mollett, 259–65. NATO ASI Series E, Applied Sciences no. 169. Dordrecht, Netherlands: Kluwer.

———. 1989b. "Fixed or Variable Catch Quotas? The Importance of Population Dynamics and Stock Dependent Costs." In *Rights Based Fishing*, ed. Philip A. Neher, Ragnar Arnason, and Nina Mollett, 467–80. NATO ASI Series E, Ap-plied Sciences no. 169. Dordrecht, Netherlands: Kluwer.

Hansen, R. G., and W. F. Samuelson. 1988. "Evolution in Economic Games." *Jour-nal of Economic Behavior and Organization* 10:315–38.

Hardin, Garrett. 1968. "The Tragedy of the Commons." *Science* 162:1243–48.

Hardin, Russell. 1982. *Collective Action*. Baltimore: Johns Hopkins University Press.

Harrè, R. 1974. "Some Remarks on 'Rule' as a Scientific Concept." In *Understanding Other Persons*, ed. Theodore Mischel, 143–83. Oxford: Basil Blackwell.

Harriss, John C. 1977. "Problems of Water Management in Hambantota District." In *Green Revolution? Technology and Change in Rice-Growing Areas of Tamil Nadu and Sri Lanka*, ed. Bertram H. Farmer, 364–76. New York: Macmillan.

———. 1984. "Social Organisation and Irrigation: Ideology, Planning, and Practice in Sri Lanka's Settlement Schemes." In *Understanding Green Revolutions*, ed. Tim

P. Bayliss-Smith and Sudhir Wanmali, 315–38. Cambridge: Cambridge University Press.

Harsanyi, John C. 1977. *Rational Behavior and Bargaining Equilibrium in Games and Social Situations*. New York: Cambridge University Press.

Harsanyi, John C., and Reinhard Selten. 1988. *A General Theory of Equilibrium Selection in Games*. Cambridge, Mass.: MIT Press.

Hart, Henry C. 1978. "Anarchy, Paternalism, or Collective Responsibility under the Canals?" *Economic and Political Weekly* 13 (52): A125–34.

Hartwick, John M. 1982. "Free Access and the Dynamics of the Fishery." In *Essays in the Economics of Renewable Resources*, ed. Leonard J. Mirman and Daniel F. Spulber, 159–74. New York: North-Holland.

Heaney, J. P., and R. E. Dickinson. 1982. "Methods for Apportioning the Cost of a Water Resource Project." *Water Resources Research* 18:476–82.

Hechter, Michael. 1987. *Principles of Group Solidarity*. Berkeley and Los Angeles: University of California Press.

Heiner, R. A. 1983. "The Origin of Predictable Behavior." *American Economic Review* 83:560–97.

Hirshleifer, Jack. 1985. "Protocol, Payoff, and Equilibrium: Game Theory and Social Modelling." Working Paper no. 366. University of California, Los Angeles, Department of Economics.

Hobbes, Thomas. [1651] 1960. *Leviathan or the Matter, Forme and Power of a Commonwealth Ecclesiasticall and Civil*. Ed. Michael Oakeshott. Oxford: Basil Blackwell.

Hofbauer, Josef, and Karl Sigmund. 1988. *The Theory of Evolution and Dynamical Systems*. Cambridge: Cambridge University Press.

Holler, M. J. 1990. "The Unprofitability of Mixed-Strategy Equilibria in Two-Person Games." *Economics Letters* 32:319–23.

Howe, Charles. 1979. *Natural Resource Economics: Issues, Analysis, and Policy*. New York: Wiley.

Hunt, Robert C. 1990. "Organizational Control over Water: The Positive Identification of a Social Constraint on Farmer Participation." In *Social, Economic, and Institutional Issues in Third World Irrigation Management*, ed. Rajan K. Sampath and Robert A. Young, 141–54. Studies in Water Policy and Management no. 15. Boulder, Colo.: Westview.

Igarashi, T. 1974. "A Traditional Technique of Fishermen for Locating Fishing Spots: A Case Study in the Tokara Islands." *Journal of Human Ergology* 3:3–28.

International Bank for Reconstruction and Development. 1985. *Tenth Annual Review of Project Performance Audit Results*. Washington, D.C.: World Bank, Operations Evaluation Department.

Isaac, R. Mark, Kenneth McCue, and Charles R. Plott. 1985. "Public Goods Provision in an Experimental Environment." *Journal of Public Economics* 26:51–74.

Isaac, R. Mark, and Charles R. Plott. 1978. "Comparative Game Models of the Influence of the Closed Rule in Three Person, Majority Rule Committees: Theory and Experiment." In *Game Theory and Political Science*, ed. Peter C. Ordeshook, 283–322. New York: New York University Press.

Isaac, R. Mark, David Schmidtz, and James M. Walker. 1989. "The Assurance Problem in a Laboratory Market." *Public Choice* 62 (3): 217–36.

Isaac, R. Mark, and James M. Walker. 1988a. "Communication and Free-Riding Behavior: The Voluntary Contribution Mechanism." *Economic Inquiry* 26:585–608.

———. 1988b. "Group Size Effects in Public Goods Provision: The Voluntary Contributions Mechanism." *Quarterly Journal of Economics* 103:179–99.

———. 1991. "Costly Communication: An Experiment in a Nested Public Goods Problem." In *Laboratory Research in Political Economy*, ed. Thomas R. Palfrey, 269–86. Ann Arbor: University of Michigan Press.

Isaac, R. Mark, James M. Walker, and Susan Thomas. 1984. "Divergent Evidence on Free Riding: An Experimental Examination of Possible Explanations." *Public Choice* 43 (2): 113–49.

Isaac, R. Mark, James M. Walker, and Arlington Williams. 1993. "Group Size and Voluntary Provision of Public Goods: Experimental Evidence Utilizing Large Groups." *Journal of Public Economics*, forthcoming.

Jankowski, Richard. 1990. "Punishment in Iterated Chicken and Prisoner's Dilemma Games." *Rationality and Society* 2:449–70.

———. 1991. "Social Control and the Freerider Problem in Small and Large Groups." Working paper. University of Arizona, Department of Political Science.

Jaquette, David L., and Nancy Y. Moore. 1978. *Efficient Water Use in California: Groundwater Use and Management*. Santa Monica, Calif.: Rand Corp., R-2387/1-CAS/RF, November.

Jerdee, Thomas H., and Benson Rosen. 1974. "Effects of Opportunity to Communicate and Visibility of Individual Decisions on Behavior in the Common Interest." *Journal of Applied Psychology* 59:712–16.

Johnson, Ronald, and Gary Libecap. 1982. "Contracting Problems and Regulation: The Case of the Fishery." *American Economic Review* 72:1005–23.

Jorgenson, Dale, and Anthony S. Papciak. 1980. "The Effects of Communication, Resource Feedback, and Identifiability on Behavior in a Simulated Commons." *Journal of Experimental Social Psychology* 17:373–85.

Kaitala, V. 1986. "Game Theory Models of Fisheries Management—A Survey." In *Dynamic Games and Applications in Economics*, ed. Tamer Basar, 252–66. Lecture Notes in Economics and Mathematical Systems no. 265. Berlin: Springer-Verlag.

Kaminski, Antoni. 1992. *An Institutional Theory of Communist Regimes: Design, Function, and Breakdown*. San Francisco: Institute for Contemporary Studies.

Keohane, Robert O. 1980. "The Theory of Hegemonic Stability and Changes in International Economic Regimes, 1967–1977." In *Change in the International System*, ed. Ole Holsti, Randolph Siverson, and Alexander George, 131–62. Boulder, Colo.: Westview.

———. 1984. *After Hegemony: Cooperation and Discord in the World Political Economy*. Princeton, N.J.: Princeton University Press.

———. 1986. "Reciprocity in International Relations." *International Organization* 40 (Winter): 1–27.

Kerr, R. A. 1991. "Geothermal Tragedy of the Commons." *Science* 253:134–35.

Keser, Claudia. 1992. *Experimental Duopoly Markets with Demand Inertia: Game-Playing Experiments and the Strategy Method.* Berlin: Springer-Verlag.

Kim, Oliver, and Mark Walker. 1984. "The Free Rider Problem: Experimental Evidence." *Public Choice* 43 (1): 3–24.

Kiser, Larry L., and Elinor Ostrom. 1982. "The Three Worlds of Action: A Metatheoretical Synthesis of Institutional Approaches." In *Strategies of Political Inquiry*, ed. Elinor Ostrom, 179–222. Beverly Hills, Calif.: Sage.

Koford, Kenneth J., and Jeffrey B. Miller, eds. 1991. *Social Norms and Economic Institutions.* Ann Arbor: University of Michigan Press.

Kotsonias, G. 1984. "The Messolonghi-Etolico Lagoon of Greece: Socioeconomic and Ecological Interactions of Cooperatives and Independent Fishermen." In *Management of Coastal Lagoon Fisheries*, ed. James M. Kapetsky and George Lasserre, 521–28. GFCM Studies and Reviews no. 61. Rome: Food and Agriculture Organization of the United Nations.

Kottak, Conrad P. 1966. "The Structure of Equality in a Brazilian Fishing Community." Ph.D. diss., Columbia University.

Kramer, R. M., and Marilyn M. Brewer. 1986. "Social Group Identity and the Emergence of Cooperation in Resource Conservation Dilemmas." In *Experimental Social Dilemmas*, ed. Henk A. Wilke, David M. Messick, and Christel G. Rutte, 205–34. Frankfurt am Main: Lang.

Kreps, David M., Paul Milgrom, John Roberts, and Robert Wilson. 1982. "Rational Cooperation in the Finitely Repeated Prisoner's Dilemma." *Journal of Economic Theory* 27:245–52.

Krueger, Ann O. 1974. "The Political Economy of the Rent-Seeking Society." *American Economic Review* 64:291–303.

Kurien, John. 1988. "Studies on the Role of Fishermen's Organizations in Fisheries Management: The Role of Fishermen's Organizations in Fisheries Management of Developing Countries (with Particular Reference to the Indo-Pacific Region)." FAO Fisheries Technical Paper no. 300. Food and Agriculture Organization of the United Nations, Rome.

Lando, Richard P. 1979. "The Gift of Land: Irrigation and Social Structure in a Toba Village." Ph.D. diss., University of California, Riverside.

Ledyard, John O. 1993. "Is There a Problem with Public Goods Provision?" In *The Handbook of Experimental Economics*, ed. John Kagel and Alvin Roth. Princeton, N.J.: Princeton University Press, forthcoming.

Levhari, D., and L. H. Mirman. 1980. "The Great Fish War: An Example Using a Dynamic Cournot-Nash Solution." *Bell Journal of Economics* 11:322–34.

Levine, Gilbert. 1980. "The Relationship of Design, Operation, and Management." In *Irrigation and Agricultural Development in Asia*, ed. E. Walter Coward, Jr., 51–64. Ithaca, N.Y.: Cornell University Press.

Lewis, Tracy R., and James Cowens. 1982. "The Great Fish War: A Cooperative Solution." California Institute of Technology Working Paper no. 448.

———. 1983. "Cooperation in the Commons: An Application of Repetitious Rivalry." University of British Columbia, Department of Economics. Typescript.

Libecap, Gary. 1978. "Economic Variables and the Development of Law: The Case of Western Mineral Rights." *Journal of Economic History* 38:338–62.

———. 1989. "Distributional Issues in Contracting for Property Rights." *Journal of Institutional and Theoretical Economics* 145:6–24.

———. 1990. *Contracting for Property Rights*. New York: Cambridge University Press.

Lowdermilk, Max K., Wayne Clyma, and Alan C. Early. 1975. "Physical and Socio-Economic Dynamics of a Watercourse in Pakistan's Punjab: System Constraints and Farmers' Responses." Water Management Technical Report no. 42. Colorado State University.

Luce, R. Duncan, and Howard Raiffa. 1957. *Games and Decisions: Introduction and Critical Survey*. New York: Wiley.

Maass, Arthur, and Raymond L. Anderson. 1986. *. . . and the Desert Shall Rejoice: Conflict, Growth, and Justice in Arid Environments*. Malabar, Fla.: Krieger.

McCay, Bonnie J. 1980. "A Fisherman's Cooperative: Limited, Indigenous Resource Management in a Complex Society." *Anthropological Quarterly* 53 (1): 29–38.

McCay, Bonnie J., and James M. Acheson. 1987. *The Question of the Commons: The Culture and Ecology of Communal Resources*. Tucson: University of Arizona Press.

McGartland, A., and W. Oates. 1985. "Marketable Permits for the Prevention of Environmental Deterioration." *Journal of Environmental Economics and Management* 12:207–28.

McGinnis, Michael D., and John T. Williams. 1989. "Change and Stability in Superpower Rivalry." *American Political Science Review* 83:1101–23.

———. 1991. "Configurations of Cooperation: Correlation Equilibria in Coordination and Iterated Prisoner's Dilemma Games." Presented at the North American meeting of the Peace Science Society (International), University of Michigan, Ann Arbor, 15–17 November.

McGuire, T., M. Coiner, and L. Spancake. 1979. "Budget Maximizing Agencies and Efficiency in Government." *Public Choice* 34 (3–4): 333–59.

McHugh, J. L. 1972. "Jeffersonian Democracy and the Fisheries." In *World Fisheries Policy: Multidisciplinary Views*, ed. Brian J. Rothschild, 134–55. Seattle: University of Washington Press.

Mackay, R. J., and C. Weaver. 1978. "Monopoly Bureaus and Fiscal Outcomes: Deductive Models and Implications for Reform." In *Policy Analysis and Deductive Reasoning*, ed. Gordon Tullock and Richard E. Wagner, 141–65. Lexington, Mass.: Lexington Books.

McKean, Margaret A. 1992. "Management of Traditional Common Lands (*Iriaichi*) in Japan." In *Making the Commons Work: Theory, Practice, and Policy*, ed. Daniel W. Bromley, 63–98. San Francisco: Institute for Contemporary Studies.

McKelvey, Richard D. 1979. "General Conditions for Global Intransitivities." *Econometrica* 47:1085–11.

McKelvey, Richard D., and Peter C. Ordeshook. 1984. "An Experimental Study of the Effect of Procedural Rules on Committee Behavior." *Journal of Politics* 46 (1): 182–205.

McKelvey, Richard D., and Thomas Palfrey. 1992. "An Experimental Study of the Centipede Game." *Econometrica* 60:803–36.

Malik, A., B. Larson, and M. Ribaudo. 1991. "Nonpoint Source Pollution and Economic Incentive Policy in the Reauthorization of the Clean Water Act." U.S. Department of Agriculture, Washington, D.C. Typescript.

Maloney, D. G., and Peter Pearse. 1979. "Quantitative Rights as an Instrument for Regulating Commercial Fisheries." *Journal of the Fisheries Research Board of Canada* 37:859–66.

Marchak, Patricia. 1987. "Uncommon History." In *Uncommon Property: The Fishing and Fish-Processing Industries in British Columbia*, ed. Patricia Marchak, Neil Guppy, and John McMullan, 353–59. Toronto: Methuen.

Marchak, Patricia, Neil Guppy, and John McMullan. 1987. *Uncommon Property: The Fishing and Fish-Processing Industries in British Columbia*. Toronto: Methuen.

Martin, Edward, and Robert Yoder. 1983a. "The Chherlung Thulo: A Case Study of a Farmer-Managed Irrigation System." In *Water Management in Nepal: Proceedings of the Seminar on Water Management Issues*, appendix 1, 203–17. Kathmandu, Nepal: Ministry of Agriculture.

———. 1983b. "Water Allocation and Resource Mobilization for Irrigation: A Comparison of Two Systems in Nepal." Paper presented at the Annual Meeting of the Nepal Studies Association, University of Wisconsin, Madison, 4–6 November.

———. 1986. "Institutions for Irrigation Management in Farmer-Managed Systems: Examples from the Hills of Nepal." Research Paper no. 5. International Irrigation Management Institute, Digana Village, Sri Lanka.

Martin, Fenton. 1989. *Common Pool Resources and Collective Action: A Bibliography*. Vol. 1. Bloomington: Indiana University, Workshop in Political Theory and Policy Analysis.

Martin, Kent O. 1973. "'The Law in St. John's Says . . . ': Space Division and Resource Allocation in the Newfoundland Fishing Community of Fermeuse." Master's thesis, Memorial University of Newfoundland.

———. 1979. "Play by the Rules or Don't Play at All: Space Division and Resource Allocation in a Rural Newfoundland Fishing Community." In *North Atlantic Maritime Cultures: Anthropological Essays on Changing Adaptations*, ed. Raoul Andersen, 276–98. The Hague: Mouton.

Martin, Lisa. 1992. *Coercive Cooperation: Explaining Multilateral Economic Sanctions*. Princeton, N.J.: Princeton University Press.

Marwell, G., and R. E. Ames. 1979. "Experiments on the Provision of Public Goods I: Resources, Interest, Group Size, and the Free Rider Problem." *American Journal of Sociology* 84:1335–60.

———. 1980. "Experiments on the Provision of Public Goods II: Provision Points, Stakes, Experience and the Free Rider Problem." *American Journal of Sociology* 85:926–37.

———. 1981. "Economists Free Ride, Does Anyone Else?" *Journal of Public Economics* 15:295–310.

Mason, C., Todd Sandler, and Richard Cornes. 1988. "Expectations, the Commons, and Optimal Group Size." *Journal of Environmental Economics and Management* 15:99–110.

Matthews, R. 1988. "Federal Licensing Policies for the Atlantic Inshore Fishery and Their Implementation in Newfoundland, 1973–1981." *Acadiensis: Journal of the History of the Atlantic Region* 17:83–108.

Matthews, R., and J. Phyne. 1988. "Regulating the Newfoundland Inshore Fishery: Traditional Values versus State Control in the Regulation of a Common Property Resource." *Journal of Canadian Studies* 23:158–76.

Maynard Smith, J. 1982. *Evolution and the Theory of Games*. Cambridge: Cambridge University Press.

Mehra, S. 1981. *Instability in Indian Agriculture in the Context of the New Technology*. Research Report no. 25. International Food Policy Research Institution, Washington, D.C.

Meinzen-Dick, Ruth S. 1984. "Local Management of Tank Irrigation in South India: Organization and Operation." Cornell Studies in Irrigation no. 3. Cornell University.

Menger, Karl. [1883] 1963. *Problems in Economics and Sociology*. Trans. Francis J. Nock. Urbana: University of Illinois Press.

Merrey, Douglas J., and James M. Wolf. 1986. "Irrigation Management in Pakistan: Four Papers." Research Paper no. 4. International Irrigation Management Institute, Digana Village, Sri Lanka.

Messerschmidt, Donald A. 1986. "People and Resources in Nepal: Customary Resource Management Systems of the Upper Kali Gandaki." In *Proceedings of the Conference on Common Property Resource Management*, National Research Council, 455–80. Washington, D.C.: National Academy Press.

Messick, David M., and Carol L. McClelland. 1983. "Social Traps and Temporal Traps." *Personality and Social Psychology Bulletin* 9:105–10.

Messick, David M., Henk Wilke, Marilynn Brewer, Roderick Kramer, Patricia English Zemke, and Layton Lui. 1983. "Individual Adaptations and Structural Change as Solutions to Social Dilemmas." *Journal of Personality and Social Psychology* 44 (2): 294–309.

Milgrom, Paul R., Douglass C. North, and Barry R. Weingast. 1990. "The Role of Institutions in the Revival of Trade: The Law Merchant, Private Judges, and the Champagne Fairs." *Economics and Politics* 2:1–23.

Miller, David. 1982. "Mexico's Caribbean Fishery: Recent Change and Current Issues." Ph.D. diss., University of Wisconsin, Milwaukee.

———. 1989. "The Evolution of Mexico's Spiny Lobster Fishery." In *Common Property Resources: Ecology and Community-Based Sustainable Development*, ed. Fikret Berkes, 185–98. London: Belhaven.

Miller, John, and James Andreoni. 1991. "A Coevolutionary Model of Free Riding Behavior: Replicator Dynamics as an Explanation of the Experimental Results." *Economics Letters* 36:9–15.

Millner, E., and M. Pratt. 1989. "An Experimental Investigation of Efficient Rent Seeking." *Public Choice* 62 (2): 139–52.

Mirza, A. H. 1975. "A Study of Village Organizational Factors Affecting Water

Management Decision Making in Pakistan." Water Management Technical Report no. 34. Colorado State University.

Mirza, A. H., and Douglas J. Merrey. 1979. *Organization Problems and Their Consequences on Improved Watercourses in Punjab.* Fort Collins: Colorado State University Water Management Research Project.

Mitchell, William P. 1976. "Irrigation and Community in the Central Peruvian Highlands." *American Anthropologist* 78:25–44.

———. 1977. "Irrigation Farming in the Andes: Evolutionary Implications." In *Studies in Peasant Livelihood*, ed. Rhoda Halperin and James Dow, 36–59. New York: St. Martin's.

Mitzkewitz, Michael, and Rosemarie Nagel. 1991. "Envy, Greed, and Anticipation in Ultimatum Games with Incomplete Information: An Experimental Study." Special Research Project 303, Discussion Paper B-181, University of Bonn, March.

Nachbar, John H. 1990. "'Evolutionary' Selection Dynamics in Games: Convergence and Limit Properties." *International Journal of Game Theory* 19 (1): 59–89.

Nachmias, David, and Chava Nachmias. 1987. *Research Methods in the Social Sciences.* 3d ed. New York: St. Martin's.

Nash, John F. 1950. "Equilibrium Points in n-Person Games." *Proceedings of the National Academy of Sciences* 36:48–49.

———. 1951. "Non-Cooperative Games." *Annals of Mathematics* 54:286–95.

Negri, D. H. 1989. "The Common Property Aquifer as a Differential Game." *Water Resources Research* 25:9–15.

Neher, Philip A. 1989. "Fishing Quota Management with Multiple Stock Objectives." In *Rights Based Fishing*, ed. Philip A. Neher, Ragnar Arnason, and Nina Mollett, 505–24. NATO ASI Series E. Applied Sciences no. 169. Dordrecht, Netherlands: Kluwer.

———. 1990. *Natural Resource Economics: Conservation and Exploitation.* Cambridge: Cambridge University Press.

Nepal Irrigation Research Project. 1983. *Sunduwari Irrigation System (Badichaur, Surkhet).* Kathmandu, Nepal: Nepal Irrigation Research Project. Mimeograph.

Netting, Robert McC. 1974. "The System Nobody Knows: Village Irrigation in the Swiss Alps." In *Irrigation's Impact on Society*, ed. Theodore E. Downing and McGuire Gibson, 67–75. Tucson: University of Arizona Press.

———. 1976. "What Alpine Peasants Have in Common: Observations on Communal Tenure in a Swiss Village." *Human Ecology* 4:135–46.

———. 1981. *Balancing on an Alp: Ecological Change and Continuity in a Swiss Mountain Community.* New York: Cambridge University Press.

Nietschmann, Bernard. 1972. "Hunting and Fishing Focus among the Miskito Indians, Eastern Nicaragua." *Human Ecology* 1 (1): 41–67.

———. 1973. *Between Land and Water: The Subsistence Ecology of the Miskito Indians, Eastern Nicaragua.* New York: Seminar Press.

Niskanen, William A. 1971. *Bureaucracy and Representative Government.* Chicago: Aldine-Atherton.

North, Douglass C. 1990. *Institutions, Institutional Change, and Economic Performance.* New York: Cambridge University Press.

Nozick, Robert. 1975. *Anarchy, State, and Utopia*. New York: Basic Books.

Nunn, Susan C. 1985. "The Political Economy of Institutional Change: A Distributional Criterion for Acceptance of Groundwater Rules." *Natural Resources Journal* 25:867–92.

O'Neill, Barry. 1987. "Nonmetric Test of the Minimax Theory of Two-Person Zerosum Games." *Proceedings of the National Academy of Sciences* 84: 2106–9.

Oakerson, Ronald J. 1992. "Analyzing the Commons." In *Making the Commons Work: Theory, Practice, and Policy*, ed. Daniel W. Bromley, 41–59. San Francisco: Institute for Contemporary Studies.

Oakerson, Ronald J., Susan Wynne, Tham V. Truong, and Stuart Tjip Walker. 1990. *Privatization Structures: An Institutional Analysis of the Fertilizer Sub-Sector Reform Program in Cameroon*. Washington, D.C.: Ernst and Young.

Oliver, Pamela. 1980. "Rewards and Punishments as Selective Incentives for Collective Action: Theoretical Investigations." *American Journal of Sociology* 85:356–75.

Olson, Mancur. 1965. *The Logic of Collective Action: Public Goods and the Theory of Groups*. Cambridge, Mass.: Harvard University Press.

———. 1969. "The Principle of 'Fiscal Equivalence': The Division of Responsibilities among Different Levels of Government." *American Economic Review* 59:479–87.

Ongkingko, Petronio S. 1973. "Case Studies of Laoag-Vintar and Nazareno-Gamutan Irrigation System." *Philippine Agriculturist* 59 (9–10): 374–80.

Orbell, John M., Robyn M. Dawes, and Alphons van de Kragt. 1990. "The Limits of Multilateral Promising." *Ethics* 100 (4): 616–27.

Orbell, John M., Alphons van de Kragt, and Robyn M. Dawes. 1988. "Explaining Discussion-Induced Cooperation." *Journal of Personality and Social Psychology* 54 (5): 811–19.

———. 1991. "Covenants without the Sword: The Role of Promises in Social Dilemma Circumstances." In *Social Norms and Economic Institutions*, ed. Kenneth J. Kofford and Jeffrey B. Miller, 117–34. Ann Arbor: University of Michigan Press.

Ostrom, Elinor. 1965. "Public Entrepreneurship: A Case Study in Ground Water Basin Management." Ph.D. diss., University of California, Los Angeles.

———. 1986a. "An Agenda for the Study of Institutions." *Public Choice* 48 (1): 3–25.

———. 1986b. "A Method of Institutional Analysis." In *Guidance, Control, and Evaluation in the Public Sector*, ed. Franz-Xaver Kaufmann, Giandomenico Majone, and Vincent Ostrom, 459–75. Berlin: de Gruyter.

———. 1989. "Microconstitutional Change in Multiconstitutional Political Systems." *Rationality and Society* 1:11–50.

———. 1990. *Governing the Commons: The Evolution of Institutions for Collective Action*. New York: Cambridge University Press.

———. 1991. "A Framework for Institutional Analysis." Working paper. Indiana University, Workshop in Political Theory and Policy Analysis.

———. 1992. *Crafting Institutions for Self-Governing Irrigation Systems*. San Francisco: Institute for Contemporary Studies.

———. 1993. "Institutional Arrangements and the Commons Dilemma." In *Rethinking Institutional Analysis and Development: Issues, Alternatives, and Choices*, ed. Vincent Ostrom, David Feeny, and Hartmut Picht, 101–39. San Francisco: Institute for Contemporary Studies.

Ostrom, Elinor, Paul Benjamin, Ganesh Shivakoti, and the NIIS Project Team. 1993. *Institutions, Incentives, and Irrigation in Nepal*. Nepal Irrigation Institutions and Systems Project, vol. 1. Bloomington: Indiana University, Workshop in Political Theory and Policy Analysis.

Ostrom, Elinor, and Roy Gardner. 1993. "Coping with Asymmetries in the Commons: Self-Governing Irrigation Systems Can Work." *Journal of Economic Perspectives*, forthcoming.

Ostrom, Elinor, Larry Schroeder, and Susan Wynne. 1993. *Institutional Incentives and Sustainable Development: Infrastructure Policies in Perspective*. Boulder, Colo.: Westview.

Ostrom, Elinor, and James M. Walker. 1991. "Communication in a Commons: Cooperation without External Enforcement." In *Laboratory Research in Political Economy*, ed. Thomas R. Palfrey, 287–322. Ann Arbor: University of Michigan Press.

Ostrom, Elinor, James M. Walker, and Roy Gardner. 1992. "Covenants with and without a Sword: Self-Governance Is Possible." *American Political Science Review* 86:404–17.

Ostrom, Vincent. 1980. "Artisanship and Artifact." *Public Administration Review* 40 (4): 309–17.

———. 1982. "A Forgotten Tradition: The Constitutional Level of Analysis." In *Missing Elements in Political Inquiry: Logic and Levels of Analysis*, ed. Judith A. Gillespie and Dina A. Zinnes, 237–52. Beverly Hills, Calif.: Sage.

———. 1985. "Constitutional Considerations with Particular Reference to Federal Systems." In *Guidance, Control, and Evaluation in the Public Sector*, ed. Franz-Xaver Kaufmann, Giandomenico Majone, and Vincent Ostrom, 111–25. Berlin: de Gruyter.

———. 1987. *The Political Theory of a Compound Republic: Designing the American Experiment*. 2d ed. San Francisco: Institute for Contemporary Studies.

———. 1989. *The Intellectual Crisis in American Public Administration*. 2d ed. Tuscaloosa: University of Alabama Press.

———. 1991. *The Meaning of American Federalism: Constituting a Self-Governing Society*. San Francisco: Institute for Contemporary Studies.

———. 1994. JOURNEY AMONG CONJECTURES: *About Constituting Order in Human Societies*. San Francisco: Institute for Contemporary Studies, forthcoming.

Ostrom, Vincent, Robert Bish, and Elinor Ostrom. 1988. *Local Government in the United States*. San Francisco: Institute for Contemporary Studies.

Ostrom, Vincent, David Feeny, and Hartmut Picht, eds. 1993. *Rethinking Institutional Analysis and Development: Issues, Alternatives, and Choices*. 2d ed. San Francisco: Institute for Contemporary Studies.

Ostrom, Vincent, and Elinor Ostrom. 1977. "Public Goods and Public Choices." In *Alternatives for Delivering Public Services: Toward Improved Performance*, ed. E. S. Savas, 7–49. Boulder, Colo.: Westview.

Ostrom, Vincent, Charles Tiebout, and Robert Warren. 1961. "The Organization of Government in Metropolitan Areas: A Theoretical Inquiry." *American Political Science Review* 55:831–42.

Oye, Kenneth A., ed. 1986. *Cooperation under Anarchy*. Princeton, N.J.: Princeton University Press.

Palfrey, Thomas R., and Howard Rosenthal. 1984. "Participation and the Provision of Discrete Public Goods: A Strategic Analysis." *Journal of Public Economics* 24 (2): 171–93.

————. 1991a. "Testing for Effects of Cheaptalk in a Public Goods Game with Private Information." *Games and Economic Behavior* 3:183–220.

————. 1991b. "Testing Game-Theoretic Models of Free Riding: New Evidence on Probability Bias and Learning." In *Laboratory Research in Political Economy*, ed. Thomas R. Palfrey, 239–68. Ann Arbor: University of Michigan Press.

————. 1992. "Repeated Play, Cooperation and Coordination: An Experimental Study." Social Science Working Paper. California Institute of Technology.

Panayoutou, T. 1982. "Management Concepts for Small-Scale Fisheries: Economic and Social Aspects." FAO Fisheries Technical Paper no. 228. Food and Agriculture Organization of the United Nations, Rome.

Pant, Govind B. 1922. *The Forest Problem in Kumaon*. Nainital: Gyanodaya Prakashan.

Parks, Roger B., and Elinor Ostrom. 1981. "Complex Models of Urban Service Systems." In *Urban Policy Analysis: Directions for Future Research*, ed. Terry N. Clark, 171–99. Urban Affairs Annual Reviews, vol. 21. Beverly Hills, Calif.: Sage.

Pearse, Peter H., and James E. Wilen. 1979. "Impact of Canada's Pacific Salmon Fleet Control Program." *Journal of the Fisheries Research Board of Canada* 36:764–69.

Piaget, Jean. [1932] 1969. *The Moral Judgment of the Child*. New York: Free Press.

Pinkerton, Evelyn, ed. 1989. *Co-operative Management of Local Fisheries: New Directions for Improved Management and Community Development*. Vancouver: University of British Columbia Press.

Plott, Charles R. 1967. "A Notion of Equilibrium and Its Possibility under Majority Rule." *American Economic Review* 57:787–807.

————. 1979. "The Application of Laboratory Experimental Methods to Public Choice." In *Collective Decision Making: Applications from Public Choice Theory*, ed. Clifford S. Russell, 137–60. Baltimore: Johns Hopkins University Press.

————. 1983. "Externalities and Corrective Policies in Experimental Markets." *Economic Journal* 93:106–27.

Plott, Charles R., and M. E. Levine. 1978. "A Model for Agenda Influence on Committee Decisions." *American Economic Review* 68:146–60.

Plott, Charles R., and Robert A. Meyer. 1975. "The Technology of Public Goods, Externalities, and the Exclusion Principle." In *Economic Analysis of Environmen-*

tal Problems, ed. Edwin S. Mills, 65–94. New York: National Bureau of Economic Research.

Pollack, S. 1983. "Long Island Sound's Lobster War Rages on Despite New Rules." *National Fisherman* 65:9–11.

Popper, Karl R. 1967. "Rationality and the Status of the Rationality Principle." In *Le Fondements philosophiques des systems economiques textes de Jacques Rueff et essais rediges en son honneur*, ed. E. M. Classen, 145–50. Paris: Payot.

Postel, Sandra. 1990. "Saving Water for Agriculture." In *State of the World 1990: A Worldwatch Institute Report on Progress Toward a Sustainable Society*, ed. Lester R. Brown et al., 39–58. New York: Norton.

Potter, Jack M. 1976. *Thai Peasant Social Structure*. Chicago: University of Chicago Press.

Powers, Ann M. 1984. "Social Organization in a Newfoundland Fishing Settlement on the Burin Peninsula." Ph.D. diss., State University of New York, Stony Brook.

Pressman, Jeffrey L., and Aaron Wildavsky. 1973. *Implementation*. Berkeley and Los Angeles: University of California Press.

Putnam, Robert D., with Robert Leonardi and Raffaella Nanetti. 1993. *Making Democracy Work: Civic Traditions in Modern Italy*. Princeton, N.J.: Princeton University Press.

Rasmusen, Eric. 1989. *Games and Information: An Introduction to Game Theory*. Oxford: Basil Blackwell.

Rawls, John. [1955] 1968. "Two Concepts of Rules." In *Readings in the Theory of Action*, ed. Norman S. Care and Charles Landesman, 306–40. Bloomington: Indiana University Press.

———. 1971. *A Theory of Justice*. Cambridge, Mass.: Harvard University Press.

Raychaudhuri, Bikash. 1968. "Fishing Rituals of the Marine Fisherfolk of Jambudwip: A Sociocultural Study." *Bulletin of Anthropological Survey of India* 17 (2): 83–116.

———. 1980. *The Moon and the Net: Study of a Transient Community of Fishermen at Jambudwip*. Calcutta: Anthropological Survey of India, Government of India.

Reidinger, Richard B. 1974. "Institutional Rationing of Canal Water in Northern India: Conflict between Traditional Patterns and Modern Needs." *Economic Development and Cultural Change* 23 (Oct.): 79–104.

———. 1980. "Water Management by Administrative Procedures in an Indian Irrigation System." In *Irrigation and Agricultural Development in Asia*, ed. E. Walter Coward, Jr., 263–88. Ithaca, N.Y.: Cornell University Press.

Reilly, J. M., J. A. Edmonds, R. H. Gardner, and A. L. Brenkert. 1987. "Uncertainty Analysis of the IEA/ORAU CO_2 Emissions Model." *Energy Journal* 8:1–29.

Repetto, Robert. 1986. *Skimming the Water: Rent-Seeking and the Performance of Public Irrigation Systems*. Research Report no. 4. World Resources Institute, Washington, D.C.

Riker, William H. 1962. *The Theory of Political Coalitions*. New Haven, Conn.: Yale University Press.

———. 1982. "Implications from the Disequilibrium of Majority Rule for the Study of Institutions." In *Political Equilibrium*, ed. Peter C. Ordeshook and Kenneth A. Shepsle, 3–24. Boston: Kluwer-Nijhoff.

Rockenbach, Bettin, and Gerald R. Uhlich. 1989. "The Negotiation Agreement Area: An Experimental Analysis of Two-Person Characteristic Function Games." Special Research Project 303, Discussion Paper B-126, University of Bonn, October.

Rogers, P. 1969. "A Game Theory Approach to the Problems of International River Basins." *Water Resources Research* 5:749–60.

Romer, Thomas, and Howard Rosenthal. 1978. "Political Resource Allocation, Controlled Agendas, and the Status Quo." *Public Choice* 33 (4): 27–43.

Roth, Alvin E. 1991. "Game Theory as a Part of Empirical Economics." *Economic Journal* 101:107–14.

Ruddle, Kenneth, and Tomoya Akimichi, eds. 1984. *Maritime Institutions in the Western Pacific*. Osaka: National Museum of Ethnology.

Runge, C. Ford. 1984a. "Institutions and the Free Rider: The Assurance Problem in Collective Action." *Journal of Politics* 46 (1): 154–81.

———. 1984b. "Strategic Interdependence in Models of Property Rights." *American Journal of Agricultural Economics* 66:807–13.

———. 1992. "Common Property and Collective Action in Economic Development." In *Making the Commons Work: Theory, Practice, and Policy*, ed. Daniel W. Bromley, 17–39. San Francisco: Institute for Contemporary Studies.

Sabel, Charles F. 1993. "Constitutional Ordering in Historical Context." In *Games in Hierarchies and Networks: Analytical and Empirical Approaches to the Study of Governance Institutions*, ed. Fritz W. Scharpf, 65–123. Frankfurt am Main: Campus Verlag; Boulder, Colo.: Westview.

———. n.d. "Studied Trust: Building New Forms of Cooperation in a Volatile Economy." In *Human Relations and Readings in Economic Sociology*, ed. Frank Romo and Richard Swedberg. New York: Sage.

Sampath, Rajan K., and Robert A. Young. 1990. "Introduction: Social, Economic, and Institutional Aspects of Irrigation Management." In *Social, Economic, and Institutional Issues in Third World Irrigation Management*, ed. Rajan K. Sampath and Robert A. Young, 1–10. Boulder, Colo.: Westview.

Sandberg, Audun. 1991a. "Fish for All: CPR-Problems in North-Atlantic Environments." Working paper. Indiana University, Workshop in Political Theory and Policy Analysis.

———. 1991b. "Sustainable Aquaculture Development: The Role of Finance Institutions in Common Property Resource Management." Presented at the International Association for the Study of Common Property, Winnipeg, Manitoba, 26–29 September.

Sandler, Todd. 1992. *Collective Action: Theory and Applications*. Ann Arbor: University of Michigan Press.

Sawyer, Amos. 1992. *The Emergence of Autocracy in Liberia: Tragedy and Challenge*. San Francisco: Institute for Contemporary Studies.

Schaaf, Jeanne. 1989. "Governing a Monopoly Market under Siege: Using Institutional

Analysis to Understand Competitive Entry into Telecommunications Markets, 1944–1982." Ph.D. diss., Indiana University, Department of Political Science.

Schlager, Edella. 1989. "Bounding Unboundable Resources: An Empirical Analysis of Property Rights and Rules in Coastal Fisheries." Working paper. Indiana University, Workshop in Political Theory and Policy Analysis.

———. 1990. "Model Specification and Policy Analysis: The Governance of Coastal Fisheries." Ph.D. diss., Indiana University.

Schlager, Edella, and Elinor Ostrom. 1992. "Property-Rights Regimes and Natural Resources: A Conceptual Analysis." *Land Economics* 68 (3): 249–62.

Schotter, Andrew. 1981. *The Economic Theory of Social Institutions*. Cambridge: Cambridge University Press.

Scott, Anthony D. 1955. "The Fishery: The Objectives of Sole Ownership." *Journal of Political Economy* 63:116–24.

———. 1979. "Development of Economic Theory on Fisheries Regulation." *Journal of the Fisheries Research Board of Canada* 36:725–41.

Scott, James C. 1985. *Weapons of the Weak: Everyday Forms of Peasant Resistance*. New Haven, Conn.: Yale University Press.

———. 1986. "Everyday Forms of Peasant Resistance." *Journal of Peasant Studies* 13 (2): 5–35.

———. 1990. *Domination and the Arts of Resistance: Hidden Transcripts*. New Haven, Conn.: Yale University Press.

Sell, Jane, and Rick Wilson. 1991. "Levels of Information and Contributions to Public Goods." *Social Forces* 70 (1): 107–24.

———. 1992. "Liar, Liar, Pants on Fire: Cheap Talk and Signalling in Repeated Public Goods Settings." Working paper. Rice University, Department of Political Science.

Selten, Reinhard. 1971. "A Simple Model of Imperfect Competition Where Four are Few and Six are Many." *International Journal of Game Theory* 2:141–201.

———. 1975. "Reexamination of the Perfectness Concept for Equilibrium Points in Extensive Games." *International Journal of Game Theory* 4:25–55.

———. 1983. "Evolutionary Stability in Extensive Two-Person Games." *Mathematical Social Sciences* 5:269–363.

———. 1990. "Bounded Rationality." *Journal of Institutional and Theoretical Economics* 146:649–58.

———. 1991a. "Anticipatory Learning in Two-Person Games." In *Game Equilibrium Models I: Evolution and Game Dynamics*, ed. Reinhard Selten, 98–154. Berlin: Springer-Verlag.

———. 1991b. "Evolution, Learning, and Economic Behavior." *Games and Economic Behavior* 3 (1) (Feb.): 3–24.

Selten, Reinhard, Michael Mitzkewitz, and Gerald R. Uhlich. 1988. "Duopoly Strategies Programmed by Experienced Players." Special Research Project 303, Discussion Paper B-172, University of Bonn.

Sen, Amatrya K. 1977. "Rational Fools: A Critique of the Behavioral Foundations of Economic Theory." *Philosophy and Public Affairs* 6:317–44.

Sengupta, Nirmal. 1991. *Managing Common Property: Irrigation in India and the Philippines*. London: Sage.

Shepsle, Kenneth A. 1979a. "Institutional Arrangements and Equilibrium in Multi-dimensional Voting Models." *American Journal of Political Science* 23:27–59.

———. 1979b. "The Role of Institutional Structure in the Creation of Policy Equilibrium." In *Public Policy and Public Choice*, ed. Douglas W. Rae and Theodore J. Eismeier, 249–83. Sage Yearbooks in Politics and Public Policy no. 6. Beverly Hills, Calif.: Sage.

Shepsle, Kenneth A., and Barry R. Weingast. 1981a. "Structure and Strategy: The Two Faces of Agenda Power." Paper presented at the Annual Meeting of the American Political Science Association, 3–6 September.

———. 1981b. "Structure-Induced Equilibrium and Legislative Choice." *Public Choice* 37:503–19.

Shimanoff, Susan B. 1980. *Communication Rules: Theory and Research*. Beverly Hills, Calif.: Sage.

Shortall, D. 1973. "Environmental Perception in Two Local Fisheries: A Case Study from Eastern Newfoundland." Master's thesis, Memorial University of Newfoundland.

Shubik, Martin. 1982. *Game Theory in the Social Sciences: Concepts and Solutions*, vol. 1. Cambridge, Mass.: MIT Press.

Sinn, Hans-Werner. 1984. "Common Property Resources, Storage Facilities, and Ownership Structures: A Cournot Model of the Oil Market." *Economica* 51:235–52.

Siy, Robert Y., Jr. 1982. *Community Resource Management: Lessons from the Zanjera*. Quezon City, Philippines: University of the Philippines Press.

Slade, Margaret. 1987. "Interfirm Rivalry in a Repeated Game: An Empirical Test of Tacit Collusion." *Journal of Industrial Economics* 35:499–516.

Smith, Vernon. 1968. "Economics of Production from Natural Resources." *American Economic Review* 58:409–31.

———. 1982. "Microeconomic Systems as an Experimental Science." *American Economic Review* 72:923–55.

Snidal, Duncan. 1985. "The Game Theory of International Politics." *World Politics* 36.25–57.

Spooner, Brian. 1971. "Continuity and Change in Rural Iran: The Eastern Deserts." In *Iran: Continuity and Variety*, ed. Peter J. Chelkowski, 1–20. New York: New York University, Center for Near Eastern Studies and the Center for International Studies.

———. 1972. "The Iranian Deserts." In *Population Growth: Anthropological Implications*, ed. Brian Spooner, 245–68. Cambridge, Mass.: MIT Press.

———. 1974. "Irrigation and Society: The Iranian Plateau." In *Irrigation's Impact on Society*, ed. Theodore E. Downing and McGuire Gibson, 43–57. Tucson: University of Arizona Press.

Straffin, P. D., and J. P. Heaney. 1981. "Game Theory and the Tennessee Valley Authority." *International Journal of Game Theory* 10:35–43.

Sturgess, N. H., N. Dow, and P. Belin. 1982. "Management of the Victorian Scallop Fisheries: Retrospect and Prospect." In *Policy and Practice in Fisheries Manage-

ment, ed. N. H. Sturgess and T. F. Meany, 277–316. Canberra: Australian Government Publishing Service.

Sutherland, Anne. 1986. *Caye Caulker: Economic Success in a Belizean Fishing Village*. Boulder, Colo.: Westview.

Tang, Shui Yan. 1991. "Institutional Arrangements and the Management of Common-Pool Resources." *Public Administration Review* 51 (1): 42–51.

———. 1992. *Institutions and Collective Action: Self-Governance in Irrigation*. San Francisco: Institute for Contemporary Studies.

———. 1993. "Integrating Local Participation and Institutional Development: A Transaction Cost Perspective." In *Research in Public Administration*, ed. James L. Perry, 2:213–33. Greenwich, Conn.: JAI Press.

Tan-kim-yong, Uraivan. 1983. "Resource Mobilization in Traditional Irrigation Systems of Northern Thailand: A Comparison between the Lowland and the Upland Irrigation Communities." Ph.D. diss., Cornell University.

Taylor, Michael. 1976. *Anarchy and Cooperation*. New York: Wiley.

———. 1982. *Community, Anarchy, and Liberty*. New York: Cambridge University Press.

———. 1987. *The Possibility of Cooperation*. New York: Cambridge University Press.

Tejwani, K. G. 1987. "Agroforestry Practices and Research in India." In *Agroforestry: Realities, Possibilities, and Potentials*, ed. Henry L. Gholz, 109–36. Dordrecht, Netherlands: Martinus Nijhoff Publishers.

Thomson, James T. 1977. "Ecological Deterioration: Local-Level Rule Making and Enforcement Problems in Niger." In *Desertification: Environmental Degradation in and around Arid Lands*, ed. Michael H. Glantz, 57–79. Boulder, Colo.: Westview.

Thomson, James T., David Feeny, and Ronald J. Oakerson. 1992. "Institutional Dynamics: The Evolution and Dissolution of Common-Property Resource Management." In *Making the Commons Work: Theory, Practice, and Policy*, ed. Daniel W. Bromley, 129–60. San Francisco: Institute for Contemporary Studies.

Toulmin, S. 1974. "Rules and Their Relevance for Understanding Human Behavior." In *Understanding Other Persons*, ed. Theodore Mischel, 185–215. Oxford: Basil Blackwell.

Tsebelis, George. 1989. "The Abuse of Probability in Political Analysis: The Robinson Crusoe Fallacy." *American Political Science Review* 83:77–91.

———. 1990a. *Nested Games: Rational Choice in Comparative Politics*. Berkeley and Los Angeles: University of California Press.

———. 1990b. "Penalty Has No Impact on Crime: A Game-Theoretical Analysis." *Rationality and Society* 2:255–86.

———. 1991. "The Effect of Fines on Regulated Industries: Game Theory versus Decision Theory." *Journal of Theoretical Politics* 3 (1): 81–101.

Tullock, Gordon. 1967. "The Welfare Costs of Tariff Monopolies and Theft." *Western Economic Journal* 5 (June): 224–32.

———. 1981. "Why So Much Stability?" *Public Choice* 37 (2): 189–205.

Tversky, Amos, and Daniel Kahneman. 1990. "Rational Choice and the Framing of

Decisions." In *The Limits of Rationality*, ed. Karen Schweers Cook and Margaret Levi, 60–89. Chicago: University of Chicago Press.

Ullman-Margalit, E. 1978. *The Emergence of Norms*. New York: Oxford University Press.

Umbeck, John R. 1977. "The California Gold Rush: A Study of Emerging Property Rights." *Explorations in Economic History* 14:197–226.

———. 1981. *A Theory of Property Rights: With Application to the California Gold Rush*. Ames: Iowa State University Press.

Uphoff, Norman. 1985. "Fitting Projects to People." In *Putting People First: Sociological Variables in Rural Development*, ed. Michael M. Cernea, 359–98. New York: Oxford University Press.

Uphoff, Norman, M. L. Wickramasinghe, and C. M. Wijayaratna. 1990. "'Optimum' Participation in Irrigation Management: Issues and Evidence from Sri Lanka." *Human Organization* 49 (1): 26–40.

U.S. Agency for International Development. 1983. *Irrigation Assistance to Developing Countries Should Require Stronger Commitments to Operation and Maintenance*. Washington, D.C.: General Accounting Office.

van Damme, Eric. 1983. *Refinements of the Nash Equilibrium Concept*. Berlin: Springer-Verlag.

———. 1987. *Stability and Perfection of Nash Equilibrium*. Berlin: Springer-Verlag.

van de Kragt, Alphons, Robyn M. Dawes, John M. Orbell, S. R. Braver, and L. A. Wilson. 1986. "Doing Well and Doing Good as Ways of Resolving Social Dilemmas." In *Experimental Social Dilemmas*, ed. Henk A. M. Wilke, Dave Messick, and Christel Rutte, 177–204. Frankfurt am Main: Verlag Peter Lang.

van de Kragt, Alphons, John M. Orbell, and Robyn M. Dawes. 1983. "The Minimal Contributing Set as a Solution to Public Goods Problems." *American Political Science Review* 77:112–22.

Vander Velde, Edward J. 1971. "The Distribution of Irrigation Benefits: A Study in Haryana, India." Ph.D. diss., University of Michigan.

———. 1980. "Local Consequences of a Large-Scale Irrigation System in India." In *Irrigation and Agricultural Development in Asia*, ed. E. Walter Coward, Jr., 299–328. Ithaca, N.Y.: Cornell University Press.

von Hayek, Friedrich A. 1973. *Law, Legislation and Liberty*. Vol. 1. Chicago: University of Chicago Press.

———. 1976. *The Mirage of Social Justice*. Chicago: University of Chicago Press.

———. 1978. *New Studies in Philosophy, Politics, Economics, and the History of Ideas*. Chicago: University of Chicago Press.

Von Neumann, John, and Oskar Morgenstern. [1944] 1964. *Theory of Games and Economic Behavior*. New York: Wiley.

von Wright, Georg H. 1951. "Deontic Logic." *Mind* 60:58–74.

———. 1963. *Norms and Action: A Logical Enquiry*. London: Routledge and Kegan Paul.

———. 1968. "The Logic of Practical Discourse." In *Contemporary Philosophy*, ed. Raymond Klikansky, 141–67. Florence, Italy: La nuova Italia Editrice.

———. 1971. *Explanation and Understanding*. Ithaca, N.Y.: Cornell University Press.

Wade, Robert. 1987. "Managing Water Managers: Deterring Expropriation, or Equity as a Control Mechanism." In *Water and Water Policy in World Food Supplies*, ed. Wayne R. Jordan, 177–83. College Station: Texas A&M University Press.

———. 1988a. *Village Republics: Economic Conditions for Collective Action in South India*. New York: Cambridge University Press.

———. 1988b. "The Management of Irrigation Systems: How to Evoke Trust and Avoid Prisoners' Dilemma." *World Development* 16 (4): 489–500.

———. 1990. "On the 'Technical' Causes of Irrigation Hoarding Behavior, or Why Irrigators Keep Interfering in the Main System." In *Social, Economic, and Institutional Issues in Third World Irrigation Management*, ed. Rajan K. Sampath and Robert A. Young, 175–93. Boulder, Colo: Westview.

———. 1992. "Common-Property Resource Management in South Indian Villages." In *Making the Commons Work: Theory, Practice, and Policy*, ed. Daniel W. Bromley, 207–28. San Francisco: Institute for Contemporary Studies.

Wade, Robert, and David Seckler. 1990. "Priority Issues in the Management of Irrigation Systems." In *Social, Economic, and Institutional Issues in Third World Irrigation Management*, ed. Rajan K. Sampath and Robert A. Young, 13–29. Boulder, Colo.: Westview.

Walker, H. H. 1983. "Determinants for the Organisation of Irrigation Projects." In *Man and Technology in Irrigated Agriculture*, 19–36. Irrigation Symposium, 1982. Hamburg: Verlag Paul Parey.

Walker, James M., and Roy Gardner. 1992. "Probabilistic Destruction of Common-Pool Resources: Experimental Evidence." *Economic Journal* 102:1149–61.

Walker, James M., Roy Gardner, and Elinor Ostrom. 1990. "Rent Dissipation in a Limited-Access Common-Pool Resource: Experimental Evidence." *Journal of Environmental Economics and Management* 19:203–11.

———. 1991. "Rent Dissipation and Balanced Deviation Disequilibrium in Common Pool Resources: Experimental Evidence." In *Game Equilibrium Models II: Methods, Morals, and Markets*, ed. Reinhard Selten, 337–67. Berlin: Springer-Verlag.

Water and Engineering Commission. 1987. *Rapid Appraisal Study of Eight Selected Micro-Areas of Farmers' Irrigation Systems*. Kathmandu, Nepal: Ministry of Water Resources.

Weimer, David L., and Aidan R. Vining. 1992. *Policy Analysis: Concepts and Practice*. 2d ed. Englewood Cliffs, N.J.: Prentice-Hall.

Weissing, Franz. 1983. *Populationsgenetische Grundlagen der Evolutionīren Spieltheorie*. Materialien zur Mathematisierung der Einzelwissenschaften, nos. 41 and 42, Bielefeld, Germany.

———. 1991. "Evolutionary Stability and Dynamic Stability in a Class of Evolutionary Normal Form Games." In *Game Equilibrium Models I: Evolution and Game Dynamics*, ed. Reinhard Selten, 29–97. Berlin: Springer-Verlag.

Weissing, Franz, and Elinor Ostrom. 1991. "Irrigation Institutions and the Games Irrigators Play: Rule Enforcement without Guards." In *Game Equilibrium Models II: Methods, Morals, and Markets*, ed. Reinhard Selten, 188–262. Berlin: Springer-Verlag.

———. 1993. "Irrigation Institutions and the Games Irrigators Play: Rule Enforcement on Government- and Farmer-Managed Systems." In *Games in Hierarchies and Networks: Analytical and Empirical Approaches to the Study of Governance Institutions*, ed. Fritz W. Scharpf, 387–428. Frankfurt am Main: Campus Verlag; Boulder, Colo.: Westview.

Weschler, Louis. 1968. *Water Resources Management: The Orange County Experience.* California Government Series no. 14. Davis, Calif.: Institute of Governmental Affairs.

Wesney, David. 1989. "Applied Fisheries Management Plans: Individual Transferable Quotas and Input Controls." In *Rights Based Fishing*, ed. Philip A. Neher, Ragnar Arnason, and Nina Mollett. NATO ASI Series E, Applied Sciences no. 169. Dordrecht, Netherlands: Kluwer.

Wickham, Thomas H., and A. Valera. 1979. "Practices and Accountability for Better Water Management." In *Irrigation Policy and the Management of Irrigation Systems in Southeast Asia*, ed. Donald C. Taylor and Thomas H. Wickham, 61–75. Bangkok: Agricultural Development Council.

Williams, John T., and Michael D. McGinnis. 1988. "Sophisticated Reaction in the U.S.-Soviet Arms Race: Evidence of Rational Expectations." *American Journal of Political Science* 32:968–95.

Williamson, Oliver E. 1975. *Markets and Hierarchies: Analysis and Antitrust Implications.* New York: Free Press.

———. 1985. *The Economic Institutions of Capitalism: Firms, Markets, Relational Contracting.* New York: Free Press.

Wilson, James A. 1982. "The Economical Management of Multispecies Fisheries." *Land Economics* 58 (4): 417–34.

———. 1990. "Fishing for Knowledge." *Land Economics* 66 (1): 12–29.

Wilson, Rick K., and Roberta Herzberg. 1984. "Voting Is Only a Block Away: Theory and Experiments on Blocking Coalitions." Paper presented at the Public Choice Society meetings, Phoenix, 29–31 March.

Wittman, D. 1985. "Counter-intuitive Results in Game Theory." *European Journal of Political Economy* 1:77–89.

Wynne, Susan G. 1989. "The Land Boards of Botswana: A Problem in Institutional Design." Ph.D. diss., Indiana University, Department of Political Science.

Yamagishi, Toshio. 1986. "The Provision of a Sanctioning System as a Public Good." *Journal of Personality and Social Psychology* 51 (1): 110–16.

———. 1988. "Seriousness of Social Dilemmas and the Provision of a Sanctioning System." *Social Psychology Quarterly* 51 (1): 32–42.

Yang, Tai-Shuenn. 1987. "Property Rights and Constitutional Order in Imperial China." Ph.D. diss., Indiana University.

Yin, Robert K., and Karen A. Heald. 1975. "Using the Case Survey Method to Analyze Policy Studies." *Administrative Science Quarterly* 20:371–81.

Young, H. P., N. Okada, and T. Hashimoto. 1982. "Cost Allocation in Water Resources Development." *Water Resources Research* 18:463–75.

Contributors

Arun Agrawal teaches at the University of Florida in the Political Science Department, and with the Tropical Conservation and Development Program. After his Ph.D. at Duke University, he spent a year and a half at the University of California, Berkeley, on a postdoctoral fellowship, and at present he is working on two research projects related to institutions and resource management. His major research interests include resource management, development, indigenous institutions and technology, and social movements.

William Blomquist is associate professor of Political Science at Indiana University, Indianapolis. He received a Ph.D. in Political Science from Indiana University, Bloomington, in 1987, and is the author of *Dividing the Waters: Governing Groundwater in Southern California*.

Roy Gardner is professor of economics at Indiana University and Cooperating Scientist, Economic Research Service, USDA. He is the author of articles on game theory and its applications in the social and behavioral sciences. He is most recently author of a forthcoming book, *Games for Business and Economics*.

Elinor Ostrom is codirector of the Workshop in Political Theory and Policy Analysis and the Arthur F. Bentley Professor of Political Science at Indiana University, Bloomington. She is the author of *Governing the Commons* and *Crafting Institutions for Self-Governing Irrigation Systems*, coauthor with Robert Bish and Vincent Ostrom of *Local Government in the United States*, and coeditor with Richard Kimber and Jan-Erik Lane of the *Journal of Theoretical Politics*.

Edella Schlager is an assistant professor in the School of Public Administration and Policy at the University of Arizona. Her research involves developing, refining, and testing theories of collective action and institutional choice primarily in relation to the governance of common-pool resources. Her articles have been published in *Land Economics* (with Elinor Ostrom) and the *Journal of Environmental Economics and Management* (with Steven Hackett and James Walker).

Shui Yan Tang is assistant professor in the School of Public Administration, University of Southern California. His research interests focus on how institutional arrangements affect the way citizens and government officials govern water resources and financial transactions. He is the author of *Institutions and Collective Action: Self-Governance in Irrigation*.

James Walker is Associate Director of the Workshop in Political Theory and Policy Analysis and Professor of Economics at Indiana University. His principal research focus is the use of experimental methods in the investigation of individual and group behavior related to the voluntary provision of public goods and the use of common-pool resources. Recent publications include "Group Size Effects in Public Goods Provision: The Voluntary Contributions Mechanism," *Quarterly Journal of Economics* (with R. Mark Isaac); "Rent Dissipation in a Limited-Access Common Pool Resource: Experimental Evidence," *Journal of Environmental Economics and Management* (with Roy Gardner and Elinor Ostrom); and "Probabilistic Destruction of Common-Pool Resources: Experimental Evidence," *Economic Journal* (with Roy Gardner).

Index